Dietmar Eberle

9×9

A Method of Design

From City to House Continued

Birkhäuser
Basel

MANAGING EDITORS

Florian Aicher
Dietmar Eberle

EDITORIAL TEAM

Franziska Hauser
Pascal Hofmann
Marcello Nasso
Stefan Roggo
Mathias Stritt

Table of Contents

Assistants,
junior assistants, and students
of the chair

Tobias Abegg | Daniel Abraha | Albert Achammer | Stephan Achermann | Martin Achermann | Nick Ackermann | Joël Adorian | Corinne Aebischer | Dominik Aegerter | Benno Agreiter | Christian Aguayo | Fabio Agustoni | Philippe Airoldi | Reem Al-Wakeel | Matthias Alder | Pun Alfred | Timothy Allen | Evran Alper | Jonas Altorfer | Karin Ammann | Desirée Amport | Deborah Andermatt | Fabiano Andina | Rahel Angst | Cyril Angst | Erkan Anil | Valentin Annen | Manuel Arnold | Martin Arnold | Roman Arpagaus | Claudio Arpagaus | Flurin Arquint | Marco Assandri | Gamze Atas | Alexander Athanassoglou | Cheuk Fan Au | Jean-Jacques Auf der Maur | Zoe Auf der Maur | Franziska Bächer | Hannah Bächi | Lutz Pablo Bachmann | Olivia Bächtold | Matthias Baer | René Bähler | Alcide Bähler | Catherine Bakkers | Sophie Ballweg | **Michèle Bär** | Runa Barbagelata Villafane | Marco Barberini | Sarah Barras | Emely Bauhofer | Chantal Baumann | Alexander Baumann | Adrian Baumberger | Simon Baur | Thomas Beekhuis | Mario Beeli | Andreas Beerli | Michael Beerli | Pawel Bejm | **Anouk Benon** | Isabelle Bentz | Lea Berger | Itamar Bergfreund | Philip Berkowitsch | Giorgia Bernasconi | Ruben Bernegger | Robert Berner | Jan Berni | Lucia Bernini | Tamara Bertone | **Krishna Bharathi** | Karin Bienz | Gregor Bieri | Sara Bieri | Sebastian Bietenhader | Emanuel Biland | Marco Bill | Elias Binggeli | Fabian Francesco Bircher | Simon Birchler | Martina Bischof | Stephan Bischof | Mario Bisquolm | Frederic Biver | Daria Blaschkiewitz | Davide Blasi | Daniel Blatter | Charline Blatter | Carmen Blättler | Philipp Bleuel | Benjamin Blocher | Eliane Blöchlinger | Fatima Blötzer | Simone Blum | Nadia Blumer | Katja Blumer | Franz Bohnacker | Jana Bohnenblust | Peter Boller | Raphael Bollhalder | Beni Bollmann | Gianni Bonacina | Annamaria Bonzanigo | Tiffany Bibi Borradori | Frédéric Borruat | Giulia Bosia | Anita Bossart | Marco Bosshardt | Misel Bozic | Philip Braem | Michèle Brand | Vesna Brandestini | Luca Branger | Julien Brassel | Alex Braun | Bob Braun | Leonie Braunschweig | Livia Breitenstein | Grégoire Bridel | Ivica Brnic | Michael Broggi | David Brückmann | Arno Bruderer | Jonas Brun | Jonas Bründler | Roman Brunner | David Robert Brunner | Lorenz Brunner | Ueli Oskar Brunner | Nils Büchel | Nicole Bucher | Antoinette Buchs | Valentin Buchwalder | Michael Buehler | Marc Buehler | Debora Buehlmann | Daniel Buergin | Daniel Bühler | Ole Bühlmann | Nicolas Burckhardt | Geraldine Burger | Joel Burger | Manuel Burkhardt | Lars Burkhardt | Patrick Thomas Burri | Ariel Burt | Isabelle Burtscher | Cosimo Caccia | Mihaela Caduff-Ene | Daniel Calvo Fernãndez | Sandro Camenzind | Gregorio Candelieri | Alessandro Canonica | Ursina Caprez | Marcel Carozzi | Jerome Carre | Rémy Carron | Rachelle Carroz | Simone Cartier | Filippo Cattaneo | Ria Cavelti | Fortunat Cavigelli | Sabrina Cervenka | Yong Cha | Stéphanie Chanson | Andre Chatelain | Stéphane Chau | **Dalila Chebbi** | Beining Chen | Ruizhi Cheng | Sylvie Chervaz | Tsz Tuen Cherry Cheung | Man Lok Christopher Choi | Julie Christ | Sasha Cisar | Geraldine Clausen | Aldo Coldesina | Flavia Conrad | **Sabrina Contratto** | Benjamin Cordes | Christian Cortesi | Caccia Cosimo | Utku Coskun | Valentino Crameri | Lucio Crignola | Eliane Csernay | Jimena Cugat Perez | Lorenz Dahinden | Gruber David | Sören Davy | Samuel Dayer | Rossella Dazio | Géraldine De Beer | Arthur De Buren | Marine De Dardel | Gino De Giorgio | Livio De Maria | Kerry De Zilva | Jonas Debatin | Anna Dechmann | Danny Deering | Janek Definti | Christian Dehli | Fernando Del Don | Massimo Della Corte | Selin Demir | Anna Denkeler | Marco Lino Derendinger | **Stephan Derendinger** | Demian Derron | Gabriela Dévaud | Flavio Diethelm | Maximilian Dietschi | Emmanuel Claude Diserens | Raphael Disler | Jan Dlabac | Bettina Dobler | Timon Dönz | Carol Dörig | Kevin Constantin Dröscher | Louise du Fay de Lavallaz | Christoph Dubler | Olivier Dubuis | **Basil Düby** | Lou Dumont d'Ayot | Isabelle Duner | Nicolas Dunkel | Maximilien Durel | Svenja Egge | Deborah Eggel | Harry Egger | Marius Eggli | Christine Egli | Natascha Egli | Jonatan Egli | Jasmin Egloff | Andy Egolf | Viviane

Ehrensberger | Miro Eichelberger | Tobias Eichenberger | Jan Eicher | Philipp Eigenmann | Josephine Eigner | Alana Elayashy | Benedikt Elmaleh | Maurin Elmer | Matthias Elsasser | Mira Elsohn | Roy Engel | Noemi Engel | Sebastian Engelhorn | Jann Erhard | Anil Erkan | Janine Erzinger | Ladina Esslinger | Alain Ettlin | Fojan Fahmi | Sacha Fahrni | Ivan Fallegger | Mevion Famos | Riet Fanzun | Christina Farragher | Adelina Fasan | Daniel Fausch | Laura Favre-Bully | Sarah Federli | Deborah Patricia Fehlmann | Nina Feix | Bruno Felber | Nicolas Feldmeyer | Samuel Fent | Adrian Fergg | Vanessa Feri | Marco Fernandes Pires | Manuela Fernandez | Diego Fernandez | Manuel Fernandez | Andreas Feurer | Amélie Fibicher | Erik Fichter | Stefan Fierz | Simon Filler | Leandra Finger | Monika Fink | Maximilian Fink | Sara Finzi-Longo | Carsten Fischer | Valentin Fischer | Noe Fischer | Annina Fischer | Jens Fischer | Stephanie Fischler | Anna Flueckiger | Hans Flühmann | Luca Fontanella | Caspar Forrer | Kay Forster | **Susanne Frank** | Nils Franzini | Michael Frefel | Michelle Frei | Michel Frei | Nicole Frey | Sandra Frey | Andreas Friedli | Anna Friedli | Christina Friedrich | Jonas Fritschi | Maximilian Fritz | Noël Frozza | Sarah Fuchs | Daniel Fuchs | Noriaki Fujishige | Sabina Furger | Michael Furrer | Sandra Furrer | Rico Furter | Sandro Gämperle | Adrian Gämperli | Julian Ganz | Nicolas Ganz | David Ganzoni | Carlos Alberto Garcia Jaramillo | **Valérie Gass** | Reto Gasser | Alix Gasser | Roy Gehrig | Pascal Genhart | Eva Gentner | Flurina Gerber | Mirjam Gerth | Judith Gessler | Lea Gfeller | Deborah Giaccalone | Giulia Giardini | **Bartelomeus Gijzen** | Valentin Gillet | Kathrin Gimmel | Tommaso Giovannoli | Reto Giovanoli | Michaela Gisler | Giardini Giulia | Lea Glanzmann | Katharina Glomb | Maude Gobet | Markus Goetz | Patrick Goldener | Daniela Gonzalez | Felipe Good | Felix Good | David Gössler | Uwe Gottfried | Adriel Graber | Benjamin Graber | Nina Graber | Fatma Graca | Gregory Graemiger | Mara Selina Graf | Lukas Graf | Julien Graf | Marco Graff | Fabrizio Gramegna | Valentina Grazioli | Candelieri Gregorio | Livia Greuter | Sarah Greuter | Christian Grewe-Rellmann | Alexandra Grieder | Louise Grosjean | Lorine Grossenbacher | Lisa Grübel | Vera Gruber | David Gruber | Florian Grunder | Lea Grunder | Reto Gsell | Sascha Gsell | Sascha Gsell | Wen Guan | Michael Gugg | **Martina Guhl** | Lowis Gujer | Martina Guler | Mathias Gunz | Simone Gutknecht | Kristel Guzman Rocabado | Niklaus Gysi | Ann-Cathrin Gysin | Oliver Haab | Lion Haag | Reto Habermacher | Lena Hächler | Mahela Hack | **Raphael Haefeli** | Manuela Häfliger | Dimitri Häfliger | Steffen Hägele | Martin Haist | Frédéric Haller | Marco Haller | Demjan Haller | Quentin Halter | Kathrin Haltiner | Liliane Haltmeier | Nikolaus Hamburger | Olivier Hames | Naomi Hanakata | Oliver Hänni | Ueli Hartmann | Florian Hartmann | Carola Hartmann | Lejla Hasanbegovic | Jonas Martin Elias Hasler | Anja Hasler | Jonas Hässig | Dani Hässig | Andreas Haug | Andreas Haupolter | Martin Hauser | **Franziska Hauser** | Jules Hausherr | Gregor Haussener | Lorraine Haussmann | Stephan Haymoz | Patricia Hedinger | Nora Heeb | Daniel Heim | Christof Heimberg | Marco Heimgartner | Fabian Heinzer | Martin Heiroth | Nadja Heitz | Christoph Heitzmann | Kaspar Helfrich | Benjamin Heller | Jan Helmchen | Pascal Hendrickx | Benedikt Hengartner | Benedikt Henggartner | Jana Henschen | Rachel Herbst | Magdalena Hermann | Lukas Herzog | Andres Herzog | Arpad Hetey | Sebastian Heusser | Victor Hidayat | Christoph Hiestand | Johannes Hirsbrunner | Cyrill Hirtz | Doris Hochstrasser | Maja Karoliina Hodel | Marc Hodel | Marcel Hodel | Christian Hoene | Florian Hofer | Thomas Jörg Hofer | Celia Hofman | **Pascal Hofmann** | Hubert Holewik | Julian Holz | **Barbara Holzer** | Jan Honegger | Anas Honeiny | Oliver Hongler | Moritz Hörnle | Lea Hottiger | Angela Hottinger | Christine Hotz | **Marcus Hsu** | Timmy Huang | Christian Huber | Mara Huber | Holewik Hubert | Ruth Huegli | Lea Huerlimann | Kristin Hufschmid | Daniel Hug | Nina Hug | Nicolas Hugentobler | Niklaus Hunkeler | Marc Hunziker | Kevin Hüppi | Peter Hutter | Roger Huwyler | Naida Iljazovic | Samuel

Imbeck | Melanie Imfeld | Mark Inderbitzin | Nicolas Indermitte | Nicole Ineichen | Martin Ineichen | Meryem Isik | Milena Isler | Marcel Jäger | Lisa Jäggli | Manuel Jakobs | Peters Jan | Jacob Jansen | Romina Janzi | Milan Jarrell | Jens Jaschek | Belen Jatuff | Simone Jaun | Aline Jean | Mélanie Jeannet | Florian Jennewein | Edward Jewitt | Sylwia Jezewska | Jie Ji | Weilan Jiang | Sven Joliat | Christian Jonasse | Vanessa Joos | Clara Jörger | Philippe Jorisch | Gopal Joshi | Marko Jovanovic | Julia Julen | Jakob Junghanss | Joni Kaçani | Simon Kaeslin | Mirjam Kägi | Peter Kai | Rabea Kalbermatten | Tim Kappeler | Kaspar Kappeler | Darius Karacsony | Nirvan Karim | Nadine Käser Cenoz | Andreas Kast | Friederike Katz | Oliver Kaufmann | Andreas Kaufmann | **Peter Kaufmann** | Katharina Keckeis | Chris Joseph Keller | Severin Keller | Yannick Keller | Thomas Keller | Ming Fung Ki | Fabian Kiepenheuer | Dorothea Kind | Eva Kiseljak | Beatrice Kiser | Andreas Kissel | Lukas Kissling | Marco Thomas Kistler | Tobias Klauser | Samuel Klingele | Nora Klinger | Daniel Klos | Judith Klostermann | Dominic Knecht | Hermann Knoblauch | Philipp Kobi | Kirsten Koch | Adrian Kocher | Moritz Köhler | Lucie Kohout | Adrian König | Anastasia König | Amanda Köpfli | Jan Kovatsch | Benedikt Kowalewski | Nina Kozulic | Georg Kraehenbuehl | Nicolo Krättli | Stephan Krauer | Martin Kraus | Simon Kretz | David Kretz | Dylan Kreuzer | Nicole Kreuzer | Markus Krieger | Dimitri Kron | Steve Kronenberg | **Henrietta Krüger** | Michal Krzywdziak | Hannah Katharina Kuby | David Kuehne | Florian Kuehne | **Nora Küenzi** | Michael Kuenzle | Yagmur Kültür | Bianca Kummer | Aidan Kümmerli | Joos Kündig | Monica Küng | Jasmin Kunst | Tamino Kuny | Fabian Kuonen | Wing Chung Lai | Lai Shun Lam | Tibor Lamoth | Mario Lampert | Andreas Lamprecht | Fabian Landolt | Melissa Lätsch | Mathias Lattmann | Fabian Lauener | Oleksandra Lebid | Franziska Ledergerber | Soo Lee | Mireille Lehmann | Jasha Lehmann | Patricia Lehner | Peter Leibacher | Barnim Lemcke | Sandro Lenherr | Gérard Lerner | Katrin Leuenberger | Lorenz Leuenberger | Cherk Ga Leung | Matthias Leutert | Magdalena Leutzendorff | Olivier Levis | Leonie Lieberherr | Christian Liechti | Marlene Lienhard | Gusung Lim | Xiao Wei Lim | Jannick Lincke | Stefan Liniger | Andrea Linke | **Mario Lins** | Yanchen Liu | Lisa Lo | Irene Lo Iacono | Kushtrim Loki | Lisa Looser | Beat Loosli | Lukas Loosli | Piotr Lopatka | Gabriel Lopes Souto | Xiao Lu | Andri Luescher | Nik Luginbühl | Julien Lukac | Herzog Lukas | Max Lüscher | Chantal Lutz | Philipp Lutz | Tobias Lutz | Minh Ly | Géraldine Maag | Alex Madathilparambil | Lea Maeder | Maja Maerzthal | Carlo Magnaguagno | Hannes Mahlknecht | Stefan Maier | Joël Maître | Michèle Majerhus | Paul Majerus | Sofia Manganas | Sabrina Maniglio | Theo Manolakis | Vanessa Mantei | Graf Mara Selina | Hodel Marcel | Simon Marti | Daniela Marti | Moritz Marti | Andrin Martig | Luca Martino | Davide Massaro | Iris Mathez | Leo Mathys | Raphael Mätzener | Miriam Maurer | Rosanna May | Marc Mayor | Hashimoto Mayumi | Dorian Mc Carthy | Eva Mehnert | Dominique Meier | Philippe Meier | Annina Claudia Meier | Florian Meier | Andreas Meier | Meret Meier | Fabian Meier | Julian Meier | Andreas Meier | Patrick Meier | Julia Meierhans | Isabelle Meister | Alexander Menke | Nicolas Mentha | Meier Meret | Friederike Merkel | Yves Merkofer | Nicola Merz | Christopher Metz | Augusta Meyer | Anja Meyer | Thomas Meyer | Anna Meyer | Andrea Micanovic | Yvonne Michel | Sasa Aleksandar Mijatovic | Marius Mildner | Natascia Minder | Mirjam Minder | **Daniel Minder** | Giorgia Mini | Roman Miszkowicz | Anna Mölk | Aleksandra Momcilovic | Andreas Monn | Franziska Moog | Leander Morf | Meret Morgenthaler | Lorenz Mörikofer | Stefan Moser | Andrea Mosimann | Manon Mottet | Marko Mrcarica | Barbara Mueller | Michi Müllener | Claus Müller | Eva Müller | Elizabeth Müller | **Thomas Müller** | Nathanael Müller | Marius Müller | Tom Mundy | Claudia Müntener | Niklas Naehrig | Taichi Naito | **Marcello Nasso** | Christina Nater | Anna Nauer | Nicola Nett | Sebastian Neu | Lisa Neuenschwander |

Nadine Neukom | Philipp Neves | Alexander Ni | Magnus Nickl | Isabelle Niederberger | Sara Nigg | Simon Nikolussi | Alessandro Nunzi | **Raphaël Nussbaumer** | Brigitte Odermatt | Katrin Oechslin | **Urs Oechslin** | Julia Oehler | Philipp Oesch | Oliver Offermann | **Patrycja Okuljar** | Kevin Olas | Fabio Orsolini | Hannes Oswald | Sebastian Oswald | Theresa Pabst | Caroline Pachoud | Clarence Dale Pajarillaga | Lilian Pala | Alexis Panoussopoulos | Fabrice Passaplan | Achille Patà | Daniela Pauli | Axel Paulus | Enrico Pegolo | Fiammetta Pennisi | Demian Peper | Leander Peper | Alejandro Pérez Giner | Baudilio Perez Pereira | Patrick Perren | Myriam Perret | Xavier Perrinjaquet | Luca Pestalozzi | Chiara Pestoni | Kai Peter | Jan Peters | Palle Petersen | Vesna Petrovic | Nora Peyer | Dario Pfammatter | Sebastian Pfammatter | Hanae Pfändler | **Markus Pfändler** | Karin Pfeifer | Stephan Pfeiffer | Andreas Pfister | Franziska Pfyffer | Tan Phan | Nathalie Pietrzko | Lambrini Pikis | Elena Pilotto | Gregor Piontek | Jan Pisani | Larissa Pitsch | Saskia Plaas | Andreas Pluess | Michael Pluess | Seraina Poltera | Petros Polychronis | Alexander Poulikakos | Malgorzata Praczyk | Michael Prager | Lea Prati | Vincent Prenner | Norman Prinz | Androniki Prokopidou | Konstantin Propp | Vincent Protic | Jakob Przybylo | Cordula Puestow | Rachel Püntener | Ferdinand Rabe von Pappenheim | Corsin Raffainer | Ladina Ramming | Luc Ramponi | Benedict Ramser | Judith Rauber | Cati Rauch | Luciano Raveane | Nadia Raymann | Corinne Räz | Lukas Redondo | Christoph Reichen | Chantal Reichenbach | Fionn Reichert | Oliver Reichling | Fabian Reiner | Michael Reiterer | Karin Renggli | Nicole Renz | Marcella Ressegatti | Robby Rey | Samuel Rey | Jannik Richter | **Florian Rickenbacher** | Simon Rieder | Berit Riegger | Maximilian Rietschel | Elisa Rimoldi | Morten Ringdal | Micha Ringger | Urs Ringli | Florian Ringli | Christian Rippstein | Tanja Risch | Raphael Risi | Daniela Risoli | Timon Ritscher | Sebastian Ritter | David Ritz | Thomas Rodemeier | Christopher Rofe | **Stefan Roggo** | Sarah Rohr | Nina Rohrer | Juan Rojas Rico | Nicolas Rolle | Rina Rolli | Gereon Rolvering | Michele Roncoroni | Stefan Roos | Armin Roost | Luca Rösch | Pascal Rosé | Martina Roser | Tibor Rossi | Arturo Roth | Nicolas Rothenbühler | Katrin Röthlin | Kathrin Röthlisberger | Francine Rotzetter | Albulena Rrudhani | Marceline Ruckstuhl | Nicolas Rüegg | **Sylvia Rüegg** | Noëmi Ruf | Tom Rüfli | Andres Ruiz Andrade | Lars Rumpel | Corinne Ruoss | **Nicolas Rüst** | Silvio Rutishauser | Elisabeth Rutz | Gabriela Rutz | Rowena Rutz | Annemarie Ryffel | Ella Ryhiner | Lino Saam | Andreas Sager | Yannick Sager | Tobias Saller | Anna Salvioni | Artai Sanchez Keller | Tobias Saner | Marchet Saratz | Christian Sauer | David Sauser | Katarina Savic | Stéphanie Savio | Alexia Sawerschel | Emil Schaad | Mirko Schaap | Niklaus Schaedelin | Roman Schafer | Tabea Schäfer | Rafael Schäfer | Stefanie Schäfer | Erich Schäli | Yannic Schaub | Angelika Scheidegger | Jakob Schelling | Stephanie Schenk | Mirjam Schenk | Samuel Scherer | **Claudia Schermesser** | Katharina Schielke | Pierre Schild | Gian-Andrea Schild | Caroline Schillinger | Tiziana Schirmer | Severine Schlaepfer | Stephanie Schleh | Jachen Schleich | Robin Schlumpf | Delphine Schmid | Chasper Schmidlin | Véronique Schneider | Silvia Schneider | Corina Schneider | **Martina Schneider** | Daniel Schneider | Eveline Schneider | Andreas Schneller | Flavio Schnelli | Rafael Schnyder | Desiree Schoen | Ekaterine Scholz | Katrin Schöne | Nik Schönenberger | Philip Schönenberger | Patrick Schori | Andrea Schregenberger | **Ulrike Schröer** | Benjamin Schulthess Rechberg | Anina Schuster | Angela Schütz | Wieland Schwarz | **Jacqueline Schwarz** | **Dieter Schwarz** | Caroline Schwarzenbach | Daniel Schweiss | Ernst Florian Schweizer | Eckart Schwerdtfeger | Danile Schwerzmann | Jonathan Sedding | Annika Seifert | Andrea Seiler | **Miriam Seiler** | Yves Seiler | **Veronika Selig** | Tatsiana Selivanava | **Gerrit Sell** | Jules Selter | Ariane Senn | Luca Sergi | Elena Sevinc | Harald Christian Seydel | Mario Sgier | Roger Sidler | Valentina Sieber | Gabrielle Siegenthaler | Felix

Siegrist | Björn Siegrist | Paul Siermann | Dominik Sigg | Fabio Signer | Daniel Sigrist | **Pia Simmendinger** | Mara Simone | Frederic Singer | Maria Skjerbaek | Aleksandra Skop | Fortesa Softa | Rina Softa | Katrin Sommer | Mario Sommer | Thomas Sonder | Gianna Sonder | Lukas Sonderegger | Nino Soppelsa | David Späh | Fabian Spahr | Florian Speier | Kerstin Spiekermann | Basil Spiess | Nicola Stadler | Cornel Staeheli | Nicola Staeubli | Lena Stäheli | Raphael Stähelin | Matthias Stalder | Ina Stammberger | Stefanie Stammer | Matthias Stark | Nina Stauffer | Verena Stecher | Angela Steffen | Henry Stehli | Petra Steinegger | Urban Steiner | Jared Steinmann | Christopher Stepan | Beat Steuri | Sebastian Stich | Juerg Stieger | Lorenzo Stieger | Fabio Stirnimann | Kaspar Stöbe | **Heidi Stoffel** | Magdalena Stolze | Michel Stössel | **Frank Strasser** | **Dorothee Strauss** | Annina Strebel | Selina Streich | Alexander Stricker | Lisa Stricker | **Mathias Stritt** | Leopold Strobl | Florian Stroh | Silvan Strohbach | Louis Strologo | Larissa Strub | Yves Stuber | Matthias Stücheli | Allegra Stucki | Reto Studer | Michael Stünzi | Florian Stutz | Chang Su | Anja Summermatter | Thomas Summermatter | Soley Suter | Christian Suter | Daniel Sutovsky | Madlaina Sutter | Christian Szalay | Bernardo Szekely | Darius Tabatabay | Nora Tahiraj | Alana Tam | Iso Tambornino | Okan Tan | Marco Teixeira | Gnanusha Thayananthan | Thomas Theilig | Chantal Thomet | Louis Thomet | Benjamin Thommen | Till Thomschke | Simon Thuner | Dimitri Thut | Andreas Thuy | Mi Tian | Patricia Tintoré Vilar | Sämi Tobler | Simone Tocchetti | Gabriella Todisco | Thomas Toffel | Tobias Tommila | Boriana Tomova | Theodora Topliyski | Matthew Tovstiga | Julian Trachsel | Simon Trachsel | Thai Tran | Felix Tran | **Gabriela Traxel** | **Eberhard Tröger** | Kathrin Troxler | Fabian Troxler | Maja Trudel | Deborah Truttmann | Kristina Turtschi | Dila Ünlü | Cristina Urzola | Viola Valsesia | Jean-Paul van der Merwe | Françoise Vannotti | **Piroska Vaszary** | Lucie Vauthey | Nicolas Vedolin | Rafael Venetz | Matteo Villa | Nina Villiger | Vladimir Vlajnic | Jana Voboril | Oliver Vogler | Bettine Volk | Gregor Vollenweider | Tessa Vollmeier | Fabrizio Thomas Völlmy | Jessica von Bachelle | Isabel von Bechtolsheim | Simon von Gunten | Anna-Marie von Knobloch | Simon von Niederhäusern | Nadine Mireille Vonlanthen | Thierry Vuattoux | Pablo Vuillemin | Aline Vuilliomenet | Milena Vuletic | Martina Wäckerlin | Nicolas Waelli | Nils Wagner | Oliver Wagner | Loo Wai | Pascal Anyl Waldburger | Martina Walker | Nic Wallimann | Patrick Walser | Renate Walter | Oliver Walter | Sonja Walthert | Jessica Wälti | Yueqiu Wang | Yeshi Wang | Céline Wanner | Jan Waser | Corinne Weber | Florian Weber | Christian Weber | Philip Weber | Moritz Weber | Micha Weber | Nadine Weger | Karin Wegmann | Corinne Wegmann | Michael Wehrli | Georg Weilenmann | Sandro Weiss | Florian Wengeler | Katharina Wepler | Vanessa Werder | Anouk Wetli | Kimberley Wichmann | Tobias Wick | Fabian Wicki | Nadja Widmer | Elisabeth Kristin Wiesenthal | Marcus Wieser | Nicolas Wild | Rhea Iris Winkler | Matthias Winter | David Winzeler | Luisa Wittgen | Martin Wolanin | Marcel Wolf | Paul Wolf | Lukas Wolfensberger | **Andrea Wolfer** | Lorenz Wuethrich | Yangzom Wujohktsang | Tobias Wullschleger | Marco Wunderli | Nicole Würth | Eva Wüst | Martina Wüst | Thomas Wüthrich | Delia Wymann | Helen Wyss | Li Andrew Xingjian | Bing Yang | Lai Man Yee | Guillaume Yersin | Jason Yeung | Han Cheol Yi | Dao Yu | Laura Zachmann | Raymond Zahno | Giacomo Zanchetta | Frederik Zapka | Andrea Zarn | Simon Zehnder | Leonie Zelger | Florentin Zellweger | Zhiyu Zeng | Kathrin Zenhäusern | Diana Zenklusen | Feng Mark Zhang | Zhou Zheng | Yuda Zheng | Viviane Zibung | Jonas Ziegler | Michèle Ziegler | Melanie Ziegler | Daniel Zielinski | Martin Zimmerli | Katrin Zimmermann | Christoph Zingg | Sebastian Ziörjen | Ding Ziyue | Eva Zohren Alewelt | Alexandre Zommerfelds | Noemi Zuest | Rafael Zulauf | Katrin Zumbrunnen | Barbara Zwicky | Christina Zwicky

Foreword

"Literature thinks in scenes. Because literature is always concrete, it does not think in concepts, but in scenes," writes the renowned Swiss literary critic Peter von Matt. He emphasizes this significant and unique feature by going on to specify: "Literature thinks in scenes, it does not translate thoughts into scenes. Wherewith it is simultaneously superior and inferior to philosophy, and the reason that one can never entirely replace the other." What he says about the relationship of literature and philosophy can most certainly be proclaimed even more roundly for the relationship of literature and science: Both say something about the world, both say something different and say it differently, both are non-interchangeable, and both irreplaceable for our understanding of the world.

How does architecture think? Together with literature, it is—with all the limitations—attributed to the arts and differentiated from the sciences. Does it think in scenes? Although atmosphere and mood have been considered part of architecture for some time now, it still does not quite hit the nail on the head. Does it think in concepts? Although architecture is highly analytical and conceptual, this also does not quite cover it. In both cases, something crucial is missing. Architecture thinks of and acts with concrete things, in the words of Dietmar Eberle: physical reality.

Architecture expresses itself in buildings—this is a concrete dialogue with the social context. The findings of the humanities, scientific technical knowledge, and insight of the arts all contribute something to it. Yet architecture is something of its very own—it melds all this knowledge together into a concrete structure in a unique design. In the first fundamental examination of the topic more than 2,000 year ago, Vitruvius defined architecture as integration—a synthesis that the architect must deliver.

This is a challenging task. That talent alone can achieve this seems questionable. So there is a need for instruction, support, and learning. Learning is not theory, but practice. A practice that presents the difference in knowledge between the teacher and the pupil and that thus presumes reflection upon one's own subject. In an interplay of intuition and tough practicing—driven by the curiosity of students—the intellectual permeation of the whole is pushed forward. This makes learning not a petrified, theoretical school building, but a living, breathing activity. In accordance with the subject, this happens much like the way one experiences a room, by walking through it; it develops step by step and, at the end, the beginning appears in a different light.

When learning is referred to as a practice, then also because it lives from practice, from the experience of the teachers. The practice of an entire career is condensed into insights that are very personally shaped. In this particular case, the practice is that of Dietmar Eberle, who began to build at a time when engagement with modernism had reached its apex. Here, he makes a statement, by visiting the construction site, by going to where things are happening and to where people are meeting. What remains: concrete things, physical reality, and real life. Drawing on this experience, the core of his teachings is based on two aspects: the context of the place and the time.

We are all familiar with it: An encounter with a foreign terrain or unfamiliar city sparks an intense effort to orient oneself. Concentrated, one tries to comprehend the structures of the place, committing the façades, activities, and atmospheres to memory. If this orientation is successful, relaxation and unaccustomed freedom sets in. This is the path to learning a design method. And almost *en passant*, one becomes familiar with the important aspects: the place, the structure, the envelope, the program, and the materiality.

And this describes the order of buildup of this method—from place to materiality. The five steps are completed by the combination of each new aspect with those that came before—four combinations. This gives us nine in total. This is the first variable of the term **9 × 9**. And the other? Each topic is unfolded in nine individual steps. This begins with an introduction to the topic, followed by a deeper essay by a guest author, and rounded off by a presentation of nine terms for associative stimulation. Then the assignments for the actual work begin, starting with an analysis, followed by the development of the city and building levels in plans, models, and finally images and/or video.

This publication reserves a very special place for the essays by our guest authors, all architects with a particular passion for theory. Vittorio Magnago Lampugnani's career has predestined him to be an expert on place. Fritz Neumeyer's writings on architectural theory revolve around structure. The relationship between the two is what interests András Pálffy, who establishes some very different characteristics. "What does the envelope of a building reveal about its soul?", asks Adam Caruso. Miroslav Šik shows us that the interplay of envelope, structure, and place has resulted today in very different schools. Silvain Malfroy examines the interaction of programmatic type and place-defined design. Eberhard Tröger takes a closer look at the relationship of materiality and atmosphere. And finally, Dietmar Eberle takes on an evaluation of architectural creation from the perspective of the everyday.

The main body of the book is reserved for questions to Dietmar Eberle about his career, followed by a presentation of his primary concerns and approaches. Adrian Meyer shines a light on the reciprocal inspiration of practice and teaching. Marcello Nasso provides insight on what exactly Eberle's teaching method actually means. The finale starts with Jia Beisi's insights on today's theory of student-teacher interaction, followed by a conversation between Michele Lanza and Marcello Nasso on the parallels between architecture and the structure of electronic media. Arno Lederer's personal view of the state of the field brings the book to a close. The publisher would like to take this opportunity to warmly thank all authors of this book.

However, this book is not only indebted to those mentioned by name. These teachings are on a subject that can only be confirmed through everyday practice. And this is possible thanks to the help of many hands. It is above all the department assistants who help ensure these endeavors. We thank the assistants Franziska Hauser, Pascal Hofmann, Mathias Stritt, and Stefan Roggo in particular, not least for their perceptions on the teaching process and the provision and development of learning material, and we thank Marcello Nasso, a former assistant, for his work in preparing the way for this book.

Florian Aicher
Dietmar Eberle

Between Architecture and Architecture Education

Interview – Florian Aicher and Dietmar Eberle

24 & 26 September, 2016
in Lustenau, Austria

F.A. | Architecture education is on the one hand the teaching of future architecture and, on the other, a summary of the principles that make up architecture. The two are interrelated and since the principles are what guide the instruction, it makes sense to begin with them.

In order to avoid getting bogged down by the basics, it may be useful to begin with a characterization: "Contour and profile are the touchstone of the architect," said a 35-year-old Le Corbusier—now that is a good place to start.

The key words contour and profile jump to the eye, and the word *form* to the mind. On *form*, the Oxford Dictionary says: "The visible shape or configuration of something; style, design, and arrangement in an artistic work as distinct from its content." Synonyms include: Structure, arrangement, layout, order, and system. In philosophy, every figure has on the one hand a form and, on the other, a material. Ever since the big bang, every formation is a reshuffling of matter, of material. Design: a never-ending shifting of matter.

What could "contours are the touchstone of the architect" mean today?

D.E. | Architecture and architecture education are, of course, two different things. Architecture, for me, is quite elementary: Defining a shape. At the end, we have the materialization of social and societal needs in a shape. I'll take a look at the concept of shape first—here, the creation of shape is still present.

I differentiate this shape into three scales. The scales can also be expressed as distances. Depending on the distance, I perceive the building differently, as something different.

First, there is the overall form, the silhouette, the shape, the building as a whole. From a distance of a hundred meters, the average building is perceived as a figure, a shape. This changes with proximity. From 50 meters, I begin to perceive constructive arrangements and geometrical principles. From 10 meters, materials, surfaces, and details become visible and add definition.

On the surface, it seems to me as if all of this can be bundled within the concept of form. From each distance, unique aspects of form reveal themselves. Different themes emerge, the overlapping of which makes a building compelling, or not. Subsuming everything under the term *form* is an inadmissible simplification.

> Architecture and architecture education are, of course, two different things. Architecture, for me, is quite elementary: Defining a shape.

One can keep on going: Each of these levels must in turn be observed from afar, from halfway, and from close up—this is how shape can be comprehended profoundly and in its entirety.

The following statement must be agreed upon without restraint: Design ability is the utmost goal of an architectural education. An architect must be able to express themself in these three dimensions using design. This remains the central task of an architectural education. I agree with Le Corbusier in that I insist: Each of the three levels and all of them together—that is design.

Today, it seems to me that a one-sided emphasis on the last dimension is prevalent—surfaces and materials. The sculpturality of the figure suffers from this.

F.A. | Design would thus mean satisfying the three scales on all levels in a way so that each is reflected in the other; so that the large scale is reflected in the small, and the small is apparent in the large.

D.E. | The different exercises used in our teaching always express these three scales. No level claims priority, the process is analogous on all levels—this is how the design acquires depth. In the end, it is about the coherence of the different distances—this is how the identity we recognize in good architecture comes about. Coherence—one thing meshes with the other; students need to learn to be proficient on all levels.

F.A. | The first step in the system is the three levels of scale; these correspond to the three distances of 100 meters, 50 meters, and 5 meters.

D.E. | A differentiated viewpoint enables us to observe different aspects of architecture, from the grand overview to smallest detail. We believe that the following five categories adequately express the complexity of architecture:

1. **PLACE** Bollnow spoke of the habitat of a building.
2. **STRUCTURE** this refers to the supporting and development structure.
3. **ENVELOPE** this is the border between interior and exterior, in particular the façade.
4. **PROGRAM** this is the use, or the spatial program.
5. **MATERIALITY** this refers to the interior surfaces of the space, including technical facilities.

F.A. | Five categories of architectural interaction, corresponded in turn by a series of numbers—in this case, there is also a temporal dimension.

D.E. | This is the result of the analysis of what actually happens with buildings—it is fully backed up empirically. Each category is inscribed with a life cycle.

How a building interacts with public space, the volumetry, the connections, the access points—in short: its situation within the place. This is what lasts the longest, what marks our cities in the long term. We are looking at much more than a hundred years.

The structure—stability, site development, and security—is a critical component that changes very little. We propose a hundred years. In some countries, it is required to guarantee these aspects of a building for one hundred years.

The envelope, the façade, is renewed sooner, for technical or aesthetic reasons. The relaunch of appearance is pushing itself more and more into the foreground, supported by technical arguments when necessary. For these building components, more than 50 years is rarely necessary.

The program, the type of use, nowadays lasts no more than a generation—that's 25 years, more or less. The values of each generation change—as do fundamental technical facilities; for example, a heating system must be exchanged after 20 years at the most.

And then there is the material: the interior, user surfaces, and so forth. These are dictated by trends, fashions, and tastes and last less than ten years.

F.A. | This is a differentiation of a building primarily according to concrete empirical criteria. However, a hierarchical order is also implied. Does this have a normative value?

D.E. | Definitely! Our values today are derived from our knowledge that resources are finite. As we know from Snozzi, architecture always causes a destruction of resources. We must therefore hold back from making it, by creating things that last. Longevity becomes a measure of quality. The dimension of time establishes sustainability. In terms of architectural design, this means that aspects characterized by longevity have priority. Sustainability is a value that justifies the validity of architectural decisions.

F.A. | This is a revaluation of architectural ideals. Fifty years ago, it would have been unimaginable to see place as having top priority.

D.E. | Back then we still learned that architecture originates from the function, which is defined by the program. According to this, place plays almost no role at all. What did we get out of this? The places that were left to us, are we happy with them? The programs from back then are long forgotten, but the place, the outside spaces, the buildings amongst one another, they have stayed. Are we satisfied with this? Giving the program preference, taken from the thinking of the user, has given us agglomeration and the devastation of entire areas. The priorities were falsely ranked, and we are now changing that. It seems to me that a consensus has now been reached: Place first. And in the end, the contribution the building makes to the place is decisive for the quality of its architecture. Today, it is possible that we maintain building fabric that is outdated and technically questionable simply because it is located in the right place; and we are stepping away from buildings that have a technically sound substance, but are situationally wrong. This is the reality.

It seems to me that a consensus has now been reached: Place first. And in the end, the contribution the building makes to the place is decisive for the quality of its architecture.

F.A. | Three levels, five categories, this is how the teaching program's model is set up. This is then taken a step further by introducing a phase to mediate or tie together the five categories. This results in the number 9.

D.E. | The repeated and uniquely different interactions result in a high degree of complexity, a densification of knowledge. The goal is a systematic approach to attaining the longest possible retention of value. This is key when we are talking about the use of resources in light of our living quality. The locale of the city, village, or countryside is crucial to attaining the right ambience – a term that applies to atmosphere as well as to the logic of how the architectural building blocks mesh with one another.

F.A. | The entire spectrum of the training program is comparable to a conceptual spectrum that ranges from elementary basic concepts to ones of great complexity. This is followed by the design – not one-dimensionally, but as an evolving development with retrogressive ascertainment. This is very challenging – Can it even be taught?

D.E. | The practice of architecture is not much different from the art of a pianist and how that is brought about. What does a pianist have to do? On the one hand, they have to master the craft. This means practicing every day. On the other hand, the knowledge (comprehension) about what is actually wanted must be continually advanced. Repetition is essential, practice creates space for personal interpretation and inspiration. Sounds stubborn. Like drilling. But that's how it is. Yes, I stand by these words.

F.A. | A new keyword: Craftsmanship. Let's compare "formation" to what happens in the kitchen. To create a meal to be served at the table, ingredients are needed. These must meet exact amount and quality requirements. They are processed, formed, in different ways – mixing, folding, kneading. They undergo a process and come out as something new at the end. Is architecture not similar to this? What are the ingredients of architecture?

D.E. | If we are talking about things being built, we must first establish that only a minimal portion of it is actually architecture. As opposed to in the arts, the functional use is the central focus of a built object – and this has been especially important not just since Loos.

Of the basic categories mentioned, the last one is the closest to us. Here, material quality – mastery of the materials – plays the essential role. This takes us back to the origins of architecture, to craftsmanship. It was so, and it will stay so. I do not think that separating craftsmanship and architecture is a viable path for the future. I do not measure architecture by its intellectual concepts, but on its material realization – this is an important point in education as well.

F.A. | This goes back to your start down the path to becoming an architect.

D.E. | Definitely! My approach to architecture is purely that of a craftsman. In the beginning, it says: We built. Why this beginning? Because we thought that the architecture taught to us then, which had never put itself at this level, was irrelevant. And thus: Exit from architecture. Enter into craftsmanship. Construction site! For the first ten years of my career, I spent summers on the building site, and winters in the office. What a gift, these summers! Building: living. The interaction of practice and theory transpires all on its own. Every practice has a theoretical background, just as theory is inspired by practice. Engaging with mind and body, that is no problem for me. Although I take the following for granted: Architecture must leave theory behind itself; it must become practical, must undergo materialization.

F.A. | This is a very operative approach, typical of your early years. Back then it went almost without saying: operative goes hand-in-hand with *cooperative.*

D.E. | Architecture cannot be carried out by one person alone, it is not a personal creation. It never was, and is today less than ever. Craftsmanship has always emphasized this togetherness in contrast to artistic genius. Construction worker, client, building authorities – all are part of the creation of architecture.

What the architect contributes that is special is the guiding idea. They formulate that upon which the others orient themselves. They supply orientation through design.

The on-site doing also needs a shape, an idea, in order for its practical advantages to develop. Later, it became clear to me: This is also true of industrial building processes. If design is neglected, then this knowledge of production spins off, loses itself in mannerisms. The overall concept of the design is replaced by partial aspects. The result is an applied art or architecture as a work process, an organizational process, participation process.

F.A. | The doing of building is also never purely individual – this is where the realization that architecture is the most social of the arts pops up.

D.E. | A built environment is social – always. Even if it is a-social. It stays social.

What was so important to us back in the day: the knowledge of craftsmanship on the one hand, and on the other the knowledge of those who were to use the building in the end. In anticipation, but also through direct participation. I have always said: As an architect, I represent all those who are not at the table right now. These are the future users, the neighbors, the precedents – the entire context. We completely contradicted the sacrosanct architectural ideals of the time – because we didn't feel that these ideas were capable of entering into a dialogue with simple people.

F.A. | Context – that is the place, but more than just the physical site.

D.E. | Building is successful when it ties local knowledge, perceptions, feelings, methods, and values together with the relatively "objectifiable" knowledge of the current state of technology. For me, the fact that the locality, every valley, each region, has its own identity remains a decisive factor. This means that the built environment does not comes first, but the mentality of the people in the context. Cultural values are much older and more important than the built objects.

In contrast to this, our landscapes today are marked by the cultural devastation of the planning ideologies of the last 50 years.

F.A. | Your launch was a decisive one: Opposition, resistance. By doing what? Building!

D.E. | Put in drastic terms: We looked into people's private lives. We lived with people, looked for solutions to problems together with people …

F.A. | … the aim of architecture is a usable and livable world, as you once put it. That sounds very down to earth.

D.E. | One can indeed see it that way. Topography, orientation, vegetation, climate, fauna, flora – these things are still neglected much too much today. But the most crucial aspect for me is the cultural identity that resides in the minds of the people.

I have already looked for my own. For the first ten years, I refused to work for property developers, municipalities, and corporations. I only made buildings for people that used them themselves. I wanted to talk directly to the people who would later use the thing themselves.

F.A. | And now you build all over the world. How does this fit together? What happened to your roots? What happened along the road from local activist to global player?

D.E. | My background is a culture with specific characteristics and values – the lost world of the farmers of the Bregenz Forest. What counted: Frugality, reduction, handling materials the right way, social responsibility, a sense of community.

When I build in the world today, then I only build where the clients are convinced that these values are making a contribution towards solving their problems. The Chinese came to us, asked what we could show them – they came because of the values that I owe to my culture and asked which solutions we would suggest for them.

I don't want my "signature" to be seen in Paris or Peking or Porto. I want the cultural identity of the location to mesh with the knowledge of our company. Of course, differences arise – the "signature" that was looked for so urgently in the 1990s is something we don't really have. We expect different designs for different situations.

F.A. | Whereby, one can assume: Design means a pleasing design, a beautiful one. This brings beauty into the game, to which timelessness is attested.

D.E. | I fully approve of beauty – and have this to add: Beauty is subject to a regional and temporal dimension. In the course of my career, I have yet to discover a timeless or placeless condition. There is one canon in one city, and a different one somewhere else. And if we fail to take a very careful look, we garner the impression that it is all the same. I am much more convinced by Rudofsky's collection of diverse anonymous architectures.

F.A. | Beauty and taste is thus tied to context, which, as we have seen, is not just physical but above all cultural – collective sensibilities and conventions. You once said that conventions are the measure of beauty.

D.E. | Yes, and it is true. Conventions cannot be globalized; they are subject to cultural, spatial, and temporal limitations. They are not generalizable; they do not apply always and everywhere.

They are limited, and therefore not arbitrary. Within a specific area of application, they of course set standards, establish coherency and validity. For those quick on the uptake, I say: Convention is what measures beauty. I do not say that convention is beauty.

F.A. | It still sounds a bit dowdy. What differentiates convention from banality, from the things that are just done as they are done?

One cannot not communicate, said Paul Watzlawick once. We consciously teach: Dialogue.

D.E. | That is a phenomenon that does not interest me, I don't even want to talk about it. It is so superficial that one simply should not do it—formalism beyond cultural identity, fashion, trends, conceptual inflation, intellectual devaluation.

When we, in light of this, begin our educational program with the concept of place, then it means that the design emerges from a dialogue between the object and the environment. This is fundamental, it is omnipresent—there is no zero-environment, no zero-dialogue. One cannot not communicate, said Paul Watzlawick once. We consciously teach: Dialogue.

I would like to see my life's contribution to the profession as having been the further development of conventions, of Vorarlberg's conventions. It is always about the form, a joining that creates something coherent, conclusive, and valid. A design must develop itself, it is not something I just find somewhere, that I see and adopt from somewhere else. Design happens when different factors are joined together into a single whole that evolves, not something that is patched together. This, of course, is connected to order. This is a joining that we recognize as being its own design, and this is always more, different, than the mere sum of its parts.

F.A. | Which conventions, collective memory, also are. Those however, are a very airy thing, while architecture is something that you can push up against. This is what Aldo Rossi seeks to bridge with his types—life experience turned into stone.

D.E. | I am skeptical about the term *types*. I absolutely do see that different cultures have developed different characteristics of coherency that can be situated within the collective memory or habits. It is important to separation conventions from their abstract state and to transplant them to a tangible place. Types make sense under these conditions, according to this understanding. There is one canon in Barcelona and there is another in Stockholm.

What I reject is the idea of the “original type”, the archetype, the primitive hut à la Laugier. That is an idealistic mind game and naïve.

F.A. | And yet you postulate the other time horizon of conventions as going beyond mere everyday up-to-dateness.

D.E. | Every human longs for a certain familiarity that provides orientation. Conventions are capable of providing that and this is what makes them important. However, they are not timeless, placeless, and absolutely valid, but are instead context-dependent. Creating familiarity makes conventions a part of architecture, which, first and foremost, does just that. What could possibly speak against this? What could be wrong with ensuring quality in expectation of radical upcoming changes?

F.A. | Some even demand new conventions.

D.E. | To me that sounds like inventing new mountains. Exhausting! I register the desire for conventions and then pick a few pleasing aspects out of a big bouquet and call it new. I don’t think it really has any future. Especially when it is actually about working on the conventions, working with them, which has as little to do with creating an exact copy as it does with overthrowing them.

F.A. | Craftsmanship, community, conventions – this results in the concept of sustainability. Is that what today’s clients – especially the international ones – are looking for when they come to you?

D.E. | Even on a global scale, we are guided by these three scales: the conventions of the place, our values and their regional background, and today’s knowledge of engineering. When we bring these into accord, the result is sustainability. Sustainability must also combine different aspects: Ecology, society, and economy.

F.A. | On the topic of economic viability: Is it that, and not beauty, that international clients and global players are looking for when they come to you? Has economic viability not fallen into a state of dire disrepute?

D.E. | I see it purely as positive! From this point of view: as a relation of used resources to return. And from the other: as an attempt to grasp something as a whole—a broadened approach. Life cycle costs are a calculation of investment, operating, and disposal costs. In the end, it is all about: How can we attain a higher use value, higher cultural acceptance while reducing the use of resources?

Economy or beauty? I say that beauty is usually economical. In Europe, beauty stands for values that are valid in the long term, this means that long-term validity is relevant. This is exactly what is provided by conventions, by social and cultural acceptance. These are expressed by likeability. This is how beauty becomes a driving point of the economy. This is how durable usability is ensured, which is sustainable.

F.A. | Beauty as a driving force of economy and sustainability—how different is this from the current dominant perception, which seems to be marked by increasing technological efficiency?

D.E. | I see this type of faith in technology as a very German phenomenon. Much ado about—well, nothing sustainable. Today more stressful than liberating. We reached back to 19th-century mechanical concepts, reacted to a problem by answering with a solution that brought out the next problem. Cascading solutions to problems and increasing complexity of technical approaches. Technology can increase the efficiency of values, but it cannot establish values itself. This is where evaluations come into play. And all at once, the question arises: Does our world become a better place to live through a new technology that we saddle on top of already existing ones and that we then have to supply with energy, check up on, maintain, and sustain? A look at new, advancing developments shows us that knowledge is taking the place of mechanics and powered machines, software is replacing hardware. The differentiation and improved efficiency of components must be put into perspective at the very least through interaction, dialogue, and recollection.

F.A. | There are continuities that reach from the early years to today, but there are also revaluations, shifts. How does architecture look after all this time?

D.E. | Thinking about temporal spaces now has greater meaning for me than when we began. This is connected to the fact that the concept of contemporary, which was such a central theme of modernity, has taken a step back. We can't separate ourselves from the past, can't create a New World for New People—that didn't work.

What has shifted for me is that in our early years, we believed in the user as the most significant measure of quality—today, this is the passerby. The passerby perceives a building as nothing more than a part of their environment. It is important, but there are also other buildings.

In the 20th century, we asked: What does a house contribute to the improvement of living conditions for the individual? In the 21st century, we ask: What does a house contribute to public space? This is a shift from the individual to the community; this means more dialogue, more contextuality, less sculpturality.

In the end, it all turns around the question: How long does a building retain its value? This appears to be an economic question, but its answer actually depends upon beauty.

F.A. | So what should we now think about the quote we cited from Le Corbusier in the beginning?

D.E. | Some things remain, contour for certain. The sentence is in one of Le Corbusier's manifestos, which are steeped in *Sturm und Drang*. But it could have been from Vitruvius, Palladio, Schinkel, Mies and all the others that came after. Whether revolutionary or conservative, contour remains the touchstone, and when students have internalized this then their designs will be convincing, whether drawn with straight lines or crooked ones.

Architecture

Dietmar Eberle

1 *Personal Observations*

Throughout the entire world, it has become standard practice to require teachers to review their work at regular intervals. This is justified alone by the fact that education should provide long-lasting effects, as well as because education must maintain its position through the passage of time. In the case of architectural education, this is especially necessary, since it is the teaching of a subject whose striving for protection and security, ascertainment and self-representation, is among the oldest undertakings of humanity.

One such revision undertaken about a decade ago was presented in *From City to House—A Design Theory*. The vicissitude in the discipline has grown no calmer since this time. What conclusions can be drawn from this? In **9 × 9**, we present a profound and up-to-date review of the approach that ties directly into the ascertainment that architecture is currently in a paradoxical state.

On the one hand, you find saviors and style icons omnipresent in word creations such as "the architecture of the web" and "the architecture of the times", "cloud architecture" can even be found. There is architecture wherever one looks. Architecture exhibitions are audience magnets, the accouterment of the new middle class with architecture cannot be ignored, and no party goes without a discussion on architecture.

This is contrasted by the repression of—and even disdain for—architecture. Deficits in usefulness, technical construction defects, planning and cost securities are sued for, and accusations of political corruption are complemented by the popularized taste judgments of a so-called "expert audience". Architecture has been declared open game. The cry of "everybody is an artist" has been replaced by "everybody is an architect".

Simplifying this to a phenomenon produced by the media would, of course, cut the story short. It is true, the field is in a state of change. Someone planning a building a generation ago could generally make do with a single structural engineer—and good craftspeople. By the end of the century, this list had grown: Site engineers, energy specialists, fire safety authorities, and exterior space designers. Instead of craftspeople, there are now salespeople for industrial building materials. Today, the table includes acoustic engineers, light designers, building material experts, equal opportunities officers, business accountants, and—now wholly inevitable—the experts of all experts: Project developers, construction planners, project managers, supervisors, and—not to be forgotten—the lawyers. This is true for more that just large construction projects with great demands and a list of regulations that are almost impossible to comprehend.

If one extrapolates this development, the conclusion is obvious: An implosion is impending. What to do? The paradoxical answer is: The design skills of the architect are needed. It has been empirically ascertained that this is one of the few qualifications not endangered by digitalization. Far-sighted project developers put their faith in design—which is, of course, dependent upon the responses of building clients, investors, and developers. One could put it in other words: Expert knowledge is overvalued, mediators are overvalued. What is needed is healthy common sense, personal judgment, and willingness to take responsibility.

These are the cornerstones of design competency—and this is how they were expressed in the earliest of architecture treatises; old and those still to be discovered. This is complemented by comprehensive expert knowledge. This knowledge must, however, be part of an ability set that has, since time immemorial, characterized the discipline like no other: Mediation and integration. Accordingly, design ability is, above all, about bringing different aspects together into a whole. And this has little to do with the graphic arts of digital computers, with all the smoke and mirrors of visualizations.

Design ability is a core competency: In the more complex processes of architecture production, the demand for it is palpably stronger. At the same time, the other end of building is also calling. There is a great interest in small projects, projects that grow up out of their surroundings. The ascertainment of their context is at the core of the social turn. It is small offices that react flexibly and directly; it is a grassroots movement that acts together with the affected people; it is local anchoring that sets the bar; it is projects that grow beyond the borders of glittering metropolises.

The diagnosis remains the same: Building quality benefits when architectural expertise is sought. It suffers when the input share of the architect is marginalized. Too often, the so-called dictates of economic benefit or functional use—without ever defining with any precision what these are—is the argument to end all arguments. But it is becoming increasingly clear that the time in which Bill Clinton issued his irrefutable statement is reaching its end: "It's the economy, stupid." A turnaround is perceptible: A new generation is remembering what was once self-evident in architecture, the most social of all arts. The increase in social engagement, practiced through new organizational forms, cannot be overlooked. And see now: What was unimaginable a mere decade ago, is now happening—graduates are finding work again, everyday work.

Therefore, the prognosis after a decade is: Architecture has a future! As a discipline that classically serves to integrate knowledge and ability, it is well positioned, for the interdisciplinary is sought everywhere. The unmistakably clear signs of a crisis are indications of a cleansing in the spirit of self-definition. And even more: The synthesizing role of architecture can be radically intensified and driven beyond the mere integration of knowledge.

2 *Craftsmanship and Architecture*

The virtual world of new media is not limited to image production. The dissemination of information—via new and conventional media alike—has reached new dimensions. The craziest skyscrapers find their way into the average living room in no time. This world is populated by stars, or architecture gurus in today's vernacular, who whisper of the strangest futures, the coming of which is announced by a few insiders. A world of pure intellect, of virtuality. Some even enjoy playing the role of the autonomous creator, the independent artist, sovereign in their own realm of ideas.

In light of this, one must establish: Architecture is not an art. While art lays claim to creating independent alternate worlds, architecture is tied to this world and has the imperative task of designing a usable and livable world. This results in having great responsibility to the public in general, a responsibility that can be divided into four fundamental aspects: cultural input, usability, economic viability, and lifespan.

In terms of these categories, responsibility means aligning with the tangible world we live in. Architecture is a physical practice; it is about material things. It shares this with craftsmanship, without which architecture—despite certain utopian visions—cannot be imagined. Craftsmanship that is, of course, at the height of the times, that is aware of its own material cyclicality. The social turn of recent years is not alone in confirming this connection.

The explosion of information together with a dragging capacity to process it creates a dissonance that is not always easy to resolve. Craftsmanship is well aware of the tensions between excessive demands and the limits of individuals. It answers with cooperation and knowledge based on experience. This cannot be described as an accumulation of information, but rather as integration, and includes evaluation, classification, and the opening of relationships. The physical dimension of such knowledge is obvious, and its qualities come naturally to our neurology, as opposed to the pure collecting of information. Such empirical knowledge combines understanding, experience, initiative, and networking. This is why it is able to process information dynamically on the one hand, and provide complex, responsible solutions on the other. Craftsmanship has always provided this kind of integration, and is thus today capable of assimilating modern technologies without problem. For this reason, empirical knowledge will become more important.

The following should be made fruitful for the professional profile of the architect: Experiential knowledge and responsibility leading to generalizing skills that are increasingly shifted to the forefront. The various demands must be weighed, resources must be used in reasonable ways—this requires a holistic viewpoint. The architect also bears responsibility for those who are not at the table. The social aspect must be bolstered. Efforts to include preliminary planning steps—key words: project development—must be welcomed. The interface between architects and producers also needs to be improved—and digital media provide excellent tools for this. Overall, bridging the gap to the practice of building is gaining in importance.

3 *Beauty as a Cultural Aspect*

The differentiation of art and architecture of course does not mean that aesthetics in architecture are obsolete. Beauty is not incidental to architecture, it is essential to it—a social art. Hans-Georg Gadamer emphasizes this: "What is seen as beautiful cannot be identified as specific recognizable characteristics of an object, but is instead testified to by subjective viewpoints: An increased sense of living in a harmonious equivalence of the powers of imagination and reason. It is a stimulation of our mental powers as a whole, an open game." According to this, architecture plays an important role in allowing beauty to unfold in people's lives.

Architecture is the environment that imprints people most. This imprinting always happens in a place. In architectural development, place and an understanding of place are the central starting point. This means augmenting the topographical and physical aspects of a place with cultural ones. This includes not only history, but also the attitudes and mentalities of the residents, the people who live there and have made the place what it is today. An architect tracks these resources of a place down, evaluates them, and ties them into their design—it is the context with which the building enters into dialogue.

This dialogue is not a one-sided or mechanical process. It can only succeed when fed with commitment. "One must take a position or have taken a position in order to understand another position," ascertains Italian philosopher Luigi Pareyson. Personal inclinations and interests, client wishes, and societal and public concerns must be brought into line in a balancing act that includes the future implications of the project: "Without this connection and an intense dedication to what a project should become, architecture as we imagine it will not be brought into existence," emphasized Jacques Herzog recently.

A building must primarily be socially accepted and culturally valued on the level of perception. The significance of architecture lies in its contribution to the public and that it is perceived by everybody, even those who never set a foot inside the door. Architecture is made up of what everybody likes, and by this I mean collective acceptance more than personal taste. The challenge is therefore to answer to these collective sensitivities, which are essentially based on locally anchored conventions. In this context, anonymous architecture, which lies well within convention, grows in significance.

Starting with this point means maintaining equal distance from, on the one hand, private taste and, on the other, academic rules that dictate sacrosanct judgments of proportion, massing, and materials. The everyday actions, approaches, and values that come together to create a distinct local identity have priority. Convention is what measures beauty. It aims for self-evident pragmatism, not for spectacularity. This quality is attributed a high value because it will endure in the long run. Beauty stimulates a cultural acceptance that affords a property more value than any technical innovation can. An investment in such beauty will be a profitable one, as it ensures the permanence of the real estate. The true significance of a structure will, in the end, be in its long-term and permanent contribution to public life.

4 *Resources and Time*

Someone who brings up cultural resources cannot fail to mention natural resources. The way we handle these resources can only be called depletion—even if one takes into consideration that the warning voices are not always in unison. Belief in technical feasibility is taking over the most remote corners of the world, and the positive effects of technical intervention are being neutralized by the rebound effect. Building plays a considerable role in this development; in highly developed societies, approximately half of the primary energy demand is used for the construction and maintenance of buildings. High demand for comfort is tied to a high use of resources. This behavior has little future and is not a viable model for developing countries. Keeping it up would result in a global collapse.

Architects have a tremendous impact on resources through their decisions on material use, construction methods, and the operating costs resulting from these. This is why they are so crucial to actuating a change in direction. Perspectives on this have shifted tremendously in recent years. The tunnel vision focused only on saving energy in the construction phase has given way to life cycle observations; a systemic view of building has taken the place of technical interventions. This brings the matter of how anonymous housing typologies have optimized the use of local resources back into focus, particularly when contrasted with architecture's trust in technology of the past century. It has meanwhile been empirically proven that a departure from this outpacing use of technology can be quite on target when looking to save resources and increase our quality of life. But no matter what the path looks like: The goal is socially and culturally valuable architecture dedicated to a caring and frugal use of our limited resources.

Seen from this viewpoint, construction is also resource management. The means that must be used in each case need to be efficiently designed and in relation to the desired quality. Ever briefer cycles of technical innovation are contrasted by enduring and usable structures. If one is speaking of quality, then the single most important requirement of a building today is longevity. This is still contrasted by a point of view focused on amortization periods of 30 to 35 years, often for technical reasons. The result of this is that innovation produces economically calculated demolition sites that bear no value for subsequent generations and then block forthcoming innovation. The complete refurbishment of existing buildings, in and of itself a highly questionable undertaking, will never be possible in this way.

Breaking with the line of thought that perceives buildings as a mere fulfillment of purpose will become inescapable. When a building garners its value from social and cultural acceptance, the primary objective of fulfilling a use can be replaced by the intrinsic value of the building, which is the result of duration and beauty. Resource conservation based on durability converges with the intrinsic value of beauty—making economy and ecology compatible. This supposed conflict of interest must be revaluated by looking at the question of the measure of time that is applied when assessing a building. A lifespan of a century or more puts construction costs in an entirely different light. Focus must be shifted from building costs to a longer duration of value. Higher quality standards and higher construction investments guarantee future value. This is the increase in value provided by architecture.

At the end of his life—one certainly not lacking in eventfulness—William S. Burroughs said that the last resource of humanity is time. When everything else runs out, we will still have time. Beginning to handle these resources carefully right now—creating things that endure and allowing them the time needed to ripen—is a wise addendum to the careful handling of natural resources.

5 *The Building as a Whole and Technical Subsystems*

A building can be seen in very different ways. If the cultural context is included and durability is a prerequisite, then the following five aspects must be considered:

THE PLACE, the context of the building—topography, climate, infrastructure, culture, and mentality—is a system with a life span of much more than 100 years.
THE STRUCTURE of the supporting framework and site development has a life span of more than 100 years.
THE SKIN of the building, both the façade and the roof, has a life span of around 50 years.
BUILDING uses change faster than expected, experience shows changes after about 25 years.

> MATERIALS, surfaces, effective use areas, and technical facilities are subject to mechanical and everyday wear and tear and rarely last more than ten years.

It is clear that the aspect of time dictates the scale; public site impact endures longest, with use and facilities trailing at the end. This is a revaluation of the design values previously considered valid. These observations lead to the following consequences:

- Public space gives a building specific qualities and characteristics.
- The value of a building is determined by its measure of openness to use conversions.
- The structure creates the prerequisites for this, which include a robust framework, divisibility of installations, and adequate site development.
- The interior—both the architecture and the technical facilities—leads its own relatively detached life that meets the needs of the users.

All of these aspects contribute to creating a valuable structure. However, it is necessary to differentiate. On the one hand, there is the public impact of a building, and on the other the private. The one is planned for durability and stability and the other for flexibility and variability, softness. This differentiation does not just apply to inside and outside, the building itself can also be divided into public and private. One is the classic terrain of architecture, the other increasingly the domain of design and interior architecture.

6 *Design Competency*

The quality of a structure is dependent upon a bringing together, something intimated by the five aspects. The architect's actual core competency is the ability to shape, to integrate various aspects into a whole of which one can say, together with

Alberti, "that reasoned harmony of all the parts within a body, so that nothing may be added, taken away, or altered, but for the worse."

Architecture is synthesis creation. Cultural values, usability, economic efficiency, and life expectancy must be integrated, which could be a more current version of Vitruvius' abstract triad of *utilitas, firmitas,* and *venustas*. Facing the concrete head on, Alberti stated: "The Conclusion is, that for the Service, Security, Honour and Ornament of the Publick, we are exceedingly obliged to the Architect; to whom, in Time of Leisure, we are indebted for Tranquility, Pleasure and Health, in Time of Business for Assistance and Profit; and in both, for Security and Dignity." In other words, the physical reality of a building is as present as the user in their sensual physical body.

The dimension of time unfurls itself in architecture. Using place as the starting point dictates that time is present in the form of history—unique, multi-layered, local history. In European cities, a wide variety of value concepts, technical developments, and social changes have come about in concrete forms and great abundance. Compared to this, almost nothing is more boring than the entirely predetermined place of a satellite town, born of a single principle.

The diversity of a city that has been able to evolve can be seen throughout our wealth of history. It is visual proof of what Josef Frank ascertained: "Our time is the entirety of history as we know it. This thought alone could be the foundation of modern architecture. [...] A human has a gothic skeleton and a classical skin, but there is nothing that makes the skeleton more genuine than the skin." Time is present here in two ways: Frank speaks of the historical eras that are reflected in building types. These types make up the history of the architectural discipline, which is essential to the creative ability of the architect.

And Frank speaks of our time. Every design begins now, in the present. He looks back and casts his eye on the future. Creative ability means bearing witness to this crossroads; this is what underpins its authenticity. And because this is about the physical reality of building, realization is key; this is applied building technology. Having a solid grip on the current state of construction technology is the logical consequence of this.

So, architecture is synthesis creation that reflects on the conditions of the site, enters into a dialogue with these conditions from the standpoint of the present time, and has mastery in its own discipline. Architecture becomes holistic when it is able to tie various, supposedly conflicting aspects together. In Semper's words, to knot them into "the original bonding of all things".

7 *Method*

Teaching is based upon a premise: Architecture can be taught. This sounds paradoxical, and a certain irritation cannot be denied—after all, every design is highly specific and personal. However, by maintaining this premise nonetheless, we accept an interplay like that proposed by Friedrich Schiller in his work *On the Aesthetic Education of Man.*

He writes of play. Playing necessitates players and an interplay, which has rules. Rules contradict the freedom of the player, but where does this freedom go when the game falls apart from a lack of rules? This unsolvable contradiction can only be playfully solved: Playfully—playing out their freedom—the players confirm the rules, which are only relevant when a player is playing. "Man is only completely a man when he plays," concludes Schiller.

One can thus deduce: Education does not contradict the development of an architect. Instead, it gives them tools, teaches about structure and the rules of the game. This fortifies the methods practiced here, which must provide three things: System, hierarchy, and simultaneity. The system assures security, hierarchy provides order, and simultaneity enables development.

The system says that each project must be processed according to a binding method. In consecutive steps, each project is examined and processed according to the five categories. These are joined by additional combinations of categories to result in a total of nine steps that can be applied to thoroughly evaluate each project. This is carried out based on a specific urban situation, and includes inspecting the actual site.

Hierarchy means that the five categories and their combinations must be processed in a specific and well-planned order, which represents an evaluation of content. After this, there is the path from the immediate to the mediated. The place is the beginning; each step taken creates a successive densification. The complexity increases, yet the project remains structured. Giving place utmost priority would have been unthinkable a mere generation ago. At that time, architecture was thought to emerge from its program, its use. This change is an expression of a revaluation that gives the integration of architecture into the social, cultural, and spatial context definitive priority.

Simultaneity says that this hierarchy, which evolves from simple basic concepts to complex interactions, is set up so that each consecutive step is able to reach back and access the starting point. In this way, the complexity of the task can evolve while basic concepts are still refined with each step. Analysis and design alternate when working on a project, as do group and individual work. The simultaneity of these different aspects stimulates the development of concepts and actions for each phase.

This vitality is reinforced by the task developing in two different ways: On the one hand, the place of the building is examined, as is the converse, the building in the place. This includes a change of scale. On the other hand, the evolution of the question according to three different urban contexts is taken into consideration.

Of course, the least part of teaching is mastering the learning material. Working with the learning material allows one's own individual skills to develop. In this, it is once again a craft—admittedly an unusual one—that is used as a model: Every musician knows that the path to success is paved with practice, practice, practice. In light of this, we go through the assignments and exercises again and again. But this is not enough: Musicians must engage with their music, study how others interpret it, where it comes from and what it could be used to say today. At the same time, the examination of how people think of certain topics today and how they thought in the past—theory and discourse—is given great significance.

What can be taught should also allow evaluation. Of course: This program has so many different levels that the question of criteria can be a difficult one. The answer can thus only be an approximation.

The first step is to determine if and to what degree the assignment was fulfilled—also in comparison to the work of fellow students. And therewith the quantification ends. Another criterion is the intensity with which the assignment was taken on and completed. And finally, it is about the independence of the idea. Certainly, the last two evaluation points are based on soft criteria—this doesn't make the situation any easier, but we are all familiar with the coexistence of stringent and tolerant thinking.

It is clear that the last two evaluation points cannot be judged with a formula. Something comes back into play that has been mentioned several times already: Context and experience. The topics are worked on in the studio, the teacher and the pupils meet each week for a half a year. These meetings, whether in a group or individually, are required by the project and are a process of—more or less intensive—reciprocal give and take; structurally, however, they are never a one-dimensional cause-and-effect system. The passing of time that this studio work requires makes it possible to develop an image of the tendencies, capacities, and dedication of the participants•

Practice and Teaching

Adrian Meyer

It was the early 1960s, and storm clouds were gathering. My architectural education was like the ball in a pinball game, its erratic movements the syllabus. The doctrine of the time concentrated on the great masters, and was rooted in the incipient instability of the term *modernity*. In light of the dynamic of budding cultural processes, the mantra of never-changing assertions was wearisome. Aldo Rossi's *L'architettura della città* undermined Hilberseimer's modern concept of the city and Venturi's *Complexity and Contradiction* scratched at the dogma of "International Style" from the year 1932. Kerouac blew the fanfare of the Beat Generation, Truffaut and Godard wallowed in the melancholy images of the Nouvelle Vague, and Dylan bluntly taunted the "Masters of War" about the Vietnam disaster.

My antennas were set to receive, but not ready to tread the worn-out path of modernism.

There had to be other ways than sitting in on what was the architectural equivalent of Latin class. Something to nourish hope that architecture still held aspects of enlightenment going beyond mere rules of grammar. A hungry young wolf doesn't want to have the slain prey placed meekly at its feet—it should rather be forced to pick up the scent, to search for lost footprints in the fog. But what to do, when one is practically force-fed with Corbusier as propaganda—with Gropius as the Minister of Defense for modernism? We would have much rather learned about how Corbusier's dogma of *cinq points* related to his late designs of the Maisons Jaoul, the chapel in Ronchamp, and the Philips Pavilion. Or about why Gropius fought so bitterly with Rudolf Schwarz about his purported betrayal of modernism after the war that even Mies van der Rohe joined the side of the church builder and city planner from Cologne? Or how Aalto's work relates to the northern classicism of Asplund and Lewerentz?

But there was no reaction to this, no useful dispute, no real examination leading forward. In the middle of these sprouting doubts of the established educational agenda, a for me quite adventurous journey began into the realm of questioning—a journey into Posthistoire literature, smack at the center of questioning the very concept of history, as well as the cartwheeling influences of metabolism, brutalism, and structuralism, of Archigram, the Vienna movement, and Team X. Questioning the dogma of modernism is all well and good, but which paths can then be trusted? What now, oh curious dilettante? Now there you stand, dizzy with confusion. Influences that you cannot connect or join. Each movement cancels out the next one. Postmodernism, an alleged new meta-language, is peeking up over the horizon. But there it stays standing with feet of clay, despite the philosophical blessings of Welsch and Lyotard, searching for the typical recipes of patricide.

It certainly would not have harmed me to feel along the footsteps of Schinkel, Semper, and the generations that followed with just a touch more humility.

Where did the history that resulted in these modernist theories come from, and to where did the paths beyond it lead? It would have provided something to hold on to—courage to speculate, to gain a little more perspective in the stirred up dust of the history of reception. And now this very footing, which I had absolutely refused to accept when offered by the theory-distant proponents of modernism, was lacking. My mental state at the time was akin to a wanderer preparing to mount the Matterhorn in house slippers with next to no supplies. Dripping wet and badly shaken, I soon returned to base camp.

Somewhat more patient, somewhat less intent upon refusal, I decided to follow the difficult path through the stations of historical architectural education, to delve into theories, and to search out the "where from" and "where to".

After the failed start of a world of monotheism and one of polytheism, I began to investigate the matter more pragmatically. My uncle, an architect in Germany and a champion of the Stuttgart School of Bonatz and Schmitthenner, gave me a book by Hans Döllgast on drawing houses. Wonderful little sketches and watercolors nourished my curiosity for this very special form of architectural writing. And then I discovered the rapid ink lines of Mendelsohn and the broad chalks of Kahn. A world revealed itself to me that stuck its head, gut, and hand wholeheartedly into the game, and a whole cosmos opened up, one that long outshone my remaining deficiencies. A little drawing, I thought, a little practice, I thought—it would be enough to at least recognize some of the great roots of architecture. The seeming ease of sketching and the "drawn" paintings of Alberto Giacometti led me headfirst into my error of thought. I could not imagine Giacometti's energy and tenacity, and how he strove to see things at their core, as they really were. After all the time of Surrealism, after the death of his father, and an existential crisis during the Second World War in Paris, his heads and figures became increasingly minimal. Searching for the essence, he found his way to an extremely fragile means of expression in plaster, clay, and bronze. His search was accompanied by nagging doubts: "I do not see much further in painting and drawing, yes. There is no space, one must create it, but it does not exist, no" (ca. 1949).[1]

And then, with bare hands, he worked the wet clay—worked it away and away—until, let us say, it left the state of being a figure and began to approach his own inner image. All this was accompanied by the knowledge of failure, if not without a certain gathering of knowledge.

[1] Alberto Giacometti: *Werke und Schriften. Entweder Objekte, oder Poesie, sonst nichts*, Verlag Scheidegger & Spiess, Zurich, 1998, p. 227.

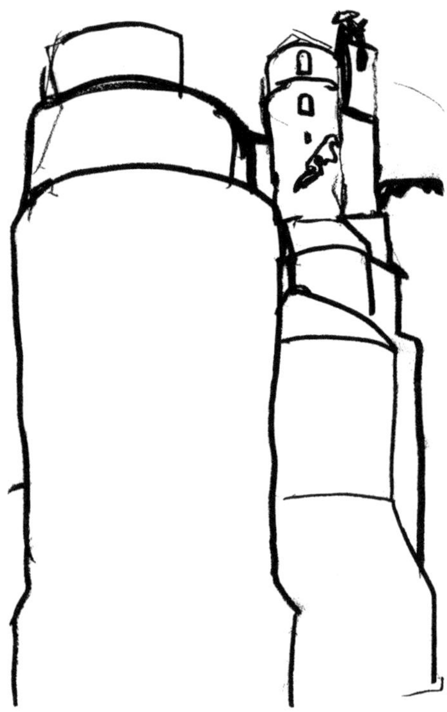

Louis I. Kahn, Buttress Tower sketch, St. Cecile Cathedral, Albi, France 1959

After I had at least understood that nothing of nothing leads to nothing, I began my intense and inspiring years of learning and wandering.

I learned to construct and to build in an architectural environment enriched by drawing and thinking. A fascination for architecture that, in accordance with its purpose, supported itself with the art of building and saw the unnamable and the idea-filled as something desirable was what stayed with me. Between the poles of reason and emotion, architectural design finds its connection on a larger scale, to the city, to the urban.

In New York and Philadelphia, I learned from the points of view of emigrated European architects—Saarinen, Kahn, Neutra, and Mies van der Rohe. The galleries and museums, with their stock of minimal and conceptual art, became my visual schools. After my return, I at least knew how much I did not know.

Around the world, students began to break up the existing structures at institutes of higher learning. Criticism of capitalism hobbled the classic design classes of architectural faculties. In the late 1960s, sociological debates threatened to blanket what was now the "suspicious" field of architecture at the ETH as well. The theoretical vacuum that resulted became, in a certain way, the flag that lured the wide-awake, leftist mind of Aldo Rossi from Milan to Zurich.

The charismatic shaman brought new life to teaching there. He tied his theoretical approach to the academic nature of city and architecture in teaching to his already flourishing architectural practice. Through his buildings, he tested, so to speak, his theory of the semiotics of architecture in the city. The risk he took, of miscalculating reality by asserting a theory, strengthened his credibility as a teacher, architect, and theoretician. In these uneasy times full of uncertainty, this was exactly what everybody was looking for—not for the ideology, which of course was also part of it, but the unagitated stance of a thinking, acting, and teaching architect.

It was a time of the transition from dogmatic modernism in architecture to something else, something that was as yet unnamed. Influential Bernhard Hoesli recognized very early on the opportunities arising from this: "The fixed points that make it possible for teachers and students to orient themselves have shifted. In their place, we now see a great number of different tendencies. The weather is starting to change."[2]

[2] Ákos Moravánszky, Judith Hopfengärtner: *Aldo Rossi und die Schweiz. Architektonische Wechselwirkungen*, gta Verlag, Zurich, 2011, p. 80.

Debates were contradictory, the first wave of modernism criticism by Jacobs, Venturi, Mitscherlich, Rossi, and others receded and was taken up again as a reaction by Collage City and Delirious New York. A time of reflective modernism began, in its classicistic, dogmatic, and expressive form.

Now I really wanted to know for certain, and threw myself into the adventure of building, together with my partner Urs Burkard. This adventure is still going on today—an oeuvre has emerged, a design approach joined with a theoretical foundation of classic radicalism that has withstood the continual shifting of new *isms* with poise and aplomb.

And then, suddenly, a wake-up call from the daydream of designing and building. There I stood on Hönggerberg Mountain, fulfilling Loos' definition of a "mason who studied Latin", not knowing what had happened to me. Behind the many expectant faces of my students hid a myriad of questions: Where from, why, how, and where to? Now you cannot just waltz up with the infallibility of the great masters. No—always nicely stomping the cement dust from your shoes before entering the holy halls of learning. I liked to spice up the stew of history and theory, statics and construction with a few ingredients from the inexorability of actual building. A drafting class emerged from this, the acceptance of which I didn't have to chase down a single time. Not even in Vienna, where, after having retired from the ETH, certain students at the TU had to cut and paste fifteen thousand cardboard bricks in order to transfer their own vault designs into a model the size of a person to understand the statics of it.

One foot in teaching, the other in practice. However, the practice is beset by increasingly strong storm winds. The occupational profile of an architect is changeable and will, in terms of required competencies, be reevaluated. Compared to this, an architectural school is like a protected harbor for ships to practice their maneuvers, with all damages covered. It is the privilege of an architect who is also a teacher to understand the conflict that emerges from each particular framework not as threat, but as an enhancement of one's own design energy.

I do not experience school as an insular universe within an increasingly fast-moving world; rather, it takes part in the discourse on the tensions connected to this. I see school as an "energetic field", from which works can arise with qualities that develop in the best of cases with almost no precedent. School becomes a laboratory in which inspiration can be anchored and absorbed. The teaching program becomes a vessel of exchange, an important cultural nursery, the conditions of which are not entirely removed from practice, but also not entirely dictated by the pragmatism inherently necessary to practice.

During one's years of study, it is possible to learn how to situate projects within a greater whole—let's call it the city—to put them into relation without the dangers of the professional routine of designing. It is these relationships to the city, and not the thinking about a mere object, that lead to the much-needed meaningfulness of a design. Not every building task is an exception in what has become a blur of the city as a whole; not every task warrants a break. Here, I push against unnecessary formal complications, which does not mean that we will traverse naturally occurring borders in order to reassess the "traditions of modernism" without the weight of its dogmas, or to search for the fine line between "fascinating clarity" and "meaningless functionalism".

Teaching also means moderation, tying together different levels of knowledge and experience. It should lead to thinking in networks and complex structures. Teaching has an exciting relationship with practice. Research results, which I understand as encompassing scientific theoretical research along with the "field research" of practicing architects, are developed within the thought laboratories of schools. The projects that are created in this laboratory usually remain on paper, unlike in practice. They profit from a special state of being undisguised and must not primarily deliver solid proof of their effective built capabilities. Because of this, they have a half-life that has proven beneficial. One can take part in an ongoing development, can sail through overly routine processes and influence the process by adding or subtracting. The theoretical level and scientific research are, so to speak, the continual and profound element at universities, the proximity to practice is indispensible—yet not the sole prerequisite—for asserting oneself in the architecture school of the future.

As a practicing architect, I feel where the wind is blowing and, as a teacher, I take this meteorological data into the classroom. Louis Kahn, who was a great architect and an influential teacher, said something along the lines of: "Schools began with a man under a tree who did not know he was a teacher, sharing his perceptions with a few others who did not know they were pupils. The pupils thought about what had been said and about how good it was to be near this person. They wanted their children to listen to such a person as well. Soon, rooms were built and the first schools came to be. The building of schools fulfills a human desire."[3] Derived from this, and this was and still is incredibly important to me, the freedom of architectural education, bound to a position of equalizing polarities, should be lived like the freedom of independent learners.

[3] Vincent Scully Jr.: Louis I. Kahn: *Makers of Contemporary Architecture*, George Braziller, 1962.

A Method of Design: Observations and Insights

Franziska Hauser and Marcello Nasso

Professor Dietmar Eberle taught his course titled "Architecture and Design II" to a class of 50 to 70 second-year students in the Department of Architecture of the ETH Zurich from 1999 to 2017. During these 18 years, he and his assistants trained over a thousand architects.

Like every course, this one is also an ongoing, ever-evolving process that involves many people, but which is based on sound thought. The basic thinking behind Eberle's course is outlined in the following as an interplay of theory and practice.

Course Organization and Structure

The students mainly experience this time of learning collectively, in a central location. At the beginning of the second year, each student is assigned an individual drawing table in the studio, where he or she can think and work outside of official class hours.

Second year is an important moment in the architecture program: The students have been at the university for just one year and have only a bit of practice in the task of converting a three-dimensional idea into a plan or a model. The design course directly confronts the students with architecture and tries to open them up to this discipline on an intellectual and practical level. The aim of the course is to sensitize the architecture students to their haptic and phenomenological experiences in a continual examination of place, and to teach them to design methodically.

At the start of the semester, six groups are formed of eight to twelve students each. An assistant instructor is assigned to each group. They accompany and supervise the architecture students during the two days of classes as a group, in teams of two, and individually.

The lesson takes place in the professorship's studio for two full days each week, and is planned for an entire year of study, in two semesters. The fall and spring semesters each last

13 weeks. During this time, between seven and nine assignments are carried out that deal with different topics and aspects of architectural design. A final exercise assigned at the end of each semester tries to combine the acquired skills and apply them together in an architectural design project.

All assignments are carried out at real building sites. At the beginning of each year's course, the materials needed to carry out the work are produced collectively; this includes models of the building sites and their surroundings at a scale of 1:500, and various base drawings. During the fall semester, the aim is to reconfigure, add to, and improve the existing built fabric of the site. A detailed analysis of the existing context is an important part of every exercise. In the spring semester, the building site is fictitiously cleared, and the students continue to work on the already known sites by designing new buildings. Each exercise consists of an analysis that deals with the place at an urban level, and a design assignment on the level of the building.

The students objectively approach the building sites by doing a detailed analysis of the urban space. Their tools of analysis are walks through the city, videos of the area, urban history research, investigation of the infrastructure, and documentation of street sequences (views) around each of the building sites. They put their findings together in a presentation for the whole class.

In the design portion of the exercise, which is done in pairs, students work on the various topics step-by-step. The resulting design schemes are presented in one or two A0 format drawings, and are presented to the professor and assistant before the whole class. The contents of the A0 layouts are pre-defined: concept text, plans, images, or model photos. The models are placed next to the A0 drawings and show the design in three dimensions.

Professor Eberle takes part in discussions with the students in the studio, but he himself never sits at the drawing board to correct individual projects. After each exercise is finished, it is subjected to a comprehensive critique. These reviews are like a workshop; rather than dealing with different examples theoretically, Professor Eberle delves into each individual project, discusses architectural issues directly with the design, and thus passes on his experiences from theory and practice to the students.

At the end of the first semester in the fall and the second semester in spring, guest critics are invited to discuss each of the individually developed design projects.

Course Progression

Specific building sites in the immediate vicinity are the starting point of each exercise. Each year, three specific building sites in Zurich are selected by the department for discussion. One of the three building sites is located in the medieval old town, one in one of Zurich's Foundation Era districts, and one in a modern context or in a suburban area. During the first semester, the students rotate from one building site to the next, thus becoming acquainted with all three types of contexts.

These three historical periods—the Middle Ages, the Foundation Era, and modernity—were chosen because they represent important periods in the growth of the city of Zurich, and of many other Central European cities as well.

The individual exercises on the architectural topics of **PLACE, STRUCTURE, ENVELOPE, PROGRAM,** and **MATERIALITY** are carried out on the building sites and, through this, a method of analysis and design is learned.

The course is based on the conviction that place, represented by each of the building sites, is the reference system and thus the driving force and resource for the development of an architectural project, regardless of whether we are dealing with an urban or rural context.

An understanding of the neighborhood through abstract measurements—density, height, adjacencies, and dimensions—and as experienced by the senses—the atmosphere, the milieu, and the material texture of the built fabric—forms the basis of this process-oriented method of design.

The degree of built density and the percentage of public amenities in each location are essential features that illustrate the differences among the individual districts. The quality of the city as a whole is linked to the composition of the various districts and their different densities. It is not about one specific setting, but the change and the mix of different districts and settings.

For the students, engaging the context always begins with a walk through the city to the building site. These walks through the city make the link between the theoretical method of design and the physical experience of the building sites comprehensible.

If we look at the urban fabric of European cities, it becomes clear that the old town centers that evolved naturally from the Middle Ages and the Foundation Era districts characterized by similar building types are shaped more by anonymous buildings than by the individual work of a particular architect.

In support of this realization, Professor Eberle points to the book, *Architecture Without Architects*, published by the architect and cultural philosopher Bernard Rudofsky in 1964, as a catalogue to his exhibition of the same name at MOMA in New York. Eberle adds:

> *Behind these anonymous buildings is a collective memory, which is typical of our different cultures. This collective memory is what we find so important as a resource for architecture when we make it today. A great wealth of experience and knowledge is contained within these anonymous buildings. It is not the famous designer, but precisely the knowledge that is present in the collective memory that is the resource to which we attach such great importance. One must not underestimate the fact that through the academization of our profession, conditioned by the division of labor in our societies, much of this knowledge has been lost.*

1	2	3	4	5	6	7	8	9
Place		Place		Place		Place		Place
	Structure	Structure		Structure		Structure		Structure
			Envelope	Envelope		Envelope		Envelope
					Program	Program		Program
							Materiality	Materiality

Course structure, by Prof. D. Eberle

In this regard, the core question we ask ourselves, namely, with which methods of working and thinking these buildings were made, must be answered and reformulated in order to develop an awareness of our contemporary architecture.

If we want other results, we also need different methods of approach and of architectural thought.

While in the 20th century, many buildings were examined from their internal organization outwards, in the 21st century we are interested in the question of what these buildings contribute to the public space of the place. If we thought from the inside out in the 20th century, I believe that in the 21st century we must think more from the outside—of the public space—in. This approach will create the longevity that we want so much, socially, economically, and ecologically, and that we wish to see as the task for architecture in the 21st century.

Dietmar Eberle

The Methodology and Structure of Exercises

In Professor Eberle's course, a building is understood as the superimposition of five architectural parameters that have wholly different life cycles.

These architectural parameters are:

PLACE
STRUCTURE
ENVELOPE
PROGRAM
MATERIALITY

The building is designed with the aid of these five parameters and their interconnections, in constant dialogue with the site context. The topics are related systematically and form a hierarchy in terms of meaning and value, with longevity as the main criterion. Place has the highest degree of longevity, while the materiality of the surfaces is the most transitory. The five architectural themes are studied and worked on in sequence by the students. The exercises are supplemented by four additional assignments, each of which requires a combination of previously acquired skills. The five themes are reflected on in a progressive linkage, and become more complex with each step. With the last topic, a synthesis is achieved and the architectural design emerges as a whole.

Through the process of building one upon the next, we can grasp the building in its entire complexity and thus create the preconditions for its longevity.

Exercise 1 PLACE

Place occupies the first position in this chronological sequence. It involves finding an appropriate idea about massing, as well as setting it in relation to the public space. This is based on the conviction that the building massing and the densities connected to it in relation to the immediate environment form the basis for creating the atmosphere of the place. How can this massing concept be integrated as compactly as possible into the place and the topography, and thus the design of the public space improved?

Exercise 2 **STRUCTURE**

Next is a detailed study of the subject of structure. Which kind of load-bearing structural system; what type of construction; and what kind of vertical circulation system are possible for the selected massing? What types of structures are found in the urban fabric and the context of the building site?

Exercise 3 **PLACE STRUCTURE**

Having separately analyzed the place and structure, and viewing each as a step towards design, we join them together at this stage. From the massing concept for the site, the corresponding load-bearing structure and a suitable circulation system can now be developed as a means of defining a building type.

Exercise 4 **ENVELOPE**

How is the massing expressed; how are the openings articulated; and what proportion of openings does the envelope have? How are these interfaces and the related thresholds between exterior and interior designed, fabricated, and built? The massing developed in the previous exercises is now given a building envelope.

Exercise 5 **PLACE STRUCTURE ENVELOPE**

(Design project, end of fall semester)

Before modernism, the envelope was understood in the classical manner, as an autonomous system. Although it consisted mostly of the same material as the structure and made direct contact with it, the façade connected directly to the adjoining street and to the public space it faced. In this sense, the façade was primarily influenced by the place, and meeting structural requirements was a secondary task.

In his *Practical Aesthetics*, Gottfried Semper argued for a clear separation of the bearing masonry walls and the cladding of their surfaces. He sees the surface as a garment, and hence a wrapping for the supporting structure.

In all Germanic languages the word Wand [wall], which has the same root and basic meaning as Gewand [garment] directly alludes to the ancient origin and type of the visible spatial enclosure. [...] Scaffolds that served to hold, secure, or support this spatial enclosure had nothing directly to do with space or the division of space. They were foreign to the original architectural idea and were never form-determining elements to start with.

Gottfried Semper: *Style in The Technical and Tectonic Arts; Or, Practical Aesthetics. A Handbook for Technicians, Artists, and Friends of the Arts.* Translated by Harry Francis Malgrave and Michael Robinson. Getty Publications, Los Angeles, 2004. Volume One, Chapter 4, Textiles: B. Technical/Historical, p. 167ff and p. 248.

Professor Eberle's course distinguishes structure and envelope as separate systems, following Semper's division between "structural frame" and "spatial enclosure".

I regret that a clear notion of the individual elements of architecture, as formulated by Gottfried Semper in the 19th century, was replaced by functionalist theories in the 20th century. The functional programmatic approach of the 20th century was more efficient, and apparently it could solve the problem of demographic growth in the cities more quickly. However, as we now know, these solutions were only valid for a short time.

Dietmar Eberle in conversation with Marcello Nasso

Exercise 6 **PROGRAM**

For what kind of program—use or function—can the building, whose structure and façade design on its building site are already defined, be designed? How will the spaces be arranged and the corresponding uses most efficiently accessed horizontally?

Exercise 7 **PLACE STRUCTURE ENVELOPE PROGRAM**

To a large extent, structure determines the building. Putting it before the program has consequences. In terms of program, it must be posited that the openness of the building, which makes flexibility of use possible, is determined by the strategically precise design of the structure. The program is therefore understood independently from the structure and can easily respond to the different uses for the building that history will record over time.

The fact that the structure and the envelope result primarily from place and are not found in the program or the functions was pointed out by Aldo Rossi back in 1966 in his book *The Architecture of the City:*

> *This theory arises from an analysis of the urban reality; and this reality contradicts the notion that preordained functions by themselves govern artifacts and that the problem is simply to give form to certain functions. In actuality, forms in the very act of being constituted go beyond the functions which they must serve; they arise like the city itself. In this sense, too, the building is one with the urban reality, and the urban character of architectural artifacts takes on greater meaning with respect to the design project. To consider city and buildings separately, to interpret purely organizational functions in terms of representation, is to return the discourse to a narrow functionalist vision of the city. This is a negative vision because it conceives of buildings merely as scaffoldings for functional variations, abstract containers that embody whatever functions successively fill them.*

Aldo Rossi: *The Architecture of the City*, translated by Joan Ockman and Diane Ghirardo, MIT Press, Cambridge, 1982.

A hint by Ignazio Gardella, one generation older, may indicate just how much Italian thinking emphasized the autonomy of form in relation to program:

We must speak much more about form than about the function of form; ultimately, about the concept of form; but Raphael already wrote this in his letter to Count Baldassare Castiglione.

Ignazio Gardella: *L'architettura secondo Gardella Ein Gespräch zwischen Antonio Monestiroli und Ignazio Gardella*, Laterza, Milan, 1997.

Exercise 8 MATERIALITY

The quality of the surfaces determines the atmosphere of a building. The immediate proximity is critical. For the passersby in the city, this means first and foremost the street level, and the interface of building and street. Their gaze takes in the collective transitions, from the street to the apartment doors, then the entrances, the circulation system and the apartment entrances, up to the surfaces of the apartments, including services and modern fittings. Ceramic tile and self-leveling floors; niches and walls, differently wallpapered or alternately plastered; paneling, cabinets, wardrobes, and doors made of precious woods; and carefully forged light fixtures and railings, leading with steps of solid wood or stone to the upper floors of the building—the spectrum seems to be unlimited.

Exercise 9 PLACE STRUCTURE ENVELOPE PROGRAM MATERIALITY
(Design project, end of spring semester)

If we observe the street views of the old town and the Foundation Era districts, it quickly becomes clear that these are always strongly influenced by the ground floor entrances. Due to its importance in defining identity, this spatial sequence must be carefully designed from the entrance to the stairwell. In doing so, care must be taken that the ground floor has a generally different character than the upper floors. This character, this identity, is largely formed by materiality.

With this final topic of materiality, we link the five architectural themes into a programmatically open building or building ensemble that as a whole is integrated into the neighborhood, defines the public space, and thus creates a new place in a lasting way.

Exercise Sequence and Book Structure

The encounter with place and the dialogue with it in relation to the design method take place on different levels. The approach to place and the assignment is met with the preparation of a response in the form of a design scheme. This process happens incrementally for each topic. The way students approach each topic is always similarly structured.

The introduction to a new subject begins with a guest lecture. The exercise document approaches the topic in a short text. Then the terminology is given and explained, followed by the assignment of the analysis portion, and finally the assignment of the design portion.

The Essays: While talks by guest lecturers and Professor Eberle serve as an introduction to a new topic in the course, there are also essays in the course book. In them, an author approaches the respective topic from their personal perspective and against the background of contemporary architectural theory or practice.

The Terminology sections are a more associative selection of subject-specific expressions. They aim for a deeper understanding of the subject area and encourage further engagement with it.

The Analyses are the first part of an exercise at the scale of the city and are worked on in groups in preparation for the design work. In the exercises on place, structure, and envelope, the main phenomena of the three selected building sites are presented in relation to the surrounding neighborhoods from the Middle Ages, the Foundation Era, and the modern era. In the program topic, analyses of selected buildings are carried out in smaller groups. Individual building types are evaluated for characteristics, compared to one another, and then contrasted to empirical, ecological, and economic indicators. The compactness of massing, the ratio of usable area to floor area, and the ratio of openings to building envelope are investigated. The analysis on the subject of materiality includes project-specific information on materials and the study of design precedents. Both the physical and the phenomenological qualities of the materials are important, but the primary goal is to investigate the use of these materials as a user interface.

The Assignment is the practical part of each exercise. The core of the one-year course ultimately consists of a practical and empirical approach to architecture through making and doing. All knowledge and experience is based on a direct approach to a precisely formulated assignment. Following the topics, the complexity of the building as a whole is developed.

Content and Objectives

The contents of the tasks to be performed in the assignments are explained as follows.

The Concept Text is a written sketch. In contrast to the transient nature of speech, the written word is constrained to a fixed form. The concept promotes the theoretical precision of the design. Another advantage of text is that it archives the spoken word and can be stored in books, libraries, and networks, and the stored concepts, theories, and histories thus become accessible.

The Plans, as a conceptual representation, represent design concepts and are the most important specialized technique that must be practiced. Like language, a design drawing makes it possible to define, record, and convey ideas and concepts to others by means of sections and projections. At different scales, complex shapes, structures, and assemblages can be displayed with horizontal and vertical sectional drawings. Along with the drawing itself, the ability to imagine space must also be trained.

The Model deals with the project haptically, in all its dimensions. It makes it possible to simulate and control an existing or an imaginary reality. This department places great emphasis on the model; Professor Eberle teaches that only models can deal directly with the question of dimension—lengths, widths, and heights—and only the large scale makes all dimensions accessible as an image of built form.

Images and Photographs record interior and exterior spatial configurations and atmospheres, as the painting and the vanishing point perspective once did. Moving on from the model, the technique of pictorial representation serves as a tool to capture the atmospheres of unrealized situations.

The conscious and accurate handling of the written language in the concept, the perfect use of graphic representation in the plans, the precise execution of three-dimensional models, and the practiced and correct use of visualization tools in images ultimately ensure that the very personal story, the unique character of the design, flows into all topics, and thus becomes part of the architecture. Method is not a limitation of personality, but a tool with which to give it expression.

> *The methodological approach does not prohibit the personal accent, and in the final analysis, not even the question of taste; on the contrary, it is clear that this personal accent is inherent to every architecture, every age. I am convinced that our taste is the joy of the method*•

Ernesto Nathan Rogers: *Esperienza dell'architettura*, 1958.

Class trip to Israel,
Spring Semester 2015

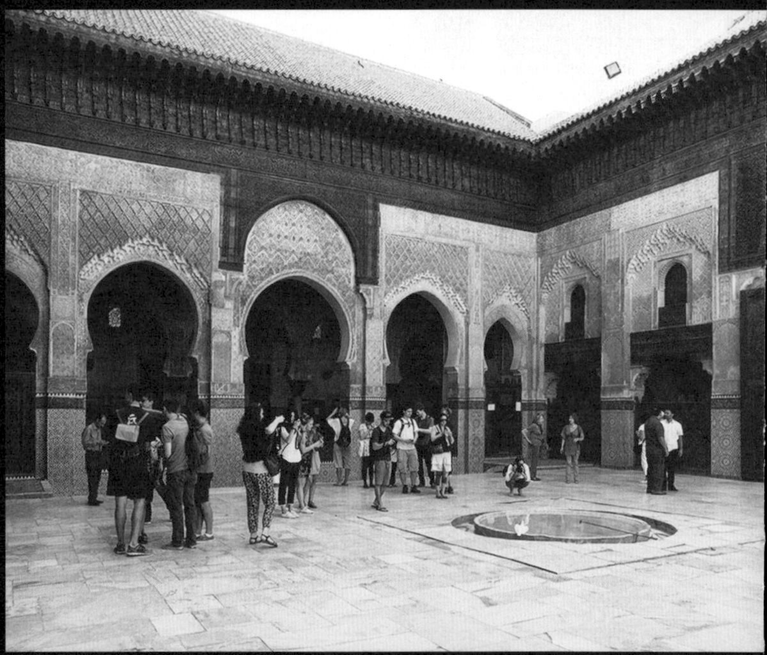

Class trip to Morocco,

Bas Princen, *Blvd (Xiamen)*, 2009, © Bas Princen

1
Place

1 Place

The original Old German meaning of the word *Ort* (place) is the point, the outmost end of something, especially that of a weapon or a path. This point protrudes and can be identified. The bargeboard (German: *Ortgang*) of a roof, for example: That is where the roof definitively ends.

Related and yet distinct is the significance of place as a location, an area: A site that is singled out, that differentiates itself from the surroundings by being limited and easily defined. Place also has something akin to a center. Such a place is a locale, an *Ortschaft*. Here, *Ort* is joined with *schaffen* (to create), place-creation. People and place are related to each other, which can create identity.

How Did Humans Get to a Place?

In the eyes of Martin Heidegger, place is tightly tied to things. Humans remain in a relationship with things and other humans—associating with them as an everyday matter, not observing or calculating. Man has always been in relationships of proximity and distance to things. This association is what allows things to have so many different connections. "Event character" (Guzzoni 2009, 108f.) is what makes a place. The personal space of a thing is the place. Place is created by the woven fabric of relationships between the things. In this vein: "Things establish places that connect to become spaces" (Führ 2000, 161).

In his lecture "Building, Dwelling, Thinking", Heidegger illustrates this with the example of a bridge. "The bridge swings over the stream 'with ease and power.' It does not just connect banks that are already there. The banks emerge as banks only as the bridge crosses the stream. The bridge expressly causes them to lie across from each other. One side is set off against the other by the bridge. [...] With the banks, the bridge brings to the stream the one and the other expanse of the landscape lying behind them. It brings stream and bank and land into each other's neighborhood. [...] The bridge lets the stream run its course and at the same time grants mortals their way, so that they may come and go from shore to shore. Bridges initiate in many ways. [...] The bridge *gathers* to itself in *its own* way earth and sky, divinities and mortals. [...] Thus the bridge does not first come to a locale to stand in it; rather, a locale comes into existence only by virtue of the bridge" (In *Poetry, Language, Thought*, trans. by Hofstadter 1971, 354–356).

So is it only things such as bridges—structures—that make places? That would neglect the interplay of things and their sites. Even though the bridge distinguishes such a site along the stream: "Nor do the banks stretch along the stream as indifferent border strips of the dry land," explains Heidegger, "But only something *that is itself a locale* can make space for a site." Heidegger accentuates how people interact with things that create places; each site must freely accommodate, must be open to a such locale.

Christian Norberg-Schulz put special focus on the topic of place during the 1970s, shifting the accent with the term *genius loci*. Place is fundamental to *genius loci*, it is the totality of concrete things. This interaction gives the place atmosphere, and aura. This, in turn, gives people a purchase, a place they can "align and identify with, experience as meaningful". Capturing the *genius loci* becomes a prerequisite of things being harmonious. To what degree the capturing itself is design remains open. Understanding the *genius loci* is an attempt, an approach—upheaval and failure included. This gives place a historical dimension; its perception is dependent upon the development of the observer's senses, on their cultural and social background. Convention and knowledge shape the understanding of the individual.

Place is special, unique, concrete, and incarnate. Architecture theorist Juhani Pallasmaa addresses the relationship to one's own body. He speaks of the body as the very locus of place, specifying: "There is no body separate from its domicile in space, and there is no space unrelated to the unconscious image of the perceiving self" (2005, 40).

Places such as these are in danger – from indifference and disassociation through media. Marc Augé characterizes such non-places as: "The space of a non-place creates neither singular identity nor relations; only solitude, and similitude" (1995, 103).

Architecture in Place

Vittorio Magnago Lampugnani

1

Architecture always belongs to a place—simply because it is physically built somewhere, or is intended to be. Even architectural projects that are only drawn are predominantly intended for a specific place. Only in the most rare of instances are radical, pure architectural utopias placeless, as the etymology suggests.

Architecture does not content itself with simply occupying its reserved place. It exerts an influence upon the site. It enters into a relationship with what exists there, interfering with and altering pre-existing relationships. It modifies the place, and sometimes even creates a new one.

To do that, it must address the place from the very start, right in the design phase. It must become involved with it, examine and interpret it, write it down, strengthen, condense, transform, and possibly counteract it. It must enrich it in whatever way it can.

Definitions

In the German language, a place *(Ort)* is a point of departure or arrival, a boundary, the prominent point of a tool, a demarcated point or section of space, the residential square of a middle-class community; it is also a plaza, a spot, an area, a town, a village, or a city. In Old German, the word meant a point or sharp corner; in any case, a precisely determinable point in space that has no appreciable surface area.

The Greek word *topos*, originally meaning place, denotes both a point that can be precisely located and the quality of spatiality that defines itself through its boundaries. The meaning also extends to "theme", as well as "commonplace", a stereotypical turn of phrase, a linguistic image, a paradigm, a motif. In classical rhetoric, it is a general standpoint from which arguments can be made.

The Latin word *locus* also means a point, as well as a location, a space, a place, or a spot; it also designates a locality or terrain, a territory, acreage, or field, as well as an abode or dwelling.

At the same time, it stands for an accountancy, an object of investigation, origin, birth, rank, position, period, moment, opportunity, possibility, occasion, situation, condition, circumstance, or relationship. In ancient Roman mythology, the *genius loci*, literally "the spirit of the place", was a protective spirit that watched over religious sites like temples and cultic spaces, as well as the countryside, cities, squares, buildings, and individual rooms within buildings. It later came to denote the spiritual quality and atmosphere of a place.

The Italian word *luogo* and French *lieu* are both derived from *locus* and are largely equivalent to it; *endroit*, originally similar to "here" or "there", emphasizes the peculiarity and distinctiveness of a *place*. The English word place, which evolved from the Greek *plateia* and the Latin *platea*, implies an area of space with an imprint made by humans.

Physical Places, Cognitive Spaces

The breadth, even the relative disparity of these definitions points to the complexity of their object. This complexity also applies to the place of architecture, which ranges from open country to highly densified cities and can also occupy one of the seemingly infinite places located in between. It is defined by its position, its size, its delineation, its boundaries, its topography, its soil structure, its surroundings, and its interconnection with those surroundings.

The *geometria* situs, or, for Gottfried Wilhelm Leibniz, the *analysis situs*, referred to the geometric description of places, until replaced by Johann Benedict Listing's topology; its physical description is devoted to the various empirical sciences. Its material qualities can make a place something special, even unique, or something normal, ordinary, common. Either way, it will be about a point demarcated in space, about a place—a physical place.

Beyond such clear, concrete, material, and thus empirically observable and objectively measurable factors, a place is also a cultural construct in which human perception, knowledge, and memory merge. It arises from the interpretation granted it by an individual or a social group. Acting as instigators of such a process are artists, especially poets and painters, and scholars, particularly historians: they discover places and underpin them with associations that are eventually taken over and shared by many people. For example, Mont Ventoux in Provence, France, which became known due to Francesco Petrarc's ascent in 1336 (and above all the narrative that the poet wrote to the humanist Dionigi di Borgo San Sepolcro), or Montagne Sainte-Victoire, to which Paul Cézanne devoted hundreds of paintings, all the way up to the Lorraine Motel in Memphis, Tennessee, where Martin Luther King was shot by a racist in 1968 (and

Paul Cézanne, *Montagne Saint-Victoire*, oil on canvas, 1887

Source: Philip Conisbee/ Denis Coutagne (eds.), *Cézanne in Provence*, exhibition catalogue, Washington et al. 2006, Fig. 69

which was remodeled and repurposed as the National Civil Rights Museum). But an individual's childhood memories are also able to invest parts of inhabited spaces with emotions and meaning: they usually belong to that person only, and remain an individual phenomenon. Here and there, however, something turns up that can be described relatively vaguely, but somewhat appropriately, as identity.

All Places Are Made by Humans

The evocation of a socially or personally significant place is obviously and indisputably a human achievement. But not only are cognitive places made and designed by people; physical places are as well, and indeed the entire range of them. For rivers and lakes, meadows and forests are predominantly artificial formations, as much as houses, bridges, streets, squares, and cities. These artificial formations are based on many motivations that are ideological, political, economic, and especially functional. They can originate from such geographical conditions as topography, soil content, locally available building materials, or the climate. They can be demographic, medical, hygienic, legal, and technical. They may have to do with local traditions, rites, habits, mentalities, cultural conditions, or trade relations. Rarely (but still at times) the motives are aesthetic. As a rule, the drivers of design are different: the aesthetic is a result, perhaps even a side effect, but often a side effect that is part of the intent, albeit *en passant.*

Such impulses and influences never affect the formal composition of a place all at once, and never with equal weight. Sometimes it is ideological goals that shape the human habitat; sometimes utilitarian or even cultural factors. But they act simultaneously and uniformly just as seldom as they act singularly and exclusively. Form is always a product of different influences.

Form can come about through planning, design, use, care, and conservation, but also by neglect and inactivity. It can be as intentional as it is unintentional. And it can occur in all manner of manifestations, from a radical intervention that alters a place to the point of being unrecognizable, right down to the most minute refinement. The intensity and intent of form are different, but even in this difference, they are effective in every single place.

Every place is thus created by humans, physically and intellectually; and every part of the human habitat is a place, albeit with differences: a meadow in the Swiss Alps on the
1 western shores of the Lake of Uri, though formed by generations of Alpine farmers, is not a place in the same way a late renaissance town square in medieval Paris is a place. The work of the Alpine shepherds of Seelisberg was almost exclusively utilitarian, whereas, in addition to functional needs, the goal of the French architects was monumentality. If, however, an alliance of the three original Swiss cantons of Uri, Schwyz, and Unterwalden was struck with the Rütlischwur on this meadow—as legend has it—then the meadow becomes a place which not only matches Place des Vosges, but can even possess a stronger sense of identity than the architecturally sophisticated Place Royale of Henri IV.

In his 1979 book titled *Place and Placeness,* the Canadian geographer Edward Relph argued against the notion of omnipresent places, at least potentially, and maintained that some (urban) places would not only look the same, but also feel the same and offer the same kinds of weak, if not non-existent, experiences. A decade earlier, Michel Foucault had already postulated an extensive placelessness for his heterotopes, places outside of all places. The French sociologist and cultural philosopher Michel de Certeau coined the notion of non-places in his 1980 *Arts de Faire,* the first volume of *L'Invention du Quotidien.* Marc Augé, ethnologist and anthropologist, took it up in his *Non-Lieu. Introduction à une anthropologie de la surmodernité* published in 1992, using it to characterize monofunctional urban and suburban spaces, such as shopping centers, train stations, airports, and highways, which he deemed ahistorical, uncommunicative, and void of identity. However, this state of affairs doesn't seem to be irreversible: shopping malls end up as social gathering places in socially vulnerable urban and suburban areas due to the security they offer, train stations end up as ruthlessly commercialized yet multifunctional places of encounter, and Steven Spielberg's cheerful and melancholy 2004 film *The Terminal* has revealed a latent,

Film still from *The Terminal*
by Steven Spielberg, 2004

domestic, almost too home-like quality of the airport. Thus, under certain circumstances, non-places can transform or change themselves back into places.

Architecture in Confrontation with Place

Any construction impinges on a concrete human artifact and a cognitive construct of society. Intentionally or unintentionally, it comes face to face with the works, the thoughts, and the dreams of people who have already worked on or with the place. This confrontation must be as conscious as possible – and as respectful as necessary.

It can take very different, almost opposing forms. There are farmhouses that seem to grow out of the landscape, so to speak, because they are built with the same stone on which it rests, and they trace the forms of the slopes to which they cling; and there are others that superimpose themselves on the landscape with keen determination, made of foreign-looking materials like brick or plaster, with vast cubic massing. The prairie
1 houses of Frank Lloyd Wright from the turn of the last century use the materials and colors of the natural surroundings in which they nestle with their windmill floor plans, while Ludwig Mies van der Rohe's Farnsworth House in Plano, Illinois, from the early 1950s, hovers like a purist abstract sculpture of steel and glass about one-and-a-half meters above a forest clearing, and its elemental volume stands out proudly against the picturesque landscape along the Fox River. These kinds of buildings that attempt to contrast place empathically engage it just as intensely as those that cultivate a critical mimesis with it. And both can equally avoid the "dissonance" lamented by Adolf Loos in his brilliant essay titled "Architecture".

Architecture's confrontation with place is even more pronounced and more complex in the city than in the landscape, because there it is shaped in the most aware and intense way by humankind, and charged with the strongest meaning. Here too, the relationship oscillates between the extremes of imitation and rupture.

In his Hôtel Tassel of 1892–93, an urban residence built on a vacant lot in Brussels, Victor Horta adopted the bay window from the neighboring buildings, an element that formed the street front in its constantly varied repetition, and turned it into an elegant protrusion in the lively Art Nouveau façade. On the other hand, in his own home on Rue Franklin in Paris built 1903–04, Auguste Perret broke with the architectural conventions of the late 19th-century Parisian townhouse and instead of stone, used reinforced concrete and ceramics on the façade, penetrated the front outside wall to open up the back rooms and give them more light, made floor heights lower, and let the ten-story building (in contrast to its seven-story neighbors) tower in the sky far above the traditional maximum roof height. Both architects, as different in their approach as they were, (also) came from the special places in which they intervened carefully as well as critically.

There are other cases, of course. In 1924, when Gerrit Thomas Rietveld attached his Haus Schröder to a row of buildings in Utrecht, choosing a totally different scale and a totally different architectural language, he ignored its (sub-)urban

Gerrit Rietveld, Haus Schröder in Utrecht, 1924

Source: Frank den Oudsten, archives

and architectural context with blasé ruthlessness. He was solely concerned with transferring the formalistic experiments with elementary geometries and primary colors that he had previously made in furniture design, and as one of the radical De Stijl painters, to architecture. He was indifferent to place—and his architecture shows it.

Two Urban Architectures as Design Experiments

The delicate balance between adaptation and contrast manifests itself in urban architecture in all its complexity. For even where it programmatically subjugates itself to the place, it still causes ruptures and creates new functional and spatial situations; and even when it strives to create something new and unusual, it does not hesitate to relate itself more or less directly to the existing context.

One of the most outstanding examples of a gentle (and highly creative) approach to an urban place is the Piazza della Santissima Annunziata in Florence. Built at the start of the 14th

1

Piazza della Santissima Annunziata, Florence, veduta from Vol. 1 *Vedute pittoresche della Toscana*, 1827

Photo: Dagmar Keultjes

century, the originally humble-looking square in front of the church of the same name received an elegant eastern front between 1419 and 1445, in the form of the loggia of the Spedale degli Innocenti, with which Filippo Brunelleschi created one of the first works of renaissance architecture. Even the alterations his pupil Francesco della Luna made to the original design during construction (and which the master sharply criticized) barely diminished the compositional perfection of the colonnade. It inspired Antonio di Tuccio Manetti, a humanist, architect, and biographer of Brunelleschi who built the church's baldachin portico, co-designed by Michelozzo di Bartolommeo and Leon Battista Alberti.

Roughly a century later, as Antonio da Sangallo the Elder, together with Baccio d'Agnolo (actually Bartolomeo d'Agnolo Baglioni) was commissioned by the Ordine dei Servi di Maria (Order of the Servants of Mary), the same group that ran the

Santissima Annunziata Basilica, to connect a series of residential buildings with an arcade element, he decided to give the square a sense of unity, which is presumably what Brunelleschi had intended. Then he did something unheard of: he copied the opposite loggia designed by Brunelleschi, and built its mirror image on the west side of the square between 1516 and 1525. In other words, one of the greatest and successful talents of late renaissance architecture took a back seat and subordinated himself to the place that Brunelleschi had imagined as a vision and built only as a fragment.

The Loggia dei Servi di Maria was not completed until 1720, with slight deviations from Sangallo's drawings. In the meantime, Giovanni Battista Caccini had added a colonnade to the façade of the church, into which he incorporated Manetti's canopy: this, too, inspired by Brunelleschi's model. To make the arches of the three arcades the same height, the columns in front of the church, which had no staircase, unlike the other two buildings, were made taller. Thus, over the course of three centuries, a harmonious open space was created by different builders from different epochs, working in unison and refining an idea that was formulated earlier.

Around seventy years after Brunelleschi's Florentine Spedale degli Innocenti arcade, and thirty years before Sangallo completed it as a spatial formation, a completely new and unique place was built all in one go, in the astonishingly brief period of three years, ruthlessly inserting itself into the urban fabric: the Piazza Ducale in Vigevano. It was built for Ludovico Maria Sforza, known as il Moro, the Duke of Milan. Ambrogio da Corte was in charge of finances, Ambrogio Ferrari oversaw the technical aspects, and Donato Bramante and Leonardo da Vinci

Piazza Ducale in Vigevano, photo 2015

were probably among the project's designers or, at the very least, generated ideas for it. As a new social center of the small town near Ticino (and a noble entrée to the castle located practically next door, which was converted into the Sforza residence at the same time), a modern forum was to be built according to the guidelines in Leon Battista Alberti's treatise, *De re aedificatoria* (1443–1452), and its source, Vitruvius's *Ten Books on Architec-*
1 *ture*, to help legitimize the dignity of the dubious Sforza dynasty
as a new interpretation of ancient *topos*. By no later than 1489, Ludovico was in possession of a bold plan. Demolition work on the buildings south of the existing market street and the Palazzo del Comune across from it began in 1492. In 1494, the rectangular square, 135 by 40 meters, lined with continuous arcades and completely uniform, two-tone façades painted with illusionistic architectural motifs, was opened. To create a sense of enclosure, the streets opening onto the square were arcaded in the same way.

The formal ideal also determined the following interventions in the architecture of the public square, strengthening it further: demolition of the ramp projecting deep into the square and serving as a gateway to the castle above and to one side of it, and closure of the southwestern corner of the square; the street intersections on the west and north sides that were originally emphasized by triumphal arch motifs were integrated into the regular arcaded row; and lastly, the new cathedral at the narrow eastern side of the square was given a concave-shaped façade designed by Juan Caramuel y Lobkowitz, a Spanish bishop, mathematician, and military engineer, integrating the Via Roma into its baroque *trompe l'oeil* composition.

In Vigevano, the creation of a new place (the square) was a rude intervention in the dense urban fabric that references an ancient, idealistic place (the Roman Forum). The result of this political and artistic act of violence became such a powerful topos itself that it became the model for a global genealogy of squares: from the Plaza Mayor in Madrid (1580–1619) to the Place Royale in Paris (now the Place des Vosges, 1605–1612), to countless monumental squares of the 18th and 19th centuries. Its apodictic elementary form determined and guided subsequent modifications, up to and including the new cathedral façade. While the square, previously designed as an urban plaza and a palace square, was transformed into a church square *sui generis*, spatially, it followed the succinct logic of the original project.

Architecture as the Creation of Place

The intensity and success of architecture's confrontation with place cannot be measured by whether this engagement results in adaptation or contrast, but whether it strengthens, clarifies, and enriches place. And whether architecture itself also benefits from place, whether it becomes denser and richer. For as the previous examples of urban architecture have shown, it is by no means always the case that a given environment—rural or urban—is conditioned by architecture. The opposite situation can also happen: that a given kind of architecture shapes the environment.

There are buildings that, due to their use, location, scale, and excellent form, become anchors and catalysts of urban growth. They outlast generations of buildings, are appropriated by the most diverse of social systems, are constantly changing their function and meaning, and always remain recognizable thanks to their architectural form. In addition, their influence radiates into the environment and not infrequently influences adjacent development.

One example of this phenomenon is the ancient Roman amphitheater. It lost purpose after the Empire collapsed; in addition, all over Europe, as well as Asia Minor and North Africa, cities fell to ruin and were depopulated. Nevertheless, the great ancient architectural monuments survived. In Nîmes, the Visigoths transformed the amphitheater into a fortress that encircled a small settlement of about 2,000 inhabitants; the remainder of the original city was abandoned. The theater of Arles was treated similarly. In Lucca, the elliptical ancient Roman building was completely integrated into the medieval urban fabric and used as housing and commercial space; the arena was also partially built over. In 1838, Lorenzo Nottolini, an engineer and architect, designed a scheme to re-open the inner square and subsequently carried it out. In Florence, the outline of the demolished amphitheater is still recognizable today in the streets and can be traced in the floor plans of the buildings that sprang up in its place.

The Colosseum *(amphitheatrum flavium)* is especially emblematic in Rome. Construction began under Emperor Vespasian in the 1st century AD, after an artificial lake built by Nero in the valley between Palatine, Esquiline, and Caelius was filled in; the monument was finished in 80 AD during the reign of Titus. The last gladiators fought there in 435; wild animal baiting continued up to 523. After that, the structure fell into disuse until the 10th century, when it was turned into a small settle-
1 ment, with the former arena serving as a square. At the start of the 12th century, it was integrated into the sprawling system

Antoine Lafréry, drawing of the Colosseum in *Speculum Romanae Magnificentiae*, 1602

of fortresses and residences of the Roman aristocracy of the Frangipani, who later had to relinquish portions of it to the Annibaldi and Orsini. After that, the building was used as a stone quarry for the Cathedral of Orvieto, Palazzo Venezia, the Cancelleria, and Palazzo Farnese.

Pope Sixtus V wanted to turn the ruins into a large spinning mill for wool as a way to boost the Roman economy. Working at his behest, in 1590 Domenico Fontana designed a scheme that placed workshops on the ground floor and workers' dwellings on the floors above. In 1707, Carlo Fontana (no relation to Domenico) proposed converting the Colosseum into a plaza for a church designed on a centralized floor plan; in 1744, the former arena was consecrated as a memorial to martyrs. In the meantime, the great ancient ruins were so overgrown with vegetation that they looked rather like a spectacular mountain range; botanists have been studying the special varieties of species growing there since the mid-17th century. Around 1800, work got underway to expose and gradually restore the amphitheater, initially clearing away the debris and dirt, then removing the vegetation in 1870, after Garibaldi's troops conquered Rome. The church's interpretation then had to yield to the nation state, whose politically dictated restoration work was

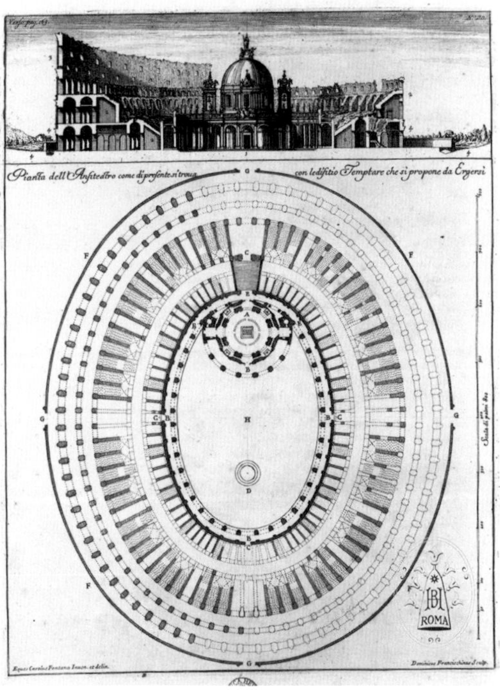

Carlo Fontana, project for the conversion of the Colosseum into a centrally planned church, 1707

rough on the building. The redevelopment of the surrounding city district, largely carried out under the fascist regime, subjugates itself to the dominant presence of the giant structure.

Worthy of note in the case of ancient Roman amphitheaters is that while there was a wide variety of schemes for their re-use and conversion, some of which were implemented, rarely was demolition ever considered, or even carried out. The explanation that people did not want to abandon such a large structure out of utilitarian and economic concerns is only part of the truth. The other part has to do with respect for materialized creative and artisanal labor, for achievement, scale, and form, and for its enigmatic layering of meanings. In short, respect for architecture itself.

1 In fact, architecture has an inherent ability to take on a life of its own and create places by virtue of its presence: not only visually, economically, and functionally, but also, and mainly, in the awareness of its inhabitants, users, and visitors. Forms, events, emotions, and meanings are deposited in largely unfathomable stratifications; changes in use always bring on new connotations. In the historical process, the only constants are place and architecture, which, beyond its original purpose, gains its own autonomous value. This value is closely tied to the form and authenticity of the buildings; should one or the other be lost, the value vanishes as well. This is the reason why demolished squares, streets, and buildings that are restored to their original state usually end up as an optical backdrop: the spiritual substance, the events and meanings that became architecture, are irrevocably lost. The facsimile, recognized as such, becomes an empty stage set.

Place as an Asset

The confrontation with place is not a matter of course for architecture: there have been and still are efforts, especially since the early 20th century, to abandon this engagement in favor of pure abstraction. And yet, it is a categorical imperative today, perhaps even more so than in the past: the landscape and the city, and also everything belonging to and between them, the rivers, the lakes, the meadows, the forests, the fields, the gardens, the parks, the hamlets, the villages, the roads, the canals, the bridges, and the dockyards must all be protected and maintained. They are an important part of our cultural heritage. The ongoing work to enhance them must be careful, responsible, meticulous, and creative.

However, to continue to work on place is not merely a duty within the scope of a contract between the generations and a concession to our environment, its culture, and its history. It most of all benefits the new project. For if a place is a space with character, it makes sense for design work to connect to, or at least embellish that character. The tasks of thinking, drawing, and building must therefore not begin at zero and define themselves entirely from themselves, but instead retain an anchor. Only extraordinarily narrow-minded or extraordinarily insecure architects will perceive this anchor or feel this influence as dictatorial, manipulative, or limiting. For all the rest, confrontation with place provides a fruitful, precious stimulus, whether it be general or specific, abstract or figurative, avant-garde or traditional; and regardless of whether they wish to stand out or fit in.

No really good architects have ever allowed themselves to be hemmed in or dominated by the place where they are to build. But no really good architects have ever ignored place, either. When Richard Neutra built in the Alps, he responded to them differently than Heinrich Tessenow did; Carlo Mollino responds differently than Ignazio Gardella; Paul Schmitthenner unlike Lois Welzenbacher; and Rudolf Olgiati unlike Edoardo Gellner—but all of them respond. Their buildings stay independent. Their authorship is still recognizable. However, their projects become more complex, richer, and better.

Every place slated for redevelopment needs a new architecture, an architecture that vibrantly enhances it and perhaps even makes it speak. Every architecture needs a place it can measure itself against, and from which it can project even more boldly into that cultural new territory that it is called upon to create.

Identity | From Latin *idem*: The same. The sum of characteristics that make up the nature of a unique individual. Concordance with oneself or others, the sameness of two objects, logically: a = a. Psychology defines the identity of an individual as the development of personal maturity allowing one to function as an adult. This is how identity is formed. If it is thus an outright construct, as is today often critically noted, or if it is at the core of existence, is something of a chicken or the egg question: It is not entirely relevant to our everyday lives.

Genius Loci | Latin: The spirit of a place. In antiquity, it was believed that the aura or atmosphere of a cultic site affected the place and the people there. The modern era bestows a spirit upon all places, particularly since the development of the English Garden, to which Alexander Pope attributed a "genius of the place." *Genius loci* has personality, is enduring, and is a companion of the *Zeitgeist*, or spirit of the times. It is the greatest inspiration for architects like Lois Welzenbacher. Starting in the mid-1970s, Christian Norberg-Schulz became the foremost theoretician on *genius loci*, saying that—anthropologically—it gives a person an existential foothold by providing orientation, identification, and meaning.

The Figure-Ground Phenomenon | According to Gestalt psychology, a form is recognized as a figure when it sufficiently distinguishes itself from a homogeneous background. Urban figures, city spaces, and buildings can be studied and designed using a figure-ground diagram. The interaction of positive and negative spaces can reveal a variety of insights. Giambattista Nolli, in a 1748 plan now named after him, delineated the public buildings of Rome. In the classical city, the shapes of places were prevalent while, in contrast, the modern era is dominated by the figures of buildings. In the 21st century, efforts to create more defined urban figures are increasing.

Public Space | In everyday speech, this refers to areas that are accessible to all. Public can be expressed by the phrases "relating to the commonality" and "representing the entirety of people concerned". The opposite of public is private—that which belongs to a single person, an individual entity, or a small group of people. These private areas are closed to the public and, conversely, private development on public space is also limited. In a civic society with property as a fundamental element, a space is only entirely public when the space is public property.

Topology | From Ancient Greek *topos*: Place, space, also a theme or motif. Topology is the study of the relative positions of geological objects, the characteristics of an area. Also: The theory of place. According to Tomáš Valena, *topos* is the antonym of *type*. While *type* describes generalities and ideals, *topos* defines the unique, particular, and individual. Geography and history are truths specific to such unique sites. The unique character of a design emerges through the dialectic of type and topos.

Rossi Plan | This term goes back to architect Aldo Rossi (1931–1997). While he was teaching at the ETH Zurich, from 1972–74, the ground floor layout for the entire Zurich inner city was developed. Since then, the ground floor plan of a city or neighborhood is called a Rossi Plan. This method of representation helps distinguish and understand the interplay of structures, building types, and forms in the urban fabric. A Rossi Plan is not just an analytical instrument, it is a direct tool for integrating new designs into an existing context.

Scale | How long is the coast of Ireland? Strictly speaking, this question can't be answered—it depends upon the scale. Am I seeing it from a bird's-eye view (That of a mudhen? A bald eagle?)? As a hiker? Through a magnifying glass? Each object stands in relation to a plurality of things. The big picture is just as important as focus and detail—this is what gives rise to a change of scale. For the premises of a buiding, a scale with a high denominator is useful, usually 1:200 or more. The building itself is generally depicted on a scale of 1:100 and 1:50 (execution plan). For details, 1:20 to 1:1 are common.

Context | From Latin *contexere*: To weave together like a fabric, connecting or joining creates something new. The same is true of design, which says that each single thing is part of a network of relationships from which it both receives and gives meaning. In the 1970s, system theory and ecology emphasized the central significance of context for each individual element. This is especially true of built structures and their surroundings. Accordingly, a structure is never fully valid solely on its own.

Vernacular | From Latin *vernaculum*: Native, homegrown. English: Commonplace, an everyday appearance. Vernacular architecture: Everyday architecture, popular, anonymous. Coined "architecture without an architect" by Bernard Rudofsky in 1964. Starting in the 1930s, the discovery of everyday American culture, seen in American pop and Robert Venturi's "Main Street is almost alright." During the late 1960s, Ivan Illich proclaims vernacular values to be the sociopolitical alternative to the industrial age of the Chicago Boys.

PLACE

The topic of this assignment is place. For the purpose of the exercise, this will be limited to urban space. Place is created by the context of physical elements such as geography, buildings, exterior spaces, and circulation, and also by societal elements such as social interaction, the economy, and the culture, mentality, and conventions of the inhabitants.

City Level

The topics of this exercise are place as a building site and its specific context. We will take a closer look at what creates the character of a place. The on-site situation will be objectively documented and analyzed; facts will be collected. In parallel, the atmosphere of the building site context will be assessed and documented.

Specifications

Project work will be carried out as a group exercise per building site. To be completed:

- *Basic maps*
  Basic maps are to be made on all three scales according to the presentation guidelines and used as a basis for ongoing design development.
- Figure-ground diagram 1:5,000
- Neighborhood plan 1:1,000 including roof perspectives, topography, and vegetation
- Site plan 1:500 including open spaces and the ground floor footprints of the context

- *Site model*
  A site model on a scale of 1:500 must be made for each building site. The development perimeter and existing buildings must be integrated as an insertion model.
- Building roof heights and styles and the height and extent of vegetation must be assessed on site and displayed by the model.
- Structural contours must be made in reasonable increments.
- The model must show a north point.

- *Video*
  In this section of the assignment, the neighborhood of the building site will be documented on video. It is important to capture the character of the place. Three urban spaces and architecturally relevant phenomena, to be clearly defined by the students in advance, must be examined

Requirements

- Cadastral map
- Findings from the city walk

Goal

The goal is to recognize, understand, and be able to express the characteristics of a place. Based upon this, various interpretations will be deliberated.

The plans on three scales will be used as a foundation for drafting and designing exercises.

The figure-ground diagram shows the relationship of built and unbuilt space and enables conclusions about the three building sites. The complementary representation of built areas and voids makes neighborhood structures more legible and makes it possible to see open space as an autonomous urban element.

Working on the model is essential to dissecting the design task: The building of the site model defines the requirements of the volumetric study.

Using images and sound, the video makes it possible to experience and express the place from a new perspective.

Gordon Matta-Clark, Conical Intersect, Paris, 1975

© 2017, ProLitteris, Zurich

Dundee City Arts Centre

© David Chipperfield Architects

1

Site model

Building Level
The task is to design a volumetric addition to a building or building ensemble in an urban environment. The focus of interest is on the sense of place. Crucial design factors are the existing buildings and the urban development context. The added volume should effect a change to the urban fabric that improves the existing situation.

Specifications
Project work will be done in groups of two. The planned expansion volume must be included graphically in the plans and as a collage in the photo montages. The presentation must be a DIN-A0 plan and include the following:

- Figure-ground diagram 1:5000
- Neighborhood plan 1:1000 including roof perspectives and topography
- Site plan 1:500 including open spaces and the ground floor footprints of the context
- Photo montage showing a before and after site comparison
- Written explanation
- Implementation model of the existing buildings with added volume 1:500

Requirements

- Figure-ground diagram 1:5000
- Neighborhood plan 1:1000 including roof perspectives and topography
- Site plan 1:500 including open spaces and the ground floor footprints of the context
- Photos of the existing buildings of each site
- Site model 1:500
- Findings from the city walk
- Findings from analysis
- Crafting Notebooks I + II

Goal

In the first phase of the assignment, the focus was on connecting to the place. Here, the focus is on the impact of the building volume on the place. Each and every intervention to an urban context creates a spatial change. These interventions must improve the urban context, otherwise they cannot be justified. The design study with a volume addition to the site model helps make an accurate estimation of changes to the urban fabric. The model of the volume is primarily a means of expression for the design concept, with the perspectives of the urban area serving as a further means of appraising the intervention.

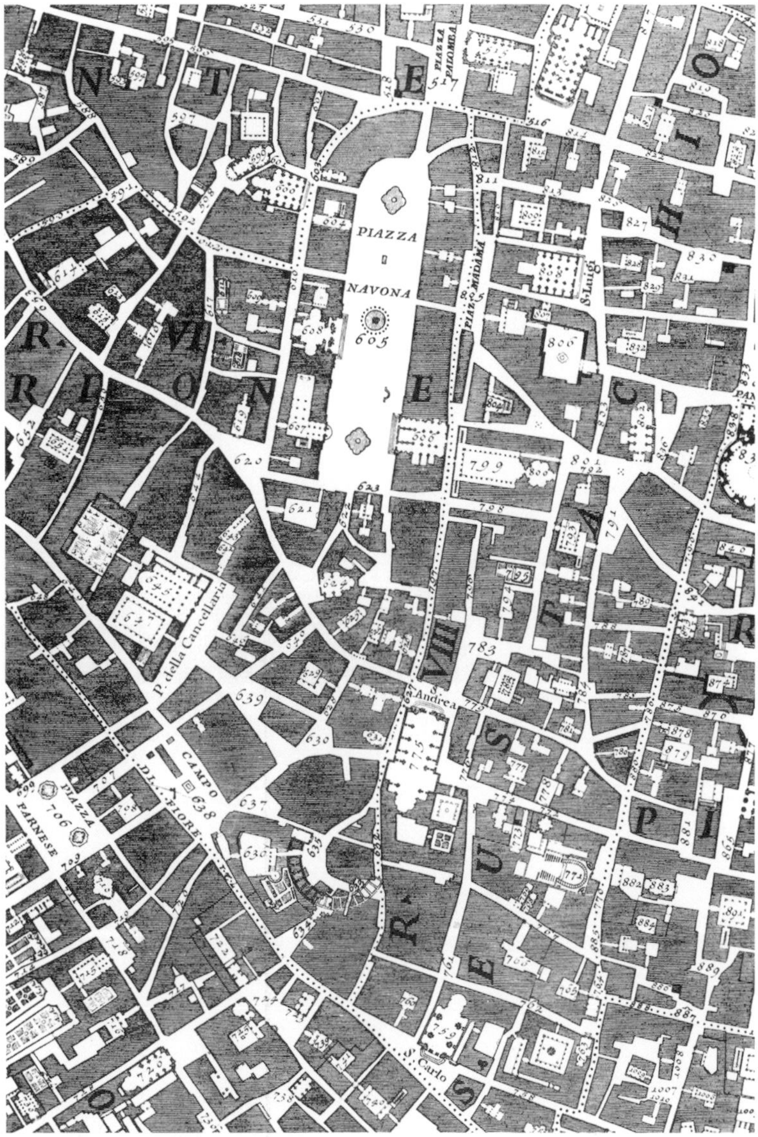

Giambattista Nolli, map of Rome, 1748, detail

Figure-ground Diagram

Area Plan

MIDDLE AGES

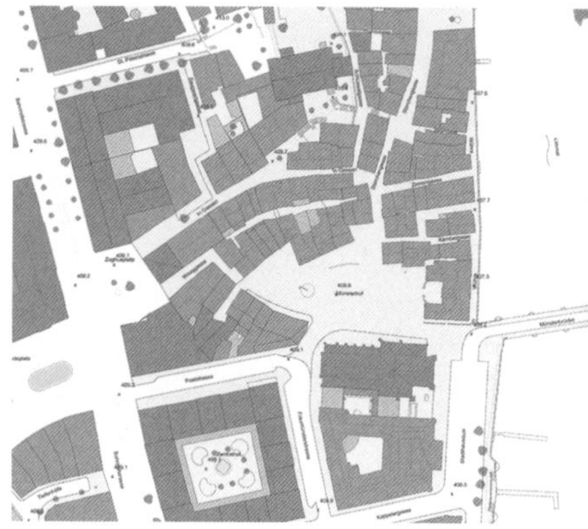

FOUNDATION ERA

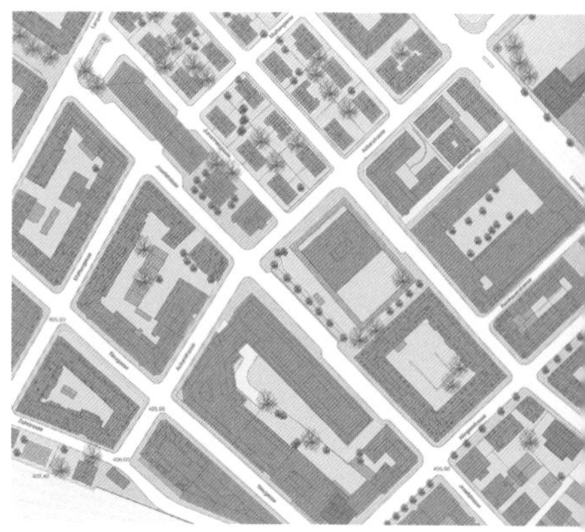

MODERNISM

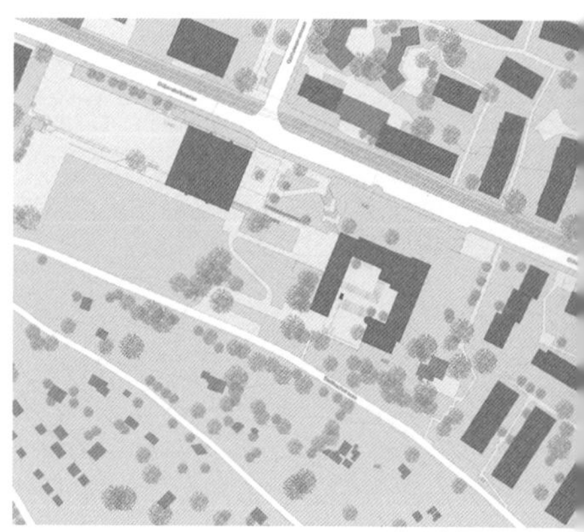

Site Plan

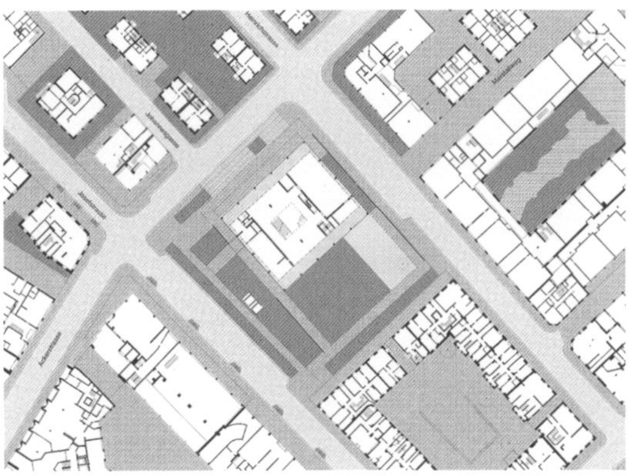

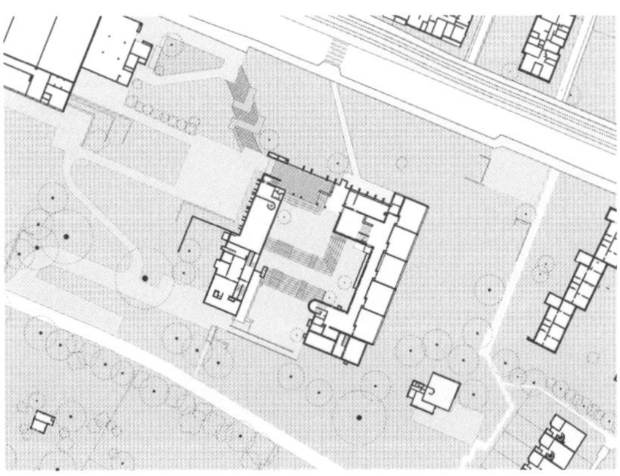

Site Model

MIDDLE AGES

FOUNDATION ERA

MODERNISM

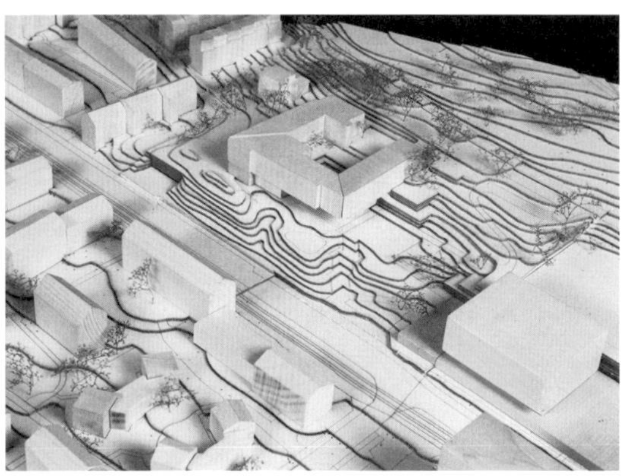

Video

MIDDLE AGES

FOUNDATION ERA

MODERNISM

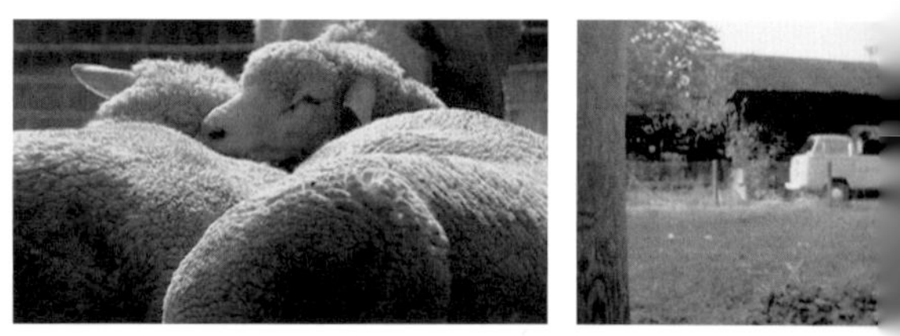

1

1

1

MIDDLE AGES
City Walk

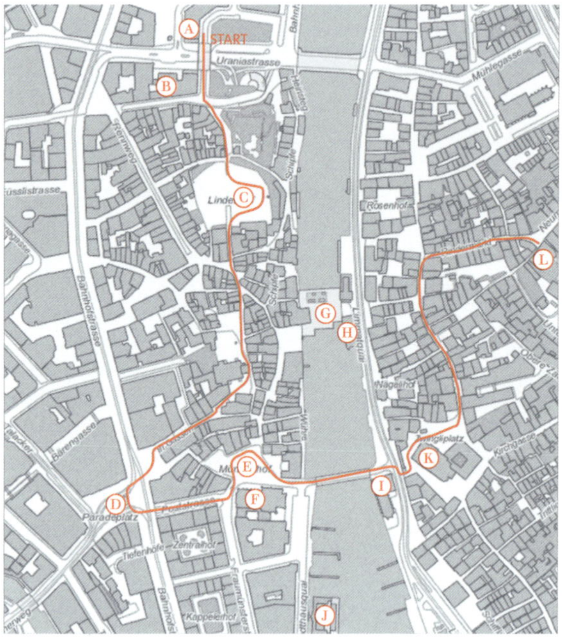

A Amtshaus
B Urania-Sternwarte
C Lindenhof
D Paradeplatz
E BUILDING SITE – Münsterhof
F Fraumünster
G Rathausbrücke
H City Hall
I Helmhaus
J Frauenbad
K Grossmünster
L Model of the city

FOUNDATION ERA
City Walk

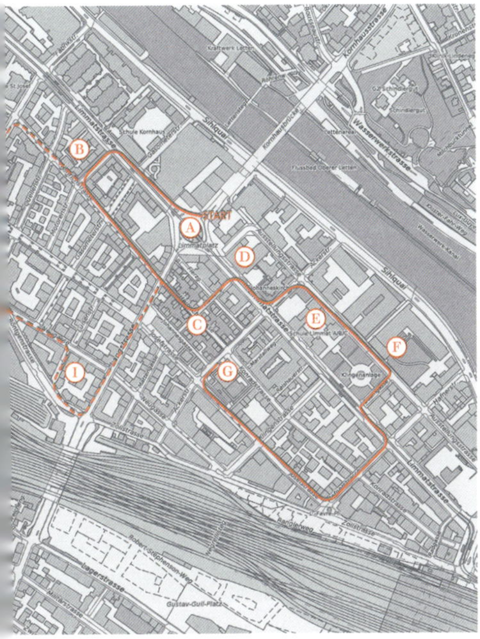

A Limmatplatz
B Limmathäuser Urban Settlement
C Fierzgasse
D Industrial Quarter Union Hall
E Limmat schoolhouses and gymnasiums
F Museum of Design
G BUILDING SITE – School of Fashion and Design
H Röntgenplatz
I Apartment building with the Riff Raff Cinema and Bistro

MODERNISM
City Walk

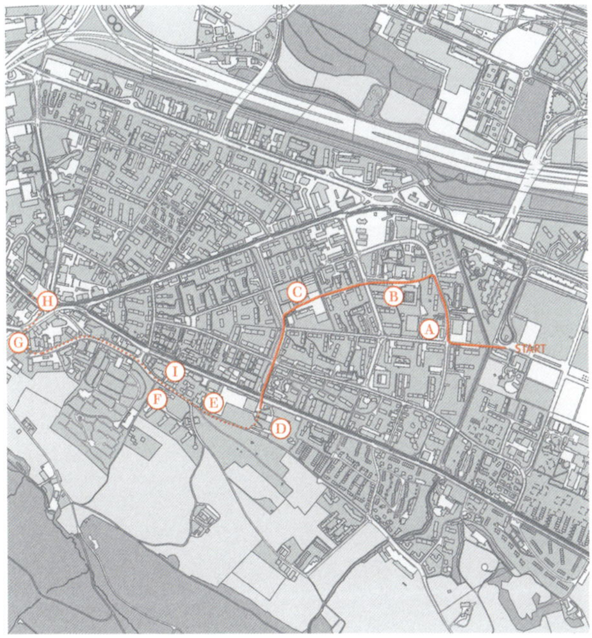

A Hirzenbach Complex
B Hirzenbach School Complex
C Glattwiesstrasse green space, Luchswies Schoolhouse
D St. Gallus Catholic Church
E Probatei Schoolhouse and Kindergarten
F BUILDING SITE – Stettbach Schoolhouse
G Schwamendingerplatz
H Schwamendingen village center

MIDDLE AGES

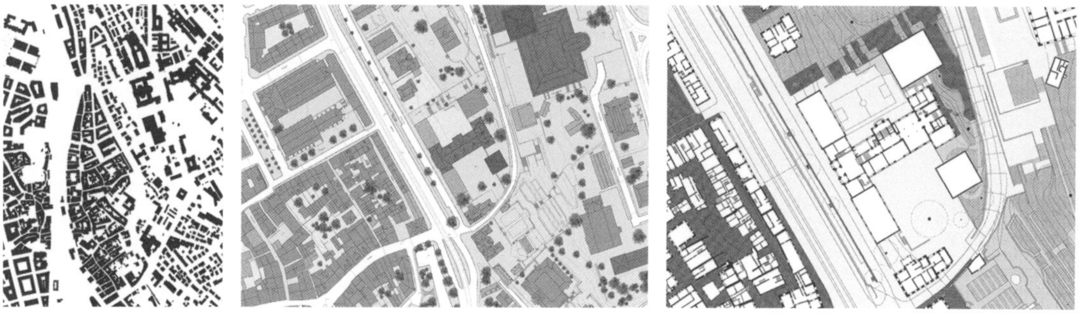

Anastasia König
Amanda Köpfli
13 AS

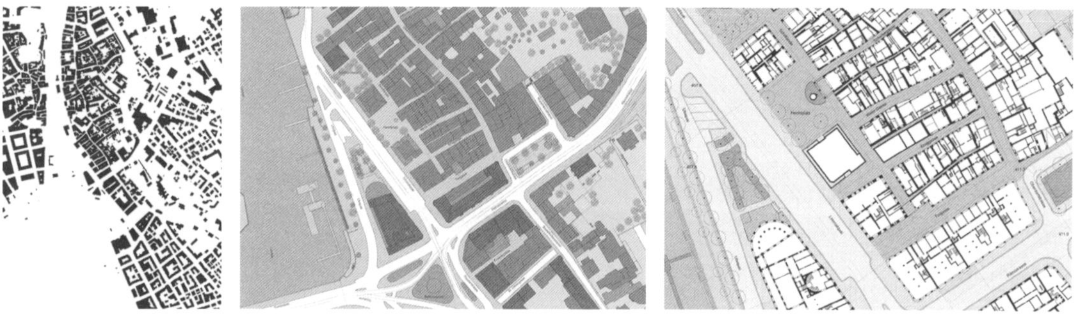

Okan Tan
Thierry Vuattoux
15 AS

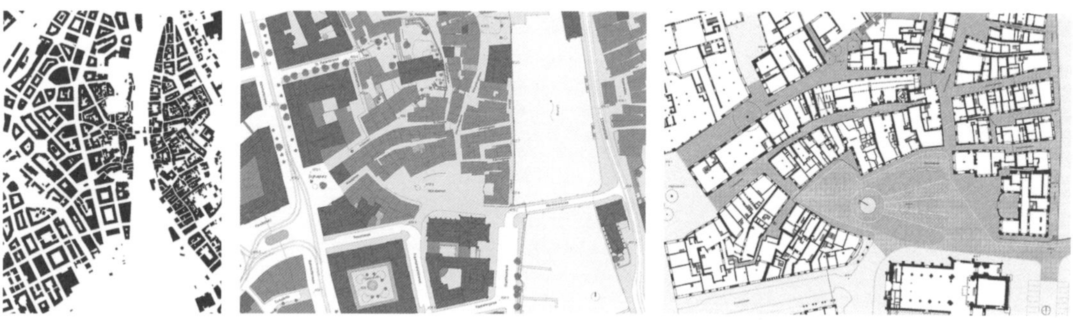

Nicola Merz
Sebastian Pfammatter
16 AS

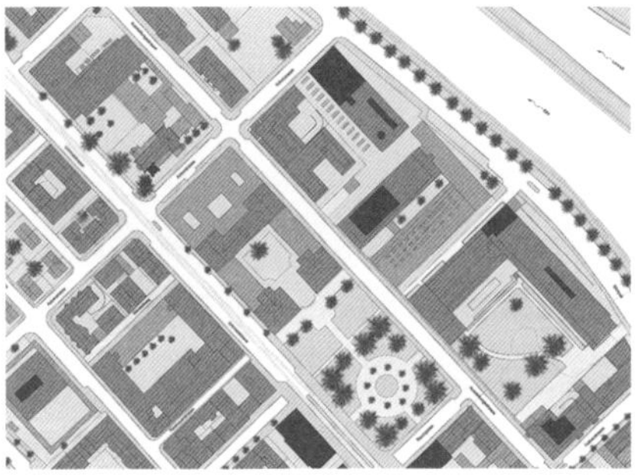
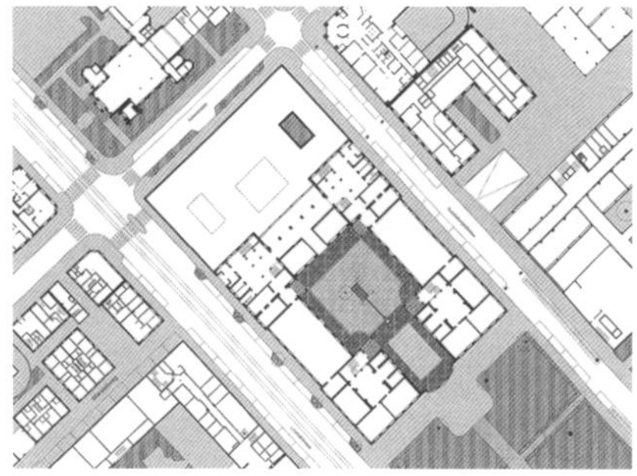

Maximilian Fritz
Valentina Grazioli
13 AS

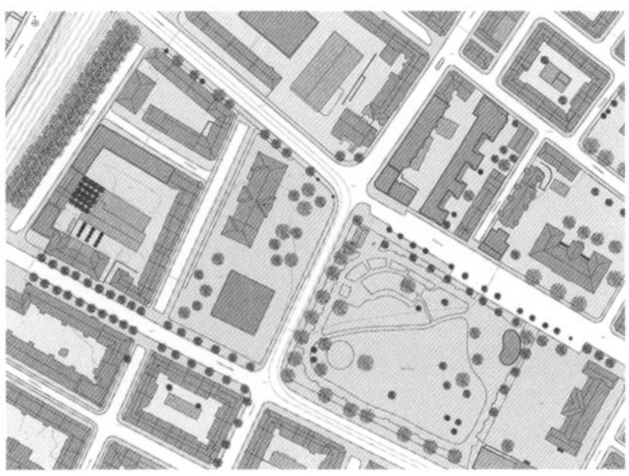

Stefan Fierz
Max Lüscher
15 AS

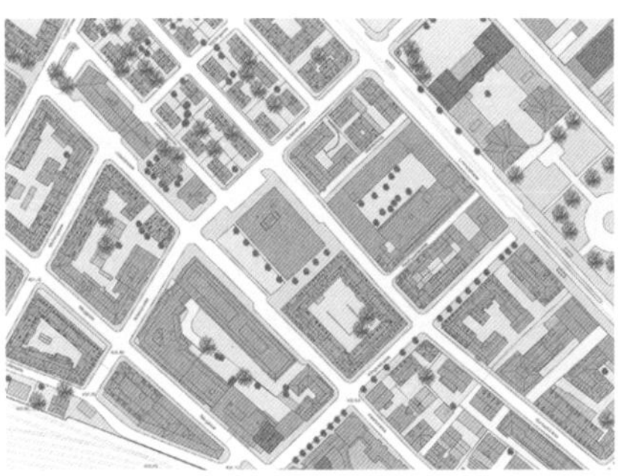
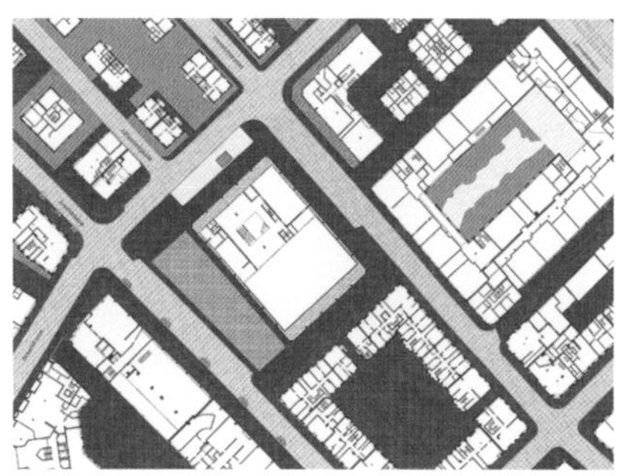

Julian Holz
Milan Jarrell
16 AS

MODERNISM

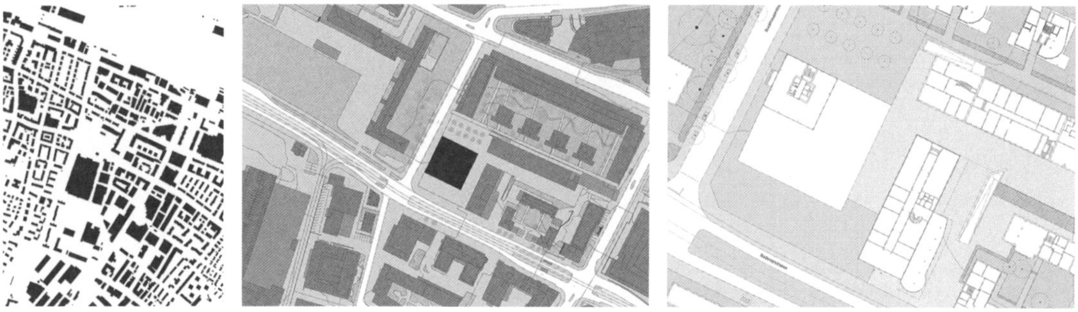

Kushtrim Loki
Han Cheol Yi
12 AS

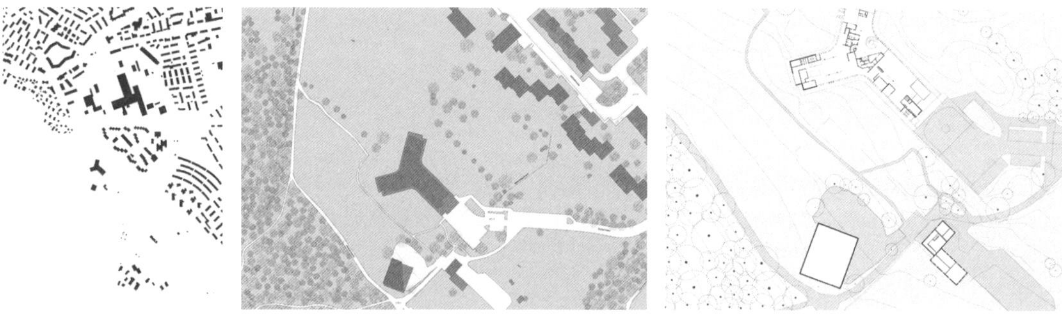

Mevion Famos
Manon Mottet
15 AS

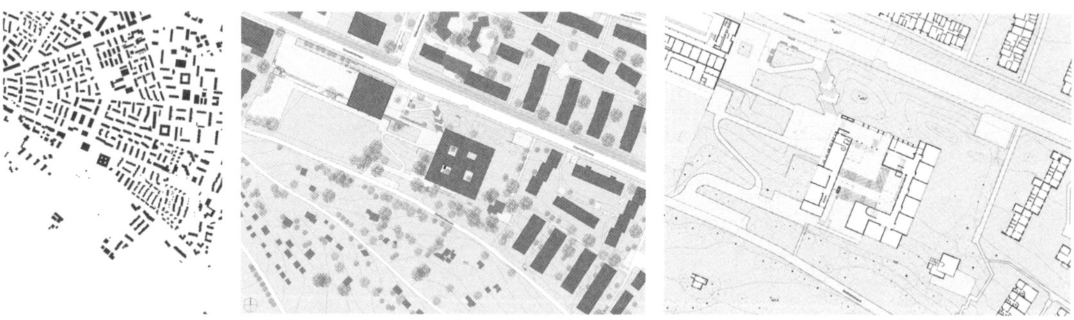

Utku Coskun
Janek Defînti
16 AS

MIDDLE AGES

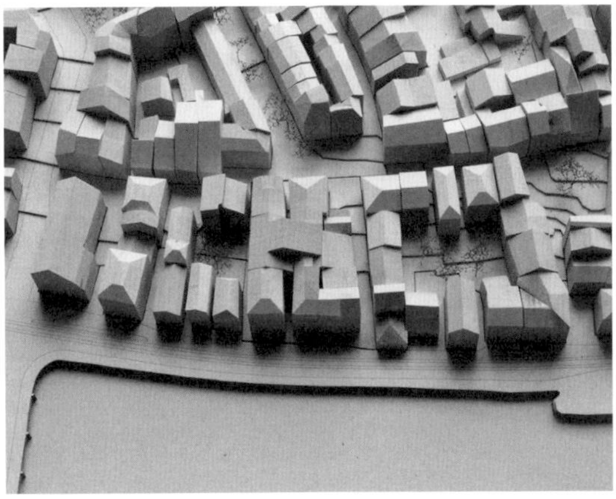

Nils Franzini
Enrico Pegolo
12 AS

Rafael Zulauf
12 AS

Okan Tan
Thierry Vuattoux
15 AS

FOUNDATION ERA

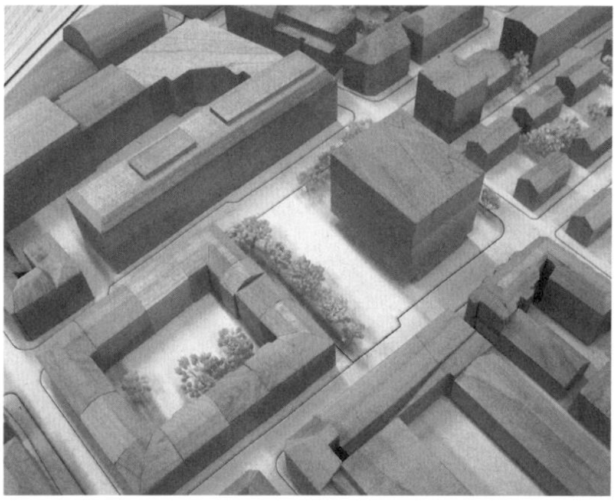

Monica Küng
Yueqiu Wang
12 AS

Philipp Lutz
Jean-Paul van der Merwe
10 AS

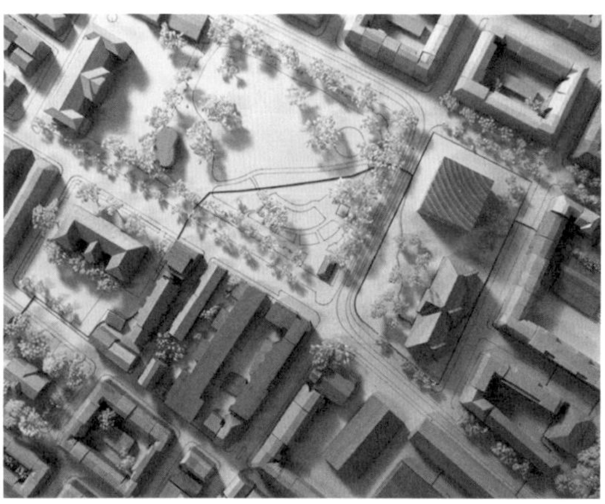

Stefan Fierz
Max Lüscher
15 AS

Lea Gfeller
12 AS

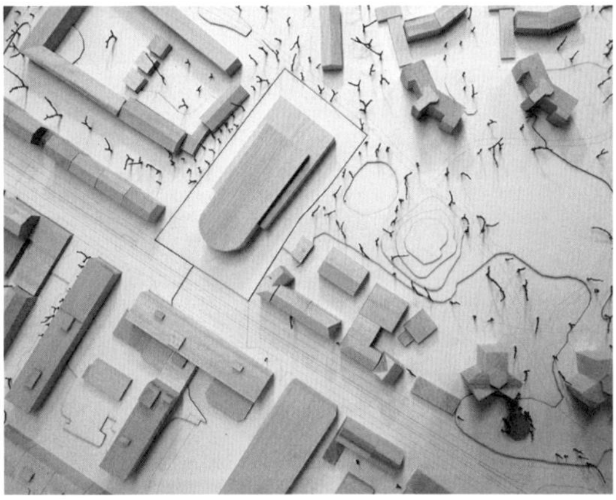

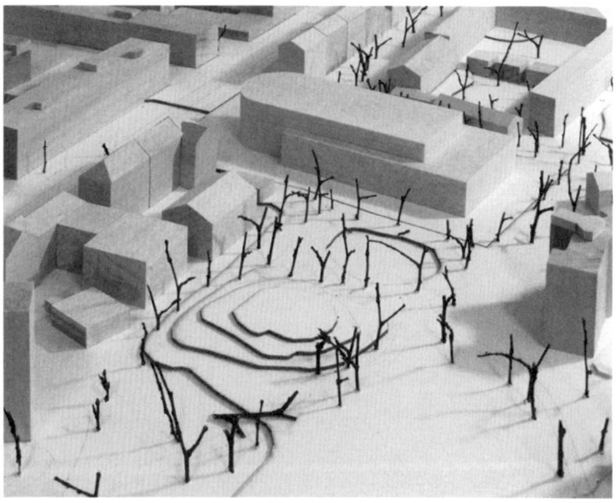

Stefanie Schäfer
Caroline Schwarzenbach
14 AS

1

MODERNISM

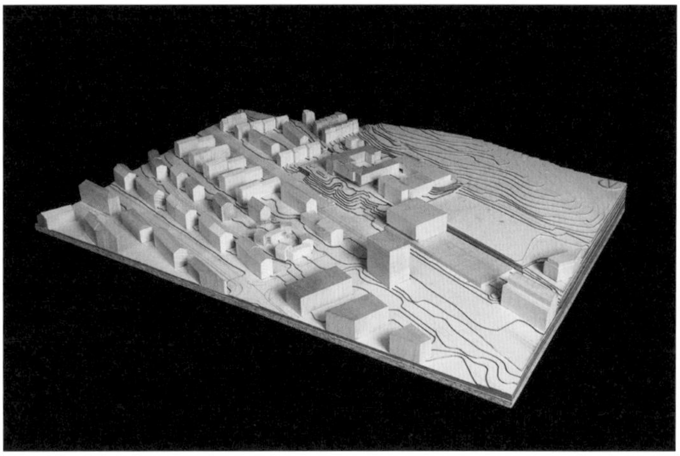

Alessandro Canonica
16 AS

Mevion Famos
Manon Mottet
15 AS

MIDDLE AGES

Claudio Arpagaus
Valentin Buchwalder
11 AS

MIDDLE AGES

Martin Achermann
Nicole Bucher
14 AS

Andrin Martig
08 AS

Okan Tan
Thierry Vuattoux
15 AS

FOUNDATION ERA

Florian Hartmann
Christoph Hiestand
09 AS

Luciano Raveane
Tibor Rossi
10 AS

Theresa Pabst
07 AS

MODERNISM

Marco Derendinger
Fabian Heinzer
13 AS

1

Alexandra Grieder
Johannes Hirsbrunner
14 AS

Fabio Orsolini
Lambrini Pikis
09 AS

Georg Aerni, 2876-3, Bandra, 2007 © Georg Aerni

2
Structure

2 Structure

Structure is a system that organizes a limited number of elements according to clear rules. Structure is relational in that it describes elements with certain characteristics among themselves and the structure as a whole. Structure is granted a fundamental power of order, often with timeless validity.

Structure became the core topic of a school of thought termed structuralism, which replaced the decisionism of the Existentialists with concrete scientific orders in the mid-20th century—reaching architecture through linguistics (Chomsky) and ethnology (Lévi-Strauss). Revolts against the international style by team X (1953–1981) showed early structuralist tendencies (Candilis, De Carlo, van Eyck). Modular orders are characteristic. In 1960s Holland, a separate school of thought dubbed structuralism coalesced around Jan van Eyck, Herman Hertzberger, and Piet Blom. Proponents of megastructures (Friedman, Constant, Schulze-Fielitz) radically emphasize structure, sometimes technically (Archigram), sometimes utopian (Superstudio).

Even though the impact of this school of architecture was limited, the concept of structure has been a strong component of architectural vocabulary ever since.

Building structure, for example, describes the interaction of constructive and spatial orders. The latter is differentiated into primary and secondary uses. By differentiating between served and servant rooms, Louis Kahn brought attention to the fact that space for construction is decreasing, while that for operating is increasing.

The structural system must be placed in a coherent correlation to the spatial structure. This is influenced by the dimensioning and spacing of the main structural and technical elements, as well as the size and proportion of effective spaces. Grids and modules facilitate coherency. The structure of the construction and the site development is a crucial aspect of the endurance of a building structure. While uses are changing at an increasing rate, and façades are restored or replaced, the serviceability of a building structure can be maintained for a very long time if conceived well.

An area that structure has had tremendous impact on is urban development. Based upon the morphological research of Saverio Muratori, Aldo Rossi played a key role in setting standards in this field. Cities are understood as a system of building and urban space types—analogous to a modular order. Building types, building eras, and building functions create distinguishable development patterns. We differentiate between closed and open constructions. In one case, this can be the natural growth of an old town or a perimeter block; in another this may be a ribbon development or a freestanding group of solitary houses or buildings.

Despite the great variety of different development patterns, the relationship of built and open space—the density—remains a decisive distinguishing feature of a city. Figure-ground diagrams make these connections especially clear. Building development, open spaces, and solitary buildings should be in a balanced ratio to one another—the shape of a building should be given equal consideration with the shape of open space. Weighting one more than the other puts the entire city in question—this is equally true for both dense construction without public space and a surplus of open space.

On the Use and Abuse of Theory for the Architect

Fritz Neumeyer

2

1 *See, Marvel, Think*

In order to provide an image of the relationship between practice and theory in architecture, I would like to start with an illustration that should be considered with some care and is not without an ulterior motive. It is one of the enchanting washed pen drawings of Malbork Castle near Danzig, today's Gdansk, in 1794, by architecture student Friedrich Gilly at the age of 22. He was accompanying his father, Prussian state architect David Gilly, on an official journey to the castle, built by the Teutonic Order in the late 13th century. The purpose of the journey was to evaluate the possible use of the ruinous hulk of a castle fortress. The results of the journey, and the different significance father and son accorded to the building, shall not be discussed in detail here. Rather, our focus is on a particular Gilly drawing showing the Malbork Castle refectory.

It is one of the most remarkable sketched self-portraits by a young architect I know. What is so remarkable in this image? With self-assured pen-strokes, Gilly delineated the gothic ribbed vaults and conjured the airy spatial expanse and depth of the hall onto his sheet in a photographically exact perspective. While Gilly garnished his drawings of other halls of Malbork Castle with knights in armor, banners, and furnishings, the refectory, which he admired exceedingly, remains completely empty. Here, the space itself suffices, or rather, it offers itself to the young man who, the only person present, stands in the foreground of the drawing. Leaning against a central column, one leg resting in front of the other, he stands there, looking upwards into the vault. It can hardly be doubted that Gilly saw himself in this solitary figure, experiencing, making this space exclusively his own. In fact, the gaze Gilly develops on this space in his description of Malbork Castle, dating from 1796, is unique. In his text, Gilly praises the "glorious arches of the Knights' ancient refectory hall", emanating from single points in three granite columns, each hewn from a single block. What is remarkable is the association that forces itself on Gilly when looking at these arches with their vaults, and what he writes merits our attention: "The vaulting seems to shoot aloft like a rocket from each pier and converges at the crown in alternating points."[1]

This is a remarkable comparison, translating the grandiose tectonics of apparent defeat of earthly weight and transcendence of matter into a dynamic image. The gothic construction, usually compared to the branches of a tree, transforms into fireworks, is dramatized in Gilly's eyes: the ribs of the vault mount towards each other into the vaulted sky along their arcs like rockets, and explode into star patterns "in alternate points" at the apex of their paths.

In his pen-and-ink drawing, Gilly seems to have portrayed himself in the midst of this architect's daydream. Lost in his thoughts, he leans against the refectory column, in a pose that suggests leaning against a tree, gazing upwards into the branches in the sky, in the vaults of which the rib construction ignites its fireworks. Gilly's gaze into eternity dreams itself beyond the vault of the roof into infinity, as though there were no lintels, as though the building stood in space merely in the abstract contours of its ideal lines of construction.

In contrast to his father David Gilly, who, as a "state architect", proposed the demolition of the central palace, seemingly without a second thought, in order to have a large barn built from its stones, the architect's scion is enthused by this building, admires the "truly admirable boldness"[2] and uses it as a starting point to dream himself into the beyond of architecture, into a nearly matterless momentary edifice which fireworks draw into the nighttime sky with their sparkling curves, as a scaffolding of space; an ephemeral, winged emergence of an occurrence, or, in current parlance, into an architectural event.

In the 20th century, it is no longer historical monumental buildings but purely technological marvels that tempt many a young architect into daydreams. For a modern architect of the early 20th century, the architecture of the past hardly has the

[1] Friedrich Gilly: "On the Views of Marienburg, Castle of the Teutonic Order in West Prussia, Drawn in the Year 1794 by Mr. Gilly, Supervisor at the Royal Building Administration", in: *Friedrich Gilly – Essays on Architecture.* Published by the Getty Center for the History of Art and the Humanities, translated by David Britt, 1994, pp. 109–110.

[2] Ibid., p. 109.

potential to arouse. What now rises into the firmament as a kind of fireworks and gives wings to the architect's imagination are the technical structures of the modern age of industry: constructions and machines begotten by the engineer, the master of technology and science and the guarantor of progress.

What was, for Friedrich Gilly, the "marvelous daring of the structure" of gothic halls, will be the image of a skyscraper in construction for Mies van der Rohe in 1922. Just as Gilly ignores the space-occluding lintels of the rib construction and thus reconverts the building into a kind of shell, van der Rohe aims to strip the skyscrapers of their stone façades and replace them with a skin made of glass. His marvel at the slender frame of the steel construction striving skywards motivated him to perform this radical operation, as van der Rohe reveals in the very first sentence of his explanation of his project of a glass high rise at the Friedrichstraße station: "Only skyscrapers in construction show the daring constructive imagination, overwhelming us with the impression of the towering steel skeletons."[3] This sublime image was "completely destroyed (...) by walling up the fronts"[4]; architecturally conserving it was the intention of van der Rohe's shell aesthetics, known as "skin-and-bones architecture". Van der Rohe later left it behind in his high-rise buildings in the U.S., returning to the image of ribs or pilasters to symbolize the constructive frame on the surface of the structure.

2

In 1923, Le Corbusier demanded this appreciative view of the new technological miracle buildings with his famous finger-pointing section "Eyes That Do Not See" as an obligatory attitude. With this sentence, he rubs his colleagues' noses, who—struck with myopia or blindness—were still clinging to the architecture of the past, in the modern arsenal of ocean liners, airplanes, and automobiles, aiming to understand this as the new architectural obligation and to carry out the inevitable revolution of architecture in the spirit of the New Age. Corbusier's references to the spirit of the New Age were his machine-like, white, floating buildings, lifted off the ground in a quasi-aeronautical existence.

[3] Mies van der Rohe, appeared without title in: *Frühlicht*, Hochhäuser, 1922, p. 122.

[4] Ibid.

The "International Style" has canonized this aesthetic into an orthodox convention. Even today, it is nostalgically cultivated as the only true language of architecture by architects who identify as modern.

Since Corbusier, we have lived through a whirl of revolutionizing architecture in the name of *zeitgeist*, or, rather, *zeitgeisten* in the plural, which clearly can prove capricious and erratic. Technology, from the first machine age through to our present "electronic age", has remained the preferred instance of normativity from which the seemingly inevitable imperatives for the revaluation of architecture's values have been derived. After a century of architecture that must constantly be lifted to the height of the times as defined by state-of-the-art technology, a veritable post-revolutionary state of exhaustion has set in. Architecture somehow seems to be paralyzed by an excess of supposedly innovative impulses, sated by its constant regurgitation of stale utopias, exhausted by its unceasing experimentation with extravagance and the supposedly unique and novel. The city had and still has to lend itself patiently as a playing field for modern architects, something clearly apparent everywhere today. It is hard to imagine that this dreary situation began a hundred years ago with colorful architectural dreams of a better world.

Architects like to dream. Why not, after all, if they take care to stay grounded and abide to van der Rohe's dictum: "While we want to stand with both feet firmly on the ground, we want to reach with our head to the clouds."[5] Illusions, however, must collapse at some point. When you leave the firm ground of architecture too far behind, someone needs to come along who calls the architect back from their utopian dreams at the edge, or even already far beyond, of architecture; someone who puts their feet firmly back onto the ground and re-roots architecture in reality.

Friedrich Gilly's fate was similar, though only posthumously. The acclaim accorded to Gilly's Malbork Castle drawings stimulated their publication in large-format copper plates,

[5] Fritz Neumeyer: *Das kunstlose Wort. Mies van der Rohe: Gedanken zur Baukunst,* dom Publishers Berlin, 1986.

etched in aquatint by Friedrich Frick from Gilly's original drawings. Gilly died in August 1800 and only lived to see the production and distribution of the first sheets. In the production of the remaining sheets, the delivery of which dragged on until 1803, Frick went beyond Gilly's drawings.

Gilly neither saw the series nor got a chance to have his say in the introduction, which was printed after his death. Frick had rewritten the history of Malbork Castle, and changed the priorities: According to Frick, in his introduction, it had become necessary to commission a new building survey, because Gilly's sheets "were not only mere sketches, but also fashioned with some imagination".[6] Gilly's emotional vision no longer satisfied

[6] Wilhelm Salewski (ed.), *Schloß Marienburg in Preußen. Das Ansichtswerk von Friedrich Gilly und Friedrich Frick. In Lieferungen erschienen von 1799 bis 1803*, Dusseldorf, 1965, preliminary report, p. 1.

2

Marienburg Castle in Prussia, refectory. Pen drawing by Friedrich Gilly, 1794, portraying himself leaning against a pillar

©HdZ 5661 of the Berlin Art Library, State Museum of Prussian Cultural Heritage the publisher who was anxious to ensure “historical accuracy”.[7] The building researcher and scientist corrected the romantic visionary and, so to speak, appointed himself the theoretical guardian of the rapturous artist.

[7] Ibid.

The refectory engraving published by Frick bluntly illustrates this process. The view of the space remains the same as in Gilly's drawing, but now, Gilly no longer leans against a column lost in his solitary dreams. In a procedure reminiscent of photomontage, his figure was simply moved a step forward, away from the column, with its posture nearly unchanged. Gilly now stands freely within the room; he no longer listens to his own dreams, leaning back against the column, but must instead

2

The same room represented by Friedrich Frick in: *Schloss Marienburg in Preussen. Das Ansichtenwerk von Freidrich Gilly und Friedrich Frick.* Published in sections from 1799 to 1803

follow the explanations of a knowledgeable theorist who has been assigned to him. The latter now directs the gaze of his pupil in a teacher's pose, his arm and index finger extended, and clearly instructs him, true to the motto "eyes that do not see", in what is worth seeing. Whether Gilly would still have marveled now is an open question. What is clear is that Frick unambiguously puts himself forward in his role as the publisher and building historian aiming for accuracy, quasi as the director of artistic imagination. Gilly was no longer able to defend himself against theoretical intrusions of this kind.

The quiet triumph of the modern, explanatory, scientific, theoretical mind over the artistic imagination with its tendency to glorify things also becomes apparent in other sheets from Frick's Malbork publication. With systematic, quasi-anatomical meticulousness and building-block didactics, the building is

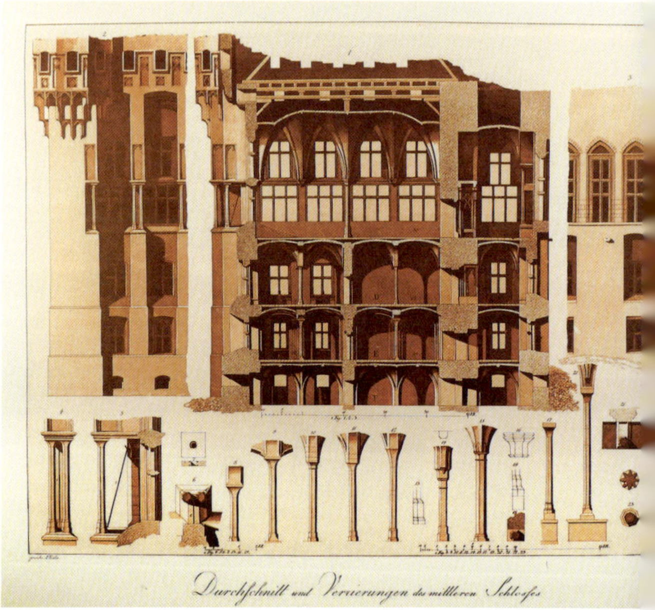

Sectional view of the refectory with ceiling, ibid.

dissected into its architectural elements and catalogued, reminiscent of Durand's demonstration of his design method in his *Précis*. The systematic mind reclaims the architect's utopia and returns it to concrete architectural reality, in which architecture cannot exist without a conscious combination of parts into a harmonious whole. A part of this art of building, according to the modern interpretation, is turning back in one's footsteps, the analytical process of a conscious, systematic dissection as a necessary anatomical operation and condition for the organization of a building kit.

The possible uses of theory for architecture and the architect can hardly be demonstrated more clearly than in the comparison of these two images of the Malbork refectory. This example conveys the practical significance of theory in the sense of Vitruvius' "demonstrate and explain". Theory requires us to look

Underside of the refectory ceiling, ibid.

more closely after our initial amazement instead of dreaming ourselves into the object in the throes of sentiment and soaring up into another sphere and letting ourselves be carried away. Theory, in the words of Nietzsche, must "courageously stay at the surface": it has to address concrete phenomena with patience and may not take refuge in an idealized backworld or superworld. Such idealism, to Nietzsche, was essentially nothing but cowardice in the face of reality.

In order to know what and how we see, we need theory. It requires a cool analytical gaze and a knowledge of knowledge and its conditions. Theory should explain and not romanticize; it should help avoid errors. The task of theory is not to establish truths, but mainly to avoid self-delusion. For the theory of architecture, this means answering to oneself, beyond artistic fancies and intellectual fashions, enlightening oneself, developing one's own architectural judgment; namely on the different levels of architectural activities, conception, production, and interpretation. When talking about the academic theory of architecture, its task would be to educate architects in the reasoning of architecture; for their own use and for the benefit of the discipline.

All this sounds very well and should spontaneously excite confidence and sympathy for theory and the theorist. But what happens when the theorist themself is the dreamer and the romantic who, in the name of theory, and preferably in the name of aesthetic theory, loses sight of architecture—if it was ever in sight—and dreams themself into the idealistic beyond of architecture?

In this case, we would have to complement the theorist with an architect possessing an essentially architectural feeling—turning the Malbork image upside down—who rocks the ivory tower of abstraction and opens the theorist's eyes, which do not see, to the concrete conditions of the discipline. From time to time, this kind of architect actually does exist.

Adolf Loos was one of them. His *Architektur* essay, dating from 1909, eloquently pits the basic reality of architecture, a specific purpose bound to general life, against the artistic tendencies of his period; a basic reality that also constitutes an intrinsic condition for the artistic existence of architecture. Architecture is a social art. In this sense, Loos says: "The artist only has to serve himself, the architect has to serve the community."[8] Architecture had been understood in this sense since the Renaissance, as we know from Alberti, who holds architecture accountable in the service of the city and of urban development.

It is also from this perspective that Loos says the following: "A house must please everyone. This distinguishes it from a work of art, which doesn't have to please anyone." And his words, "A work of art is a private matter of the artist. A house is not,"[9] are directed against an artification and academization of architecture in the name of aesthetic theories and concepts that can only lead to formal arbitrariness and "nervous vanities". Architecture is the wrong address for both of them.

Van der Rohe was an architect of similar caliber. In 1923, he vented his frustration with avant-garde architecture only motivated by art theory—as promoted by the DeStijl movement, for instance—in his famous manifesto BAUEN, and concludes with the seemingly atavistic call, "to liberate construction from aesthetic speculation and to return building to what it should exclusively be, namely BUILDING." Incidentally, the handwritten original manuscript of the text reads: "to return it to what it has always been".[10]

In my generation, it was Hans Kollhoff who referred the issue of architectural form and architectural quality back to BUILDING with a verve comparable to Loos and van der Rohe. However, with his plea for tectonic thought and feeling and an architecture in which mechanical skills reassert themselves in the sense of the art of joining, he made few friends amongst theorists and architecture colleagues.

Those who do theory as a narcissistic speculation were called, in Gilly's time, "theoreticians" and "philosophizers". In 20th-century architectural theory, this species has numerous representatives. In current architectural theory, it is in great demand. Today's media-staged architectural showbiz demands the trademark of an idealistically spectacular image, valorized

8 Adolf Loos: *Architektur* (1909), in: ibid., *Trotzdem*, Innsbruck 1931, p. 101.

9 Ibid.

10 Mies van der Rohe: "BAUEN", in: *G* No. 2, September 1923, p.1. Handwritten version in: Fritz Neumeyer: *Das kunstlose Wort. Mies van der Rohe: Gedanken zur Baukunst*, DOM Publishers Berlin, 1986, p. 300 f.

by pseudo-philosophies and all sorts of strange conceptual inventions that are barely concerned with architecture any more. A lack of substance and orientation are not disadvantages, as the diffuse and ambiguous can always be sold as an inventive conquest of uncharted territory to an architectural profession that is prone to new awakenings and has lost touch with history.

As we know, there are theoretical fashions, and the shelf life of theories has decreased enormously. Thus, art theory, and with it architecture theory, celebrate a new "turn" every decade: from the "semantic turn", the "linguistic turn", the "pictorial turn", and the "spatial turn", to the recently proclaimed "material turn".

The need for theories to explain and glorify ever-new "innovative" trends is enormous. Often, however, it is only about frantically generating the impression of having one's very own theories. In a period of theory-prone trends, such display behavior is almost obligatory for an architect to make sure they are perceived as a protagonist of the *zeitgeist.*

This theoretical theater of acquisition is a traditional part of the autocommunication rituals amongst the avant-garde. What is at stake is the theoretical legitimization of supposedly radical innovative artistry, with a reference to sociology, philosophy, chaos theory, quantum physics, biology, or whatever else is currently the height of discursive fashion. The "use" of such interdisciplinary acrobatics that allow for insights into everything and nothing is their ability to avoid any imposition on concrete architecture.

2 Architecture is a social, function-bound art. It must serve a living purpose and has the task of housing the people of this world. It must thus take forms of human community into account and provide them with fitting constructive and spatial expressions. This is the meaning of architectural form, and no theory that wants to call itself a theory of architecture may ignore this specificness of purpose. Any theory of architecture that aims to void this basic condition in the name of any type of philosophy loses sight of its objective, and therefore forfeits its *raison d'être.*

Architecture is least of all a theoretical or purely aesthetic reality. The purpose of architecture is not first and foremost to produce aesthetic showpieces that demonstrate modernity or illustrate a philosophy in three dimensions. It also doesn't befit it to simply pay homage to the spectacular, as though the most important task of architecture was to stand out and attract attention. In architecture, aesthetics cannot be separated from use. Buildings are not primarily constructed as sculptures or "images", but as places of residence and of passing time. Buildings are also, as Walter Benjamin aptly put it, "received in a twofold manner: by use and by perception. Or, better put: tactilely and visually."[11]

For the tactile, i.e. physical perception of our presence in a space we use, obviously different modalities of perception apply than for the primarily visual perception that occurs when we stand in or in front of a building contemplating it. Visual perception, which Benjamin calls "contemplation", is in contrast to the other, "tactile" perception arising from use. In tactile perception, our attention is not focused on observing, and our attitude to the building is in a state of "distraction", as Benjamin calls it, because when using a building all the senses are used in addition to the eyes.

Architecture as an aesthetic reality is therefore perceived consciously, in a state of concentrated attention, as well as unconsciously, in a state of relaxed attention, in casual observance. And this latter state of casualness, which refers to feeling and use and is always linked to what we call our mental state, would also have to come into its own in the aesthetics and theory of architecture; because architecture—contrary to other arts—is not primarily produced to elicit feelings, i. e. for the sake of an aesthetic phenomenon.

[11] Michael W. Jennings, Brigid Doherty and Thomas Y. Levin (eds.): "Walter Benjamin: The Work of Art in the Age of Its Mechanical Reproducibility," *The Work of Art in the Age of Its Technological Reproducibility, and Other Writings on Media,* trans. Edmund Jephcott, et al., The Belknap Press, Cambridge/London, 2008, p. 40.

3 Let us return to the question of the use and abuse of theory for the architect. As has become clear, the relationship between theory and practice is not a one-way street, and neither is the relationship between the theorist and the architect. Both need each other; what is important is basically only to know who needs whom at the proper time.

In Nietzsche's essay "Of the Use and Abuse of History for Life", which I appropriated in my title, things are similar. Without memory, humans are not able to live, according to Nietzsche's argument. Neither, however, can humans who only live in their memory, never forgetting. The essence of all historico-philosophical theory therefore is: One must remember at the proper time, and be able to forget at the proper time. Basically, the relationship between theorist and architect is not much different. They only have to draw close at the proper time, and also take leave at the right moment.

The question of what architecture needs theory for was answered by Marc-Antoine Laugier, one of the first modern thinkers who aimed to free architecture of all redundancy and to define its immovable laws, in his *Essai sur l'architecture*, published in 1753, in the following manner: "(...) it is not sufficient to know how to work; it is above all important to learn to think. An artist should be able to explain to himself everything he does, and for this he needs firm principles to determine his judgments and justify his choice to that he can tell whether a thing is good or bad, not simply by instinct but by reasoning and as a man experienced in the way of beauty."[12]

[12] Marc-Antoine Laugier, *An Essay on Architecture*, Hennessey & Ingalls, Los Angeles, 1977, p. 1.

This statement of self-enlightenment goes far in its demand for knowledge. It states that for architects, it is not enough to know how to do something; they must first and foremost have to know "on the basis of thought" why and wherefore it is done—and, with a view to the object-fixated architecture of our time, we might want to add: and where it is done. And finally, according to Laugier, architects must also be conversant in "the ways of beauty" of architecture, i.e. how it impacts our senses as an aesthetic reality. The theory of architecture therefore encompasses the logics of mental and manual production as well as the logics of perception and reception in the social and cultural reality of the five human senses.

Architectural theory should not only teach the architect to think "about" architecture, but in a sense, also to think "in" it. Just like a musician thinks and feels in music, a painter in images, an architect should be able to think and feel "in" architecture.

If we are to meet these requirements, the issues are the essence and the phenomenality of architecture as an art with very specific characteristics that define its unique characteristics as compared to other arts and technical disciplines. What is architecture? And how is architecture? These two questions about essence and effect are questions of disciplinarity, relating to the self-conception of architecture. No one who wants the right to call themselves an architect can ignore them.

Architectural thought, like all thought, is accomplished through linguistic signs. Without language and a conceptual ability to designate, thoughts are not possible, and neither is individual thinking. Architectural theory as the systematic thought of building thus "articulates", or rather "writes" building. Without the written word, after all, the self-reflection of architecture as an independent genre is inconceivable. Without this medium, it would *a fortiori* be impossible to speak of a theory of architecture.

The importance of writing for architecture is far more than just a literary interest. For the architect, too, the written word is indispensable. As a part of the intellectual and practical work, it supports the process of development from the first design idea to the description of the concrete object to be constructed.

As a rule, architects do not have a particularly strong relationship to the written word, or to theory. They rarely write books of theoretical content, and if they do, it is mostly in reference to their own work. One of the more immediate uses of theory since Antiquity has always been, as Vitruvius says, that the architect can "leave a more lasting remembrance in his treatises".[13] Self-explanation and self-glorification have motivated architects from Vitruvius' times until today to address in writing the most diverse issues of building and to assert themselves as theorists. This is also the starting point of the dubious prospect of completely counting on the relevance of verbal and multimedia image cultivation as an architect who does not have any important works of their own. In the theory-prone, poststructuralist 1990s, a number of young academic architects seem to have adopted the belief that model construction plus philosophy will result in a first "architect's" monograph. But architecture is no more a graphic art exalted by theory than every intellectual effort really is a thought, and even less an "architectural" theory!

[13] Vitruvius, *The Ten Books on Architecture*, Harvard University Press, Cambridge. Humphrey Milford, Oxford University Press, London, 1914, p. 5.

Vitruvius already distinguished between “fabrica” and “ratiocinatio” and thus marked the conflict constituted by the fact that architecture combines the contrasting worlds of building and art, as it is both skilled manual work and an intellectual discipline. Architecture unites science and art, logics and aesthetics, the useful and the beautiful. This is why both sides can relate to each other, but also be pitted against each other in the theoretical consideration of architecture.

In other words: Aesthetic arguments can be justified by technical and functional ones, and vice versa. Architects have always made use of both options, and they have made clever use of the combination of logics and aesthetics, construction and form as a part of a strategy of self-objectification. One’s art is made to appear as science, and science is cited as an artistic argument. In this way, the theoretical legitimization of one’s own architecture is most effective.

But mainly, the theory of architecture has itself as a discipline to blame for this abstract theorizing. It loves to refer to the seasonal normativity of different ideologies, theories, and academic disciplines in the name of a new, unlimited, interdisciplinary consciousness, while its theoretical and formal capacity to cope with its own reality and experience is limited.

Casually speaking, we might say that in architecture, it is possible to promote any nonsense with a theory—you only have to surround it with an aura of scholarship. Such an aura develops when one does not know very clearly oneself what one is talking about, and the others therefore cannot understand the theory either. The cryptic has an enormous potential for magic, the clients’ willingness to believe is tremendous as long as a theory serves to put them in a state of anticipating devotion.

The best example for the devout use of a theory one knows practically nothing of, and its interdisciplinary combination with architecture, was given by Sigfried Giedion in his classic of the historiography of modern architecture, *Space, Time and Architecture*, first published in 1939 and still sold today in the umpteenth edition. With the term “space-time”, Giedion wanted to prove himself as a theorist at the height of his time, and derive possible consequences from Einstein's momentous theory of relativity for architecture, however we were to understand that. Erich Mendelsohn, who had built the famous Einstein tower, an observatory and astrophysics institute on Telegrafenberg near Potsdam in 1920, and who still had contact with Einstein at the time, sent an excerpt of Giedion's book to Einstein in 1941, most probably the chapter "The New Space Conception: Perspective". I cannot refrain from quoting from Einstein's answering letter, dated 13 November 1941, which is conserved at the Berlin Art Library in the Mendelsohn estate collection:

"Dear Mr. Mendelsohn: The excerpt of the book *Space, Time and Architecture* you sent me has prompted the following response:

It's not hard to say something new
If you go by any nonsense.
But rarer still the occasion
That the novel is rational, too.
With warm regards, your A. Einstein

PS: It is nothing but smart-assery
with no rational foundation!"

This less than encouraging comment on the theorist's interdisciplinary efforts to raise architecture to the scientific heights of the time and to join the conversation at any cost in order to get attention and acquire a status of modernity, objectivity, and normativity should give us food for thought. Intellectual fashions aside, it not only seems foolish, but simply presumptuous to try and deduce and reason one's own architectural arguments from disciplines that one knows even less about than one's own.

The modern pluralism that has emerged from the crisis of normative architectural theory, however, has created a situation in which the dependence of architecture on theory has become stronger than ever, unless one professes a theory-free "anything goes". In the openness of today's pluralism, it is hard to make do without a point of orientation. Contemporary architectural theory with its reduction of architectural thinking to other intellectual arenas and modes of thinking (cf. Michael Hays, *Constructing a New Agenda: Architectural Theory 1993–2009*, Princeton, 2010) provides little help, as it stubbornly refuses to define its subject. In these conditions, architecture can ultimately be dissolved into nothing or everything, and architectural theory can be degraded into a kind of import business into which all other schools of thought can discharge themselves.

But interdisciplinary thought is not a one-way street, and architectural theory is not only a function of applied external scholarship, but first and foremost a systematic reflection on the existential conditions and possibilities of this intrinsic cultural institution we still call "architecture". If architecture can be understood as "scripted space" (Derrida), it embodies a grand book of humanity, so to speak, in which collective and individual experience are preserved as implicit knowledge. The fact that architecture, in the sense of transdisciplinarity, can clearly also provide input for other fields of knowledge instead of only receiving it from others seems nearly forgotten.

The modern architect has acquired many eyes since Le Corbusier. The "eyes that do not see" have literally taken note of everything by now: ships, airplanes, modern art, film, electronic media, and virtual space. In this process, the architect has been able to discover all sorts of things as a possible reference. Architectural form, however, has remained a mystery to most.

It is part of the educational tasks of architectural theory to familiarize architects with their own discipline in the consciousness of continuity; i.e. to incorporate in it the full scope of history—not only the history of the 20th century—as a heritage open to continuation. Architecture, as a form of knowledge, disposes of an implicit cultural wisdom that it has collected in the course of history. I regard the reappropriation of lost sensibilities and forgotten knowledge to the benefit of "building culture" as the most eminent task of today's theory of architecture. This task is hardly new. Camillo Sitte sketched it as early as 1889 when he stated that because the beauty of the old cannot be saved, theoretical insights should at least record its "genome".[14] Who knows, it might help pave the way forward some time in the future.

As long as we, architects and theorists alike, still admire and marvel at the architecture of the past, we need not abandon this hope•

[14] Camillo Sitte: *Der Städtebau nach seinen künstlerischen Grundsätzen*, Vienna, 1889, 3rd edition (Carl von Graeser), p. 16.

View into the Marienburg Castle refectory, 2015

Photo © Fritz Neumeyer

System | From Greek *systema*: a whole made up of many individual parts, for example, the solar system. Generally: the holistic, meaningful, functional, and methodical ordering according to consistent principles of a multitude of knowledge into an overall ideology, an educational building. The goal is to counteract the splintering of knowledge, making complexity, dynamics, and self-organization visible. The complementary aspect of a system is the part, which is provided meaning by the system.

Part | Complementary to system: *Parts* or *elements* are the basic units of a system, and create a whole by interrelating with each other. A system without parts cannot be imagined, just as a game without players cannot be imagined. A part playfully reaffirms the rules of the game as well as its autonomy. The freedom of the player, and the autonomy of the part interact with the whole: Buildings make up the parts of the city, just as the city influences the buildings.

Supporting Structure | From Latin *structura*: Assembly, construction type; here referring to the supporting building elements. In statics, the supporting structure is defined as the entirety of all building parts and the foundation required for equilibrium and structural retention, while the structural system and supporting structure are understood as the arrangement and interaction of the bearing parts. It is always an interweaving of the interdependencies of the elements of a system that, in the end, guide vertical forces into the horizontal ground.

Fire Protection | The personal safety of the building users is at the core of fire protection: The details of what this means have changed radically over time. Fire protection divides buildings into fire compartments, structures their shapes, defines emergency exits and escape routes, and has a significant impact on choice of materials and construction. Extensive rules and regulations for fire protection guidelines have been compiled by associations in each nation, in Switzerland by the Swiss Canton Fire Insurance Association. Such guidelines specify all planning and execution requirements.

Site Development | In order to use a building, both its interior and exterior must be accessible and adequately supplied. The site development of a settlement includes integration with public railways and street networks in addition to utility and waste facilities, while that of a property refers to the totality of measures that must be fulfilled by law in order for a property to obtain a building permit and be considered developable. This includes road access, sewage system connections, and the supply of water and energy. Building circulation provides access to the rooms and evacuation paths for each building section; it is a system of horizontal and vertical connections that encompasses, for example, hallways, staircases, and elevators.

Space | With the dwindling of the 19th-century questioning of style, space became a central topic of architectural theory, particularly for August Schmarsow (1853–1936), who focused on the history of a sense of space. Space has become architecture's primary medium, limited and measured in three dimensions. In *The Hidden Dimension*, E.T. Hall (1966) takes a close look at people in spaces and reaffirms Heidegger's philosophy that, for people, space is not an object, since humans are and always have been in space. It is people's places and things that connect to become spaces.

Order | Life is order. The laws of thermodynamics state that a high degree of order is required to create crucial life energy; the other option is entropy, or heat death. A high degree of order means difference, differentiation, and intellectual comprehension. According to physicist Werner Heisenberg, knowledge is nothing other than order. Building opens up living processes and is always order—valuable is separated from valueless, meaningful from futile. Order is everywhere: Regulations direct the mixing of building materials and the joining of segments, there are recognized rules for technology, dimensional regulations, and special building ordinances: Overregulation is immanent. Geometric order is central to architecture, augmented by digital form. Rules are attempts at creating order. Antonyms: Collapse, dispersion, chaos.

Structuralism | A school of thought that sees all phenomena as being interconnected by a primary structure. Emerging from linguistics (Ferdinand de Saussure in the early 20th century), structuralism succeeded to existentialism in numerous scientific fields in the post-war era. Structural sociology, for example, emphasized the order of social systems, which shapes the actions of individuals and draws them closer to one another. For architecture, structure became a key concept in critiques of classic modernism starting in the 1950s. Temporal and spatial bonds took the place of limitless creative freedom. Structures create orders, which ensure both the binding and the freedom of the user. Holland is particularly familiar with architectural structuralism (Aldo van Eyck, Herman Hertzberger, Piet Blom, et al.). N. John Habraken is a theoretical pioneer whose principles of "structure and infill" describe participation.

Constructivism | A school of thought that puts constructed aspects of the world at the center—whether this be knowledge that is constructed "in one's head", a socially constructed role or gender, or architecture that is logically constructed from a few elements to serve specific functions. These elements are, on the one hand, geometrical basic forms and, on the other, highly technical structures. Any connection to place or history is rejected. The height of the movement was the Russian constructivism of 1915–1935. This can be seen in the models of Tatlin's Tower for the Monument to the Third International, with its hovering rooms shaped as cubes, tetrahedra, cylinders, and hemispheres set in a dynamic structural framework.

2

STRUCTURE

A structure is an arrangement of different elements exhibiting patterns that can be understood as an ordering of the elements amongst each other and as a whole. Areas populated by humans are structured, increasingly complex, and increasingly dense. Cities are highly structured formations.

Individual buildings, building groups, and exterior spaces create the fabric of the city. Different eras, cultures, and building tasks contribute to the built structure, which remains in effect over a long period of time. However, individual buildings are also structured; supporting structure and circulation structure both have lasting impacts. Use patterns, in contrast, have a shorter life span.

In order to be sustainable, a building structure should allow the use to change, and adapt to the structure of the place.

City Level

The focus of this exercise is on the structure of the neighborhood, the building site, and the existing buildings. The aim is demonstrate the structural rules they are subject to and help define various structural topics. It is important to connect the rational analysis of a place with personal perceptions and to subsequently find a means of representation. The analysis of the existing buildings will create the basis for the assignment at the building level.

Specifications

Project work will be carried out in groups, one group per building site, and presented in a presentation. Each group must complete a:

Structural analysis of the neighborhood

- Historical development
- Topographical structure
- Development structure
- Traffic infrastructure/ publictransport/privatetransport
- Use distribution
- Public and private outdoor spaces
- Public and private green spaces

Analysis of existing buildings

- General information about the building and architect
- Concept of supporting structure
- Building construction/materials/ engineering
- Circulation concept
- Evacuation concept

Requirements

- Figure-ground diagram 1:5000
- Neighborhood plan 1:1000
- Site plan 1:500
- Plans for existing buildings
- Cadastral maps
- Findings from the city walk
- Crafting notebooks I + II

Goal

A place can only be understood when its structures have been analyzed in detail. The more comprehensive the knowledge, the more justifiable decisions can become. Decisions are no longer arbitrary or purely subjective, but are instead based upon a grounded analysis and thus comprehensible.

Ruedi Walti, *Water Supply Structure XI*, C-print

2

Lena Hächler
Patrizia Hedinger
AS 15

Building Level

The focus of this assignment is on static structure as the primary system for the creation of built spaces. The structure is what gives the building order. Access routes and room modules of different sizes are set into this order. A well-conceived combination of these elements can create interesting spatial qualities.

Specifications

This exercise will be done in groups of two. It must be submitted as a DIN-A0 plan that includes

- Floor plan and cross-sections 1:200/1:250
- Three photos of the interior
- Written explanation
- Sectional model of the building structure, 1:50

Requirements

- Findings from the analysis
- Crafting notebooks I + II

Goal

The goal is to understand that a building requires structural order. Static and spatial structure, circulation, and transitions from interior to exterior spaces must be in harmony with one other. In the cross-sections and floor plans (classic means of presentation), the chosen order must be recognizable. Spatial qualities, problems, and solutions should be visible in the model. The challenge is to order large and small span lengths—including circulation—using an intelligently selected supporting structure.

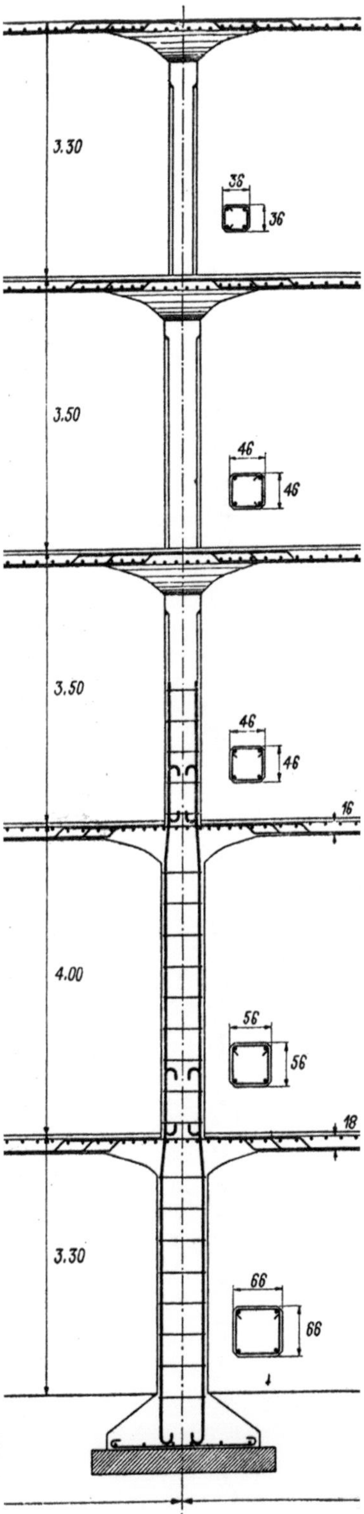

Robert Maillart, mushroom ceiling, Maillart system

Robert Maillart, Confederate Grain Stores, Altdorf, 1912

2

MIDDLE AGES

Building structure

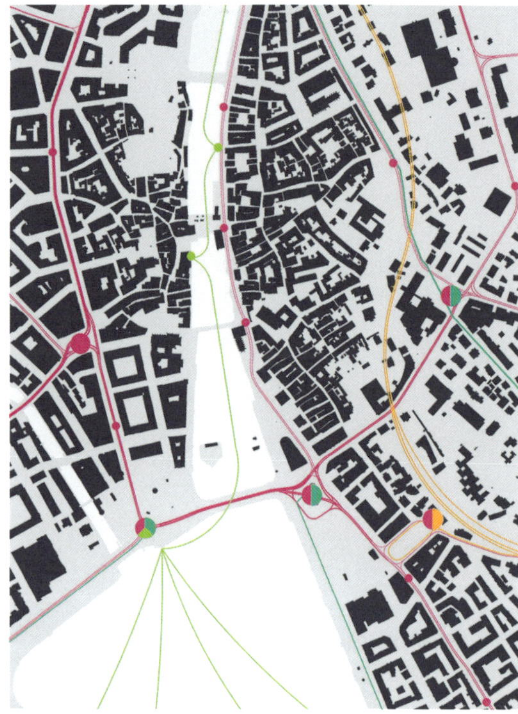

Traffic

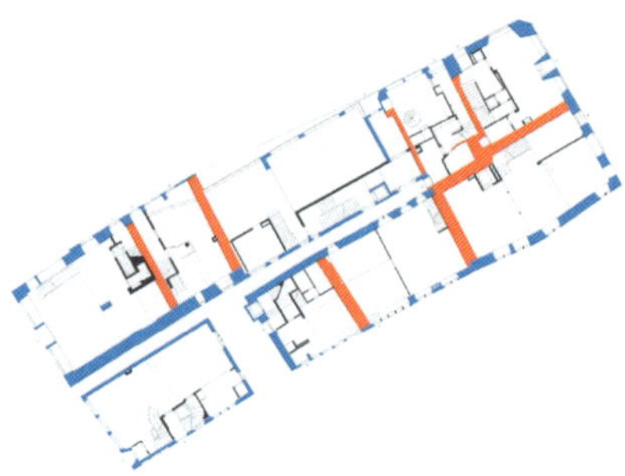

Bearing structure

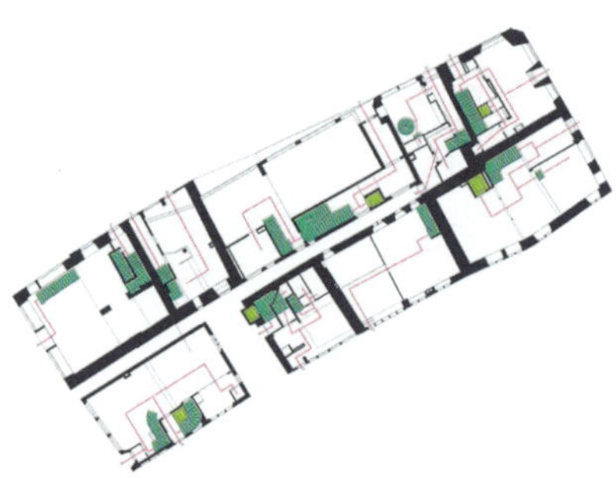

Circulation

Use distribution

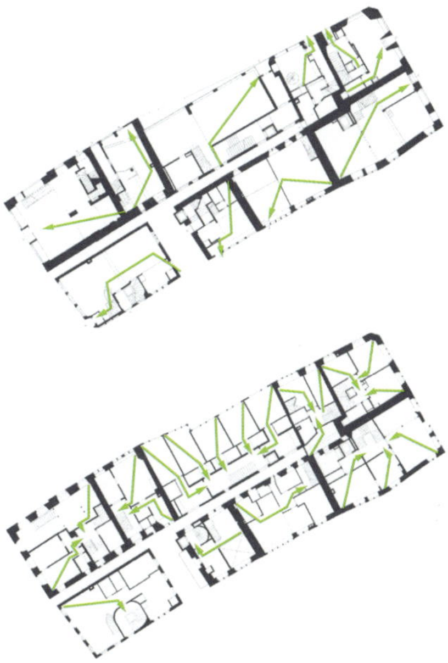

Evacuation routes

2

2

FOUNDATION ERA

Building structure

Traffic

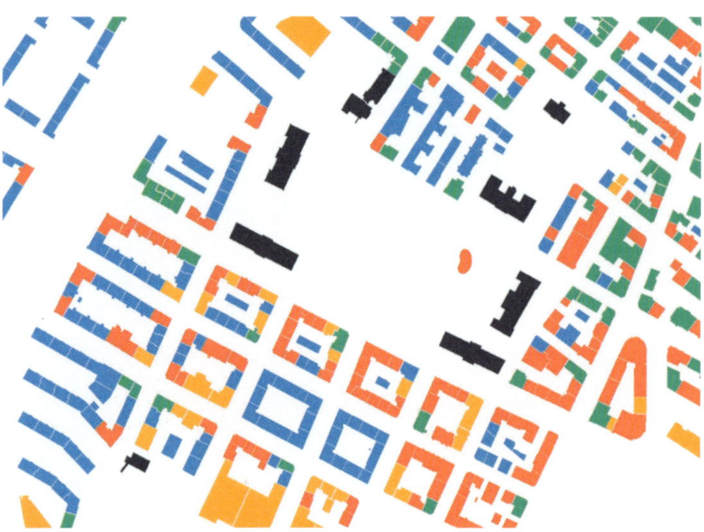

Use distribution

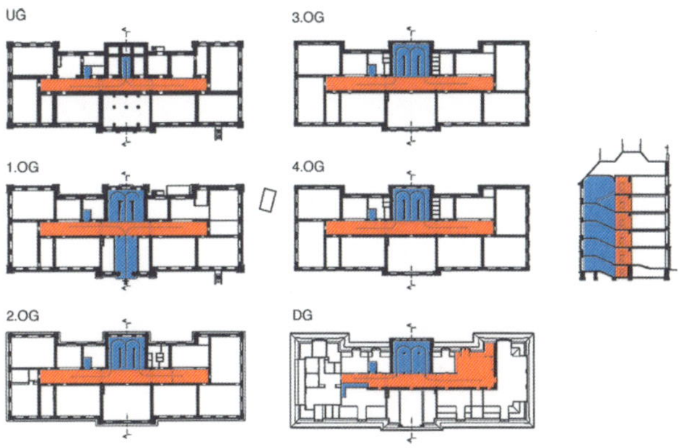

Circulation

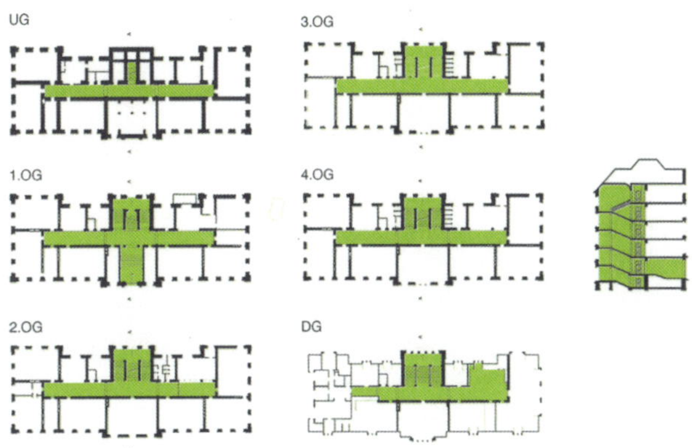

Evacuation routes

MODERNISM

Building structure

Traffic

Ground floor use distribution

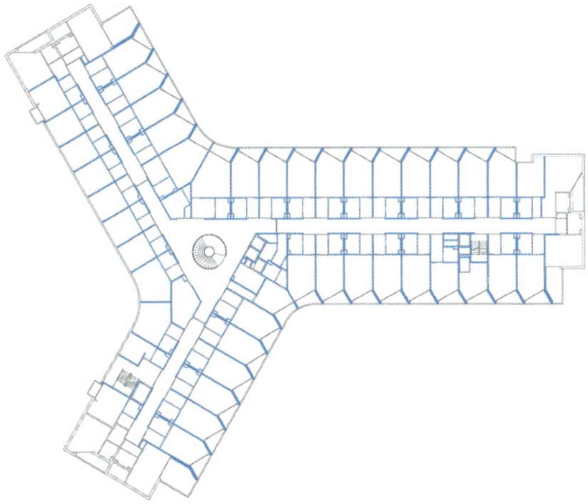

Bearing structure

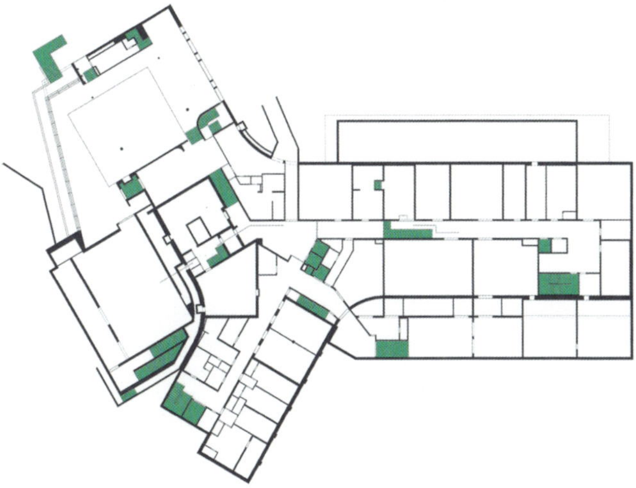

Circulation

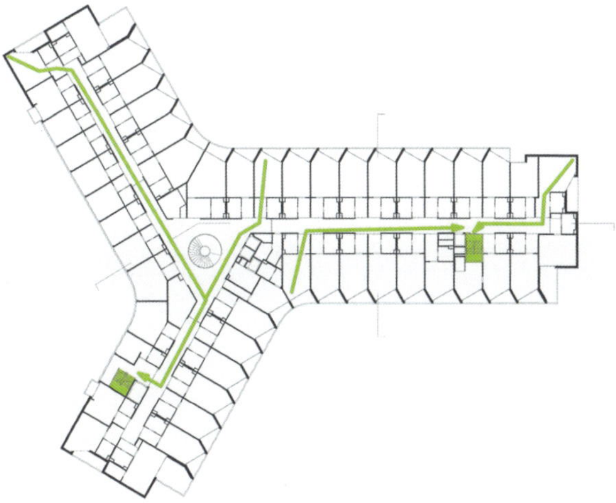

Evacuation routes

2

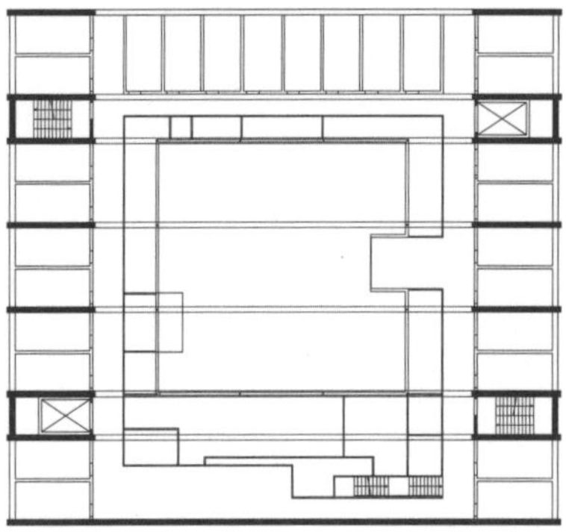

Mario Sommer
Andrea Zarn
08 AS

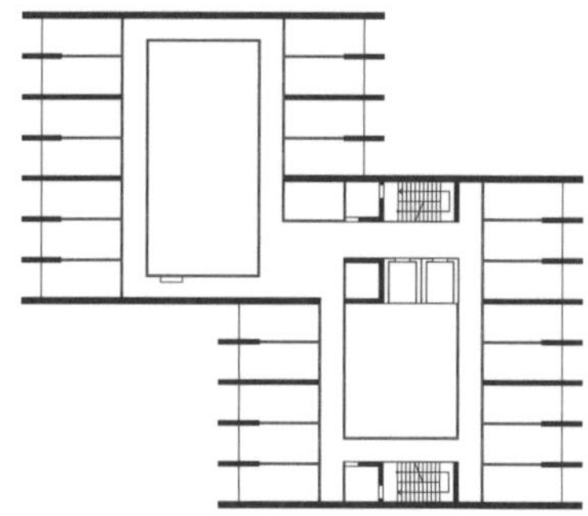

Norman Prinz
Konstantin Propp
Katrin Sommer
09 AS

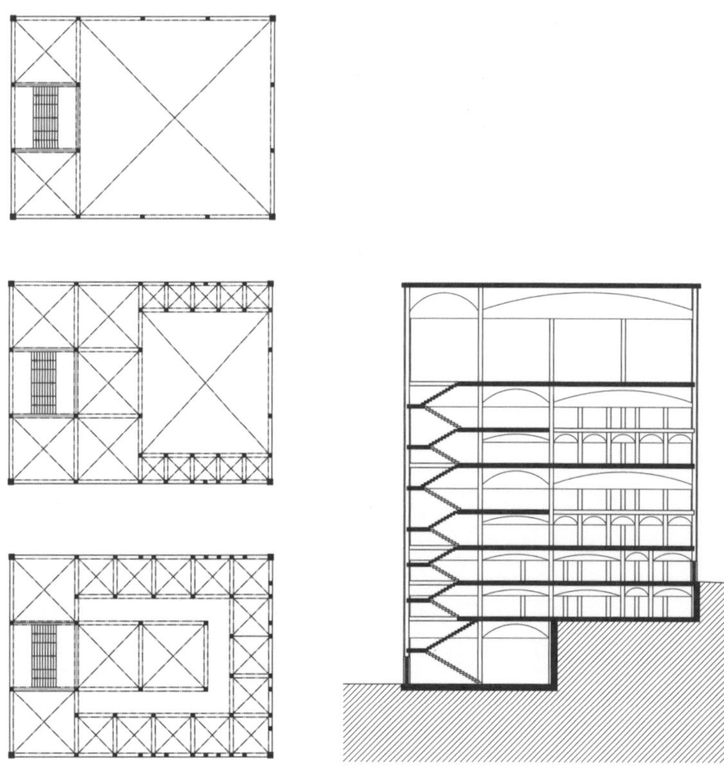

Tabea Schäfer
Pablo Vuillemin
13 AS

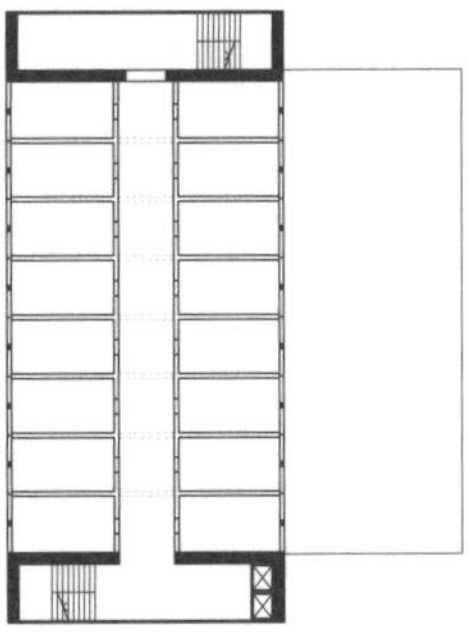

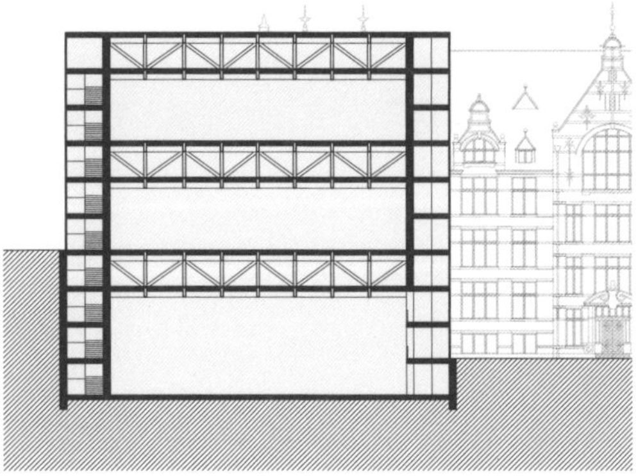

Paul Wolf
Alexandre Zommerfelds
13 AS

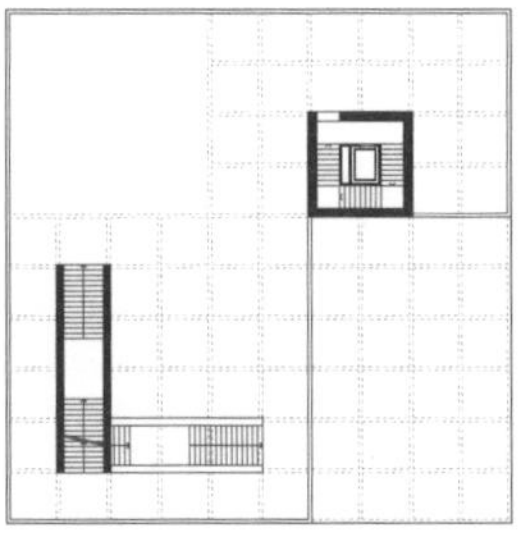

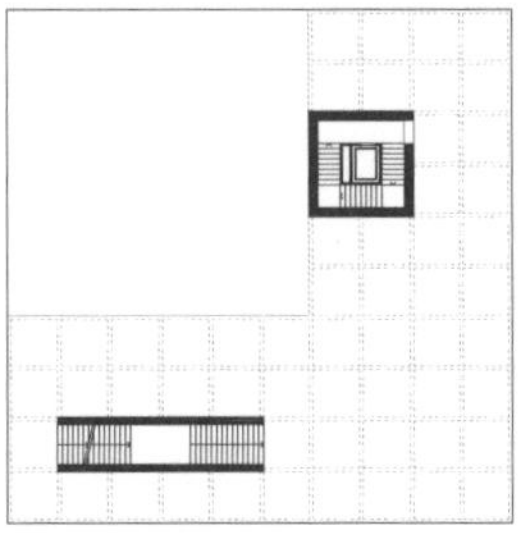

Julian Trachsel
Jan Waser
09 AS

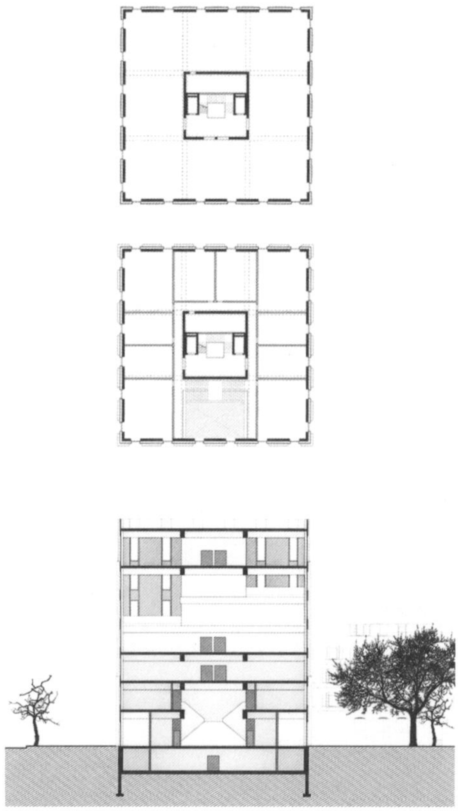

Alfred Pun
14 AS

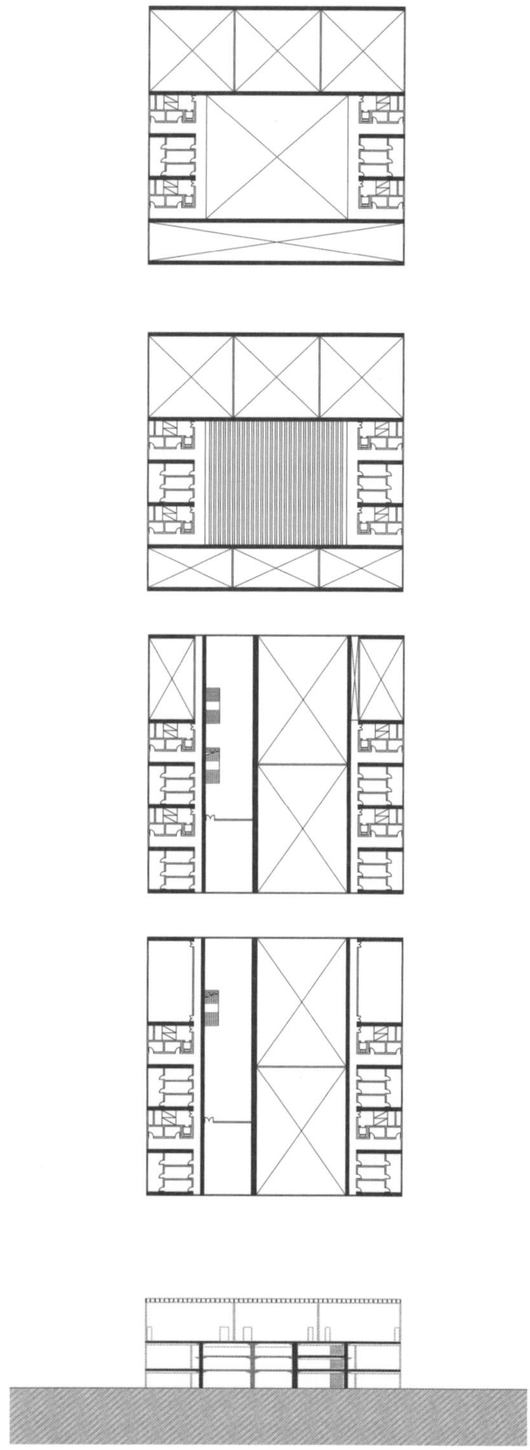

Alexander Poulikakos
Feng Mark Zhang
14 AS

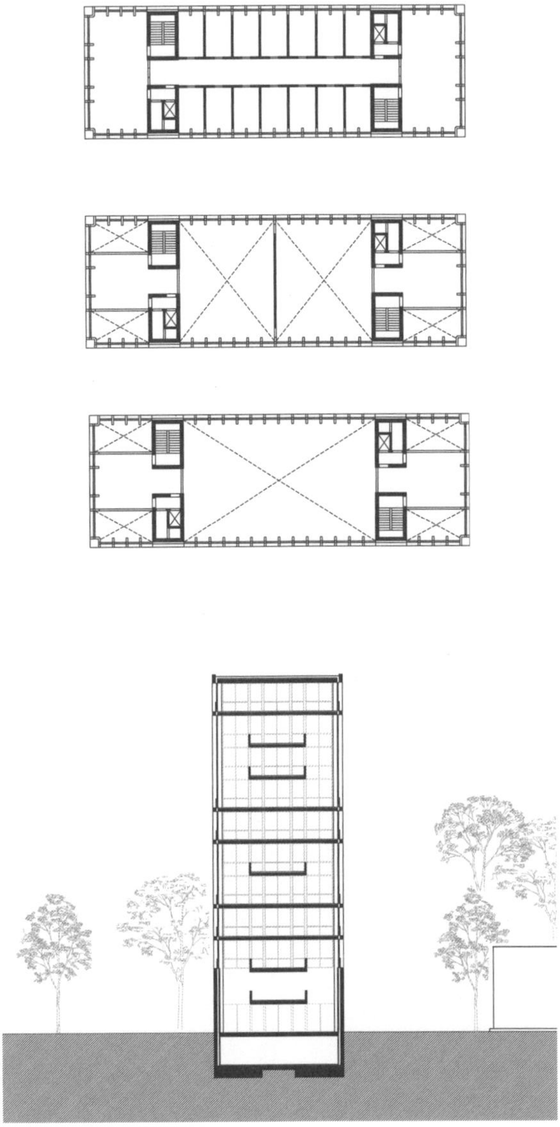

Magdalena Hermann
16 AS

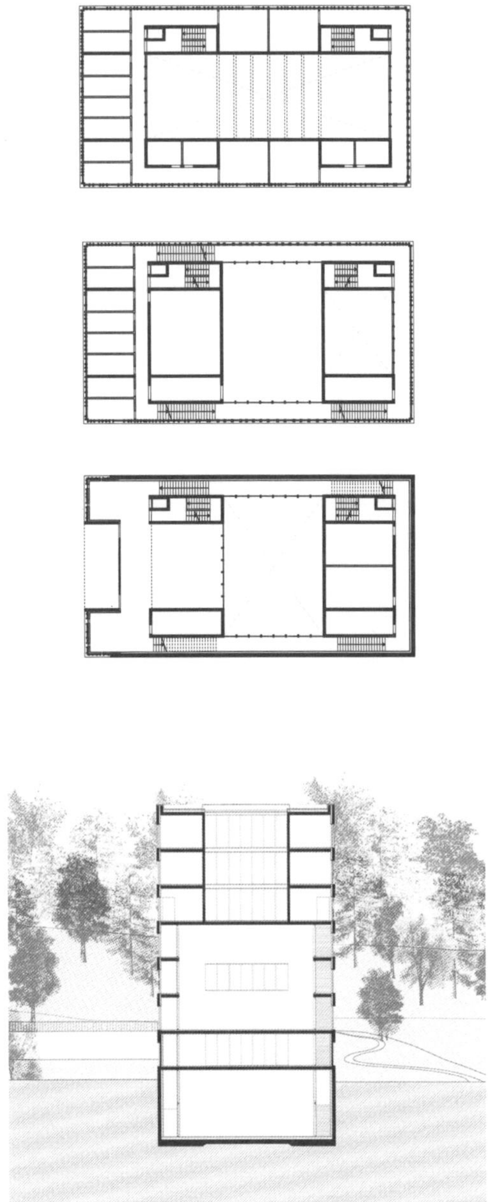

Samuel Dayer
16 AS

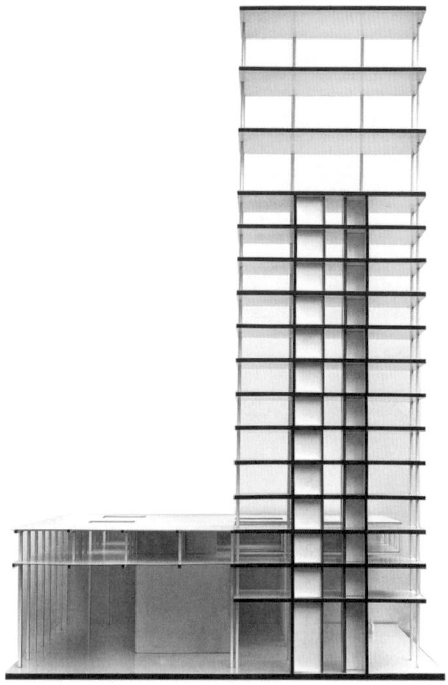

Andreas Monn
Leopold Strobl
12 AS

Julian Trachsel
Jan Waser
09 AS

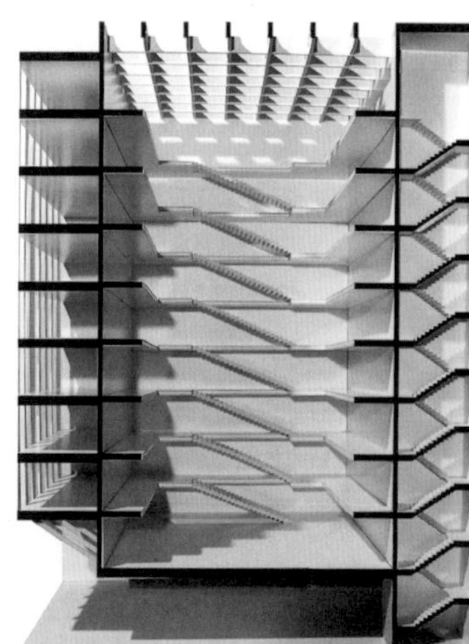

Katharina Glomb
Kirsten Koch
Magdalena Leutzendorff
09 AS

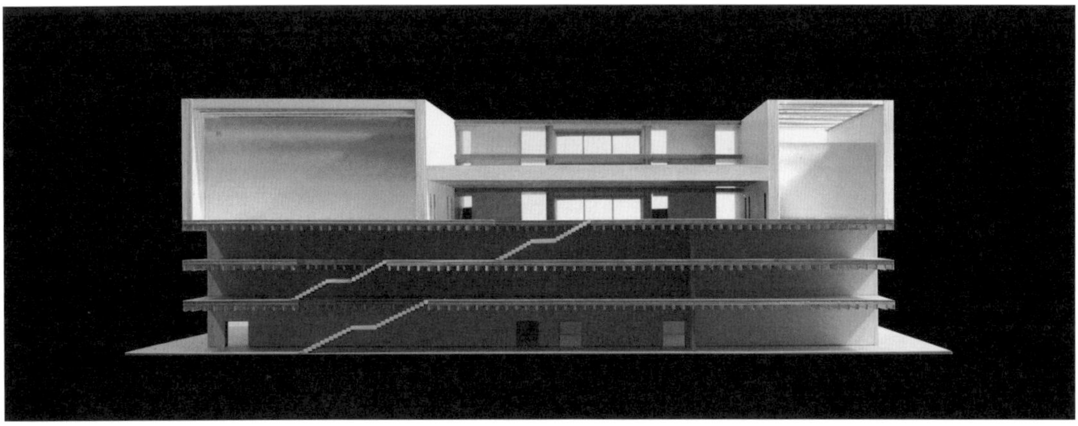

Alexander Poulikakos
Feng Mark Zhang
14 AS

2

Tabea Schäfer
Pablo Vuillemin
13 AS

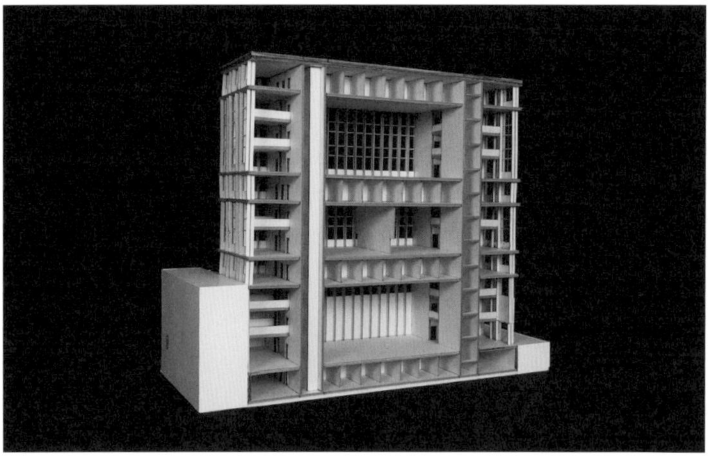

Magdalena Hermann
16 AS

Timothy Allen
Thierry Vuattoux
15 AS

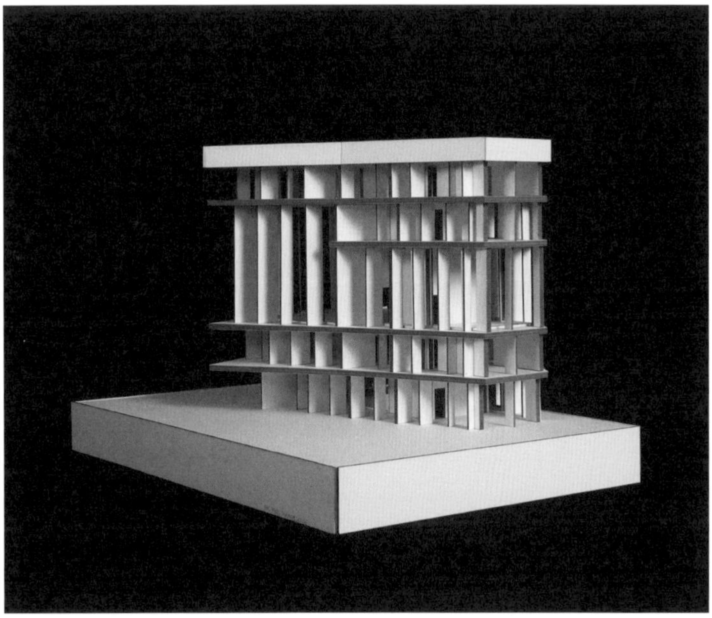

Samuel Dayer
Louise du Fay de Lavallaz
16 AS

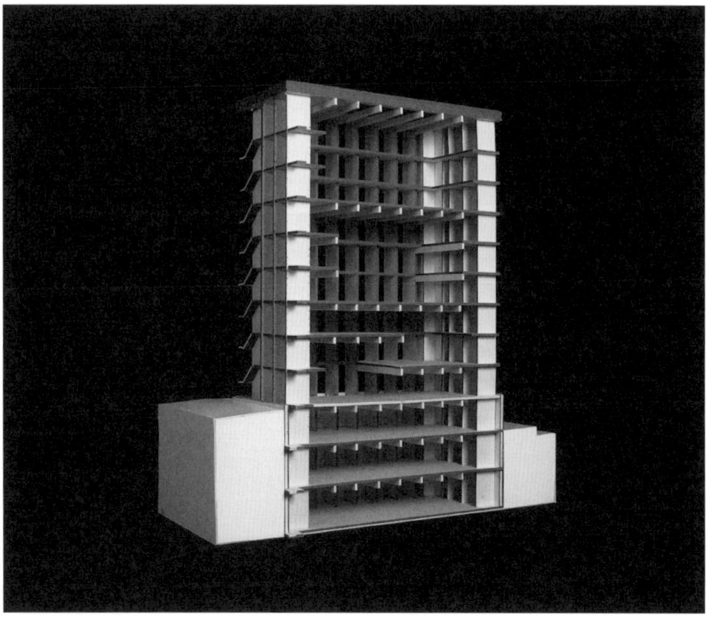

Milan Jarrell
16 AS

2

Lorenz Brunner
Leander Peper
12 AS

Mahela Hack
Jonas Martin Elias Hasler
13 AS

2

Paul Wolf
Alexandre Zommerfelds
13 AS

Beining Chen
Androniki Prokopidou
14 AS

Maximilien Durel
15 AS

Pablo Vuillemin
13 AS

Lena Hächler
Patricia Hedinger
15 AS

Andreas Monn
Leopold Strobl
12 AS

Bas Princen, *Reservoir (Concrete Rundown)*, 2005, © Bas Princen

3
Place Structure

3

Place Structure

Place is a site—limited, definable, concrete; it has physical properties. The structure is a relational system of interactions, with a tendency to openness. Place and structure appear at first glance to be indifferent or even resistant to each other, prove, however, to be interwoven when a closer look is taken. The place is inscribed with structures of greater or lesser clarity, and structures exhibit traces of the place. An enchanted place is intertwined with the path of the sun, of paths, of the passing of time; while a supporting structure reflects at the very least the place upon which it is grounded.

Place and structure permeate each other in the locale, blatantly: they grow together to form the city. During the post-war era, Italy's architectural discourse on cities often spoke of the contamination of place and structure. Linguistics describes contamination as the creation of new words from the merging of two existing ones. The word *motel*, for example, a combination of *hotel* and *motor*, is a mash-up, ambiguous, an impure term. This kind of intermingling occurs in the city permanently. The special place and the general structure enter into a new composition, neither a copy nor a break.

The powers that build cities also experience overlapping. Cities are formations that owe their existence to a very special will to design, and through this create structures from what is generally valid. "Urban architecture [...] is willed as such. [It] is a means in the formation of the city, such elements which originally start out as means tend to become ends; ultimately they *are* the city. Thus the city has as its end itself alone," writes Aldo Rossi. There is nothing else to say about the formations of the city, "beyond the fact of its own presence in its own artifacts" (1982, 162). The temporal structure solidifies into a quality of the place. The place is now marked by the structure. It is essential to understand the structure of the city, in order enter into a coalition in the right way.

This is especially effective in the relationship between public and private space. The distribution of these two types of space and the formation of their transitions characterizes the urban structure. But structure is not an isolated construction; rather, it unfolds itself within the context. Representing a city using a ground floor plan, such as taught by Rossi at the ETH, and which in turn was based on plans made by baroque architect Giambattista Nolli, illustrates the structure of the relationships among each other and to the whole.

It can be ascertained that these references are neither one-dimensional nor one-sided. Bearing structures are influenced by the place in many ways, and obtain identity through the place; yet a supporting structure—and occasionally also the access structure—can in turn also impact the place. The interaction of the two is not one of mere reflection; rather, it is open to interpretation. This comparativeness becomes especially meaningful when the relationship is fragile. The quality of the design depends on its success.

The interaction of place and structure is subtle—studying it is crucial to the design methodology. Differently evolved types of cities suggest different processes. In strongly marked places, such as an old town or a Foundation Era neighborhood, an analogous structure of ongoing construction is an obvious one; in a modernist city the open settlement structure includes the implementation of a classical structure. (FA/MN)

Construction and Place

András Pálffy

3

Construction is often overlaid by a projection with which the handling of physical laws is explained to an absolute extent, in which the logic of seams and their structural clarity render all other formal aspirations obsolete. This proposition for a hegemonic physics then becomes particularly loaded in an almost mystical fashion if a structural configuration, in its perfection, is shifted into the foreground so strongly that the perception of its formal presence is completely displaced by that assertion. The pure external expression of internal structural forces is as equally unviable as the notion of architectural plasticity liberated from structural necessity. There are always two sides, and neither can be reduced to the other.

The relationship between structure and form cannot be resolved in this way, irrespective of which of the two plays the dominant role in design. Both notions of construction run parallel throughout architectural history, and thus cannot be deemed unique to any one era.

The simultaneity of the two approaches to architecture is very clearly illustrated in the origins of modernism, in the work of Otto Wagner and Auguste Perret. While Wagner focuses on construction with multiple layers, Perret prefers monolithic building structures. Both architects were still strongly influenced by classicism, poised at the threshold of the rise of modernism, but they worked on their notions with the technical capacities of the time, albeit starting from very different positions. If the technological advances stemming from the industrial revolution, especially glass and steel construction, were concealed under the weight of classical façades – in the development of the Ringstrasse in Vienna, for example – for Perret and Wagner, they form a visible, fundamental part of their work that may be regarded in each instance as the starting point of regional modernism.

The possibility of industrialized fabrication certainly assumes and supports the development of the two principles of construction. Monolithic systems are copied in the production of precast concrete construction, and the use of serially produced steel frame structures leads directly to multilayer (composite) construction.

Regardless of whether the building is done industrially or by hand, regardless of the time it takes to complete it, nothing alters a universal constant whose validity has changed very little up to this moment, yet at the same time is the cause of numerous misunderstandings.

Transitions and borders stemming from the character of construction materials are treated according to functional necessity. A canon of construction details ranging from open to concealed joint designs allows for a vast number of variations on the

Jabornegg & Pálffy, Oberammergau Passion Play Theater (2003–2008), convertible covering of the open-air stage

Photo © Ivan Nemec

theme. The starting point for the design of ornament is frequently projected onto this space of transition, which superimposes a narrative on these gaps. The belief that modern architectural principles are responsible for the demise of ornament is only partly true, especially as this development can be explained less by technology than by culture.

In the 19th century, the erection of a steel bridge put greater importance on structural design than on any type of aesthetic intent whatsoever.

However, the desire for an aesthetic impact is inherent in the admiration of craftsmanship and the unique traces of expertise. This doesn't concern the finished product so much as the aura of its making and all of its irreproducible features. The legacy of this attitude of the Arts and Crafts movement is very much present in modernism, especially as the latter's ideals of quality is predicated by the causality of structural clarity and legibility.

In the history of modernism, connections and joints that reveal themselves fast become the object of aesthetic aspiration, the profile and setting of which ultimately always have an inherent formal character that lies within the range of ornamentation.

An aesthetic aspiration that consistently eludes these principles within the framework of modernism is best seen in the work of Mies van der Rohe. Steel members merge into one another with no visible points of construction; the fastenings are hidden in the background, and the constructive effect of the form is pushed into the foreground. The reduction to the essentials is the primary objective in this design strategy, and it aims to make clear statements about the architectural concept and less about the technical assemblage. Regardless of the materials used, the buildings of Mies deeply convey the representation of a modernism whose rules of the game consistently take them back into the shadows of classicism.

“Give meaning to form, and give form to meaning,” is a saying by Mies that leads directly from pictorial representations to spatial truths that place no constitutive parameters at the center of perception, but rather the totality of spatial effect, a spatial meaning.

On the other hand, Le Corbusier understands the structural significance of construction as an essential element within a *système de structure*, in which the universality of structural members and functions is called for. This thinking represents the desire to view architecture as a structural whole rather than as an arbitrary sum of processes. Construction becomes the mainstay of a concept into which it also integrates itself as needed.

Construction has the potential to define the massing and scale of a building within a given context. Construction can make its load-bearing behavior visible, or conceal it just as easily. Construction can express how a building is made, or distance itself from that expression.

Today’s technical possibilities have continually expanded the potential applications of construction, which are, however, still constrained by dichotomies just as much as they were in the past.

There are many dichotomies to be mediated here: new social demands, which are always being expressed with new theoretical concepts, stand in opposition to respect for craftsmanship and all its traditions as well as its new potential; the desire to invent new concepts and forms competes with the perpetuation of existing construction practices and ideas. And at the same time, these contradictions must not result in random disorder and haphazardness, but should always remain visible and comprehensible and lead to concrete perspectives and demands.

Thoughts on construction are usually confined within the contours of a building, and is thus associated with the building, not with the extended context.

But this self-contained logic is only an apparent one, of course. One always goes beyond the spatial envelope of a building, and then the pronounced reference to context becomes an essential basis of the architectural act that blends into clearly defined presences, and only comes to know its meaning within this truth, with all its frictional surfaces and oppositions.

It is no longer the aura of an object-like presence that is at the center of perception, but rather the actual potential of an intervention in an environment. However, the result of these efforts also results in an autonomy and specificity that can only be repeated under considerable constraints. The copy quickly becomes a quotation from which the original meaning is difficult to extract and decipher.

At this point, construction becomes the decisive moment of a change that is also frequently consigned to the notion of more construction. The complexity of the task is not new, and is illustrated in the history of architecture by the numerous transformations that came about for widely divergent reasons. Irrespective of this fact, to design within these structures requires a knowledge of traditional forms of construction, with their composite or monolithic configurations, in order to be able to translate existing spatial patterns into the spatial demands of the present.

The tradition of the confrontation between context and change has been increasingly blotted out by modernism and its explicit focus on the new—and thus also on a radical form of change. Consequently, history is more about a silent juxtaposition of contrasting intervention and restoration, which, embalmed and sealed, easily triggers associations with plastic surgery.

The polarization of contradictory presences points to the necessity of negotiating aspirations of historical truth, and as such, on one aesthetic truth. One truth is very clearly crystallized from this task: a radical freedom that not only allows for new design, but also the continuation of the old.

To be able to bring meanings to one clear denominator and to unfold their spatial qualities at the same time is one aspect that becomes the point of departure to strive for and generate typologically distinct, yet highly specific, designs within a given context. In this way, in terms of content, architectural form, and materiality, precision becomes the definitive reference for essential propositions, regardless of the quality of the act.

On this basis, the program, spatial quality, and constructive logic are distilled into a language that can also be deployed in completely different tasks within the interaction of construction and place.

However, it is here where it becomes clear that the oft-postulated desire for truth in construction and its potential principles may be regarded as obsolete, regardless of whether it blends into a building or a context. Outside of the aura of the absolute, construction is always being re-oriented to quotidian conditions and their immanent contradictions, and must be refined to align with the possibilities of the present●

Ground Floor | Ground level floor plan of a building, usually sectioned horizontally at a height of one meter. Parterre, *Rez-de-Chaussée* = at street level. Generally has a different use from the floors above it, but is joined by the supporting structure and circulation. The ground floor is the intersection of the verticality of the building with the horizontality of the site; the privacy of the dwelling with the public of the city. Since building and city meet on the ground floor, the representation of this level is especially important, for example, for Aldo Rossi's way of observing the city (Rossi plan).

Way/Street | Way: from moving, distancing oneself. Related to *weaving:* moving oneself, tying together. Street, from Latin *strata:* a cobblestone path, or *strenere:* to spread, cover. Related to *strew:* spread, cover, disperse. The linear dimension of movement and connection is complemented by the surface creation of the fabric. Paths, or ways, fortified into streets, create a network that structures a territory, particular the tightly woven space of a city. There is a wealth of such structures—which can be differentiated geometrically—such as those in antiquity, the Middle Ages, the Foundation Era, American cities, and many more.

Square | An area in a settlement reserved for public purposes and surrounded by construction. The basic purposes are cultural, economic, and political. In antiquity, the *polis* gathered in the *agora*; in the Middle Ages the function of a marketplace with municipal buildings took precedence: in the Renaissance and Baroque, representation was at the forefront. For planned urban expansions in the 19th century, squares and public parks were used to decoratively and geometrically structure the urban road network or to emphasize lines of sight. This rationalist rapprochement, by Otto Wagner, for one, contradicts the urban architecture of Camillo Sitte with its narrow lanes and plaza-like expansions as in an organic network.

Granularity | Granularity describes the size of individual elements in a grouping, for example, the grain size of gravel used for a grading curve. The size distribution of elements influences the characteristics of the grouping; the granularity affects the ability of the elements to enter into dialogue. The goal is a balanced distribution. The term is used in urban development and refers to both the size of the objects under study and their relationships to one another. These are usually buildings, but can often be uses. European cities, with a typical mix of building sizes and uses (with the exception of industrial areas), are described as having a complex granularity up into the mid-20th century.

Figure-ground Diagram | Map of the city showing solid black areas on a white background, whereby black usually represents built volumes and white the areas in between. The most striking graphic illustration of the interplay of heavy, black matter and airy, white unbuilt voids. The reversal of this plan, with built areas in white, emphasizes the network of public space.

Standardization | A crucial step for the industrial revolution was the standardization of screw threads in England in the 19th century. Complex economies are based on exchange, and thus on comparability and standards. In Germany, the DIN standards were a significant milestone. The standard used in Switzerland is the SIA 400. The enormous body of norms and standards reflects the complexity of modern-day construction. Standards create objectivity through quantification (T 30, 1.0 W/m^{2}K), are application-oriented, reflect the state of technology, and define production and implementation. They have a significant impact on building and become questionable when creativity is limited.

Hierarchy | From Greek *hieros:* holy and *arche:* guidance. Actually "holy rule", in general order relations, ranking, and rule of precedence. As a rule, clear domination and subordination—whether in a social or political hierarchy of power or logically with ascending and descending orders of meaning. When designing, this is helpful to target and define priorities, for example, for the use or the framework of the building being planned. The word segment *archi*, Ancient Greek for *head* or *leader*, is also a root of the word *architecture*.

Morphology | From Greek *morphé:* shape and *logos:* meaning. The study of the origins, development, and evolution of forms and shapes. Morphology examines the principles of composition and the rules of classification of living organisms, objects, and historical, societal, linguistic, and aesthetic phenomena. In architecture, morphology focuses on the evolution of design, thus expanding on the classifications of typology. Design principles and rules of order for the creation of form and the changing forms of building elements, buildings, and built areas over the course of different time spans are the topic of morphology.

Typology | From Ancient Greek *typos:* archetype and *logos:* meaning. The classification of objects that originate from an archetype that has excellently designed and typical characteristics, yet also includes formations that are less clearly developed. Typologies can be differentiated according to fundamental criteria. A fundamental design method in architecture particularly since the works of Saverio Muratori (1940s) and Aldo Rossi (as of the 1960s) that sees design and context as being reciprocal; for Thomas Valena, type and place are what constitute architecture.

PLACE—STRUCTURE

Place, as a specific settlement area, is structured. The development structure of the city is made up of closed volumes and open urban spaces. This corresponds for the most part with the division of private and public space. Particular significance is attributed to the interface of the "main entrance façade". This is concurrent with the special situation of the ground floor, an area that ties public space with the private functions of the upper floors and their structural and circulation systems.

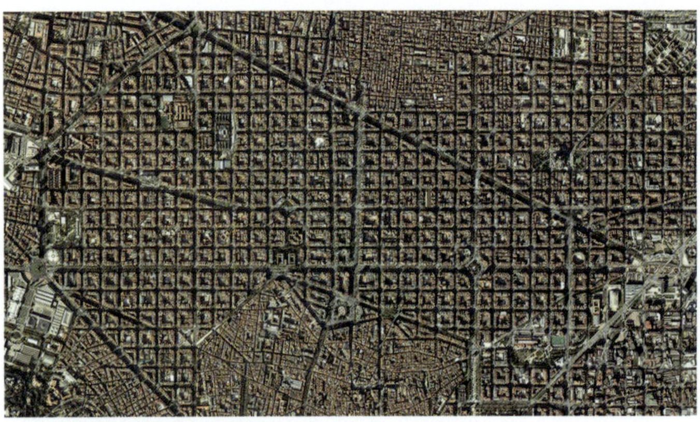

Aerial photo Eixample de Barcelona, 2004

Original plans for the expansion of Barcelona, 1859, detail

Building Level

The starting point for this exercise is the structure of the existing buildings and an understanding of their rules. The basis for this is provided by the structural analysis of the existing buildings carried out in the previous exercise.

The assignment is to draft an addition and structurally upgrade the existing building by clarifying the structure and improving its spatial characteristics. For this purpose, the expansion strategies developed in Exercise 1 will be examined and further developed using the findings on structure gained in Exercise 2.

The intervention consists of an addition to the bearing structure of the existing building and the definition of a circulation system that makes it possible to meaningfully join all proposed rooms.

Specifications

Project work will be done in groups of two. It must be submitted as a DIN-AO plan that includes:

- Figure-ground diagram 1:5000
- Neighborhood plan 1:1000
- Site plan 1:500
- Floor plan and cross-sections 1:200/1:250
- Three model photos
- Written explanation

- Sectional model of the building structure, 1:50
- Insertion model of the existing building with addition 1:500

Requirements

- Status maps
- Site plan 1:500
- Fire safety regulations
- Findings from the analysis and structural model
- Findings from the city walk
- Crafting notebooks I + II

Goal

The goal is to gain an understanding of how to structurally order a building. Static and spatial structure, circulation, and transitions from interior to exterior spaces must be in harmony with one another. The chosen order must be recognizable in the cross-sections and floor plans. Spatial qualities, problems, and solutions must be visible in the model. The existing structure—including circulation, entrances, and choice of materials—must be in conformance with modern-day needs and standards.

Constructed frames of apartment buildings at 860–880 North Lake Shore Drive

Structural model
Timothy Allen
Thierry Vuattoux
AS 15

MIDDLE AGES

Simon von Guten
Yeshi Wang
16 AS

Rafael Zulauf
12 AS

Rossella Dazio
11 AS

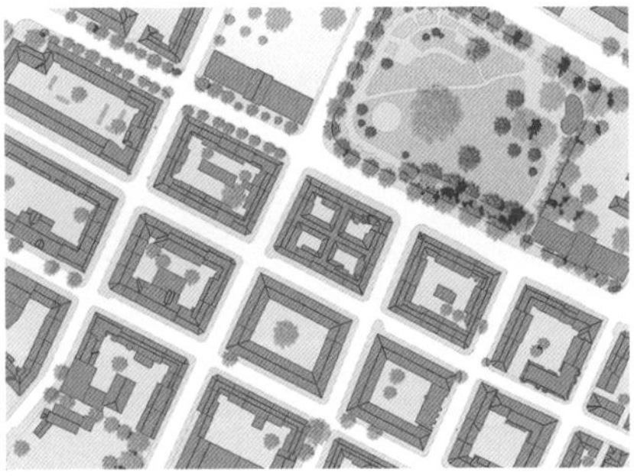
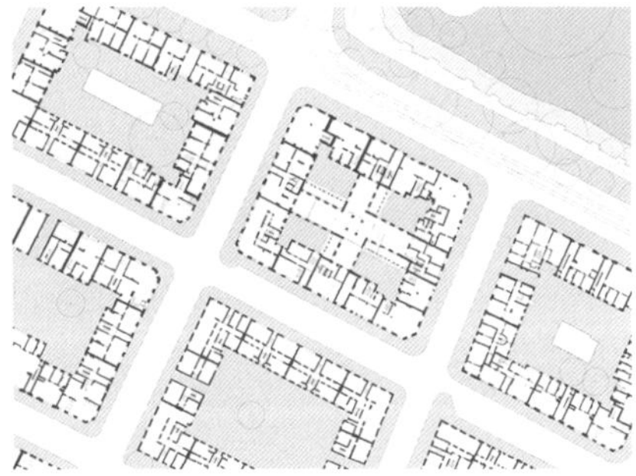

Melanie Imfeld
10 AS

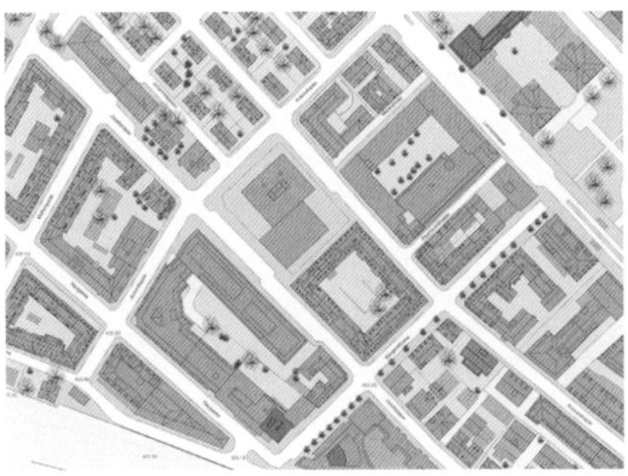
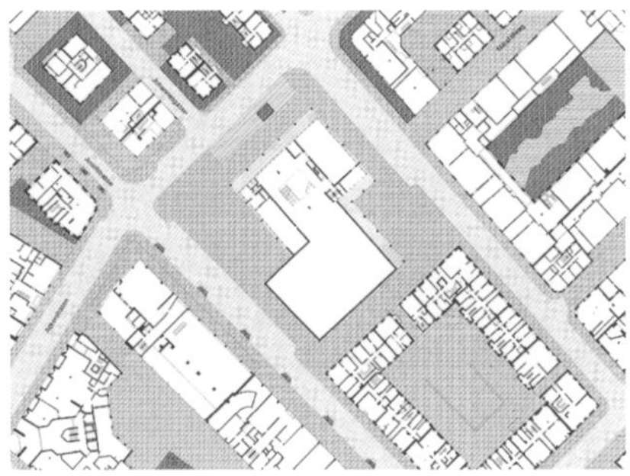

Timmy Huang
Leo Mathys
16 AS

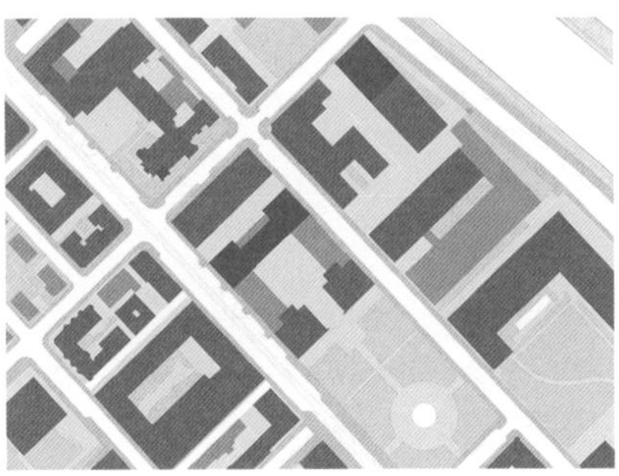

Christian Cortesi
09 AS

MODERNISM

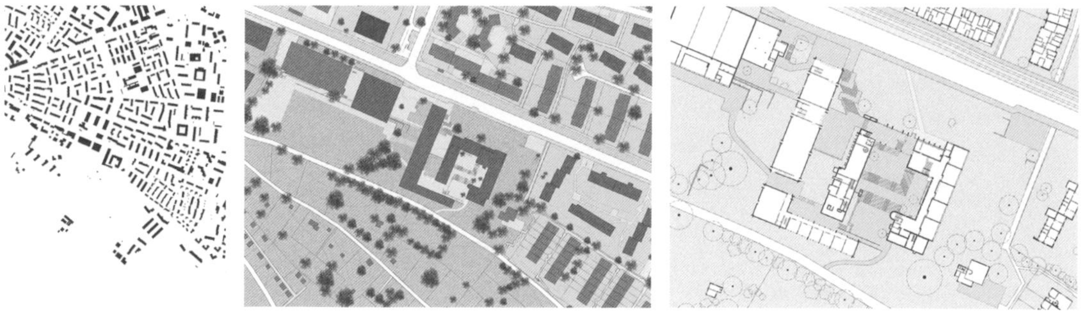

Cherk Ga Leung
13 AS

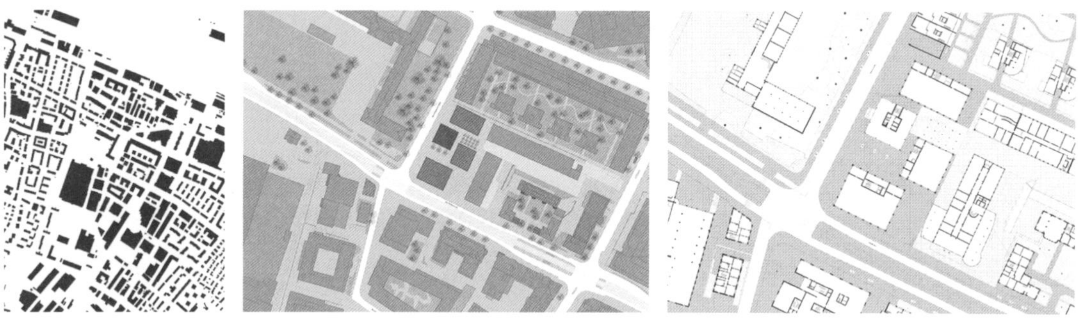

Zoe auf der Maur
12 AS

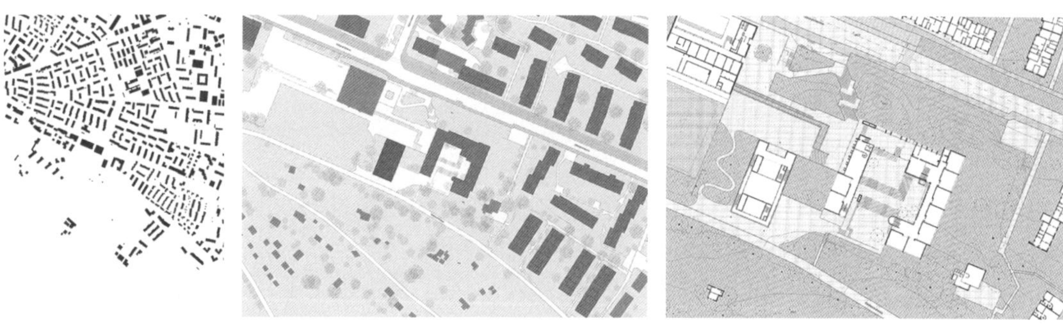

Samuel Dayer
16 AS

MIDDLE AGES

Rafael Zulauf
12 AS

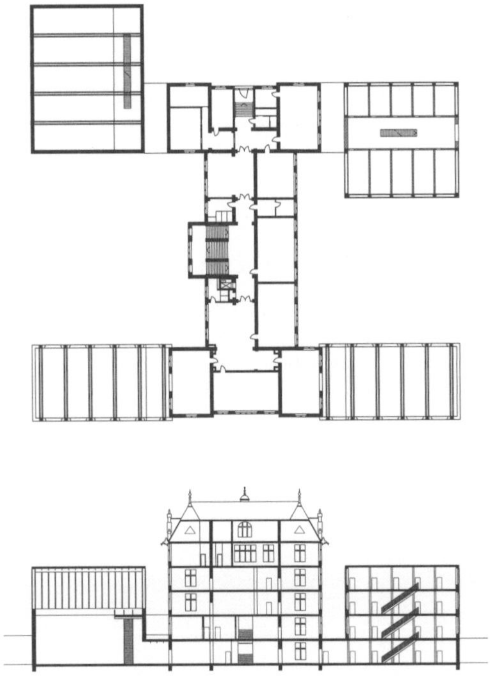

Ria Cavelti
Simon von Niederhäusern
13 AS

FOUNDATION ERA

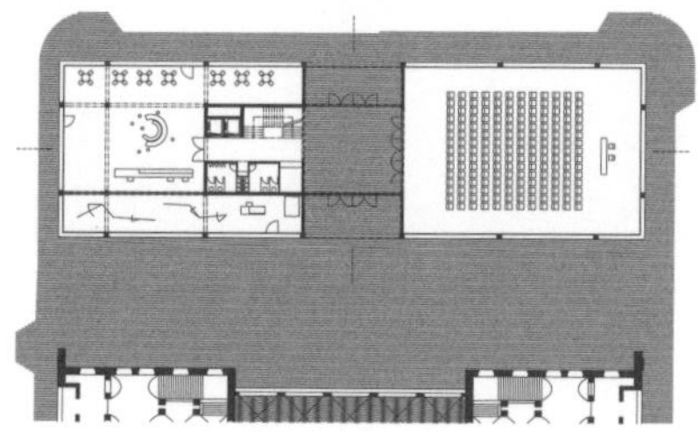

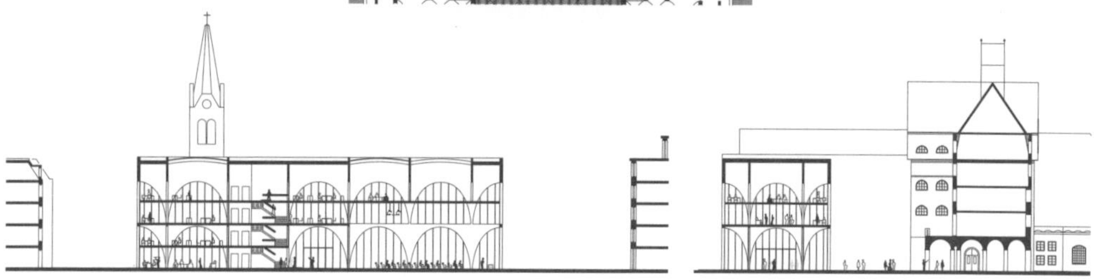

Marko Jovanovic
09 AS

Anastasia König
Amanda Köpfli
13 AS

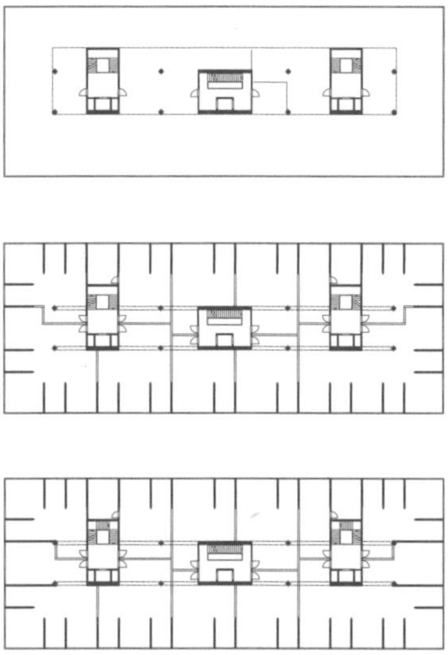

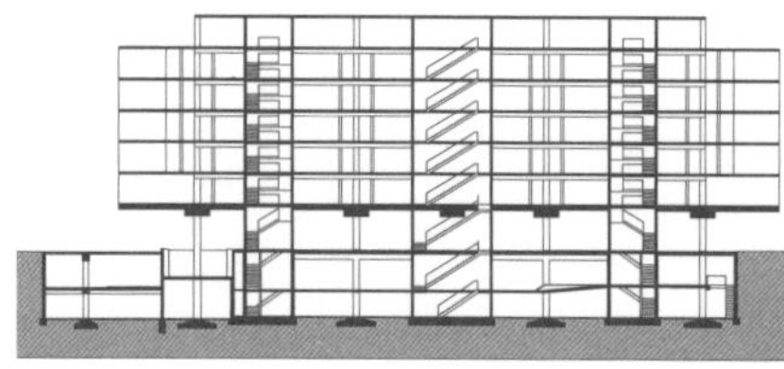

Fabio Agustoni
Giulia Bosia
Marlene Lienhard
11 AS

Elias Binggeli
Mario Bisquolm
08 AS

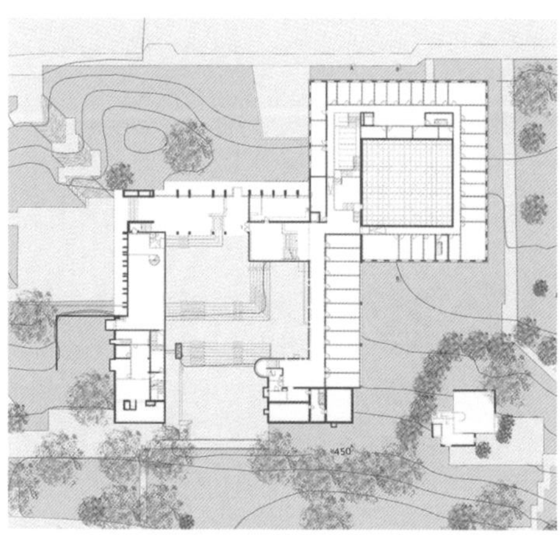

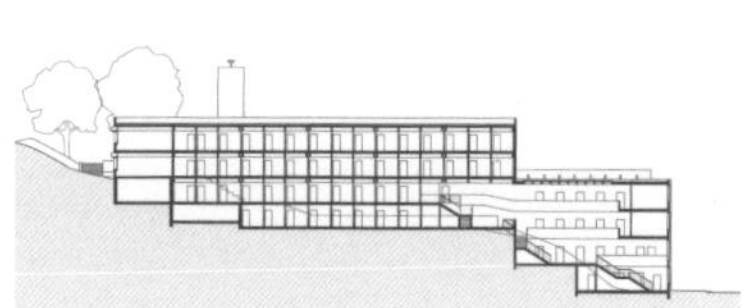

MODERNISM

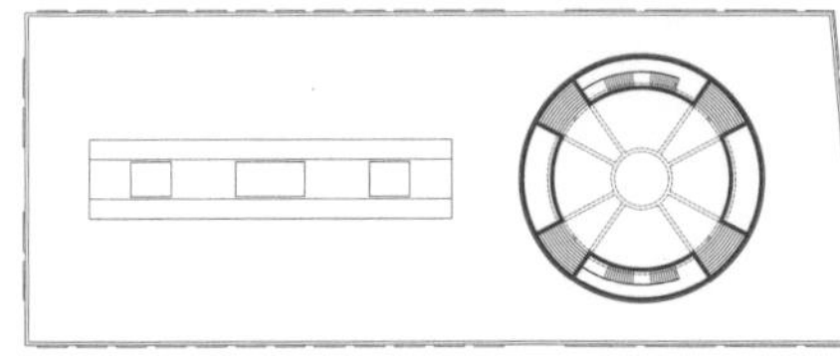

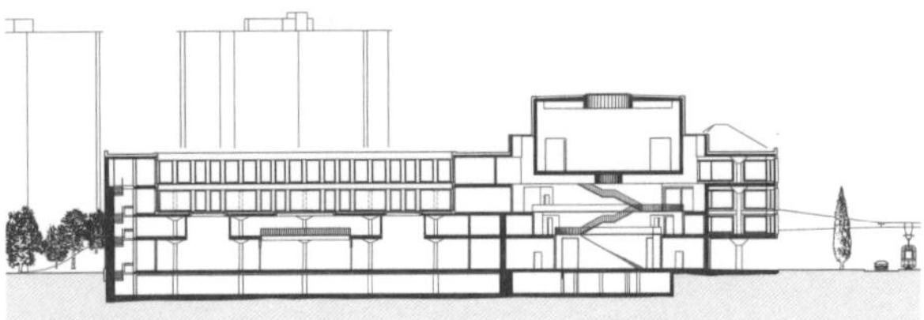

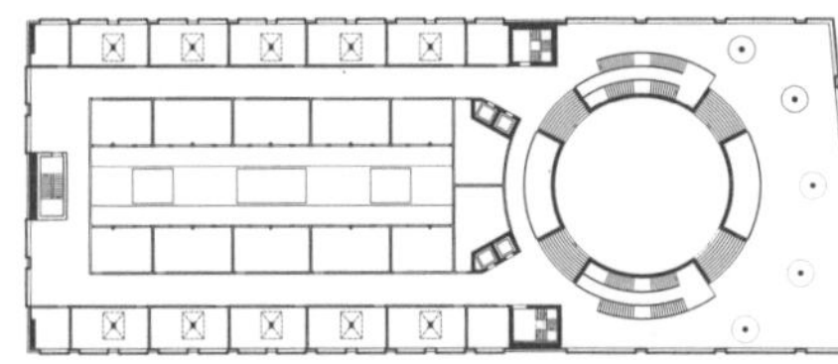

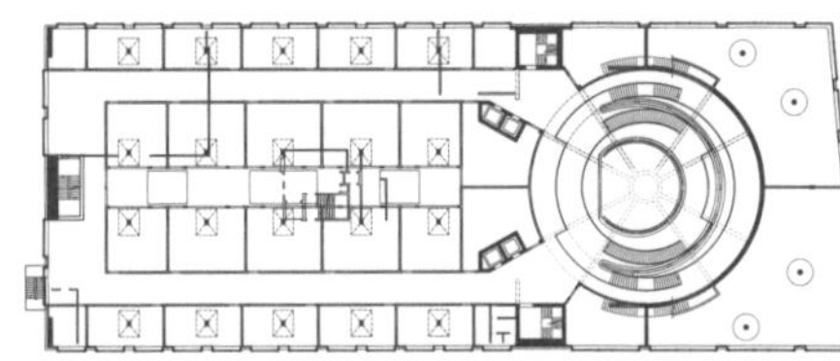

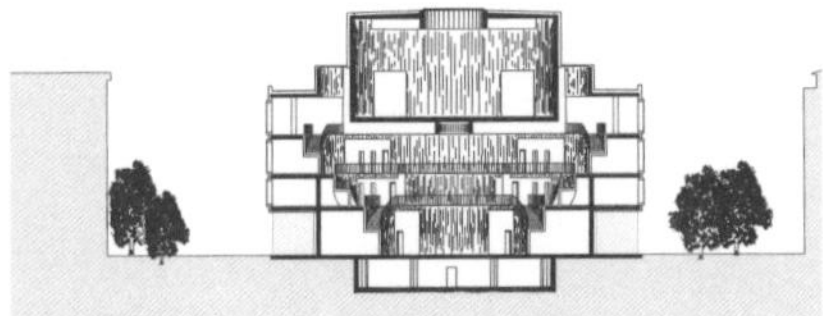

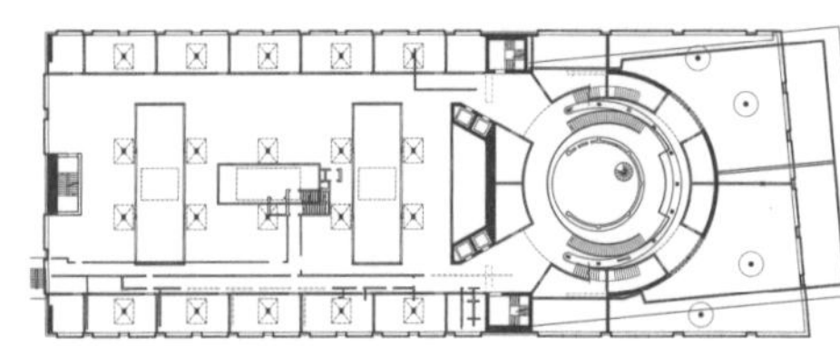

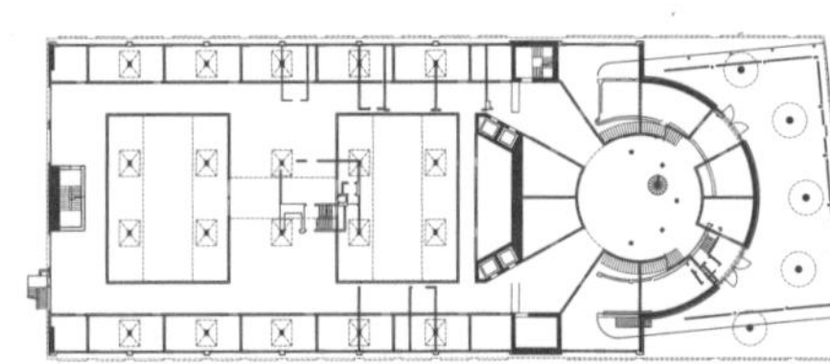

Tobias Wick
14 AS

MIDDLE AGES

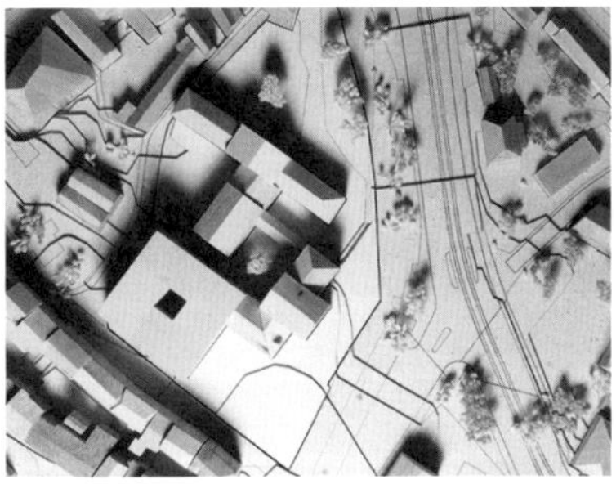

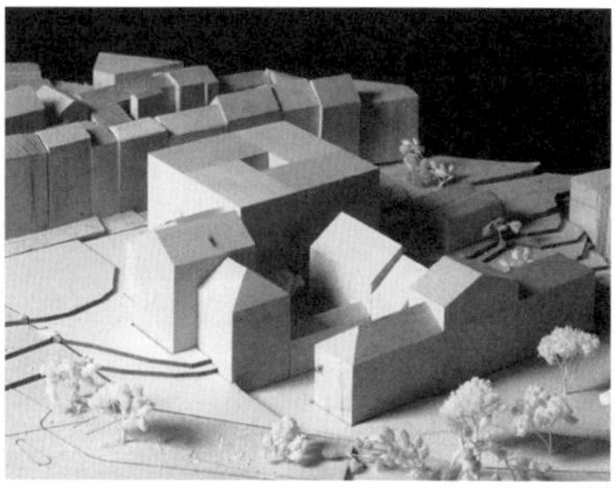

Valentin Buchwalder
11 AS

Andreas Haupolter
14 AS

Tobias Tommila
Gregor Vollenweider
08 AS

3

FOUNDATION ERA

Tamino Kuny
13 AS

Matthias Winter
Nicole Würth
08 AS

Samuel Scherer
11 AS

3

MODERNISM

Tatsiana Selivanava
13 AS

Samuel Dayer
16 AS

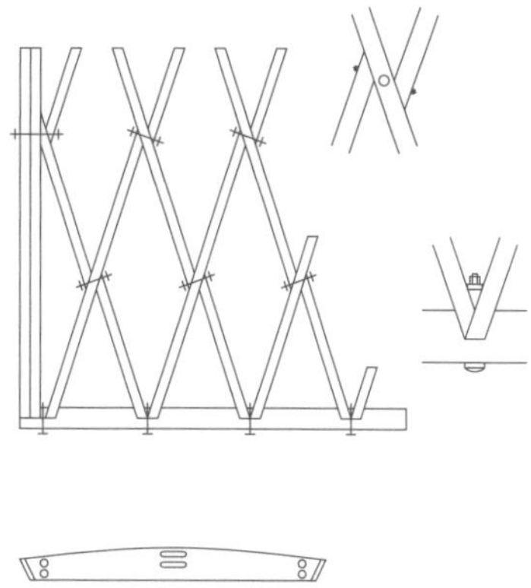

Sandra Furrer
12 AS

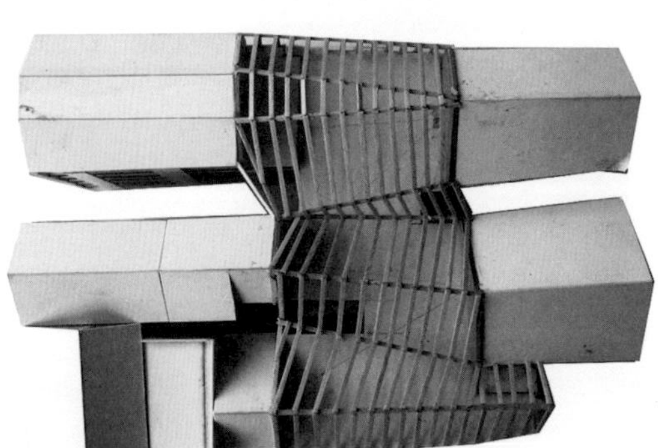

Rafael Zulauf
12 AS

MIDDLE AGES

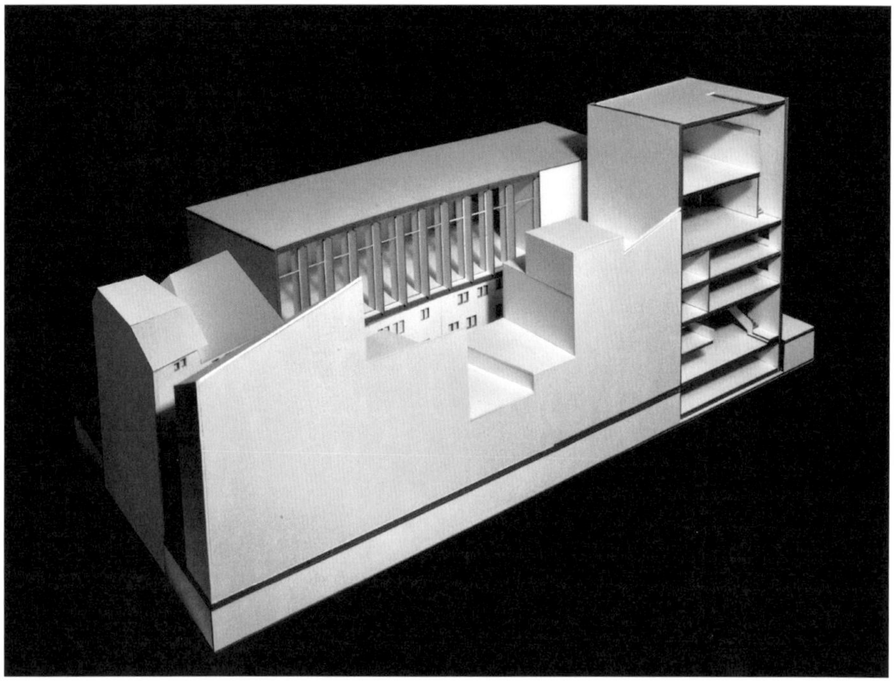

Andreas Haupolter
14 AS

Silvio Rutishauser
Stefanie Schäfer
14 AS

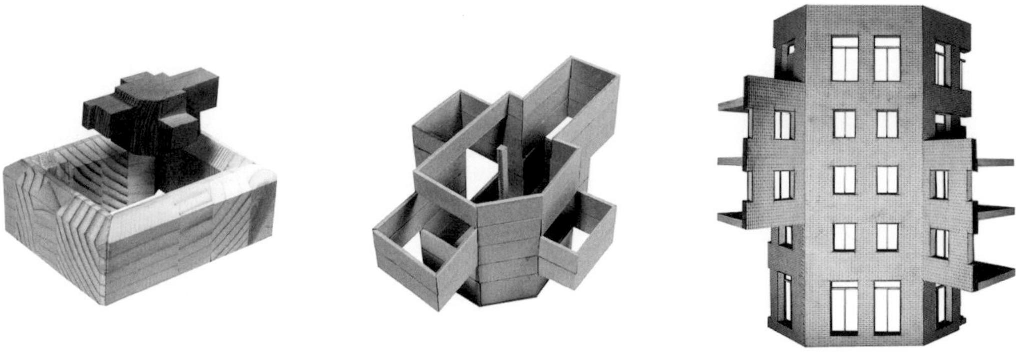

Luca Fontanella
11 AS

Tamino Kuny
13 AS

FOUNDATION ERA

Simon von Gunten
Yeshi Wang
16 AS

Nicolò Krättli
09 AS

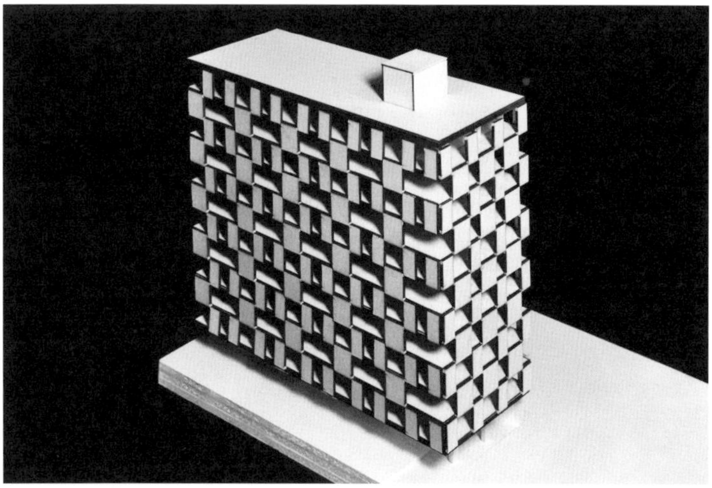

Nina Graber
Mara Selina Graf
11 AS

Samuel Scherer
11 AS

MODERNISM

Grégoire Bridel
16 AS

MIDDLE AGES

Fabio Signer
12 AS

Lucia Bernini
Tom Mundy
16 AS

MIDDLE AGES

Patrick Perren
14 AS

3

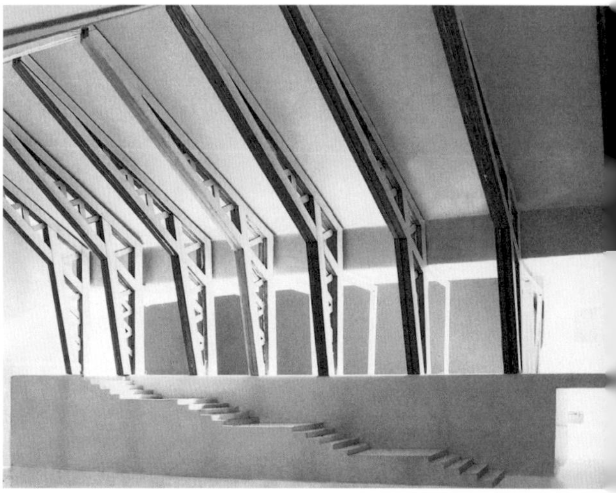

Daniela Gonzales
14 AS

Tamino Kuny
13 AS

MODERNISM

Rabea Kalbermatten
10 AS

Xiao Wei Lim
Lilian Pala
14 AS

3

MODERNISM

Adriel Graber
Mario Sgier
08 AS

Roy Engel
11 AS

3

Georg Aerni, 1834-4, Crocodile Hill, 2000 © Georg Aerni

4
Envelope

4 **Envelope**

An envelope, or *Hülle* in German, a hull, conceals, covers, hides—these are derivations of the Indo-Germanic word *hehlen*. In Old High German, this refers to the cloak and headscarf in particular. The original meaning of the German saying "*in Hülle und Fülle*", meaning "in abundance", lists two fundamental prerequisites for human life: protection (*Hülle*) and satiation, or fulfillment (*Fülle*). For, since Plato, we know that humans are imperfect, and in need of protection.

When an envelope protects, it creates space, dividing the within from the without. Creating space became a new guiding concept towards the end of the 19th century, after the debate on style ran itself into the ground. The question of style was tightly tied to the order of columns, which had long dominated architectural theory. The envelope, the wall, led a shadowy existence in comparison. And yet, a far-sighted Goethe had, in his younger years, made fun of architectural theorist Marc-Antoine Laugier, saying his "primitive hut" columns would not even be sufficient to hold together a pigsty (Goethe 1945, 4).

With the concept of space, the envelope and wall were rehabilitated in the late 19th century. As with a coat, a mantle, architecture also envelops the body. For August Schmarsow, art historian and trailblazer of the spatial concept, space is a physical experience: "This examination of the building begins with our own bodies and their effects and here is where it always returns," he explained in 1903 (105). Architecture is not an objective item; rather, it is tied to our doing, our actions.

Something similar moved Gottfried Semper, the most important architect and theorist of the late 19th century, to give special attention to the envelope. He sees the origins of enclosure in weaving. "When Semper describes the textile wall as one of the basic motifs of architecture, he is referring to the primacy of dividing space, not structural elements" (Moravánszky 2015, 124). Textiles are the very root of architecture.

Wall, dressing, winding, weaving, knotting—the social and cultural aspects cannot be overlooked. Doing—with each other, for each other, before each other—owes its very existence to textiles. The knot, "possibly the oldest technical symbol", is for Semper also "the universal symbol for the primeval chaining of things [...] which joins and commands everything" (1860, 180, 83). Traditional crafting developed through a process of change—change of action along with the change of material—into the art of building, architecture. It is craft and art—both at once.

Despite this, the envelope remains dependent upon a supporting structure—whether this be a skeleton of pillars and beams, or a supporting wall system. The envelope is generally not indifferent to this structure, instead characterizing—to borrow the word from Karl Friedrich Schinkel—the structure. The dual character remains part of the envelope—it belongs to architecture, which is usefulness and stability and provides charm. One should erect a building naked before beginning to dress it demanded Alberti, thus naming the difference between building and architecture. This is what beautifies, dresses, and typifies a building, integrating it into the cultural context and the social.

The designed envelope of the building, its façade, has its own order; it cloaks the building structure, masking something about its interior, it structural composition maybe. Finally, the façade ties the oneness of the building with the many of its context, creates relationships (always—also fissures, the rejection of an interaction), emphasizes or arranges, showing the various buildings to their place in the network of the city.

The Face is a Window to the Soul

Adam Caruso

4

This is a tale of two buildings from very different times and circumstances, both strongly representative of their times and designed by architects who would come to embody their eras in the 17th and 19th centuries respectively. There is not much in common formally between these works, or in the social situation within which they were made. This disparity is intentional and has been chosen to challenge a long-standing modernist truism, one that still underlies much of the contemporary architectural rhetoric, Le Corbusier's statement in *Towards a New Architecture:* "The Plan is the generator. Without a plan, you have a lack of order, and wilfulness. The Plan holds in itself the essence of sensation."[1]

[1] Le Corbusier: *Towards a New Architecture*, J. Rodker, London, 1931, p. 2.

Who can be sure that Le Corbusier actually meant the "ground plan" given his enthusiasm for *tracés régulateurs* and evident delight in designing elevations for his projects? Nonetheless, his dictum has been taken in the narrowest sense with generations of architects being instructed that the ground plan is a kind of circuit board, or engine that drives the architectural project. While it is certainly true that the plan wards off programmatic chaos, to say that the sensual heart of the architectural project can be discerned in the plan, is fatuous and is contradicted by one's experience of buildings throughout history. While large and complex projects undoubtedly do require careful organization in plan, it is through the conventions of elevation and section drawings that the really important work is done, where the experience of architecture can be explored and where one gains a window to the soul.

I assert therefore that, since architecture imitates nature (as do all the other arts), it cannot endure anything that alienates and distances it from what nature herself permits; so we see that those ancient architectures who began to make of stone those buildings that they once made of wood established a rule that columns should be less thick at the top than at the bottom, taking as their model trees which are always more slender at the top than at the trunk and near the roots. Similarly, because it is very appropriate that those objects upon which some great weight is placed are compressed, the ancients put bases under columns, which with their toruses and scotias appear to be crushed by the weight above. [...] Departing from what the natural order of things teaches and from that simplicity which appears in the things created by her, generates, as it were, another version of nature and deviates from the true, good, and beautiful method of building. [2]

[2] Andrea Palladio: *The Four Books On Architecture*, The First Book, The MIT Press, Cambridge, 2002, p. 51.

The villa stands on the flat table of the Veneto plain, surrounded by fertile agricultural fields that are now joined by the large sheds and open structures of industry. A robust stone pavement, very wide, leads to a monumental stone ramp with a single landing midway along its length that abruptly meets an impressive portico cut into the cubic volume of the central pavilion. Four Doric columns, two freestanding and two engaged with the body of the house, have sharply carved stone capitals and bases joined by sturdy shafts made with brick covered in stucco. The stone is cooler and harder than the stucco. The entablature of the portico is visibly made in timber which has also been coated in stucco. This large beam supports a pediment that frames the bas-relief figures of two angels embracing the family crest of the Emo family. Apart from the restrained articulation of the portico, the rest of the villa's front is made in plain, flat surfaces of stucco, with a double line marking the position of the *piano nobile* floor and a single line at the eaves of the pan-tiled roof. The six windows of the central pavilion's façade are simply cut into the stucco surface and the openings are protected with green-painted timber shutters. The effect is monumental, with the heavy vertical portico balanced by the horizontal proportion of the central façade. The compressed attic windows, like two small eyes spaced too widely apart, are pulled right up to the top of the wall and play a significant role in the composition, lending the façade a tension that is at odds with the more conventional centralizing monumentality. The position of the windows is predicated by the villa's nine-square plan and cannot be justified by antique precedent. This synthesis of temple front, Roman bath, and farmyard is pure invention, in this place for this villa. The central pavilion is flanked by symmetrical side wings, *barchesse* whose arches are unadorned. The composition

Andrea Palladio,
Villa Emo, Treviso 1584,
front view

Photo © Thorsten Bürklin

Andrea Palladio,
Villa Emo, Treviso 1584,
back view

Photo © Thorsten Bürklin

is completed by dovecotes that frame and give focus to this expansive ensemble. The rear of the villa is as rude as the front is grand. Five volumes are arranged in a line with windows and chimneys making a rhythm by virtue of their number and despite their variety in position and detail. Like the economy of only using stone for the bases and capitals of the portico columns, compositional order has also been rationed so that there is only just enough to pull the diverse parts of the villa together into a whole, but not so much to make the ensemble pompous or overbearing.

Palladio's villas, from Godi, designed in the 1530s before his first visit to Rome, to mature works like Emo, designed twenty years later and informed by a mature and fully internalized knowledge of and feeling for the architecture of antiquity, are all based on fundamentally the same premise and plan. The villas are located within a small area of the Veneto. They were itended as the centers of working agricultural complexes and are organized as central pavilions usually framed by symmetrical barchesse. Their internal organizations are also similar, versions of the nine-square plan with medium and small rooms organized about a central salon that spans from the front, representational face, to the rear working façade. If the locale, program, and organization of the villas were almost the same, why does there exist such a great diversity in the themes, compositions, and atmospheres of his façades? If form follows function, in its incorrect modernist reading, all of Palladio's villas should look more or less alike, but they do not. For their architect, as for all architects before the 20th century, the façade was as much, if not more, of a generative force in developing a design as the ground plan. Visiting the villas is to experience the nervous energy of Palladio's creativity, his excitement at seeing and understanding something new amongst the ruins of Rome, with the subjective intensity of an artist as opposed to the academic interest of an archaeologist or historian. Palladio wished to instrumentalize what he found into a new synthesis, one that would please his patrician clients and would create new atmospheres and effects that more powerfully engaged with the character of the land. If the high game of architecture is classicism, Palladio is perhaps its most influential proponent. Within the flexible and constantly developing language of his work one discovers the most ecstatic expressions of the sacred, the most opulent renderings of wealth and the most profound interpretations of territory.

4

> *The architects of this land and generation are now brought face to face with something new under the sun—namely, that evolution and integration of social conditions, that special grouping of them that results in a demand for the erection of tall office buildings. It is not my purpose to discuss the social conditions; I accept them as the fact, and say at once that the design of the tall office building must be recognized and confronted at the outset as a problem to be solved—a vital problem, pressing for a true solution.*[3]

[3] Louis Sullivan: *The Public Papers*, The University of Chicago Press, Chicago, 1988, p. 104.

Pulled up into the sky like a cliff face of garish orange, what initially appears to be the cleaved surface of uncooked earth reveals itself as a finely wrought skin of a delicate all-over surface texture. A geometrically complex ornamental pattern is cast lightly onto the square-proportioned terracotta plates that cover every surface of the building. On the main body of the volume, the pattern repeats at the same scale as the plates. On the base and cornice where the ornament is elaborated, the pattern extends over four and eight plates. The mortar-filled joints between the terracotta plates become a part of the pattern like a gridded network projected onto the surface of the building. Ornament, material, manufacture, and installation become one and the same thing, imparting a feeling that is as brutal as raw material while at the same time exquisitely refined in form. The terracotta cladding follows the steel frame of the building's structure and covers the vertical piers that set out the offices within, all the same and infinitely repeatable. Only every second façade division encases a steel column, the other piers provide office subdivisions and complete the image of the façade. The generic interior and blocky Cartesian logic of a late 19th-century commercial building is located within the gridded block pattern of the American city and in turn the Jeffersonian grid that marked out the westward expansion of the frontier, which continues

John Szarkowski,
Louis H. Sullivan, Guaranty Building, Buffalo 1894/95

John Szarkowski,
Louis H. Sullivan, Guaranty Building, Buffalo 1894/95, Detail

until it is obstructed by mountains and rivers. The idealized grid of the building is also contingent on its site, and what appears to be a consistent, just taller than cubic, volume, are actually two city façades making the corner of Pearl and Church Street with a plan that is oriented towards the original main entrance on Church Street. The terracotta building stops abruptly with each street façade, to be replaced by more utilitarian hard white glazed bricks in the light well. The Church Street façade is fourteen bays wide, seven at its base, making a centralized main entrance. The Pearl Street façade is only twelve bays, so that the secondary entrance is off-center. The individual window bays are also not consistent between the two street façades, which is not readily apparent to the eye but necessary because of the site dimensions, something which suggests that fixed proportional relationships were not paramount to the building's architect.

In 1896, at the same time he completed the Guaranty Building in Buffalo, Louis Sullivan wrote "The Tall Office Building Artistically Considered". As made clear in the title, the problem of the tall building is not a technical or social one but an artistic one. The first paragraphs of the essay set out the bald reality of the modern office building and list industry's technical solutions, the steel frame, the elevator, and caisson foundations. These are matters that Sullivan uncritically accepted since it was beyond his power to affect them. His concern was how to transform this raw material so that it was brought into the fold of architecture. When Sullivan wrote, in the same essay, that "form ever follows function", he was underlining the architect's responsibility to transform these new facts into an architecture of modern life.

> *Whether it be the sweeping eagle in his flight, or the open apple-blossom, the toiling work-horse, the blithe swan, the branching oak, the winding stream at its base, the drifting*

> *clouds, over all the coursing sun, form ever follows function, and this is the law. Where function does not change, form does not change. The granite rocks, the ever-brooding hills, remain for ages; the lightning lives, comes into shape, and dies, in a twinkling.*[4]

[4] Ibid., p. 111.

For Sullivan, the program and organization of a building did not even begin to describe what he meant by "function", which, influenced by the transcendentalist philosophy of Emerson and Thoreau, meant the very spirit of the thing that in turn was given a true and comprehensive expression by its "form". What Richardson, Sullivan, and Root succeeded in achieving was not only to give potent and meaningful form to the large and symbolically mute commercial structures they were charged with designing, they also gave voice to the young American continent.

The façade was the primary instrument of the new architecture; it would be the character of the building in the city, town, and countryside, the presence that would become a part of collective consciousness, that would express this new spirit. Construction was a part of the new architecture but only in so far as it supported and made possible the image of the building. When Sullivan was confronted with the particularly harsh challenges of practicing architecture in his times, where the forces of money and of the means of production were given new emphasis, his response was to dig deep into the history and traditions of the discipline itself. For Sullivan and his Chicago contemporaries, this formidable challenge was informed in a profound way by Gottfried Semper, whose ideas were widely discussed and debated in the architectural journals and learned societies of the time, by German born professionals, engineers like Dankmar Adler and Frederick Baumann, and by well-travelled Americans like Root and Sullivan. At the core of the discourse was the reconciliation of a historic European architecture with the speed, scale, and techniques of American practice, of the collective and long-standing development of a European artistic tradition with the individualism of America. Semper's conceptual model of the four architectural motives was compelling and useful in the new commercial architecture of Chicago. The autonomy of an artistic architectural expression from its supporting frame was a necessity in the development of the repetitive multi-story office buildings, the idea of "dressing" seems to describe precisely the artistic problem which Sullivan was grappling with in his search for an "organic" formal language, where the intuition, imagination, and inspiration of the artist would find a parallel in the formal development and materialization of the art work.

Sullivan's narrative was willfully misappropriated for the origin story of a historically unencumbered modernism, a dogma that declares the primacy of the "plan as the generator" and the transparency and simultaneity of interior space and external appearance. The work of Sullivan and his contemporaries was not about these things, and did not confuse the deployment of rational means to produce efficient buildings with making architecture that expressed rationalism and efficiency. In late 19th-century Chicago, architecture would be made to satisfy practical matters, while at the same time expressing higher cultural ideals. In this, Sullivan and his contemporaries were not any different than Palladio. He mined the ruins of ancient Rome in order to find his way of expressing the humanist values of his Venetian clients. While there was a significant economic and political shift in mid-16th-century Veneto, it was the cultural rather than the pragmatic qualities of that change that were embodied by Palladio's buildings. While he learned and was inspired by antiquity, there is nothing Roman about his architecture, it is pure invention made for its time and place but also self-consciously part of a cultural continuum. Semper's interpretation of the Italian renaissance and in turn 19th-century Chicago architecture's appropriation of Semper is similarly elliptical, personal, and poetic. While Sullivan's clients may not all have shared the high cultural aspirations of Gian Giorgio Trissino and the Barbaro brothers, his architecture, informed by the lofty ambitions of Semper's writings, filtered the entire history of art in his personal attempt to make an architecture for modern times.

Dressing/Cladding | Gottfried Semper drafted a new understanding of architecture with his theory of dressing. Not the construction is primary, he proclaimed in his seminal book *Style in the Technical and Tectonic Arts* (1860), but the wall. Humans protect themselves by dressing, beginning early with textiles. Textiles are connected threads, knots. Warp and weft create patterns. This process becomes a craft, a skill, laying the groundwork for art. For Semper, the knot is a symbol of the chain of all things. Cladding, ornamentation, and play are the beginning of all culture and for Semper, who pushed back his entire life against schematism, the root of architecture and design.

Metabolism | The conversion of materials or energy. A central concept of 19th-century scientific thought, see Justus von Liebig's *Chemical Letters* (1841), Karl Marx's *Capital* (1867) and Gottfried Semper's *Style* (1860). Semper examines how, for example, the characteristic forms of the Greek temple are transferred from wood building to stone and these, in a process of "transformative emulation", become artifacts of art. Architecture frees itself from tight material binds, gains cultural meaning, and is transformed from material to intellectual.

Ornamentation | From Latin *ornare:* To decorate or adorn, equip, embellish. Decorative patterns, often abstract figures that repeat. Images that convey neither temporal nor spatial illusions, spreading in lines or across an area. Rhythm is created through repetition; this touches the observer much like music affects the listener. This psychological dimension is rejected by the rationalist thought of modernism (Adolf Loos, *Ornament and Crime,* 1908). In contrast, ornamentation remained for Semper an anthropological constant: the act of decorating something gives it the right to exist.

Arrangement | Arrangement creates a whole from which the individual parts cannot be removed without impacting the entirety. The arrangement of the human body has long played a meaningful role in architectural theory, and connections to the human scale sought after – most commonly as the Vitruvian Man. Vitruvius made clear references to rhetoric – *dispositio* – being arrangement, demanding that statements be clearly arranged so as to be more easily understandable. For Leon Battista Alberti, arrangement is likewise indispensible to demonstrating what is ideal – mirroring, sequencing, and rhythm are the means to achieve this. In modernism, addition and repetition are dominant.

Rhythm | From Greek *rhythmós:* Symmetry, flow, structuring of time or movement. The periodic change and regular return of natural occurrences such as physical (day and night) and biological (breathing and heartbeat) processes are fundamental. Dance, arranged movement, is the original form of creating space, according to Rudolf zur Lippe. This carries through to rhythm in architecture as arrangement through the measured change of building elements. August Schmarsow states that rhythm indicates the spatial dimension of architecture, which is only fully captured through movement.

Symmetry | From Greek *syn*: Together and *métron:* The right measure, thus the interplay of measure, harmony, beauty. In Greek sculpture, the balance of the human body. Still reminiscent of the Vitruvian Man: the human body in a circle and a square. This transforms the image of the concrete figure into a geometrical order that includes point, line, and plane symmetry—a mirroring along a point, line, or plane. In architecture, mainly axial symmetries in floor plans and elevations; for main façades long equated with architectural quality. Replaced in the 20th century by free, yet still balanced distributions, in De Stijl, for example as a dynamic balance. Deconstructivism divests itself of this.

Composition | From Latin *com ponere:* To put together. The creation of a work or the creation itself. Music: Theme, development, execution, instrumentation, and performance are determined by the composer. Fine arts: The relating of design elements with a new, unique whole in an artistic creation. Architecture: Figuratively, the configuration of architectural elements according to the requirements of the architect. Modernism replaced composition with construction, artistic creation and composition are held up for ridicule.

Proportion | From Latin *pro portione:* According to ratio. The relationship of two sizes to one another; in a narrower sense, a comfortable ratio, well-proportioned. For the Pythagoreans, whole-number ratios reflect world harmony (all is a number). Octaves (1/2), fifths (3/2), fourths (4/3), etc. are acoustically and visually complete. The creation of ratios that are similar to one another occurs through proportioning, for example: Quadrature, triangulature, the golden ratio. According to Thomas Fischer, the numbers 1–6 provide the basis for all of our music and are enough to fill a building to the brim with music.

Relief | From French *relief:* The emphasized. The surface design of a plane into the third dimension. Geology: The surface design of an area. Art: An image sculpturally distinguished from the surface, i. e. the Parthenon Frieze. Architecture: Sculptural shaping of the façade. Arno Lederer emphasizes the vitality of the European city, shaped by the three-dimensional quality of façades, experienced through the light and shadow of their reliefs. The making visible of texture is replaced in the 20th century by free-form sculpturality (expressionism, Czech cubism) and graphic surfaces (curtain façades). Reliefs return in postmodernism and deconstructivism.

ENVELOPE

Together with the supporting structure and the circulation, the envelope completes the building structure. It divides interior and exterior space and ensures that the people within have a beneficial environment free of inhospitable climatic influences and all kinds of emissions. A building component with its own volume, the envelope achieves this through the interplay of insulation and retention. The envelope creates the façade, the face of the building, and profoundly marks its relationship to the context.

City Level

Information about the streets around the building site will be gathered in groups. Students will photograph the streets and supplement with sketches.

Work will be done on two different reference levels: street and single façade. Information about the streets should be gathered, compared, and evaluated according to a criteria list.

Specifications

Project work will be carried out in groups, one per building site. Findings will be presented to the other students in a presentation.

The following documentation will first be compiled in order to analyze the individual street sections (about 250 meters of the street):

- Photo montage of the street section 1:250
- Drawing of the street section 1:250

Appraisal criteria

- Plot width
- Building spacing and width
- Eaves height
- Comparative dimensions of public space
- Number of floors
- Floor height (standard floor/ground floor)
- Window to wall ratio
- Façade rhythm
- Window proportion (of a typical window)
- Photographic documentation of the existing building (façade materials, typical elements)

Evaluation

- Description of the impression created by the façade lines and their interaction with the street space and the facing buildings
- Comparison of the various streets to one another
- Characterization of single façades
- Description and representation of the organizing principles
- Listing of elements and materials
- Description of the architectural expression

- Selection of a building typical to the locale
- Comparison of the various building façades

Requirements

- Plans for existing buildings
- Findings from the city walk
- Crafting notebooks I + II

Goal

The photomontages will be used to describe and clearly show the analytical criteria of the street, various façades, and individual elements using specific examples. The student group will critically examine and evaluate the analysis, which should be independently presented. These views will serve as a foundation for subsequent exercises.

Predefined criteria and methodology will introduce the concept of façade analysis. The assessment of existing buildings reveals and clarifies possibilities for developing and designing façades. The analysis and comparisons provide insights that, together with the design ability of the student, make up an important foundation of independent façade design.

Herzog & de Meuron, Ricola Warehouse, Laufen, 1986–87, façade detail

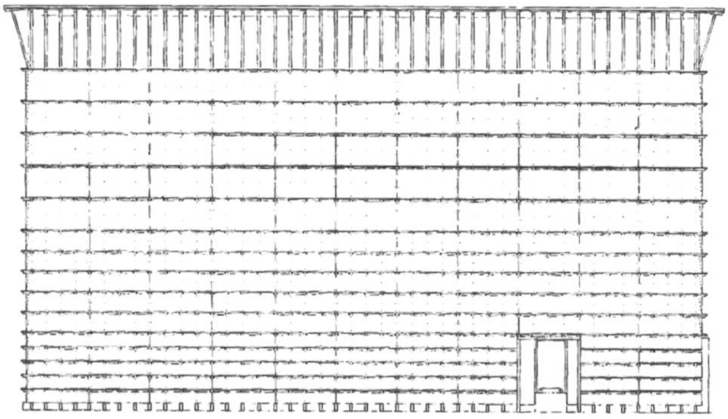

Herzog & de Meuron, Ricola Warehouse, Laufen, 1986–87, drawing

Konstantin Melnikow
Melnikov House, Moscow,
1928–31, construction photo

Building Level

The topic is the development and design of a building envelope. The streets around each building site create the frame of reference within the urban context. The entrance floor, which is the interface between inside and outside, has special significance. Choice of materials and colors will be evolved from the existing urban context.

Specifications

This exercise will be carried out in groups of two and result in a graphic representation in DIN-A0 format. The following must be submitted:

- Model photos (interior, entrance, details)
- Graphic representation of projected façade section 1:75
- Graphic representation of existing façade section 1:75
- Photomontage of the design including existing buildings 1:75
- Area plan detail 1:1000
- Graphic representation of the street with new façade 1:200/1:250
- Written explanation
- Façade model showing all relevant elements, from the ground floor to the roof

Requirements

- View of examined streets 1:200/1:250
- Crafting notebooks I + II

Goal

Knowledge gained from the analysis should be applied and developed by designing a façade. The definition and representation of one's own standpoint to the site and the assignment is added to this.

The individual steps in the process train students to make decisions on constructively and statically sound façade systems that also clearly show the architectural expressiveness of the design idea.

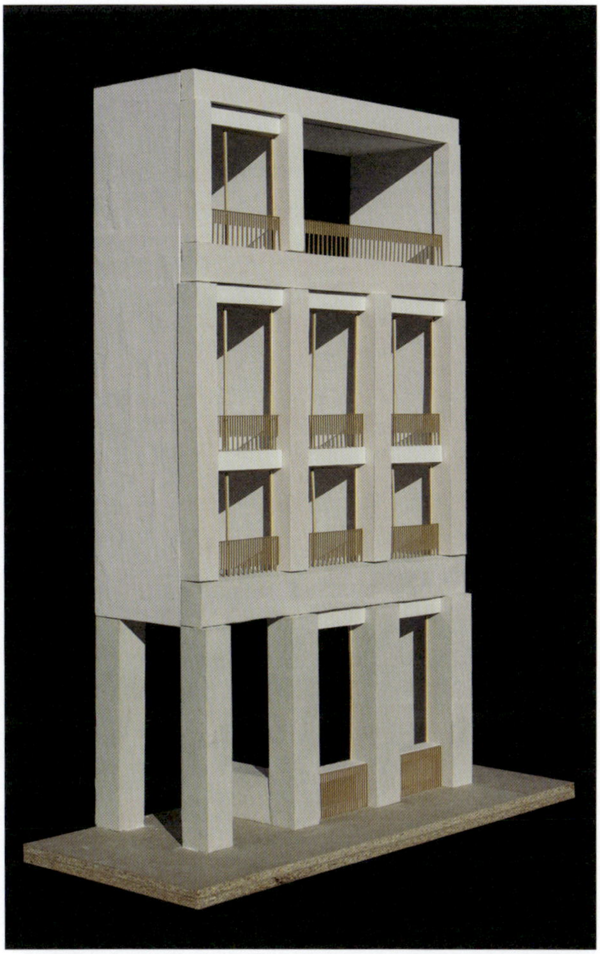

Façade model
Alexander Poulikakos
Feng Zhang
14 AS

MIDDLE AGES

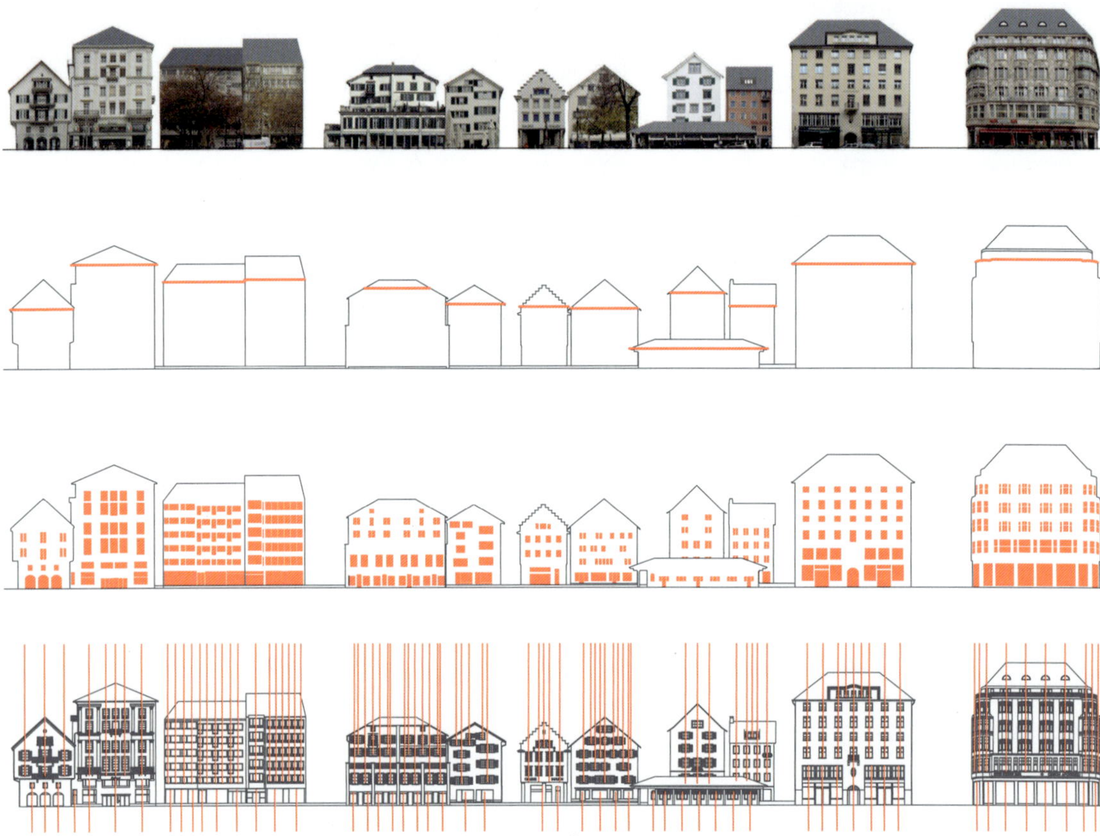

Analysis of Limmatquai
street views

Eaves height
Degree of openness
Rhythm
Materiality

FOUNDATION ERA

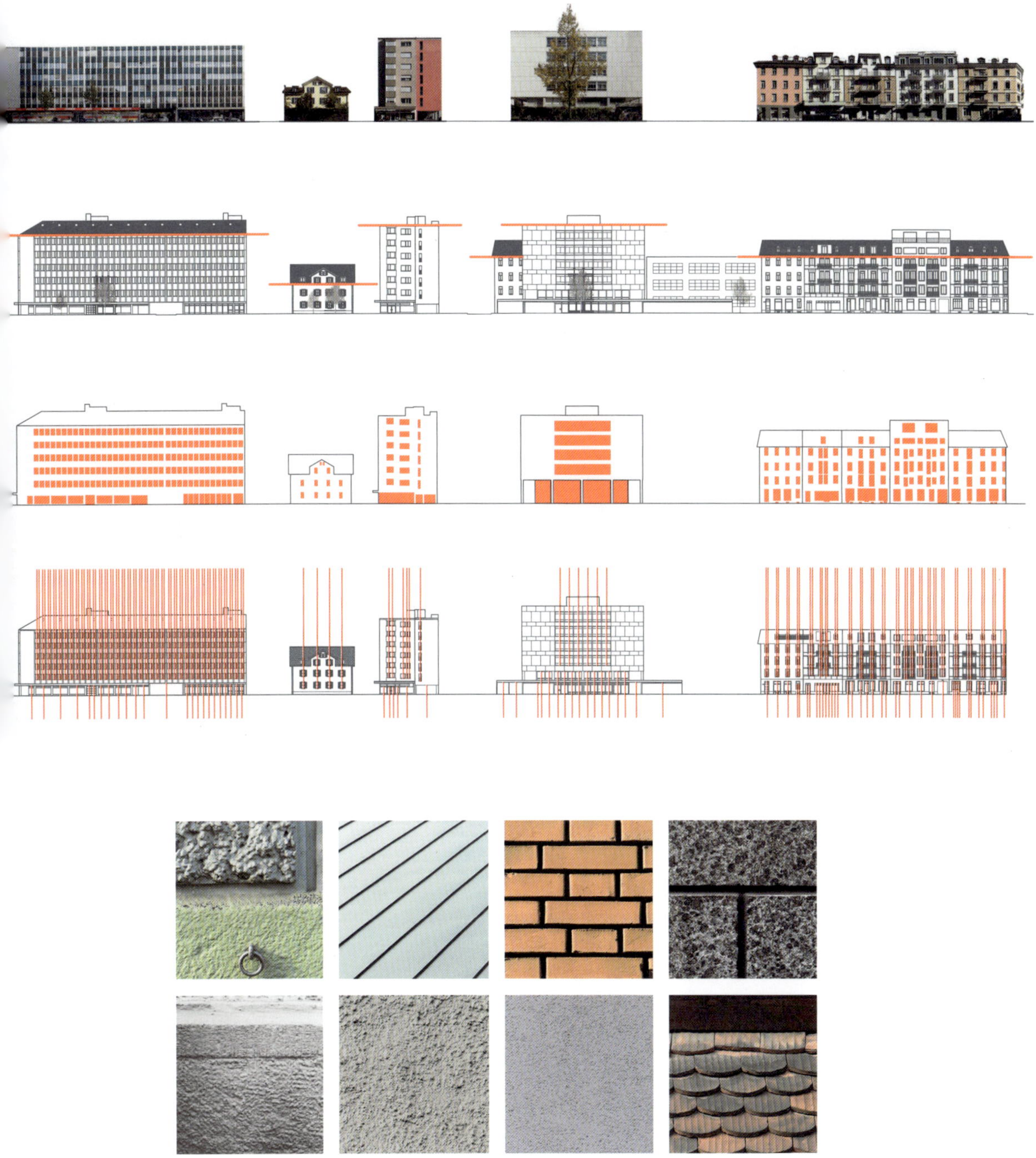

Analysis of Josefstrasse street views

Eaves height
Degree of openness
Rhythm
Materiality

MODERNISM

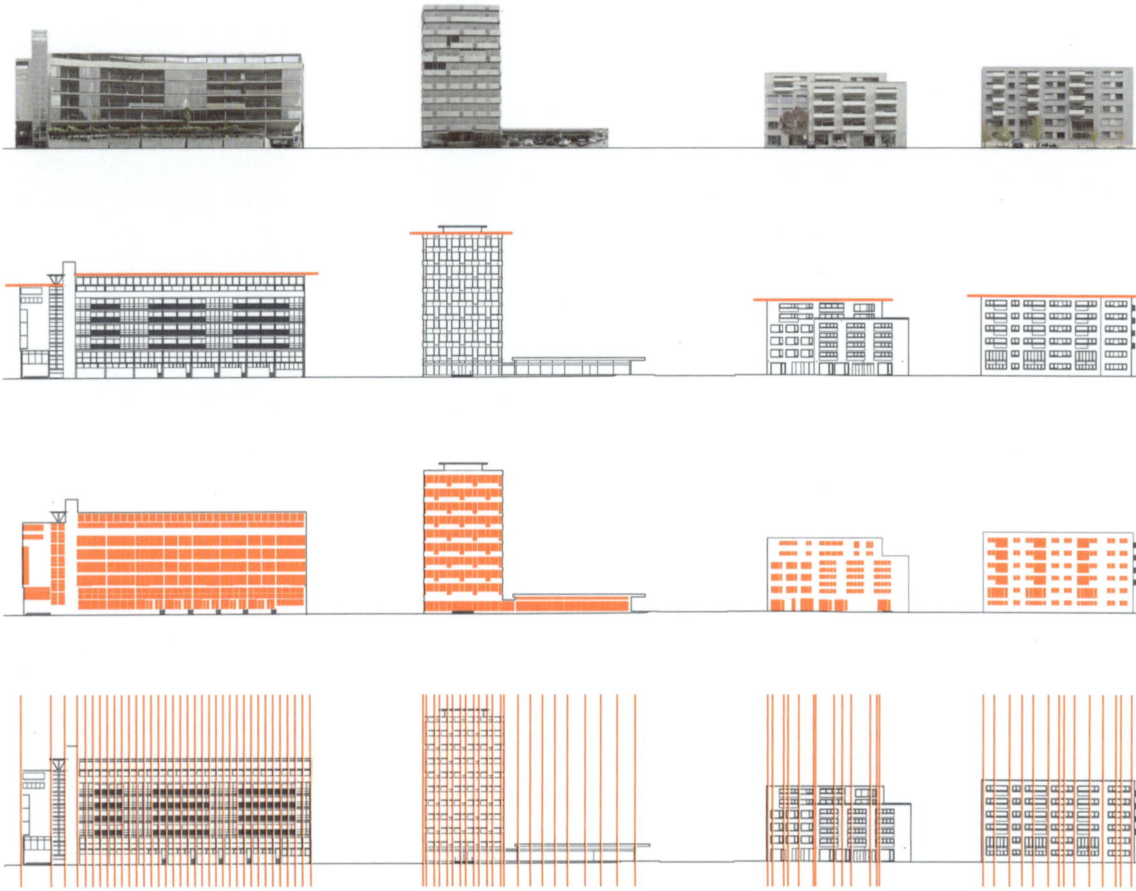

Analysis of
Buckhauserstrasse
street views

Eaves height
Degree of openness
Rhythm
Materiality

MIDDLE AGES

Samuel Klingele
Alexis Panoussopoulos
12 AS

Lucia Bernini
16 AS

Lucio Crignola
Maurin Elmer
13 AS

FOUNDATION ERA

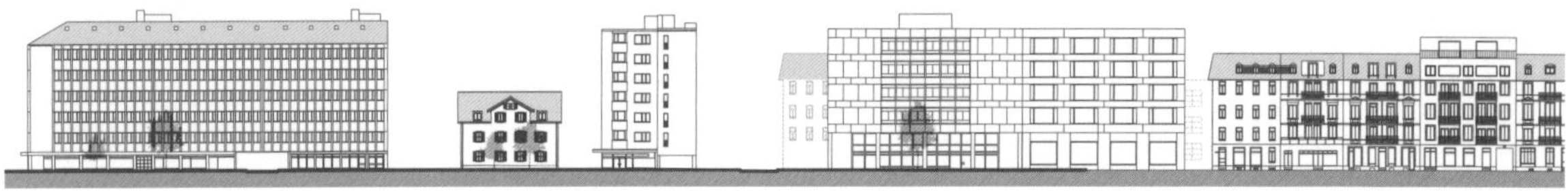

Grégoire Bridel
Rémy Carron
16 AS

Lea Grunder
13 AS

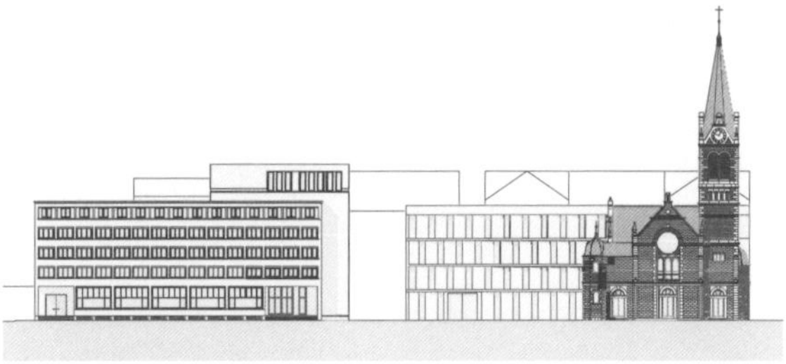

Corinne Wegmann
Vanessa Werder
08 AS

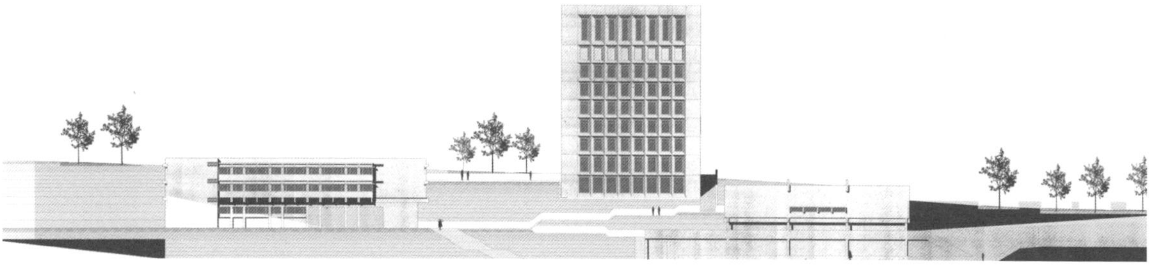

Benjamin Cordes
08 AS

Stéphane Chau
13 AS

Timothy Allen
Christian Weber
15 AS

MIDDLE AGES

FOUNDATION ERA

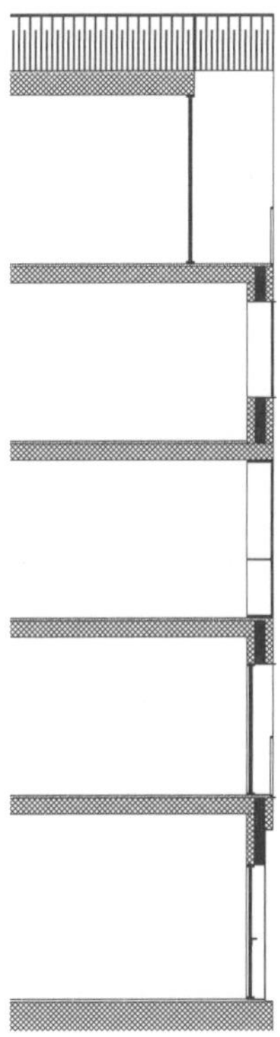

Noël Frozza
Julien Graf
15 AS

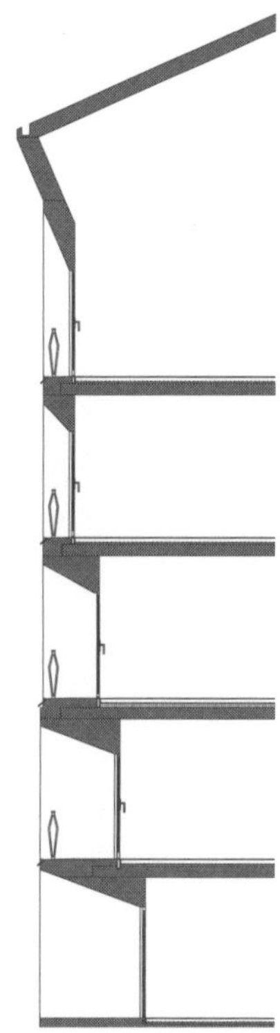

Markus Krieger
Petra Steinegger
14 AS

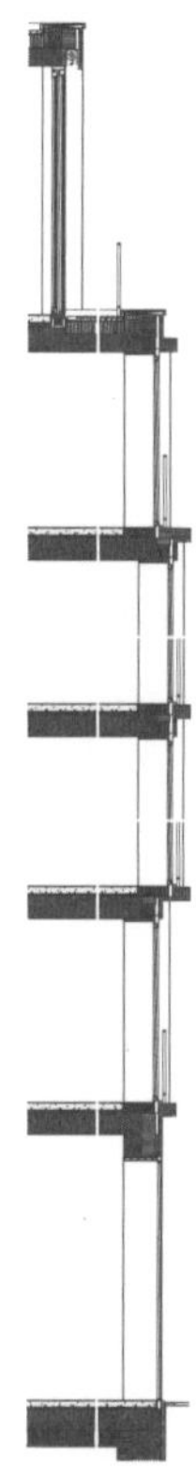

Lukas Herzog
Hubert Holewik
11 AS

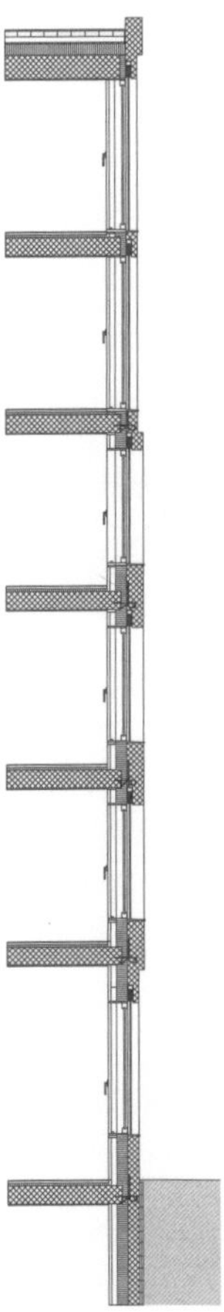

Jana Bohnenblust
Marco Fernandes Pires
16 AS

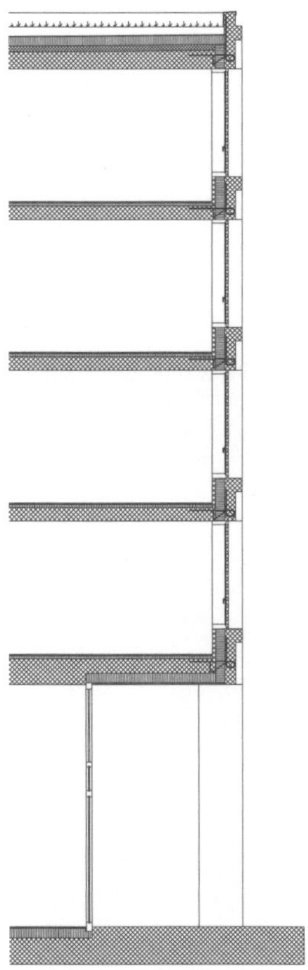

Samuel Dayer
Louis du Fay de Lavallaz
16 AS

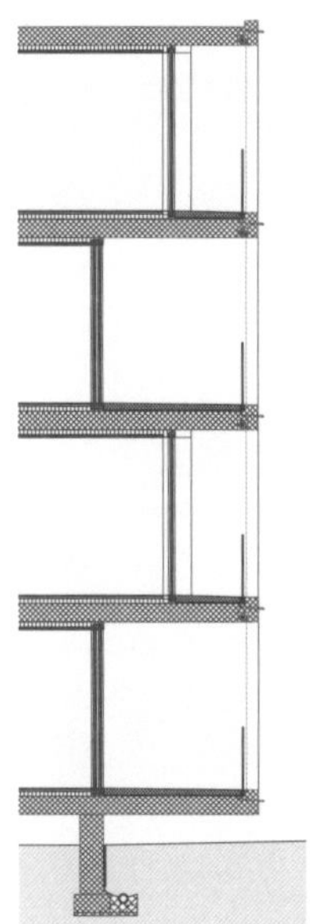

Flurin Arquint
Michael Beerli
10 AS

Larissa Strub
Lucie Vauthey
16 AS

4

MIDDLE AGES

FOUNDATION ERA

Wen Guan
Zhiyku Zeng
16 AS

Isabel von Bechtolsheim
Rafael Zulauf
12 AS

Lea Graf
Andrea Micanovic
13 AS

Isabelle Burtscher
Carlo Magnaguagno
12 AS

Grégoire Bridel
Rémy Carron
16 AS

Lucia Bernini
Tom Mundy
16 AS

Samuel Dayer
Louis du Fay de Lavallaz
16 AS

4

MODERNISM

Karin Bienz
Felix Good
12 AS

Timothy Allen
Christian Weber
15 AS

Flammetta Pennisi
10 AS

Alejandro Pérez Giner
Juan Rojas Rico
16 AS

MIDDLE AGES

Carola Hartmann
Robin Schlumpf
15 AS

Lukas Graf
Andrea Micanovic
13 AS

FOUNDATION ERA

Ria Cavelti
Simon von Niederhäusern
13 AS

Lukas Herzog
Hubert Holewik
11 AS

Sarah Federli
Lea Glanzmann
10 AS

4

Caroline Schwarzenbach
Fabian Reiner
14 AS

MODERNISM

Arthur de Buren
Jonatan Egli
11 AS

Timothy Allen
Christian Weber
15 AS

Noëmi Ruf
Lars Rumpel
13 AS

Bas Princen, *Valley (Jing'an)*, 2007 © Bas Princen

5

Place Structure Envelope

An envelope is a membrane, defined in chemistry as a thin layer separating the interior from the exterior environment. It is selectively permeable, and controls the movement of substances. Impermeability is just one of many options. In addition to dividing and masking, the envelope enables targeted exchange and hints at what could lie behind, for example, the structure of something. Masking and revealing are two equivalent qualities of an envelope.

The envelope is usually observed from the perspective of the view from outside. The building shell surrounds and limits the building, adding something of its own to the interior, giving it shape. The envelope reveals something of or about the interior. If this showing were, however, purely a copy, the envelope would not need it. Schinkel, who made constructive structure the measure of form, used the term *characterization* to express the way the envelope conveys the structure through artistic means.

However, as a boundary, the envelope always has another side. This becomes especially clear when buildings are viewed in the midst of other buildings: in the city. In this case, the outer shell of each building creates the inner shell of public space. The envelope mediates between these spheres, which is only possible if it is a physical reality. The envelope, an intimation of the interior structure of the building, contributes to the structure of urban space.

The manner in which this mediation takes place varies. Similar to the most significant of mediation tools – language – the mediation is both free and regulated, through grammar and vocabulary, which are in this case concrete structures. The place shapes this language; when the message is clearly spoken, then the building is comprehensible and contributes to the consistency of the urban space. When the rules of language are ignored, a Babylonian linguistic entanglement, a babble of buildings is the result.

This possibility exists because the relationship between envelope and place is neither clear-cut nor obligatory. The envelope also expresses the structure of the building. This can be the constructive structure, and can also have other meanings. A palazzo is not automatically located at the right place—it can also make the space it needs. New factors are added: Since Venturi and Rauch, the membrane is a projection screen for the intentions of the clients and the wishes of the public. Different situations lead to different envelopes.

The design must fulfill this interdependency. It must recognize the singularity of the place, which is shown not only by the characteristics of the envelopes. It must carefully examine each aspect and put it in relation to the newcomer, which will, for its part, reveal its innermost. (FA/MN)

References to Construction

Miroslav Šik

A livable interior is designed by putting up an encasement consisting of six elements, commonly known as the foundation, walls, and roof. These elements primarily impact us through the quality of their design and the architectural atmosphere. However, when viewed from a purely constructive point of view, architectural elements with aesthetic characteristics show another side: Structural and load-bearing building components.

This three-dimensional structure protects the interior space with a dense and stable envelope, perforated by only a few openings. The enclosure, support, and opening occurs to a large part inside of the building components themselves, with only sporadic, although significant, constructive indicators visible at the surface. If one groups these indicators by characteristic features, three types of constructive references are revealed.

Sainte-Chapelle
Paris, 13th century.

Photo © M. Šik

The first tangible type of reference uses building material and technique to weave an opulent material ambience. The abstract manner transfigures the tangibility of the construction until it is immaterial, and the figurative uses both tangible and abstract references, depending on the building component, thus creating a building atmosphere that is both adequate and conventional.

The Classic Structure

If you happen to visit the cloister of a Romanic Cistercian monastery in France, you will find within—as described by Fernand Pouillon in his novel *Stones of the Abbey*—walls with oversized, relatively precisely hewn lacustrine limestone blocks and nidged surfaces. When seen from a distance, the building appears to be greyish-white and monochrome, while from up close, this sacral architecture transforms into a polychromatic surface with bas-relief. The strong structure and the elementary materiality are perfect examples of the enthrallment of the concrete, which prioritizes building materials, structure, and seam patterns at the expense of décor and cladding.

In the church choir of Sainte-Chapelle in Paris, very high and filigree vertical pilasters sandwich stained glass to produce the extremely delicate structuring of the bearing framework, straining towards the heavens. An observant viewer will sense that this very immaterial effect has a non-architectural analogy to a veil or a screen. A second, likewise seemingly immaterial effect showed up in the late Baroque, and can be traced back to the illusionist painting—and for the time unusually long span—of the ceiling mural, which revealed no sign of conventional support structure from any of the viewpoints accessible to the public, instead hiding its highly technical timbering in the attic.

The birth hour of the figurative house will remain forever hidden to us. It is similar to the structure sketched by laypersons as the "original house", with a vertical rectangle of a room that encases the interior chamber, maybe with a distinct base with centered, cross-like window bars topped by a pointed roof and a smoking chimney. Its material and structural triad of foundation, walls, and roof, divided inside by the analogous floors, walls, and ceiling, in the current context correspond most to three different, yet conventional, building materials: the jointed stone base, the plastered walls, and the intricately clad wooden roof.

The Structure Encases

As already stated, a structure is correctly built when the interior space is encased and protected by a closed structure formed by the three building components of foundation, walls, and roof. Pictured this way, the structure presents itself as an abundance of building materials, modules, and connecting seams. The abstract shell is reminiscent of skin or a mold cast from a single material. The figural reference unspectacularly merges the two principles.

The building materials and techniques favored in the concrete style evoke a feeling of material completeness at the surface of the envelope. The ideals are powerful vertical and horizontal joints, the individual materiality of each building component, precise and slightly imprecise aspects coexisting side-by-side, and the artisanal manufacturing of select surfaces. This concrete style is threatened by all kinds of effective surrogates, which—glued to the outer wall—convey a mural impression without the strength and full-bodiedness of the true materials.

A complete liberation from the shackles of the conventional and everyday seems to be the ultimate goal of constructive abstraction. With concrete, a building material was found with which one could design almost any strong spatial body, monoliths, for example. If conventional concrete techniques—trivial panel formwork, normal granularity, and coloration—were to give way to courageous innovation, a building would emerge with a such unbendable and resistant hull as those of crystals and synthetic resin casings. If innovation in building materials, bearing structures, and building sites continues, then a new type of concrete will stream out of the silo, one that can solidify into a hornet's nets or a giant cloud, puffing up with power and ringing in the repositioning of exterior architecture with a swarm of little nubs. Until this happens, one is merely imitating Africa's plaster and clay foundlings on one's own four walls, tolerating the predictable proliferation of cracks. Until further notice, our streaming-out-of-the-silo scenario will remain just another immaterial promise of *l'art pour l'art.*

The figurative tri-structure, made up of concrete and abstract references, reflects years of construction experience and everyday use. The foundation, made of stone, seems solid and is, indeed, a strong building component. For laypersons, fully plastered walls may seem abstract, but they were perceived on the construction site in their unplastered state as being solid and material, sometimes made with brick, sometimes made with in-situ concrete, or set with a timber frame. Every person has memorized the pitched roof as a tangible and intricately shingled surface that covers the eaves and the site and reveals wooden beams from the underside. Thanks to sustainable exterior insulation, we experience the image of our own four walls no longer as something solid and hard, but as a soft and certainly also very short-lived structure. As a result of the unavoidable impact of nature, the building components stretch and shrink, and one hides their dilations behind rain gutters with a benefit. The plastering, a gruel-like lime or cement mortar to be exact, becomes an actual building material with an abstract effect through its stone granulation, pigmentation, and plastered texture. Today, centuries-old plastering techniques can be carried out with acceptable effort, making them beloved traditional décor and, on the flip side, causing plaster to appear trivial in the eyes of innovative architects.

The Structure Bears

The joined shell requires a support structure to distribute its own weight and that of the inhabitants and interior into the earth. The concrete reference disconnects several building components from the structure as visible supporting elements. The abstract structure reveals a more virtual supporting framework. The figurative support structure references a building shell with cladding.

How could one symbolize the movement of forces more concretely and expressively than with bearing elements, such as pillars or visibly plastered plates, standing like autonomous sculptures in the room? To increase the contrast to this powerful support structure, dividing walls are visually slimmed, or differentiated from the supporting skeleton using joints and materials. The era of sustainability opposes this liberation of the bearing structure to the outside, because it is almost never done without creating thermal bridges.

In the abstract style, constructive connections are referenced in a way that is by no means enlightening, instead intentionally cloaking them with dematerialization, and showing space and design as being sullied by nothing, as pure phenomena. In instances where purist design imitates exterior architectural forms, no inner eye of experience is there to test the preliminary dimensions or the stability of the constructive elements. Giant buildings that, structurally braced, hover above emptied city plazas, were darlings of early modernism, but showed these effects, however, always in combination with powerful roof beams or mega-mushrooms in the veristic manner. Made possible today by cutting edge technologies, the abstract image shows floating forms and glass volumes as a purely magical feat of bearing vastly exceeding any previous material reality.

The figurative building shell is part of the conventional construction site, it supports the structure, limits the interior space, and has sufficient apertures for building services. Because it will later be clad in a decorative layer, one can design the building shell with the sober calculations of building site and market price, with a clean surface free of fine-tuned visible qualities. Building materials, building components, and supporting struc-

Karin Gauch
Christian Center in Schlieren
ETHZ 2010
Professorship M. Šik

Tobias Häfliger
Open Air Theater in Zurich
ETHZ 2008
Professorship M. Šik

ture of the building shell are constructed in accordance with the usual rules of architecture, yet not with the dictates of purity, coherence, and composition. The decorative layer clads and protects the building shell, usually copying its contours, but only rarely reflects its materiality, often even breaking away from the structural contour with a faux plafond.

The Opening of the Structure

Each opening, each fissure in the shell and truss, weakens the structure, leaving permeable seams between the walls and the frames of the openings. Unlike a simple opening, problems arising from incoming daylight, visibility, and sometimes also security require that the apertures be complex and elaborate. The constructive style systematizes open and closed wall sections in a façade grid. In the abstract, the openings dissolve into glass walls. And in the conventional figuration, an opening becomes a recess.

Jean-Jacques Auf der Maur
zoo in Zurich
ETHZ 2011
Professorship M. Šik

Enzo Valerio
Hotel in Zurich
ETHZ 2013
Professorship M. Šik

5

Concrete openings are also nothing but passageways, apertures for light and air, although they are less like doors and windows but rather glass fillings, spanned between thin wall sections. Rows of openings with wide or highly thinned wall sections, known as grid façades, can be found in farmhouses and office buildings alike, but stylized very differently and in different materials. To achieve a maximum view to the outside, wall posts are made so thin that they gradually lose any supporting function at all, and only serve to delineate openings. If the opening dissolves into a solitary hole in a strong wall, giving way to horizontally and vertically ordered apertures, then the mural surface also vanishes, becoming a constructive system of posts and beams. Clearly marked by industrial detailing, in the concrete style, manufacturing and assembly approaches an architectural reference to auto body openings.

The abstract style replaces the diversity of materials and shapes, as the protagonist of emulation, through smooth, transparent murality. A banally suspended sunblind, disrupting the sculptural impression, secedes to the grand technology of tinted and metallic evaporated glass. Banished to the interior of the building, there is no support structure visible along the periphery of the construction. High-performance adhesives make it possible to mount the glass, delivered in mega-formats, with no visible conventional fasteners, and—thanks to a discovery that has yet to be made—maybe someday the oh-so-striking seams between two panes of glass, sealed with plastics, will also disappear. The contrast between the minimalistic detailed images on the surface of building elements and a great and profound technological expenditure remain characteristic of the abstract.

Openings are often referred to as perforations, which characterizes the constructive penetration of the structure quite well. A solitary window represents something missing, a hole in the wall, whereby only parts of the cutout can be seen in the decorative layer. Window surrounds made of four parts is a traditional and elegant solution to four constructive problems at once, and uses only a single building element. It absorbs the weight of the wall above the aperture as a lintel, limits the window shutters on the sides, and covers the horizontal capstone as a windowsill.

A profiled window flashing can protectively cover the tolerance gap between the edge of the wall opening and the jambs. An inexpensive and visually minimized solution covers only the horizontal surface with a sheet metal windowsill and clads the other three perforated edges with a decorative strip.

References and Images

In order to avoid the cheap impression of a decorated shed, references should preferably not be constructed merely as symbols stuck to the surface of the building structure, but as the tracks of true construction. This veristic understanding selects from the mass of possible constructions a solution that stages a coherently dramatic effect with the guiding spirit of the architecture. My teacher Aldo Rossi once superimposed trivial everyday snapshots he had taken of barracks and lido cabins with abstract constructions, composing an enthralling masterpiece of petty bourgeois redolence, sculptural archaism, and a playful atmosphere. In contrast, his last buildings, which are coarsely detailed and pragmatic, lack this spirit of naive earthiness. When amateurishly tempered with chaos, references to construction can sully any work of architecture. Yet, if one designs veristic and autonomous references, then they modify the architectural images to be concrete, abstract, or figurative●

Concept | From Latin *concipire:* To retain, to take in. A sketched plan, "first draft", a suggestion, intellectual fixating of the design idea, to be specified in a detail plan to follow. Critique of technocratic design and the reception of concept art (as of the 1960s, USA) are behind the steep career curve of this key word, which is today part of our everyday language. In concept art, the idea and its development are the crucial elements, the execution is secondary; dematerialization is sought after, a renunciation of the concrete panel painting. Since concepts are wont to be abstract, the concrete is neglected, often resulting in failure.

Façade | From Latin *facies:* Face. The elevation of a building, originally only the main elevation facing public space. Here, the orientation is a gain clear: from the floor of the basement to the sky of the attic, and in between the main floors. For constructive reasons, a building layer of sometimes great spatial depth mediates the public and private spheres. In modernism, façade volumes tended to become the thinned surfaces of curtain façades. Freestanding buildings have several effective elevations, and Le Corbusier's raised buildings also have top and bottom surfaces.

Process | From Latin *procedere:* To move forward, proceed. Thus, on the one hand, movement and activity and, on the other, in a direction that can be deterministic or random. Contrasting this, we have the legal definition that has the declaratory character of a decree or court ruling, certainly the result of the movement between for and against. Accuracy is crucial. Especially since the Romantic Era, the opinion that supposedly established things are the result of processes and life processes has made headway.

Character | From Greek *charaktér:* Stamp, seal. Manner, personal competence, nature, the temperament of a being. Virtuous characteristics grow through practice and habit, less from instruction. For Schinkel, character is an important part of construction and architecture, such that constructive characteristics do not have the aesthetic of an effigy, but rather give construction a fitting expression and convey its character honestly and at first glance to the viewer. This is very different from ambience and atmosphere.

Convention | From Latin *conventio:* Agreement. Rules for interacting with others, often unspoken, of practical use, not necessarily logical (for example, there is no reason that screws generally turn to the right). Convention owes its tacit manner to its proximity to the traditional, customary, not backwards—mutual agreement is the base of its validity, and it often varies by region. There is a widespread misunderstanding that rational thought alone creates meaningful and mutual agreement. Construction is shaped by convention from urban development to each doorknob—this is proven every time someone must find their way in a darkened room.

Density | Density is the ratio of the mass of a body and its volume. Figuratively, the content in relation to its expansion; in the city, the number of users/buildings in relation to an area or neighborhood, usable surface in relation to a territory. Density is a central aspect of urban planning. Once negatively associated with close quarters and bad hygiene, today positively related to diversity and richness of experience. It has become an indicator of urbanity, which should ensure socio-economic efficiency and sustainability in land use.

Resilience | From Latin *resilio*: To recoil, spring back. Refers to the hardiness or tolerance of complex systems faced with massive external or internal disruption and includes an inherent ability to learn and develop. Originally a physics term referring to highly elastic materials, today it is used in psychology, ecology, and other fields as well. Used in more recent times to denote sustainable human settlement and the planning thereof. An indicator of sustainability in combination with the complementary aspect of efficiency.

Sufficiency | From Latin *sufficere:* To suffice. In the sense of the "right measure", or the amount of resources necessary to maintain a system. The inferred reference to limits makes it clear that valuable qualities are being asked for, while efficiency calls for relationships and therefore quantities. The foundation of sustainability is based on the three pillars of efficiency (effectiveness), consistency (materiality), and sufficiency.

Mixed Use | In contrast to the shining future promised by the Athens Charter of 1933's arrangement of the city according to function, the total demolition of the Pruitt-Igoe neighborhood of St. Louis in 1972 marked its failure. Functional division is nonetheless holding strong. Mixed use is tediously becoming one of the guiding principles of urban development—socially, economically, and in construction. Together with heterogeneity and diversity, mixed used is considered the epitome of urban vitality. An ideal that is in a state of dynamic equilibrium and is constantly endangered, today by gentrification and the development of entire areas by a single investor.

PLACE–STRUCTURE–ENVELOPE

The topic of this assignment is the connection of place, structure, and envelope. Knowledge and experience from the previous tasks will be used as the basis of this exercise. A volumetric intervention to the bearing structure and circulation system will be further developed and subsequently integrated into the context with a fitting façade. The façade, or envelope, creates connections between inside and outside, reveals the interior of the building, stands within a context, and is able to integrate aspects of the context. Last but not least, its voluminous character makes an important contribution to urban space.

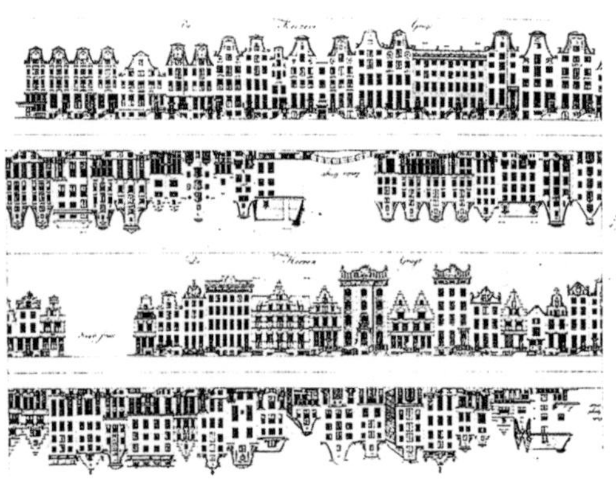

Grachtenboek (Canal Book) by Caspar Philips

Building Level

This intervention must expand the existing building or buildings by 1,000–5,000 square meters. The next step is to define a bearing structure and a circulation system enabling the organization of the rooms listed below. Finally, the intervention/addition will be completed by the addition of a building envelope that integrates with the context.

Spatial program

Middle Ages
- (expansion ca. 1,000 m^2)
- One 400-m^2, three-story room without columns
- One 200-m^2, two-story room without columns

Foundation Era
- (expansion ca. 3,000 m^2)
- One 400-m^2, three-story room without columns
- Two 200-m^2, two-story rooms without columns

Modernism
- (expansion ca. 5,000 m^2)
- Two 400-m^2, three-story rooms without columns
- Two 200-m^2, two-story rooms without columns

The remaining spaces of the addition are to be structured with single-story rooms approximately 2.7 × 5.4 meters in size.

Specifications

This exercise will be done individually. Graphic representation on two DIN A0 plans.

Plan 1 City Level
- Written explanation
- Photos of insertion model 1:500
- Figure-ground diagram 1:5,000
- Area plan 1:1,000 including roof perspectives and topography
- Site plan 1:500 with ground floor plan, open spaces, and footprints of the surrounding buildings
- Representative façade view 1:200 / 1:250

Plan 2 Building Level
- Concept sketches, photos of concept model
- Interior model photos
- Standard floor plan 1:200 / 1:250 (differentiation of new, existing, and demolition sections)
- Floor plans 1:500 (differentiation of new, existing, and demolition sections)
- A representative cross-section 1:200 / 1:250 including the context

Models
- Insertion model 1:500
- Sectional model 1:75

Requirements

- Figure-ground diagram 1:5,000
- Area plan 1:1,000
- Site plan 1:500
- Site model 1:500
- Plans of existing structures
- Fire Safety Regulations
- Crafting notebooks I + II

Goal

It is important that the concepts of place, structure, and envelope are not addressed individually, but viewed as an interdependent whole. This increased simultaneity causes complexity to increase. Students learn to recognize that good solutions can only be found by meshing these concepts together.

Adolf Loos
Villa Karma, Clarens VD, 1903–06, finished by Hugo Ehrlich, 1912

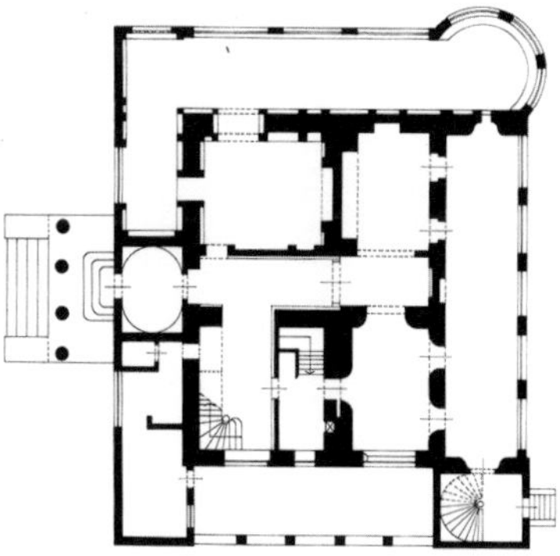

Adolf Loos
Villa Karma, Clarens VD, 1903–06, finished by Hugo Ehrlich, 1912

Model
Manon Mottet
15 AS

MIDDLE AGES

Erik Fichter
16 AS

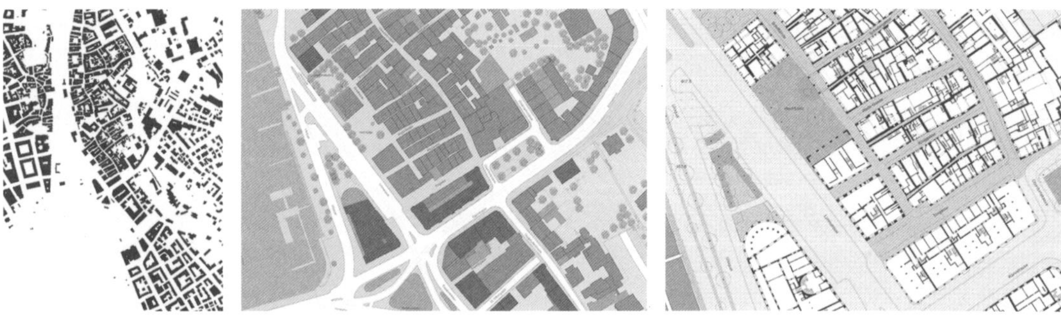

Artai Sanchez Keller
15 AS

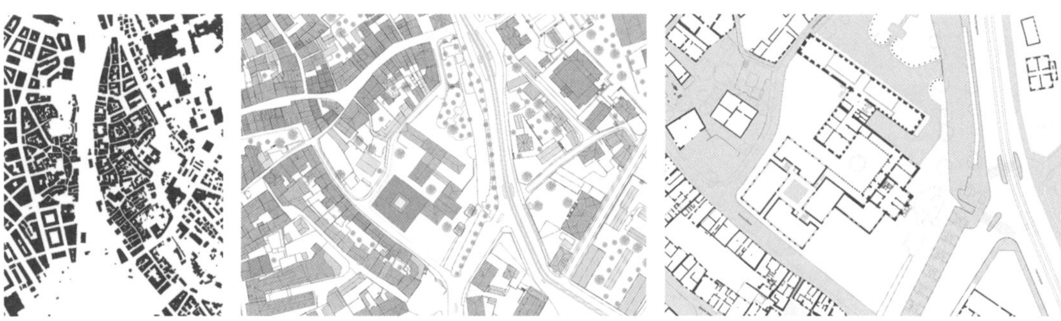

Valentin Buchwalder
11 AS

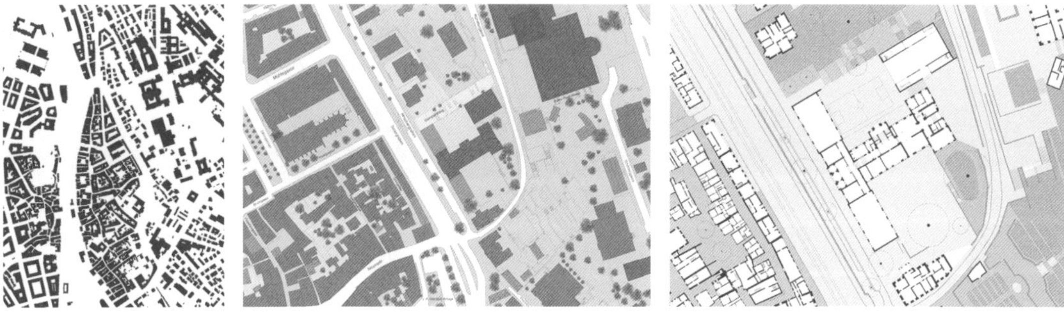

Fabian Heinzer
13 AS

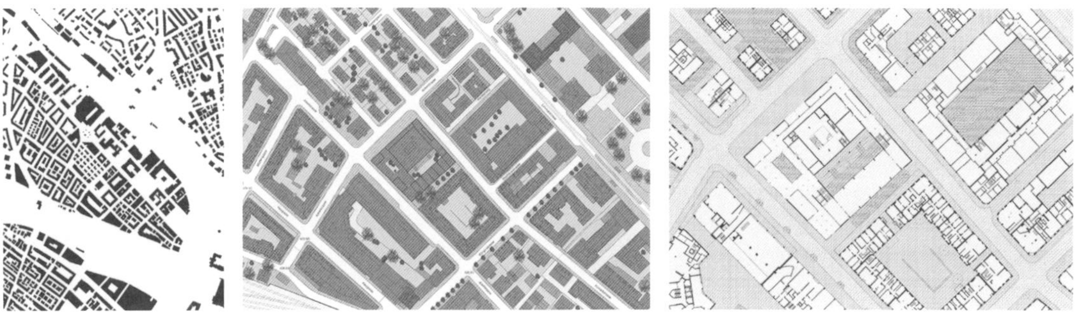

Anna Nauer
16 AS

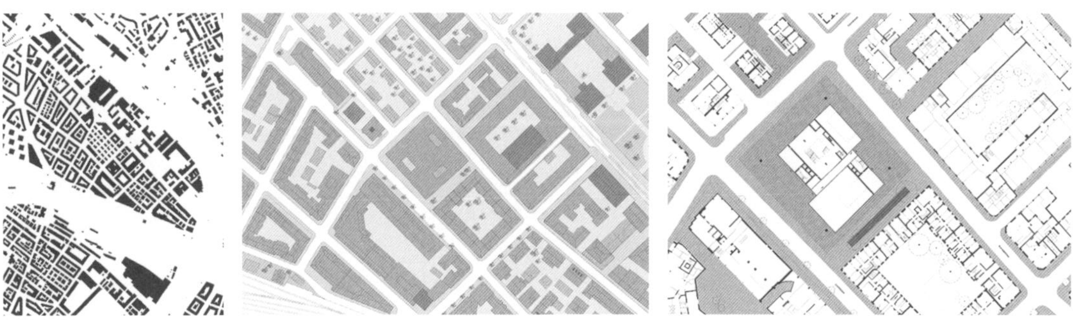

Tiziana Schirmer
12 AS

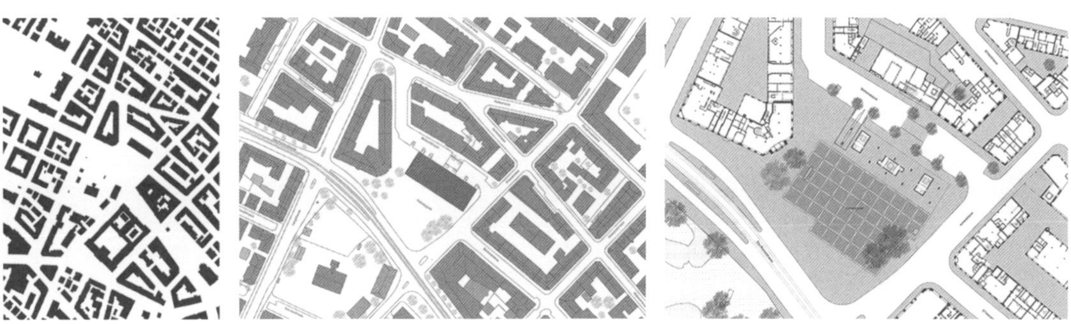

Samuel Scherer
11 AS

MODERNISM

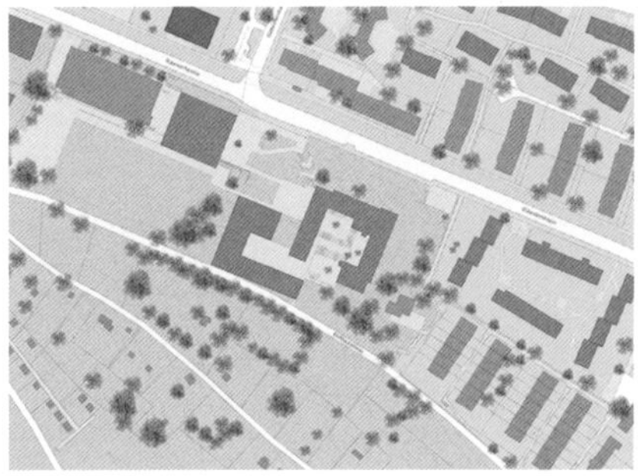
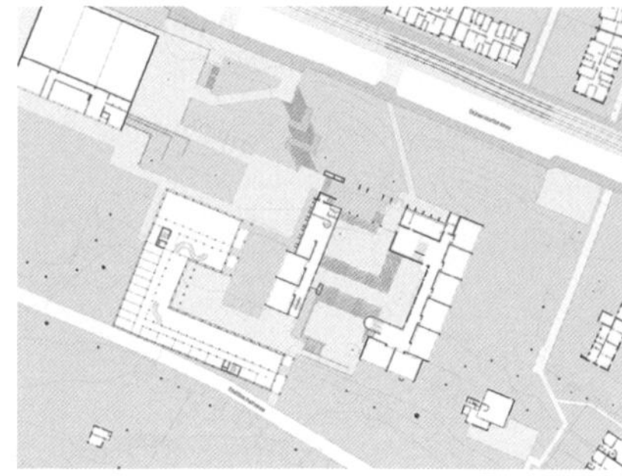

Nadine Weger
13 AS

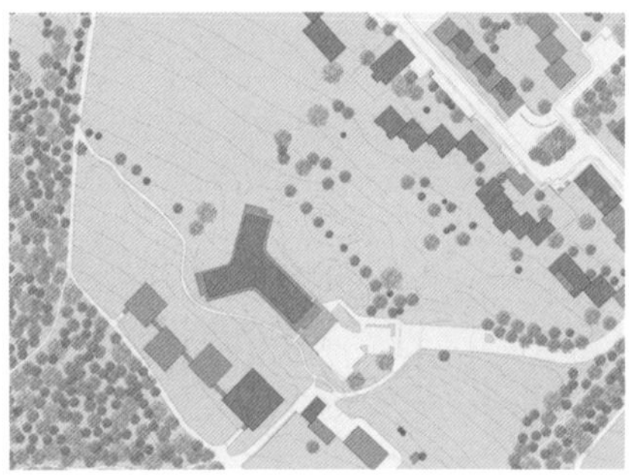
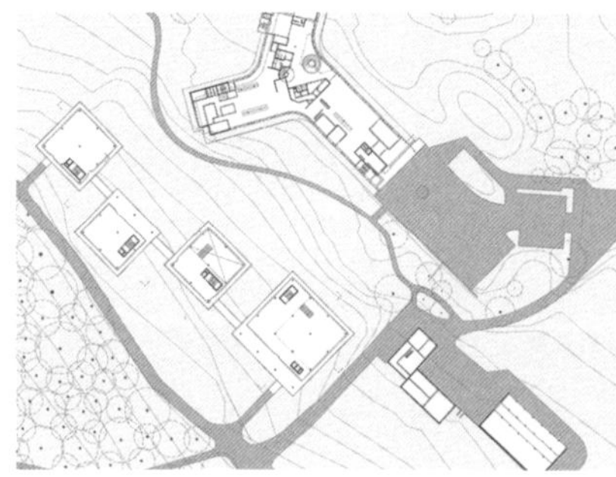

Timothy Allen
15 AS

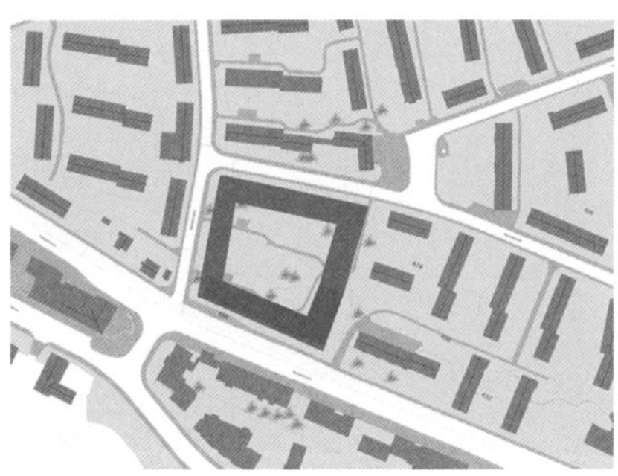

Kaspar Stöbe
10 AS

MIDDLE AGES

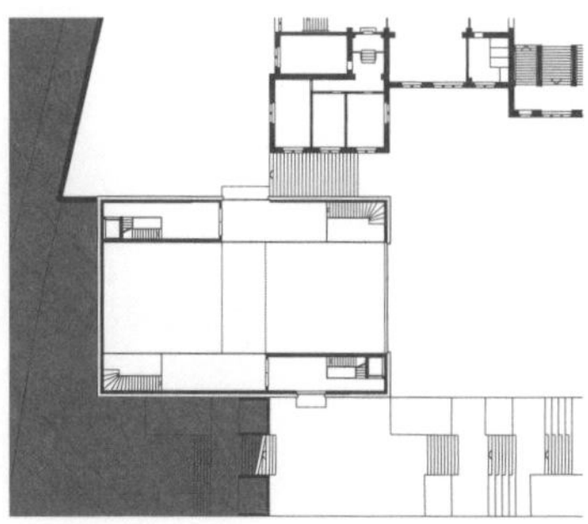

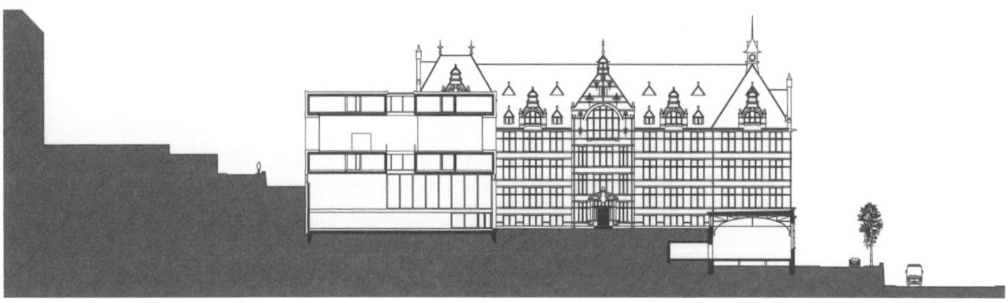

Fabian Heinzer
13 AS

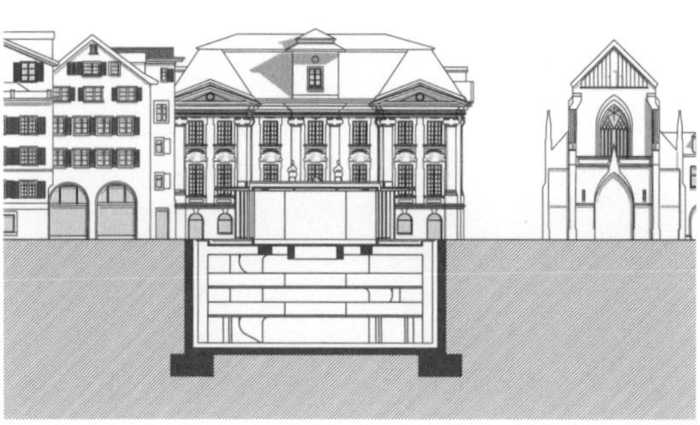

Wen Guan
16 AS

MIDDLE AGES

Feng Mark Zhang
14 AS

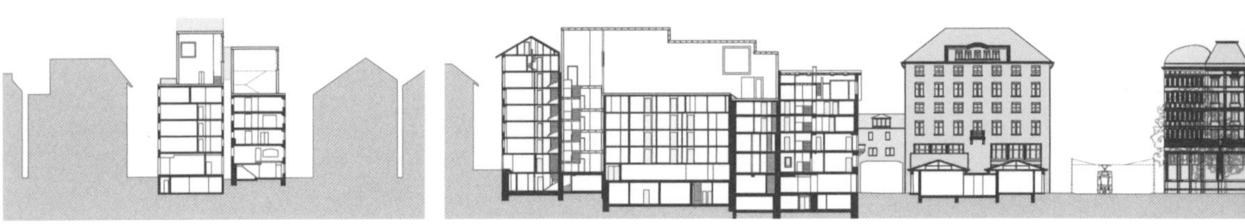

Manon Mottet
15 AS

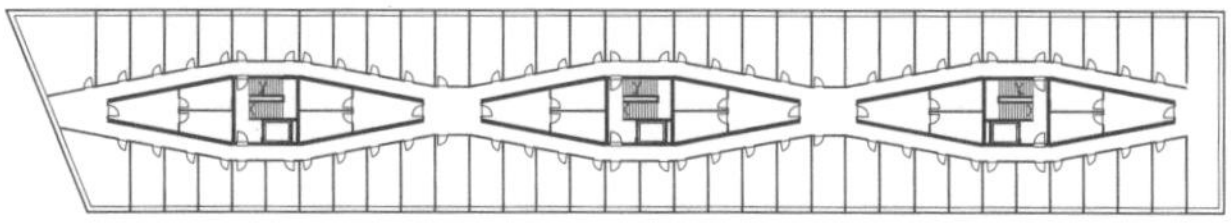

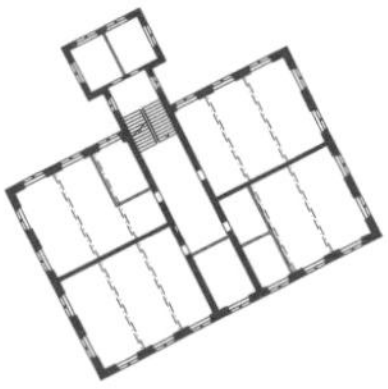

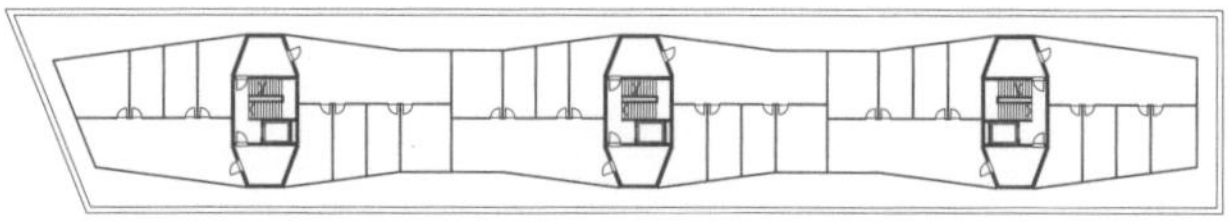

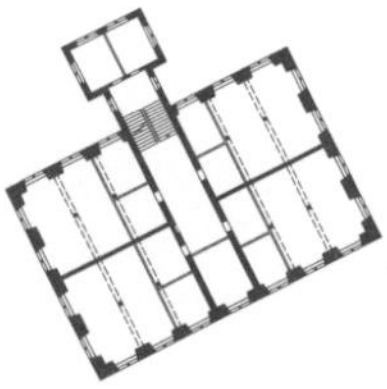

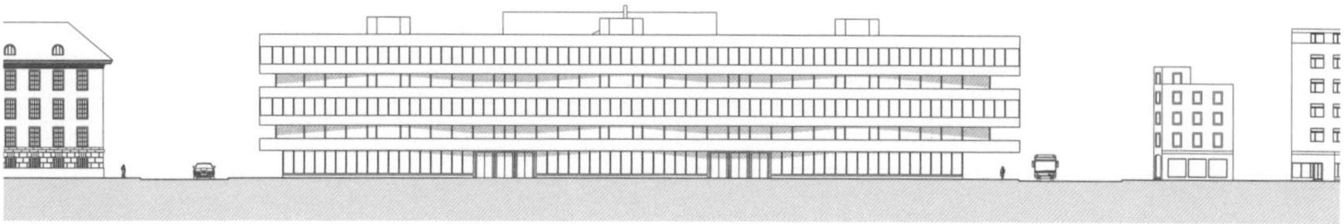

Joos Kündig
14 AS

FOUNDATION ERA

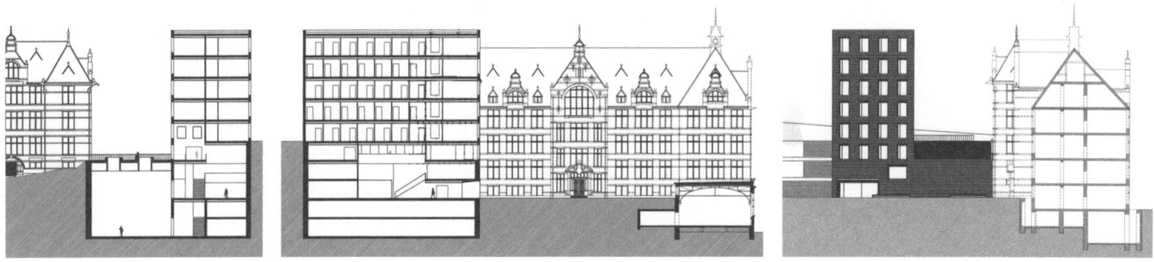

Thomas Meyer
08 AS

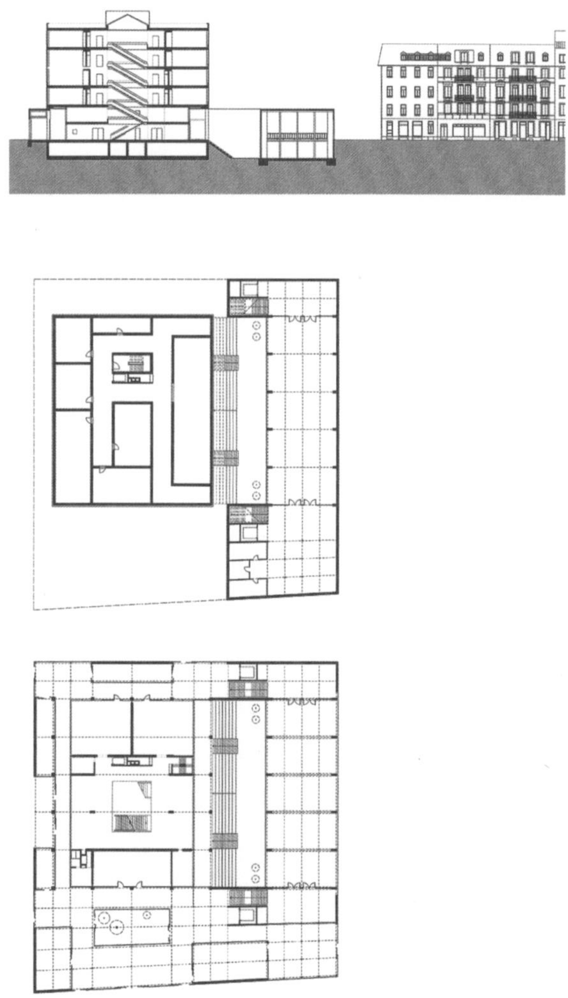

Anna Nauer
16 AS

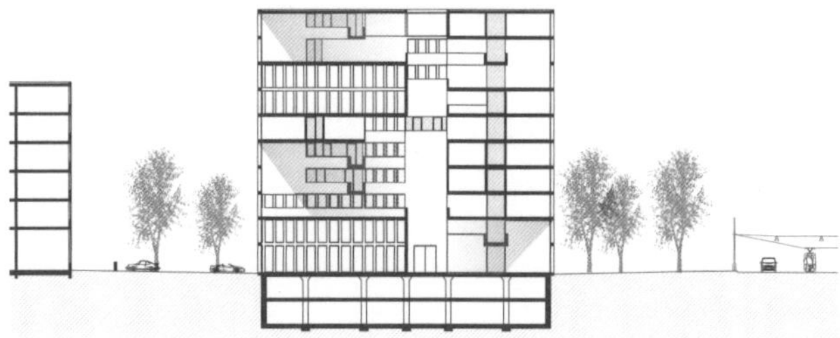

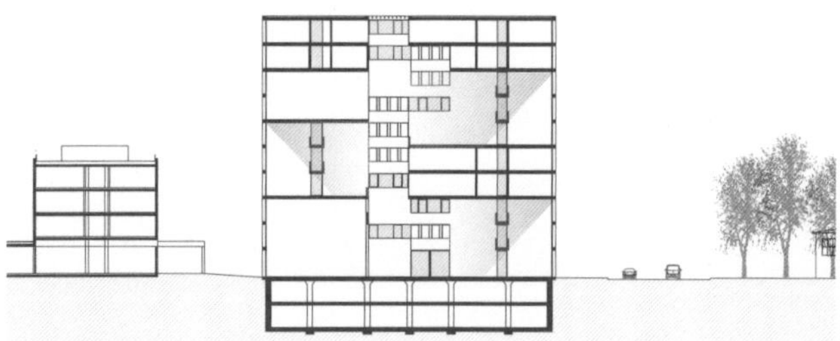

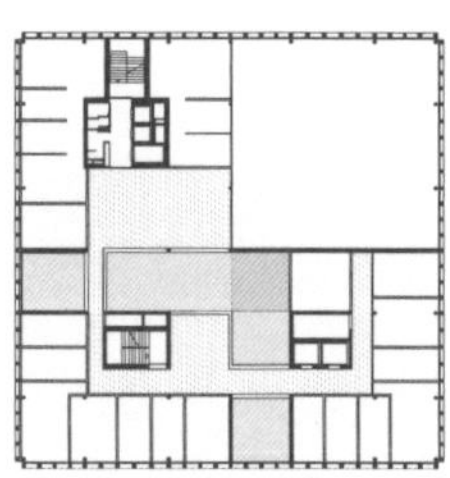

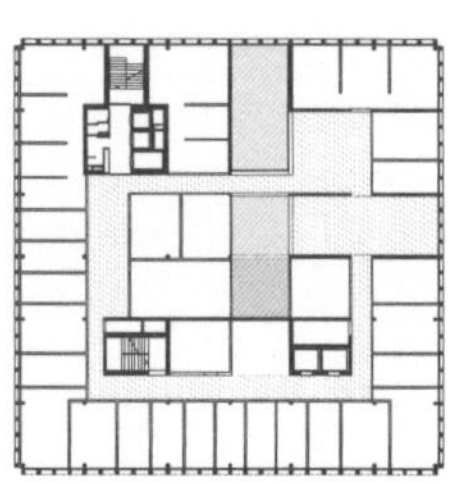

Benjamin Blocher
12 AS

MODERNISM

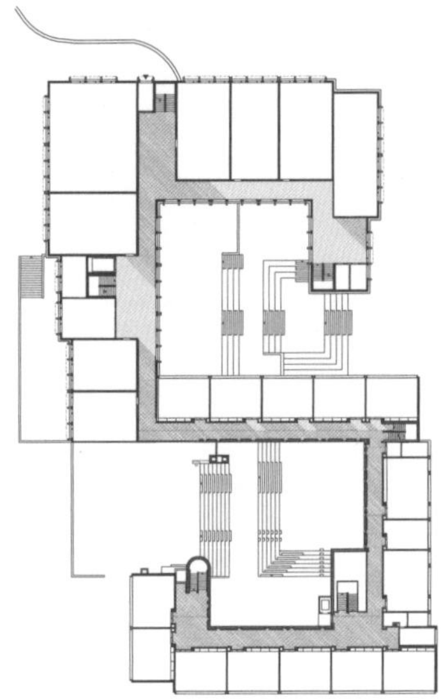

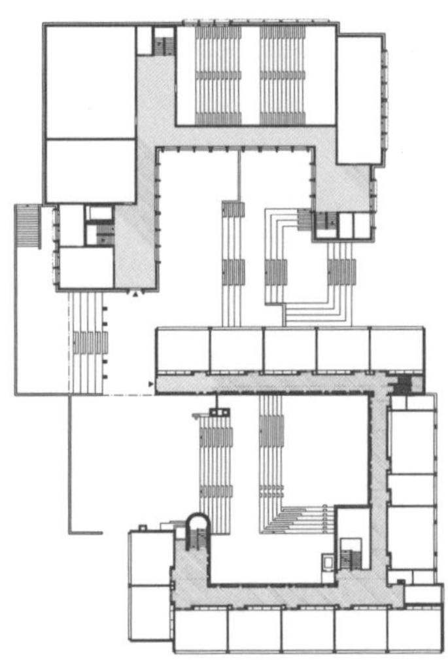

Alessandro Canonica
16 AS

MIDDLE AGES

Artai Sanchez Keller
15 AS

Erik Fichter
16 AS

MIDDLE AGES

Jonas Martin Elias Hasler
13 AS

5

Tiziana Schirmer
12 AS

Joos Kündig
14 AS

Anna Nauer
16 AS

MODERNISM

Zoe auf der Maur
12 AS

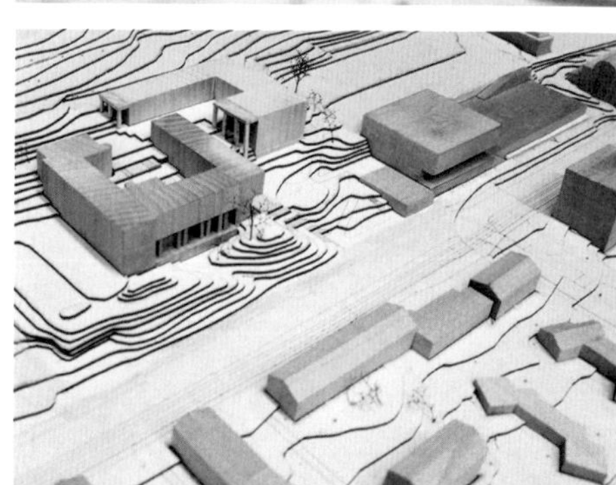

Nadine Weger
13 AS

Timothy Allen
15 AS

5

MIDDLE AGES

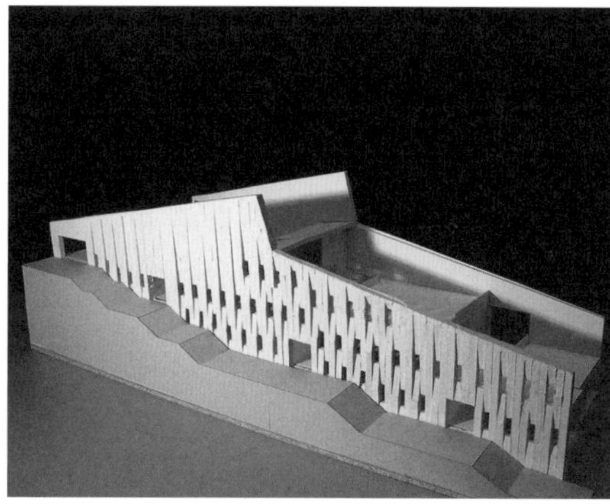

Mathias Lattmann
Fabian Lauener
08 AS

Simon Rieder
12 AS

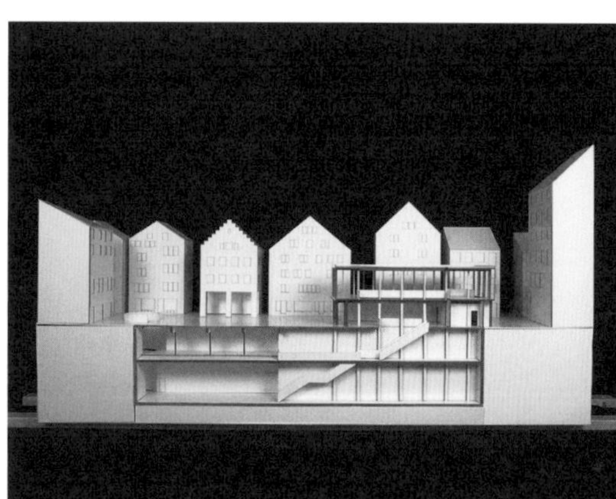

Julian Meier
11 AS

Artai Sanchez Keller
15 AS

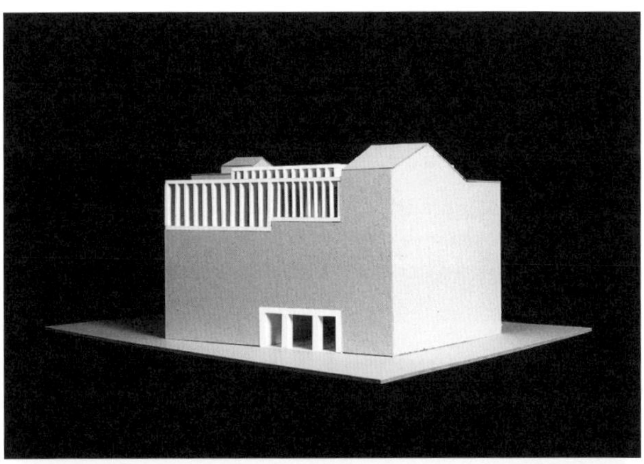

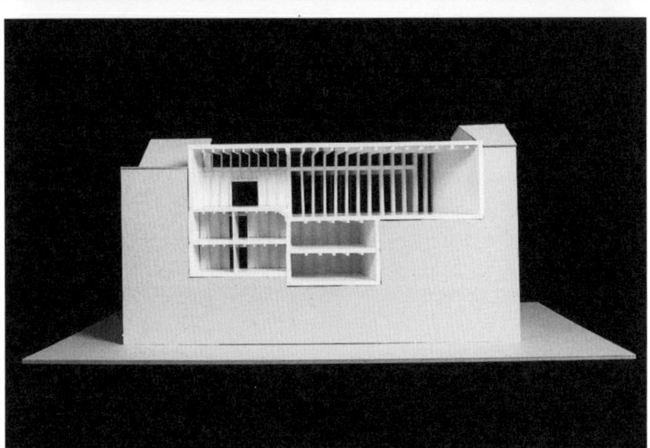

Tom Mundy
16 AS

FOUNDATION ERA

Riet Fanzun
09 AS

Tiziana Schirmer
12 AS

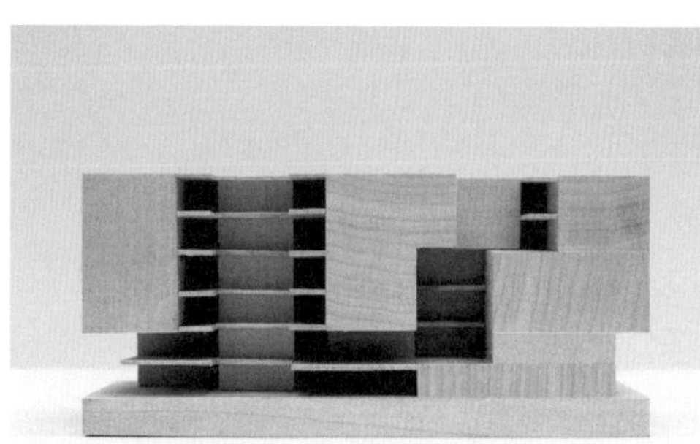

Nina Rohrer
16 AS

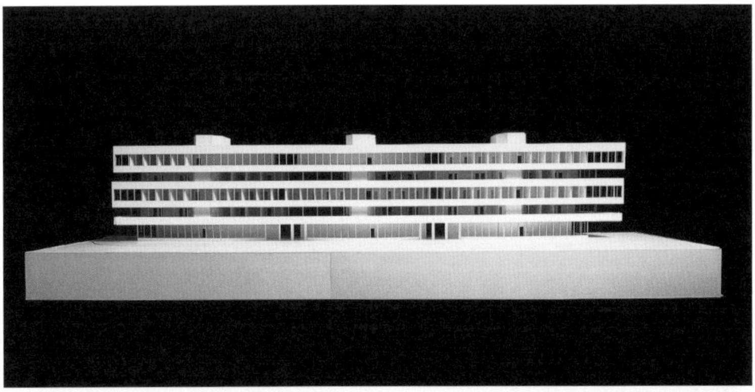

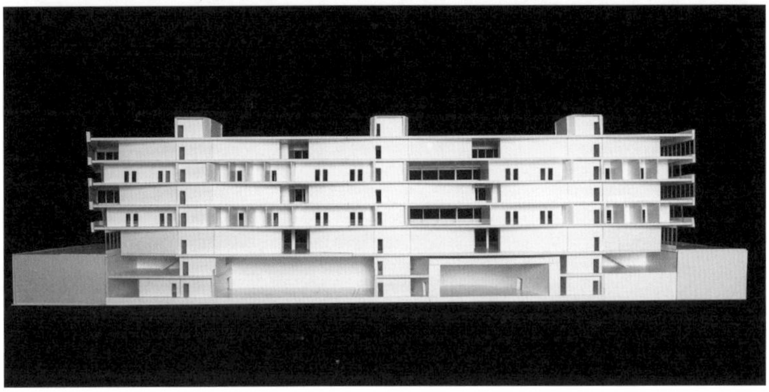

Joos Kündig
14 AS

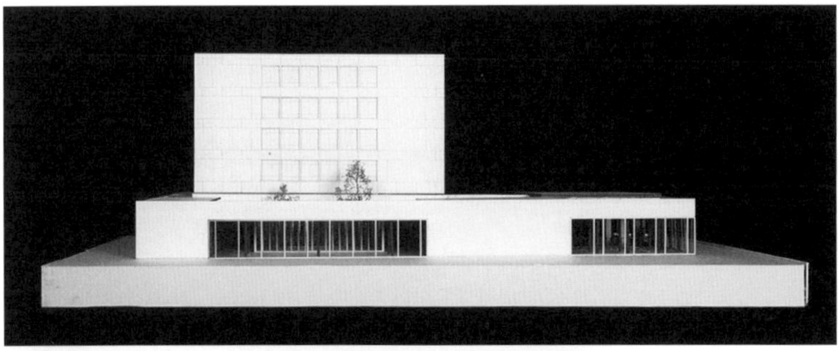

Anna Nauer
16 AS

MODERNISM

Nadine Weger
13 AS

Tobias Wick
14 AS

Timothy Allen
15 AS

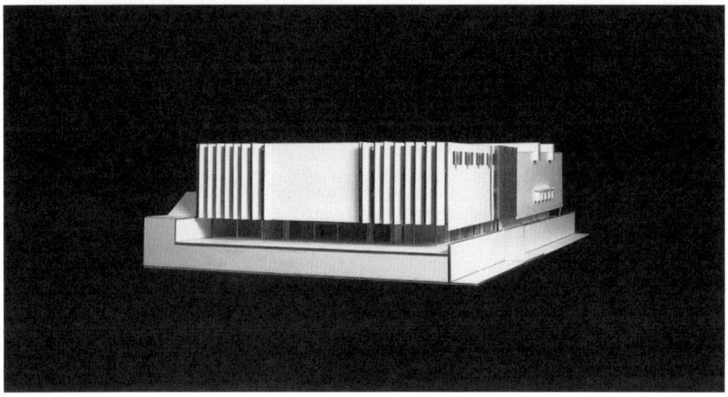

Grégoire Bridel
16 AS

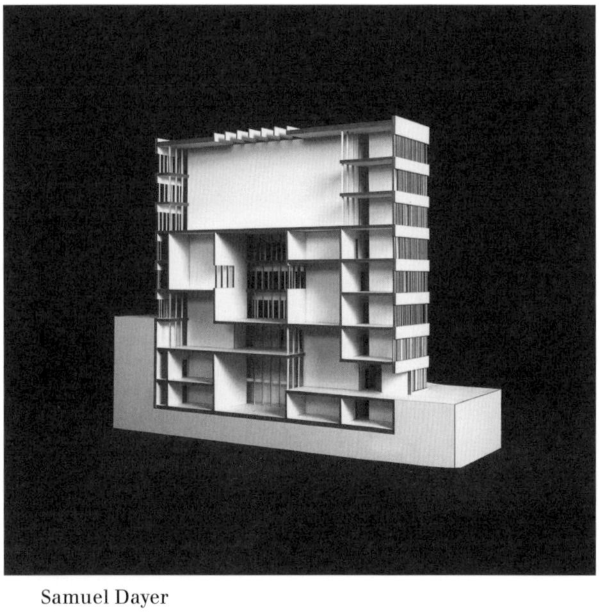

Samuel Dayer
16 AS

MIDDLE AGES

Thomas Meyer
08 AS

Lorenz Mörikofer
Xavier Perrinjaquet
08 AS

Joni Kaçani
09 AS

Jie Li
13 AS

5

Fabian Heinzer
13 AS

MIDDLE AGES

Erik Fichter
16 AS

Larissa Strub
16 AS

Peter Boller
10 AS

FOUNDATION ERA

Roy Engel
11 AS

Cosimo Caccia
12 AS

Nirvan Karim
15 AS

Nina Rohrer
16 AS

5

Anna Nauer
16 AS

MODERNISM

Noriaki Fujishige
09 AS

Timothy Allen
15 AS

Maximilien Durel
15 AS

Darius Tabatabay
16 AS

Andreas Gursky, São Paulo, Sé, 2002, C-Print, 273 × 206 × 6.2 cm
Courtesy Sprüth Magers Berleri London © Andreas Gursky / 2017, ProLitteris, Zurich

6
Program

6 Program

The word program stems from the Greek *prógramma:* Something prescribed. This can mean two things: something that precedes all further statements, or something that mandates how something must proceed. A political program, or platform, establishes something fundamental, has a foundational effect, unlike the daily pronouncements of the party. In contrast, a computer program describes the calculation steps to be undertaken when the program is used. The program or agenda of a conference is similar: It describes a progression, without providing a reason for it. When searching the internet for "architecture + program", the results provided are almost exclusively for software programs.

In today's architectural practice, the program is the foundation of a design—the spatial allocation program, the *Raumprogramm.* The client defines the "content" the building project should contain—the architect puts this into a plan. Program and plan are mutually dependent; they relate to each other reasonably—in the sense of cause and effect—and systematically—in the sense of completeness and free of caprice and chance. Program and plan are rationally connected.

This associative figure is a product of the Enlightenment. This era mistrusted anything led by any unfamiliar—religious or arbitrary—interpretation and allowed only the self-justification of a methodically clean if-then conclusion. The scientific technological thinking of modernism is founded upon this.

The attempt to found a decided modernist architecture shifted this rational self-legitimization into the center of 20th-century architectural thought. "Logic, which governs the statement of the problem and its realization," is, according to Le Corbusier, the style of our era. This all-encompassing demand for "a unity of intention" is at the root of, in his eyes, the architectural talent of the architect. "It alone, through the building programme, determines his architecture" (Le Corbusier, 1986, 4).

But who justifies the program, the building program? Is the building justified as soon as it functions as a building? Is it sufficient when space and construction are in concordance? What type of space is it? What qualities do the rooms have? Closed, open, flowing?

Acting on the needs of the time, distilling a program from this, and translating it with unobstructed logic into a plan means that: A specific moment in time is made into a general one—something that is, in light of changes in our living habits, truly venturesome. The rallying cry of modernism for timeless rationality had to follow the postulate of the New Human. Raised up to a dogma, it paradoxically did not even survive for the lifespan of a generation.

As Leon Battista Alberti stated 400 years earlier, "The Conclusion is, that for the Service, Security, Honour and Ornament of the Publick, we are exceedingly obliged to the Architect," (1755, 6) and demanded that: "Let your Building therefore be such, that it may not want any Members which it has not, and that those which it has, may not in any Respect deserve to be condemned"(64). One's ears perk up at the words, "those which it has". Something other than pure logic can be heard ringing through. For Alberti, it is fundamental: "Building consists in six Things, which are these: The Region, the Seat or Platform, the Compartition, the Walling, the Covering and the Apertures" (28). The first two at least—region and building site—cannot be logically justified. Architecture is related to what has come before it; this is joined by logic. It must fulfill the demands of both.

Program and plan are a great part of architecture—but they are certainly not everything. Architecture is grounded in its social, built, and temporal environment—it is stimulated by confrontations with them, and unfolds within this field of vibrant interaction. Bert Brecht, partial to the central planning school of thought, summed it up in his later days thus: "Go make yourself a plan! And be a shining light! Then make yourself a second plan, for neither will come right. But for this life..." Architecture, beholden to life, should renounce all lessening.

Program and Typology

Sylvain Malfroy

6

Preface

During a stay in Paris in the early 1990s, one day I thought I'd try my luck at buying tickets for that evening's performance at the Palais Garnier. On the program that night was the ballet pantomime *La Sylphide*. The box office informed me that tickets were still available, but only for seats with an obstructed view of the stage. Would that be all right with me? I declined; and as a result, will not be able to report about my first-hand experience of that concert hall. However, this anecdote makes for an interesting starting point for thinking about the relationship between program and building typology. Obviously, the idea of theater seating without a clear view of the stage bears all the signs of a logical contradiction, unless the theater in question belongs to a type in which a view of the stage is not a defining characteristic. In fact, typologically speaking, that opera house, which was designed by Charles Garnier for Napoleon III and built from 1862 to 1874, is a hybrid between "perspective theater", where the audience is mainly focused on the action on stage, and the *Selbstdarstellungsarena*, arenas of self-exhibition, where the attendees primarily wish to present themselves. By definition, a direct view of the stage belongs to the perspective theater, but it is not obligatory in the self-exhibition type of theater, in which the reciprocal visibility of seats has priority. Approximately one quarter of the seats in the Palais Garnier, that is, 500 out of 1991, are classified as *aveugles* (blind)![1]

In 1982, when President François Mitterrand decided to celebrate the bicentennial anniversary of the French Revolution on 14 July 1989 with the opening of a new popular opera house on Bastille Square, the building committee aimed to democratize the sight lines and disentangle the building types that intersect

[1] Gérard Charlet: *L'opéra de la Bastille, gènese et réalisation*, Electa/Moniteur, Milan/Paris, 1989, p. 25.

in the Palais Garnier, detracting from one another. In addition, the stage machinery had to be adapted to suit the working conditions of a modern theater tasked to provide a variety of programs affordably and in quick succession. The Bastille Opera was to become the "Beaubourg of lyric art". The geometrical arrangement of the new opera house, with its front-view rows of seating and steep balconies, comes a bit closer to the ideal of the pure perspective theater. However, many operagoers complain that this 2,700-seat hall is too big. The demand for evenly distributed visual and listening conditions in large halls remains a difficult challenge for architects to this day. Thus, the evolution of the theater as a building type has certainly not reached its finale. Its institutional function will likely undergo further changes, and the range of floor plan and building section types used will be further differentiated in the future.

To broaden the statements made so far, I would like to try to position them on the conceptual map proposed by Bernard Leupen (TU Delft) at the beginning of *Design and Analysis* in 1997,[2] and taken up since then by other authors. Where should we situate the typological distinction between peep-show type theaters and self-exhibition arenas? The roughly circular shape of the arena and its many vantage points that are bundled into a fan-shape in the design of the perspective theater seem to render the subject solely a matter of *geometry*. But this framework is too narrow to fit the generic concept of the "self-exhibition theater". Beyond the formal and geometrical relationships between the stage and the audience, the sociological dimension of this function is addressed at the same time. If we simply relegated this concept to Leupen's notion of the vessel of "society", it would lose some of its typifying power. The range of theater types is rooted not only in the variety of design principles for floor plans and sections, but also in the scope of purposes for which theaters are built. When President Mitterrand and Jack Lang, his Minister of Culture, called for a new type of state opera, they were determined to find an alternative to the Palais Garnier,

[2] Bernard Leupen, Christoph Grafe, Nicola Körnig, Mark Lampe, Peter de Zeeuw: *Design and Analysis*, 010 Publishers, Rotterdam, 1997, p. 17.

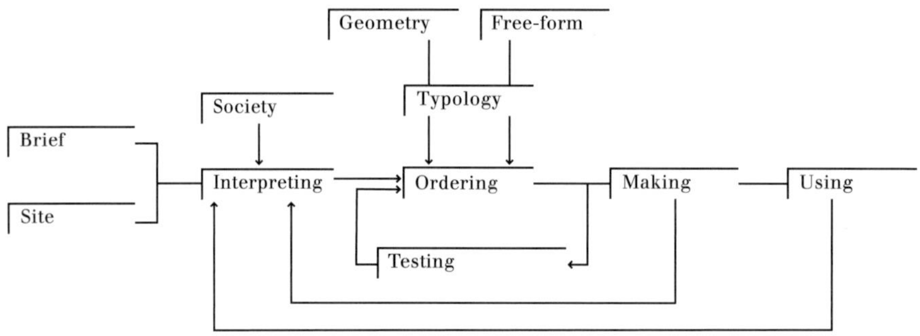

Bernard Leupen's diagram of the design process (Leupen 1997, p. 17,)
The program (or brief), which initiates the design process, is presented alongside the building site. Typology is solely defined as the formal and geometric instruments used to solve a design problem. The feedback loops indicate a method of trial and error. In this sense, Leupen's understanding of the design process may be characterized as extremely pragmatic or empirical.

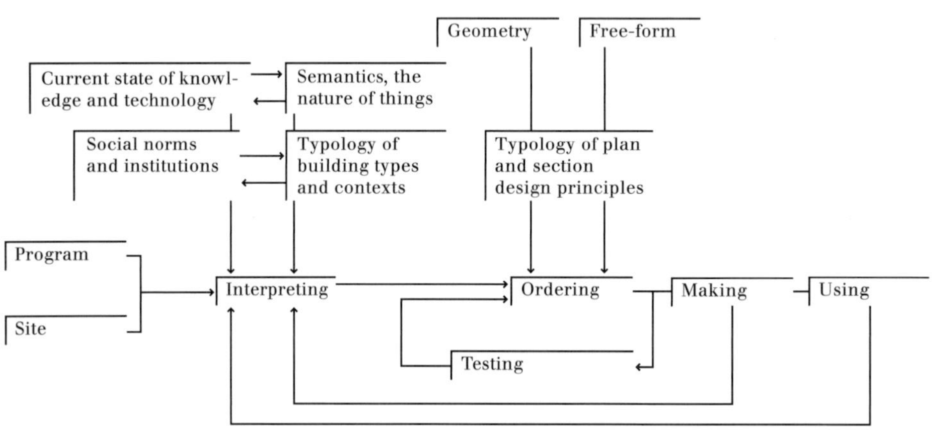

Revised version of Bernard Leupen's concept of the design process
A typology of building types and contexts is added to distill a coherent functional definition of the future building from the diversity of the components and qualities listed in the program (i.e., *what purpose* should the building serve *well*?), and to precisely identify the possibilities and needs inherent to the given situation (i.e., what *can* or *must* be done on this site?). The connection to semantics and ontology ("the nature of things") indicates that the program may be derived not only in terms of client demands and the constraints of society, but also according to the requirements of the intended goal and the specific nature of the site (i. e., what does it mean for a building *of this kind* or *of any kind* to impact a *specific* place?). In this sense, the revisions I suggest guide Leupen's diagram closer towards realism.

a venerable building to be sure, but one stuck in the Second Empire. We must adapt Leupen's diagram in a way that in addition to the geometrical transformation, such changes in social function (from the self-exhibition arena of the elite to popular opera) become typologically conceivable. Admittedly, builders, architects, and the public are not the only protagonists of theater design. Innovative theaters are also a means of opening the stage up to creative opportunities. What is central here is not audience demand, or the agenda of the public commission, but the ability of the stage performers themselves to go beyond the familiar repertoire to access the dormant potential of the theater arts. "Experimental theater" is probably the generic term that Jack Lang and the Bastille Opera building committee had in mind when they spoke of a "Beaubourg of lyric art". Here again, we need to make room in Leupen's diagram for designating the purposes and parameters that arise from an in-depth study of the "nature of the thing" itself: part of the answer to the question of what it means for a building to be the best opera house in the world surely lies in the critical discovery of what limits or distorts operatic art today and prevents it from arousing renewed interest as a living art form. Ultimately, an explicitly stated typology of urban design spaces is still missing in Leupen's overview of architectural areas of expertise. For not every building program is compatible with every piece of property. The new State Opera did not come to Bastille Square solely because the socialist President Mitterrand wanted to link it symbolically to that famous site of the French Revolution. The new cultural institution could only be built there after numerous locations were exhaustively compared, and after it was shown that the existing urban fabric and the available transportation infrastructure were suitable for grafting, and could be elevated to a new dynamic through this operation.

At first glance, the habit of mind that says that to fulfill a desire for a building, a person simply retains the services of a specialist in design seems consistent with sound judgment; however, it reduces architecture to a purely administrative role, separates the form-finding process from many critical parameters, and misses precisely that core advisory activity that distinguishes the independent practice of architecture with a corresponding professional ethos. What really differentiates architecture from the building trades? Architecture may be placed on a par with medicine, finance, law, and many other self-employed professions because it is practiced on the basis of a relationship of trust. Clients do not simply entrust architects with their desire to build in the expectation that it will be executed unaltered, but so that it will be handled appropriately and advantageously. Clients take on personal risk in the construction process; they do not have a complete understanding of their own interests, and they rely on the prudent advice of the expert. Now, how do architects demonstrate the competence needed to earn that trust? Certainly not by merely acting as artistic virtuosos who use client commissions to make a name for themselves. The bond of trust between client and architect can only flourish if the professional can demonstrate at the start an understanding of what a building commission on a given site entails, before taking the time to discuss the alternatives.

In greater depth

In Sections 1.1 and 1.2, I will explain how the identity of a building is composed of content (programmatic) and formal-spatial characteristics. I underscore the complementary nature of linguistic and formal definitions. In Section 2, I portray the architect as an interpreter of a given set of circumstances, usually consulted because of the ability to state, and provide verifiable reasoning to support, what might be done, or possibly should not be done at all. Section 3 focuses on the architectural realization of programmatic prerequisites. Programmatic requirements may be implemented in various ways and do not have to result in the design of a self-contained part of a work of architecture every time, following the dictate of "form follows function". Using the example of Adolf Loos' single-family houses, I show that the functional requirement of "suitability for home concerts" was not necessarily realized in the form of a specific room type (music room), but by a well thought-out system of circulation (interconnectable rooms). In Section 4, I return to the linguistic designation or description of the settings that the client and the designing architect evolve together. I believe that the relevant designation of what takes place should be asserted based on differentiated typologies (classification systems). Typologies of urban design, of building classifications, and of formal and geometric ordering patterns help us to understand things and relationships as they really are, and as they actually behave. In Section 5, I shift the focus to innovative typological solutions and the ways and means of recognizing them. In Section 6, I examine the prerequisites to be fulfilled when there is demand for something from a particular class of building. What you do matters, not what you say! In Section 7, I conclude this series of explorations by highlighting what the collective programming of public building projects has come to signify. I will contrast the mostly capricious negotiation of programmatic content against the background of power relations with the collective discovery of the genuine possibilities that are present in the nature of things.

6

1 *How words become spaces*

1.1 *Program as a sub-definition of the building project*

The word *program* basically refers to something written (from Greek, *gramma:* the alphabetic character, the written letter, the list, the writ) and to the initial phase of a procedure (*pro:* first, in advance) that is intended to provide or bring about something. In architecture and planning, a "program" is a linguistic reference to an object or a physical state that at the outset has no concrete form in space, but is to be determined through collaborative work. What the program lacks is a clear idea of the financial, technical, formal, and structural means necessary for the successful realization of the building project. As such, it has an essentially abstract nature that ceases to exist once it is spatially and physically realized. Together with the architectural design drawings and the detailed construction specifications, the program provides a complete definition of the planned building in terms of its desired spatial disposition. It remains a "partial definition"[3] until this synthesis of all information is present. Creating a program is a dynamic process that generally occurs in steps or iterations. Depending on the type of client and the contracting process, a certain degree of vagueness can be tolerated or even desired in the programmatic prerequisites until the phases of planning and design are completed.

[3] Nelson Goodman (3.1, 3.2) places architecture in which the concept and the completion of the work are not done by the same person in the category of "allographic arts". Allographic art can only be correctly executed if an explicit definition of the work is available. Goodman speaks then of notation. It is unusual to view the client as a co-creator or co-author of a work, although they own the created building program, the notation of the work.

3.1 Nelson Goodman: *Languages of Art*, Oxford University Press, 1969, Chapter 4.

3.2 Remei Capdevila-Werning: *Goodman for Architects,* Routledge, Abingdon/New York, 2014, Chapter 4.

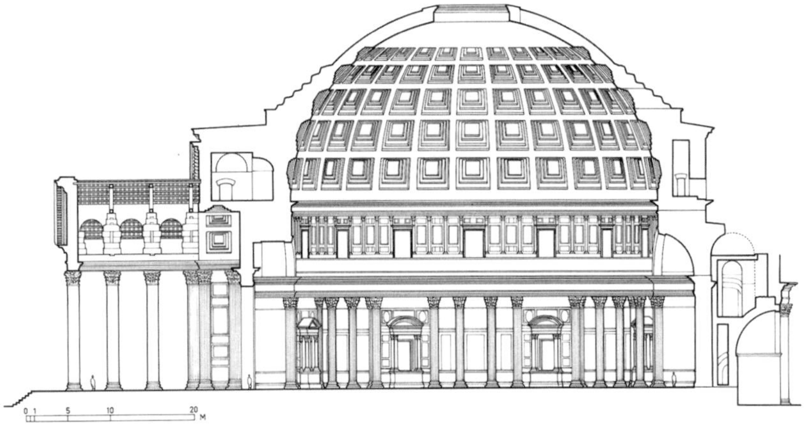

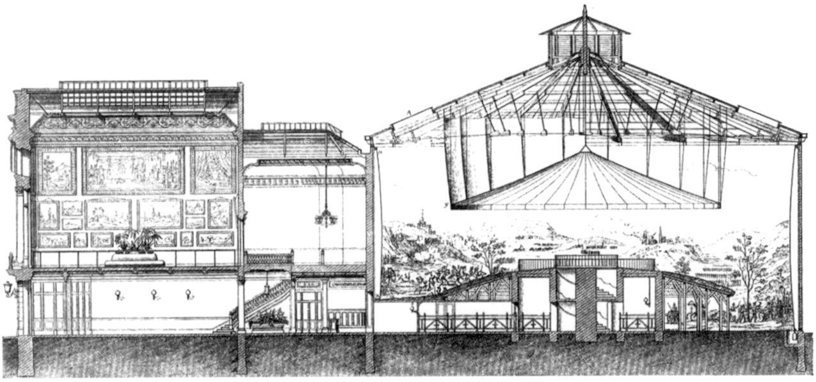

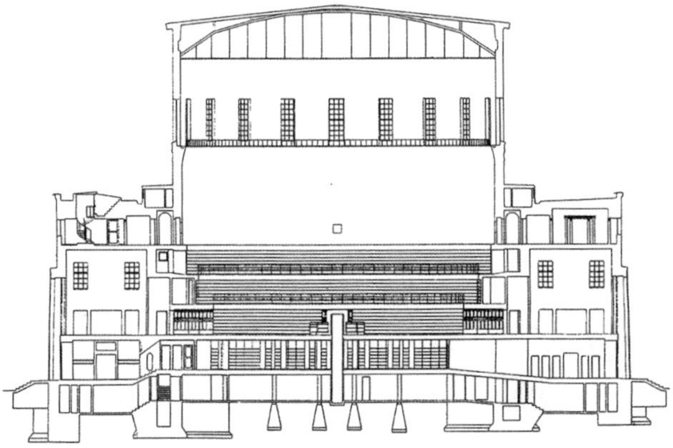

1.2 Functional and formal spatial typologies
The formal spatial typology of the Rotunda is compatible with a wide array of uses and not necessarily bound to any one specific program. The Pantheon in Rome has been used as a sacred space uninterrupted to this very day; the Panorama français in Paris was crated in 1881 as an illusion machine, but was converted to a circus as early as 1886; Asplund's library in Stockholm has been in operation with the same use since 1928.

Sources:
1) Drawing by José Conesa, from Henri Stierlin, *Hadrien et l'architecture romaine*, Fribourg (CH), Office du Livre, 1984
2) *Revue générale de l'architecture et des travaux publics*, Paris, 1882
3) Published project plan (1928), Stockholm City Library 1998

1.2 *Functional and spatial-formal typologies*

The sub-definition of the program requires elaboration. However, two possible usages of the term *building type* must be distinguished. As the program, being a *sub-definition* of the future project, contains no form or space determinants (these are the *unknowns,* yet to be determined by the designer), the building type, as described in the program, is not at all fixed. However, it is always at least functionally determined. Say a client wants a new "theater", a "school", or an "apartment building": These are classes of buildings, or building types. After the completion of the architectural design process, a building of a particular type is also present. In this case, however, the identifying features defined by the type acquire formal and spatial qualities: "theater *all'italiana*", "pavilion school", "apartment tower", and so on. Functional, formal, and spatial building types must not be linked to one another too hastily. This avoids creating programs that are merely stereotypical translations of form, which then harden into conventions. Programmatic goals may be achieved with a wide variety of formal and spatial solutions. Conversely, formal and spatial ordering patterns are applied to a wide variety of usage requirements (see p. 293). Large vaulted halls and courtyard plans are just as functionally indeterminate as housing or education are independent of fixed spatial organizational schemas.[4] The value added by the cultural contribution of a work of architecture stems precisely from the fact that, on the one hand, it always discovers new possibilities for a relatively narrow number of spatial ordering patterns. And on the other hand, it shows that the most perfect kind of artifacts we would like to find in a perfect state in our built environment may only be improved upon because they are not bound to any fixed forms.[5]

[4] Philip Steadman, *Building Types and Built Forms*, Matador, Kibworth Beauchamp, 2014.

Sylvain Malfroy, "Book Review: Building Types and Built Forms by Philip Steadman", *Urban Morphology*, 2016, 20(2), pp. 181–183.

[5] Robert Sokolowski: *Phenomenology of the Human Person*, Cambridge University Press, 2008, pp. 108–116.

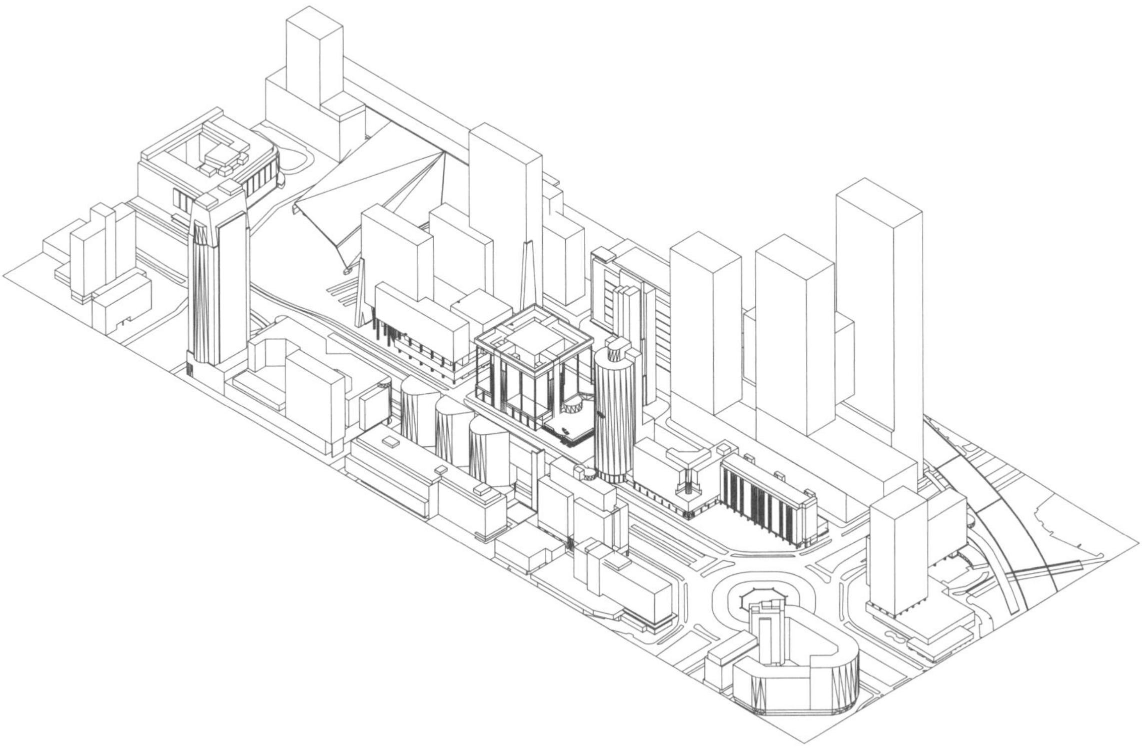

2.1 Investors without a use concept

Development project for a high-rise complex on Weena Boulevard, Rotterdam, Kaan Architecten, 2000–2005.
Volumetric study for a highly flexible, mixed-use project on a 1.3-hectare site with approximately 240,000 square meters of floor area

Source: © KAAN Architecten

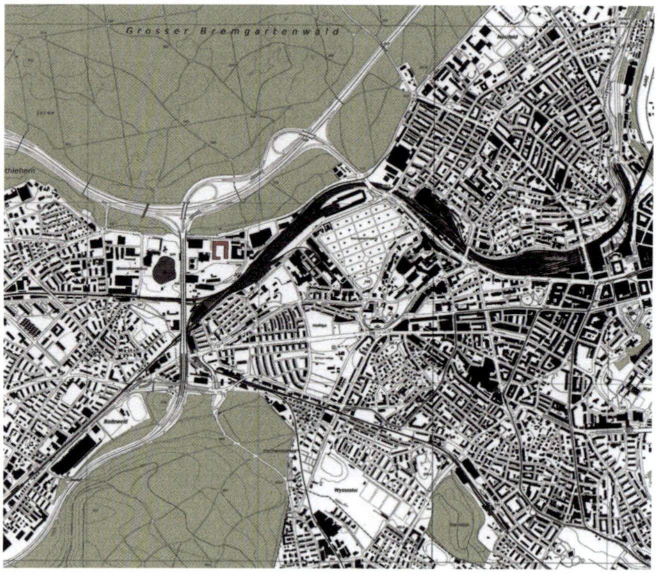

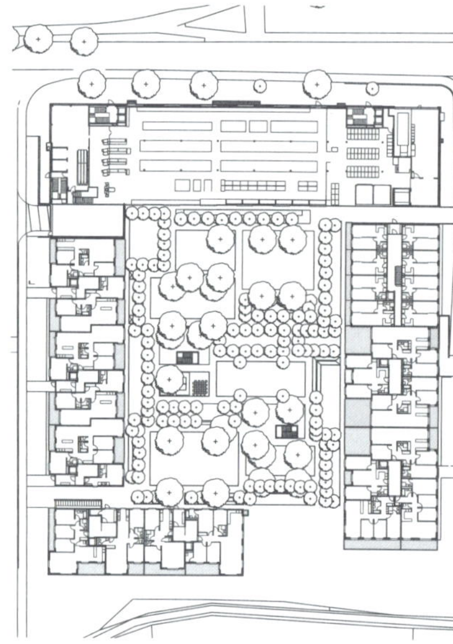

2.1 Investors without a use concept

ARK 143 (in red), residential/office/retail complex, Murtenstrasse 143, Bern, Ueli Zbinden, Architect, Zurich, 2009–2013; Bercor AG, Bern, investor.

As is typical with a project for real estate investors, the programmatic components of the building complex closely correspond to the site's features. For instance, its proximity to the university (in the upper right quadrant of the plan) suggested the inclusion of 52 student housing units, while 300 parking spaces are provided with the adjacent highway ramps in mind. A rooftop restaurant, a fitness center, and luxury penthouse apartments make the best of the beautiful views of the Alps. The fact that the project was designed as a pioneer of a public strategy to convert abandoned commercial property in a barely inhabited area (Weyermannshaus-Ost) basically led to a strong mix of uses and dwelling types. The intent was to cover the broadest possible demand, ensure the functional independence of the complex, and at the same time reduce the investment risk. The difficult challenges were turned into positive assets by promoting the project with the image of an "ark", asking future users and inhabitants of the complex to imagine themselves as small-scale trailblazers of an urban renaissance.

Size of property: 12,438 m^2, BGF 30,600 m^2 gross floor area

Sources: Photos by Laura Egger, Zurich; drawings by the office of Prof. Ueli Zbinden, Zurich

The program and the client

In principle, a single person always stands "behind" a program, whether they are a natural person (Ms. or Mr. X), or a legal entity (a municipality, a church, a cooperative, a company, or a club). This person desires something, has some sort of intention, is pursuing a goal, and expects to manifest an intention. Now, it may turn out that clients are eager to build, but lack clear ideas about the uses they would like to accommodate on their property.

.1 *Investors without a use concept*

In a lecture at the Delft University of Technology in October 2012, the Dutch architect Kees Kaan[6] reported about such a case. He had been commissioned with the design of a project for a high-rise complex with approximately 240,000 square meters of floor space on a 1.3-hectare piece of property on Weena Boulevard, near the new central rail station in Rotterdam, the function of which the client—a consortium of banks, real estate developers, and general contractors—had no concept at all at the outset. The project initially included a lavish Las Vegas-style casino, which was later dropped. Kaan was then told to design a convention center with a large public event hall, but it was clear that everything could change at any moment. This is a good example of a situation where the key to a deeper understanding of the building program is not "in the head" of the client, but is "external" to it, in the features and potential of a development site. Depending on the type of client, the objective "program" can consist of the personal and subjectively-defined needs of a single person, or the use anticipated by market demand, whose impersonal pattern and behavior must first be studied carefully.[7]

At the conclusion of this essay, we will return to the necessity of handling the programming process differently for different types of clients.

[6] Kees Kaan, Manuela Triggianese, (2014), "Complex projects: Design or planning?", in Roberto Cavallo, Susanne Kamossa, Nicola Marzot et al (eds.): *New Urban Configurations*, Delft University of Technology, Faculty of Architecture and the Built Environment, IOS Press, Amsterdam, 2014, pp. 67–78.

[7] Gabriele Bobka, Jürgen Simon (eds.): *Handbuch Immobilienbewertung in internationalen Märkten*, Bundesanzeiger Verlag, Cologne, 2013.

Hanspeter Gondring, Thomas Wagner: *Real Estate Asset Management. Handbuch für Studium und Praxis*, Vahlen, Munich, 2010.

2.2 *Explaining reasons vs. understanding objectives*

This topic, discussed here only in passing, is part of philosophical action theory. In the context of the current discussion, it is of interest to know whether the "program" is to be derived purely from the qualities and potential of the given circumstances, or from the various ideas about uses that belong to a group of people. In the first instance, the entire process of development, from the acquisition of land to the completion of a building, wants to be *explained* as a causal chain with objectively grounded reasons and site-specific causes.[8] In the second instance, the same process is grasped intentionally; that is, traced back to the meaning-laden intentions of subjects with agency, and thus wants to be understood in this way. Architecture necessitates a methodological pluralism, because architectural interventions express both the motivations of subjects with agency and the framing conditions of specific situations.[9] Hermann Schmitz argues that programs always germinate in the subjective sphere, and considers the need to objectify them, at least in part, as an indication of maturation.[10]

3 *The program as a challenge to the professional expertise of the architect*

The fact that the program is part of the building contract could easily lead to the false assumption that the task of the designing architect consists of "carrying out" the program without any added conceptual value, i.e. "to implement" it in physical built form. But nothing is more contentious than to argue that the more exacting and stringent the program, the more efficiently the architect can do the job. There is great potential for optimization in the designer's analysis of the program, provided the functional requirements to be met are not already itemized in an exhaustive and binding "room schedule" with defined allocations, fixed dimensions, and interrelationships.

8 Sylvain Malfroy: *L'approche morphologique de la ville et du territoire / Die morphologische Betrachtungsweise von Stadt und Territorium*, ETH, Department of the History of Urban Development, Zurich, 1986.

Karl Kropf, Sylvain Malfroy, "What is urban morphology supposed to be about?: Specialization and the growth of a discipline" in *Urban Morphology*, Iss. 17, October 2013, 2, pp. 128–131.

Sylvain Malfroy, Frank Zierau, "Stadtquartiere vom Webstuhl – Wie textile Metaphern ab 1950 die Komplexit.t der Stadt veranschaulichen", in Sophie Wolfrum and Winfried Nerdinger (eds.): *Multiple City, Stadtkonzepte*, 1908–2008, Jovis, Berlin, 2008, pp. 77–82.

Giancarlo Cataldi (ed.): *Saverio Muratori architetto (Modena 1910 – Roma 1973) a cento anni dalla nascita: atti del convegno itinerante*, Aión, Florence, 2013.

Urban Morphology, Journal of the International Seminar on Urban Form, Birmingham, 1997, *www.urbanform.org/online_public/*

9 Paul Ricoeur, "Expliquer et comprendre", in *Du texte à l'action. Essais d'herméneutique*, II, Seuil, Paris, 1986, pp. 161–182.

Christoph Horn, Guido Löhrer, (eds.): *Gründe und Zwecke. Texte zur aktuellen Handlungstheorie*, Suhrkamp, Frankfurt am Main, 2010.

Edward Jonathan Lowe: *Personal Agency. the Metaphysics of Mind and Action*, Oxford University Press, 2008.

10 Hermann Schmitz: *Der unerschöpfliche Gegenstand, Grundzüge der Philosophie*, Bouvier, Bonn, 1990, p. 6 f. and passim.

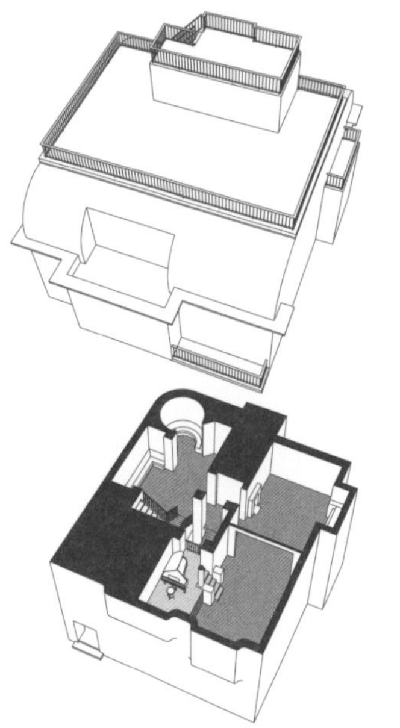

3.1 Loos' "Raumplan" as a response to programmatic demands

Villa for Hilda and Karl Strasser-Fischer, Vienna, by architect Adolf Loos, 1918–19
Axonometric view. The music room, in the southeastern corner, adjoins the dining room to the north. The piano alcove expands the space westward and is also in line with the staircase and diagonal to the salon.

Drawings: Saikal Zhunushova, Dipl. architect ZHAW, Winterthur

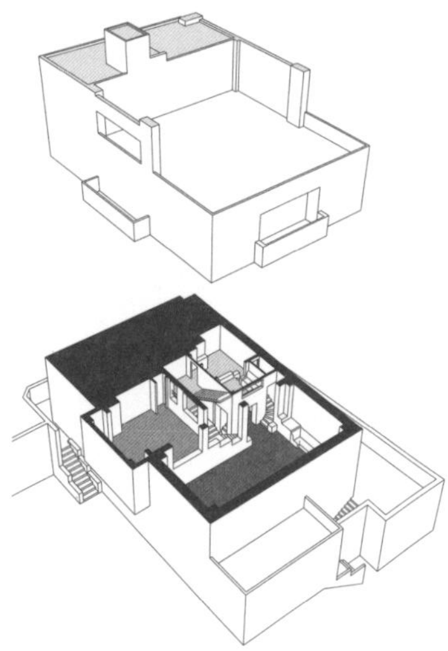

3.1 Loos' "Raumplan" as a response to programmatic demands

Villa for Frantisek and Milada Müller-Kratka, Prague, by architect Adolf Loos, 1928–30
The large salon is not specifically designated as a music room in the original plans, but its spacious layout suggests that the elaborate receptions held at the Haus Müller were arranged with music in mind. The dining room to the west opens out to the "grand salon", while towards the east, the "ladies' salon", to where the lady of the house liked to retire to play her violin, maintains visual and acoustic contact with the goings-on in the main space thanks to its wide window.

Drawings: Saikal Zhunushova, Dipl. architect ZHAW, Winterthur

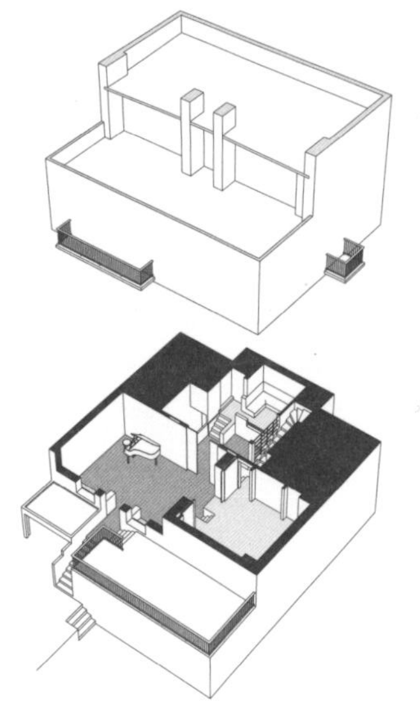

3.1 Loos' "Raumplan" as a response to programmatic demands

Villa for Hans and Hanny Moller-Wottitz, Vienna, by architect Adolf Loos, 1926–27
The patrons, themselves musicians (violin and cello), maintained close ties to the Vienna avant-garde music scene (Arnold Schönberg). The music room, in the southwest corner of the plan, opens in line with the slightly elevated dining room to the east, and connects to the hall diagonally through a pair of sliding double doors, with a reading niche on the outside wall to the north.

Drawings: Saikal Zhunushova, Dipl. architect ZHAW, Winterthur

.1 *Loos' Raumplan as a response to programmatic demands*

Let's take the series of private family homes designed by Adolf Loos: the Villa Steiner (1910), Villa Duschnitz (1915), Villa Strasser, Villa Rufer, and Villa Moller (1927) in Vienna, and the Villa Müller in Prague (1928).[11] All of these building programs—according to good old Austrian tradition—included the desire to be able to conduct regular private concerts for one's social circle. In contrast to upper-class villas, this problem had to be solved without creating a larger than average room designed exclusively for that type of social event. Instead, the programmatic demand had to be satisfied by temporarily joining together many smaller rooms, which are otherwise available for their normal functions during regular use. Thus, Adolf Loos did not respond to the functional demand of the ability to conduct private concerts with a separate music room (i. e., a specific and wholly self-contained space), but rather with a flexible interconnectivity of both axial and diagonal views through the dining and living rooms, the piano alcove, the entry hall, the reading niche, and all sorts of secondary rooms (individual uses as an integral part of the overall concept of the house). Viewed independently of such programmatic contexts, Loos' famous *Raumplan*—the considered ordering and size of interior spaces based on function—will be misunderstood as a purely formal gesture.[12] This method of spatial composition, initially developed for private houses, was aimed at optimizing the proportions and functional synergies among the various rooms of a house.

[11] Ralf Bock (2009), *Adolf Loos: Leben und Werke, 1870–1933,* DVA, Munich.

[12] Max Risselada (ed.): *Raumplan versus plan libre: Adolf Loos / Le Corbusier,* 010 Publishers, Rotterdam, 2008.

.2 *Detachable vs. non-detachable parts*

The distinction between "detachable parts" and "undetachable parts or moments" stems from Edmund Husserl.[13] This conceptualization is particularly useful for the analysis of architectural objects as composed entities, as it makes it possible to ground such elusive elements as "space" and "atmosphere". Space is never an independent part of a whole, but always exists as a "moment" that is a function of other "parts" (building materials, structural members) and "moments" (light, color, dimensions, and proportions). Loos transforms the traditional

[13] Edmund Husserl (1900–01), *Logische Untersuchungen,* Meiner (student's edition), Hamburg, 2009, Vol. 2, Part 3.

Robert Sokolowski: *Husserlian Meditations,* Northwestern University Press, Evanston, 1974, pp. 8–17.

David Woodruff Smith: *Husserl,* Routledge, London, New York, 2013, pp. 51–54, 145–147.

music room conceived as a "detachable" part of the house into a "moment" of the floor plan. Not all demands in a building program can be systematically resolved with the design of "detachable parts". The character of individual rooms and the entire building's appearance (the dignity of the public institution, the intimacy of a private room) can only be worked out in the design as "moments" of other elements.[14]

3.3 *The convergence of the best solution "for someone", and the best solution "per se"*

Adolf Loos' conduct towards his client was professional to the extent that he did not limit himself to merely carrying out their wishes.[15] Instead, he possessed the ability to separate these wishes from their conventional spatial forms and satisfy them with an innovative solution that best suited their lifestyle and individual identity. Rather than taking on the subjective perspective of the client, the architect analyzed the functional typology of the "private concert" for its fundamental characteristics, liberated it from its encrusted, time-worn manifestations of turn-of-the-century Vienna, and took it to a new spatial and formal topology. This ability to distinguish the essential from the secondary in a design program[16] is of critical importance to the discipline of architecture, as this enables it to claim its rightful place among the humanities. Architecture is equally concerned with truth (from the Greek *aletheia*, or disclosure; the revelation of reality). It does not invent its objects out of pure imagination, but rather discovers real possibilities by critically examining the existing and the ordinary.

[14] The relationships of the parts to the whole are the object of study in mereology, a branch of logic that developed around 1900 from a critique of set theory. It is currently growing in conjunction with artificial intelligence and information technology, and contains many fruitful methodological propositions for architecture theory and design methodology (14.1).

14.1 Verity Harte: *Plato on Parts and Wholes. The Metaphysics of Structure*, Oxford University Press, 2002.

Hans Burkhardt: *Handbook of Mereology*, Philosophia, Munich, 2017.

Daniel Köhler: *The Mereological City: A reading of the works of Ludwig Hilberseimer*, Transcript, Bielefeld, 2016.

Kathrin Koslicki: *The Structure of Objects*, Oxford University Press, 2008.

Sylvain Malfroy (2014), "L'espace et la ville comme ‹moments› du projet d'architecture" in Anne-Marie Châtelet, Michael Denès, Cristiana Mazzoni (eds.): *La ville parfaitement imparfaite*, La Commune, Paris, 2014, pp. 245–259.

Ariel Merav: *Whole Sums and Unities*, Kluwer, Dordrecht, Boston, London, 2003.

[15] Robert Sokolowski (1991), "The Fiduciary Relationship and the Nature of Professions", in Edmund D. Pellegrino, Robert M. Veatch, John P. Langan (eds.): *Ethics, Trust and the Professions*, Georgetown University Press, Washington, 1991, pp. 23–43.

[16] Robert Sokolowski: *Presence and Absence. A Philosophical Investigation of Language and Being*, Indiana University Press, Bloomington, 1978, pp. 130–143.

Robert Sokolowski: *A Philosophical Investigation of Language and Being*, Indiana University Press, Bloomington, 2008, pp. 99–135

6

4 *The program and conversational determination of the goal of action*

Programs are expressed in words. At the same time, we might be tempted to neglect the interpersonal moment of interaction in which the words are first invested with meaning. Removed from ongoing communication, the isolated reflection fixes on the supposedly self-contained reference of the words to things in the world. This results in such questions as: "What does a hospital even look like?" or "What is the basic appearance of a cooperative housing estate?" in a desperate attempt to reach a stable solution by means of a universal definition of the task of design. There are no final answers to such questions, as the words only actually serve the opposite purpose, of bringing things into the conversation so that their qualities can be agreed upon.[17]

[17] Robert Sokolowski: *Pictures, Quotations, and Distinctions, Fourteen Essays in Phenomenology*, University of Notre Dame Press, 1992, pp. 187–209.

4.1 *Pushing past the latest facts towards the deeper nature of things*

"Why aren't contemporary hospitals built the way they were up to the 1930s anymore, on isolated sites at the edge of town, with wonderful sunlight steaming in?" Because in most cases, ambulatory care is now the rule, claimed an associate, and the easy accessibility of a central location now outweighs other considerations in selecting sites. Once advanced, a fact can then be checked by other participants in the discussion and included in their conclusion as to whether a hygienic location with optimal sun exposure belongs to the essential features of a hospital or is merely among those that are time-bound.

"Why does cooperative housing no longer look much different than private and speculative housing?" "Because housing cooperatives are no longer recruiting their members from among firmly constituted professional groups and other social formations with common denominators as they once did, and therefore there is no longer a need for a common symbolic identifying image!" Once again, a verifiable fact is circulated that allows us to discuss the nature and historically conditioned appearance of cooperative housing, and at the same time take note of recent trends in cooperative housing design. Inserting such references into the discussion focuses our attention on what something can become, on the possibilities of its design and differentiation, and on new formal, spatial, and other characteristics that it is able to take on. This process of clarification in which different modes of perception are compared, on one hand, and on the other, facts and causal relationships are studied, corresponds to a process of truth-finding (according to the phenomenological understanding). In the end, the veil lifts a bit further on a view of the part of reality occupying us, and we have good reason to assume that the factual situation is indeed the way it shows itself to us as a collective.

4.2 *Collectively tapping into the nature of architecture*

This realistic interpretation of the reference of words is not universally shared. An opposing view takes the position that language can only process conventional meanings, and does not allow for any reference to "the things themselves". That which is architecture is a purely institutional understanding. Without relevant and verifiable facts, that which today constitutes a hospital, a courthouse, a single-family home, a promising development site, would also be a pure matter of opinion. I would like to point out here, in reference to phenomenology, that everything that can be referred to by name has an intelligibility which can be interpreted, sharpened, and objectified in discussion. Such understandings may be reached more or less deeply, but are otherwise unavailable for free manipulation.[18] It may be difficult for us to provide a universal definition of architecture. But we need not puzzle for long over the question: "Why does an architect concerned with the ethics of the profession not simply refuse to 'execute' a program in the form in which it is given, without scrutinizing it?" "Because he or she is concerned about the *true* interests of the client, and does not want to provide them

[18] Robert Sokolowski, "Discovery and Obligation in Natural Law" (2010), in Holger Zaborowski (ed.): *Natural Moral Law in Contemporary Society*, Catholic University of America Press, Washington, D.C., 2010, pp. 24–42.

with whatever seems good, but rather what is *genuinely* relevant in the given situation, in light of the known standards, the resources available, and the actual possibilities flowing from them!"

5 *The identity of the work of architecture, its internal makeup, and its relation to context*

Every time we describe a building, we cannot avoid robbing this single thing of its individuality and relating it to a general category of buildings by means of typological allocation.[19] "This theater" means the individual instantiation of the general building class of "theater" (this specific example of that type of building). Language cannot express bare particularity. If we ask such questions as: "Is this work of architecture functional?", "Is this building successful?", "Is this building perfectly completed?", and "How many buildings are there in this city?", we can only answer if we know *what* this building should be functioning as; *what* it should be good for; *at what point* might it be considered as a whole, and *what type* of buildings should be counted in the city.

Modern logic has created the notion of "sortals" to refer to those names that help us distinguish, count, or investigate the identity of things: Is this *theater* the same as that one? For two structures to be identical, they must contain the same elements. That is to say, they must have the same composition. For example, a theater that does not have a foyer, or a courthouse without holding cells, cannot be the same as a theater with a foyer, or a courthouse with detention facilities. We note that the program and type

[19] Edward Jonathan Lowe: *More Kinds of Being. A Further Study of Individuation, Identity, and the Logic of Sortal Terms*, Wiley-Blackwell, 2009.

Eddy M. Zemach, "No Identification Without Evaluation" (1986), in: *Types. Essays in Metaphysics*, Leiden, Brill, 1992, pp. 111–126.

Christian Kanzian: *Ding – Substanz – Person. Ein Alltagsontologie*, Ontos, Frankfurt am Main, 2009.

Johannes Hübner: *Komplexe Substanzen*, De Gruyter, Berlin, 2007.

Amie L. Thomasson, "Public Artifacts, Intentions, and Norms" (2014), in Maarten Franssen, Peter Koos, Thomas A. C. Reydon, Piete E. Vermaas, (eds.): *Artefact Kinds. Ontology and the Human-Made World*, Cham, Springer, Heidelberg, New York, Dordrecht, London, 2014, pp. 45–62.

are closely connected when the program lists precisely those diverse elements, qualities, and internal relationships that make up the identity of the built work, and justify its affiliation to a type (and here I am using "type" as synonymous with sortal).

5.1 *Typological differentiation as a means of substantiating programmatic intent*

When a client expresses a wish: "I really want a building of this type, except with such and such adjustments," the question arises as to whether those adjustments *significantly* or merely superficially change the composition that forms the basic identity of the given type. If the changes do indeed significantly affect the type of the building, we will have to consider how to name the new genus (the new type, or the sortal), which logically constrains the existing *differentia specifica.* Otherwise, we only have to deal with a minor variation that does not justify modifying the existing categorization. In terms of design, this means that the one program conforms to the typological classifications applicable in the construction industry and confines itself to reproducing what has so far stood the test. On the other hand, the non-standardized program seeks to produce not only "a new thing" (individual), but "a different kind" of thing.

A person who doesn't want something that already exists, but wants something that starts out only existing as words and is not yet materialized in space, is pursuing a specific intention. He or she has something in mind. I would like to call these creative desires, plans, or intentions, as they are called, *programs in the broader sense.*[20] I would like to show that creative wishes

[20] In a narrower sense, a building program is a list of usable areas that describes their individual desired characteristics and interrelationships. However, a program, or "programmatic text", can also be something like an ideological manifesto. A political party is always working on its "program", and a group of artists is likewise constituted by a common "program" (20.1).

20.1 Ulrich Conrads: *Programme und Manifeste zur Architektur des 20. Jahrhunderts,* Ullstein (Serie Bauwelt Fundamente 1), Berlin, 1964, Reprint Birkhäuser, Basel, 2001.

of whatever nature (changes in lifestyle and habits, social relations in the city, child-rearing in schools, behavior in heavy traffic, etc.) become manifest only when they act on the composition of things and thus on their typological differentiation. Conversely (from the perspective of the recipient), programmatic intentions may be identified at different scales in terms of whether something in the composition of existing types has been modified.

5.2 *A festival hall is not an opera house—typological distinction signifies programmatic intent*

Let's take a look at a famous wood engraving that was published anonymously in the German illustrated magazine *Die Gartenlaube* in 1873, which is modeled on a painting by Louis Santer titled *The Wagner Theater in Bayreuth after its Completion* (see p. 310). At that time, although the topping-out ceremony had taken place in October, construction was by no means finished, and Richard Wagner and his supporters were more desperate than ever for funding. This idealized image fulfilled a clear advertising goal in the media, which is why it interests us so much. Santer's picture did not depict a finished state, but a programmatic preview of what would finally take built form in the summer of 1876.[21]

It has to do with the composition of the building: Should the building's park-like forecourt be regarded as an integral part of the project, or be downgraded to a contextual element? In other words, is the self-contained whole of the building simply contained in the park as a contextual vessel, or is the park part of the concept and composition of the building?

Those who regard the building as a self-contained entity regard Santer's image as a conventional "opera house" looking somewhat out of place in a park. However, all other viewers who recognize the park as an integral part of the building can identify the actual building type of "festival hall" (*Festspielhaus*)

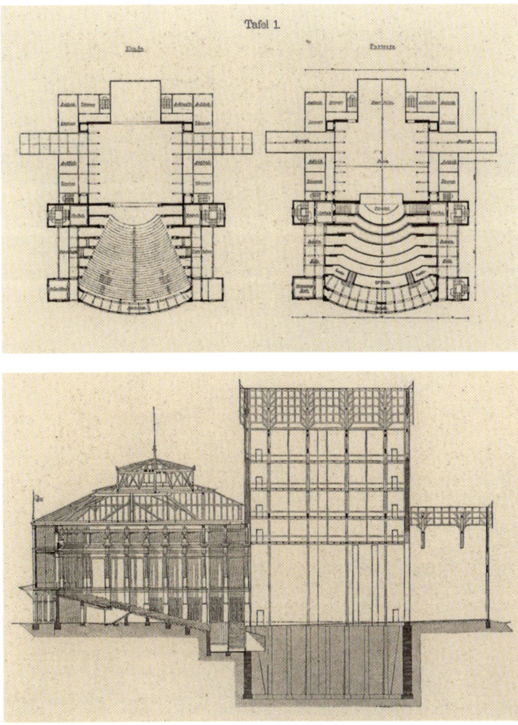

5.2 A festival hall is not an opera house
Floor plans and longitudinal section of Richard Wagner's Festspielhaus, Otto Brückwald, architect, 1873

Source: Richard Wagner: *Das Bühnenfestspielhaus zu Bayreuth: nebst einem Berichte über die Grundsteinlegung desselben*, Fritzsch, Leipzig, 1873

1 During his Zurich exile from 1849 to 1858, Richard Wagner worked on various projects aimed at the reform of the practice of musical theater production in Germany, which he published in a series of programmatic texts and open letters to his friends. He had two complementary concerns, one artistic and one political. On the one hand, he wanted to combine the relatively loose components of operatic art into an enchanting *Gesamtkunstwerk* (total work of art). On the other hand, he sought to promote the collective return to old Germanic myths (the Nibelungen) that shape identity by means of multi-day, artistically ambitious festivals based on an ancient model, and thus contribute to the emergence of a united German nation state.

Richard Wagner: *Das Bühnenfestspielhaus zu Bayreuth, nebst einem Bericht über die Grundsteinlegung desselben, mit sechs architektonischen Plänen*, Fritzsch, Leipzig, 1873, (http://dx.doi.org/10.3931/e-rara-713)

Matthias Theodor Vogt (1982), "Die Geburt des Festspielgedankens aus dem Geist der Bäderkultur" in Peter Csobadi, et al. (eds.): *Welttheater, Mysterienspiel, rituelles Theater*, Verlag Ursula Müller-Speiser, Anif/Salzburg, 1982, pp. 343–364.

Richard and Helen Leacroft: *Theatre and Playhouse: An Illustrated Survey of Theatre Building from Ancient Greece to the Present Day*, Methuen, London, New York, 1984.

Hans-Jürgen Fliedner: *Architektur und Erlebnis. Das Festspielhaus, Bayreuth*, Synästhesie Verlag, Coburg, 1999.

Patrick Carnegy: *Wagner and the Art of the Theater*, Yale University Press, New Haven, London, 2006.

Timothée Picard (ed.): *Dictionnaire encyclopédique Wagner*, Actes Sud, Arles, 2010.

5.2 A festival hall is not an opera house

The Wagner Theater in Bayreuth after its Completion, anonymous engraving emulating the oil painting by Louis Santer, *Die Gartenlaube,* 1873, Vol. 32, p. 515

The park is an integral part of the building and manifests Wagner's programmatic intentions for the *Festspiel* as a patriotic people's festival in direct contact with nature.

Source: https://de.wikipedia.org/wiki/Richard-Wagner-Festspielhaus#/media/File:Die_Gartenlaube_(1873)_b_515.jpg (public commons)

View of the Avenue de l'Opéra from the exterior balcony of the new opera house in Paris, by architect Charles Garnier, 1860–1875, engraving by Charles Nuitter, *Le nouvel opéra,* Hachette, Paris, 1875, p. 127

Much like the park for the Festspielhaus in Bayreuth, the Avenue de l'Opéra, planned by Baron Georges Eugène Haussmann, is an integral part of the new opera house in Paris and a key aid to the completion of the ambitious building program.

Source: Bibliothèque nationale de France

that Wagner envisaged from 1848 on and spent decades trying to bring about. The floor plan designed by the architect Otto Brückwald is sufficient indication that the attractively landscaped outdoor space replaces both the traditional foyer and the typically elaborate choreography of circulation in conventional public theaters. The audience is encouraged to spend intermissions outside. Wagner believed opera should be enjoyed in the immediate vicinity of the beauty of nature.

We may thus assert that unlike an expendable addition to theater architecture, this park is an *essential* feature that is *constitutive* of the identity of the festival hall. In this sense, as an integral part of the festival hall, the park embodies the *differentia specifica* that makes it possible to introduce the sub-category of "festival hall" within the more comprehensive building type of "theater architecture".

6 *Identity and normativity: What should a building be in order to be considered an instantiation of a particular type?*

The "festival hall" is not the only building type in which the connection to a park-like exterior space assumes a constitutive role. Let us consider, for example, the rich tradition of villa architecture and its widely branching and palatial typological lineage: the manor house, the Palladian villa, the bourgeois mansion, the suburban villa, the country farmhouse, the holiday villa by the sea or in the mountains, and so on.[22] To be recognized as a "villa", a building must meet certain essential identifying conditions. For example, such a building must be "freestanding" on the property, provide an "all-round view" of a "garden setting", and be dedicated to "personal use" (by owner and family). A villa whose garden has been completely paved over for a parking lot can by definition no longer be called a "villa". It has lost its typological identity and becomes something different from all things called "villa". Thus, the question to ask is, at what point does an instantiation of a certain type of building cease to belong to it and begin to embody a different identity by virtue of newly added qualities?

[22] James S. Ackerman: *The Villa: Form and Ideology of Country Houses,* Princeton University Press, Princeton, New Jersey, 1990.

6

6.2 "Urban villa" vs. "multi-family dwellings"

Redevelopment of Furglerstrasse, St. Gallen, commissioned by the Pensionskasse (government employee pension fund), by architect Dominik Uhrmeister, Berlin, 2005 (competition winner), in collaboration with Matti Ragaz Hitz Arch. Bern, 2012 (completion).

A programmed "urban villa" is not an "urban villa" *per se.* There is a critical threshold at which the excessively high density and maximized use of a land parcel are no longer compatible with the essential features of the building type. Building typology is not an "ontological free lunch"; rather, the identity and distinct qualities of individual building types are grounded in reality.

Source: Dominik Uhrmeister, Berlin

6.1 *The essence of a given type is legible only in its most perfect examples*

Aristotle once observed that generic terms contain something normative: an instantiation of a species, genus, or type is able to reveal the identity of the same to a *greater or lesser degree.* An apple of a given variety may combine the latter's properties (color, average size, taste, maturity, etc.) to a *varying degree.* A farmer knows at exactly which time of the harvest to pick which kind of fruit to be sent directly to the table for immediate consumption, which fruits to leave on the tree to ripen fully, which fruits of inferior quality to set aside for making juice and cider, and which ones belong in the compost. That is, inserted between the instantiation and the type (between the exemplar and the type exemplified) is a teleological dynamism, a purposeful straining towards excellence.[23] In other words, the set of individual specimens falling under a general genus or type can be hierarchized among themselves, according to their proximity to the perfect embodiment of the identity of that species. Most interesting of all is that the normativity of the generic term is internally validated: a knife is even more of a knife the sharper it is, because the ability to cut lies within the nature of a knife. The sharpness of the blade is an essential quality that belongs to the general class of knives, but among the many specimens of knives are blades that are sharp and some that are less sharp.

6.2 *A programmed "urban villa" is not an "urban villa" per se*

I would like to pose this series of questions regarding the normativity of the type in the example of the exhausted concept of "urban villa" and briefly discuss it in the context of the public controversy surrounding the Chrüzacker/Furglerstrasse redevelopment project in St. Gallen.[24] Does the redevelopment project really consist of "urban villas", or is the term deceptive? Is it sufficient to declare a building project an "urban villa", so that the facts are purely the result of agreement, or must the object possess certain essential features?

The "urban villa", a hybrid of urban and rural forms of dwelling, is a representation of a utopia at the architectural scale, in which the "Garden City" is immanent at the urban scale. It is a periodically recurring attempt to unite the expansiveness of the individual villa in a rural or suburban setting and the densely populated urban context, without having to put up with the inconvenience of large-scale housing complexes. The concept of the urban villa originates from a programmatic intention in the broader sense that is not so distant from that of the "festival hall". The 1984 International Building Exhibition in Berlin gave this architectural type renewed currency. The demand for urban villas in the housing market has been relatively strong since the 1990s. This housing type is especially favored

[23] Francis Slade (2000), "On the Ontological Priority of Ends And Its Relevance to the Narrative Arts" in Alice Ramos (ed.): *Beauty, Art, and the Polis*, American Maritain Association, Washington, D.C., pp. 58–69.

Robert Sokolowski (1981), "Knowing Natural Law", in ibid., 1992, pp. 277–291 (see footnote 17).

Robert Sokolowski (2004), "What is Natural Law. Human Purposes and Natural Ends" *The Thomist* 68, pp. 507–529.

Robert Sokolowski (2010), "Discovery and Obligation in Natural Law", in Zaborowski, pp. 24–43 (see footnote 18).

Robert Spaemann, Reinhard Löw: *Natürliche Ziele. Geschichte und Wiederentdeckung des telelogischen Denkens*, Klett-Cotta, Stuttgart, 2005.

[24] Sylvain Malfroy (2012), "Genese und Städtebau", in *Staufer & Hasler Architekten: Bundesverwaltungsgericht, bauen für die Justiz*, Niggli, Sulgen, pp. 18–43.

Dominik Uhrmeister: *Wohnüberbauung Furglerstrasse St. Gallen Schweiz*, www.d-uhrmeister.de/Broschuere.pdf

by members of the middle class who would like to own their own homes, but do not want to have to commute between city and country.

In 2004, the Pensionskasse, a civil servants' pension fund, of the canton of St. Gallen, sponsored a design competition for the redevelopment of the Chrüzacker estate, an area of roughly 1.5 hectares. In addition to the construction of residential units, the primary goal was increase the working capital ratio of the fund. The proceedings were coordinated with a competition for a new Federal Administrative Court building, as the Pensionskasse had sold part of its landholdings for that prestigious project. The immediate proximity to an institutional monument held the promise of attracting future buyers from among courthouse staff. Added to this was the elevated topography of the site, a sunny ridge with a beautiful view; its prior use as a seat of nobility; and the middle-class development east of the building site, which has been dominated by villas since the 1880s, peaking during the Jugendstil era. All of these factors made a redevelopment project with ten neoclassical "urban villas" seem logical.

6.3 *Calling things by their proper names*

As soon as the design of this residential complex was publicized, and even more so after the completion of its ten buildings with 129 residential units built atop an underground parking garage, a debate raged in the regional press and professional circles regarding the density of the district. In the opinion of the critics, there was an extreme disparity in the type and catchword of "urban villa" as advertised. The developer then withdrew that term from the media campaign marketing the housing complex, and replaced it with the more general term of "multi-family dwellings". The characteristics of the project as built were not fully consistent with the basic features of an urban villa: blocks five and six stories high, three flats per floor,and more than ten residential units per building, laid out with buildings spaced eleven meters apart, and underground parking that does not permit the growth of tall vegetation, demonstrably cannot claim the identity of the private dwelling in the midst of nature.

7 When the collective definition of the goal becomes the means of achieving it.

Culture and Congress Centre in Lucerne, 1990 (competition), 1995 (construction begin), 2000 (opening), by the architects Atelier Jean Nouvel, Paris, photographs by Ivan Suta. Ever since the 1980s, there were calls to separate the programmatic components of the original 1930s building that was located on roughly the same site. In a first step, the music festival sponsor, the Kunstgesellschaft, along with the hotelier association and various other lobbying groups, attempted to pressure the municipality and the canton to build a new art museum, a concert hall, a congress center, a public auditorium, and a youth center. It soon became clear that the public coffers would never have enough funds to satisfy each of these demands. A concept of cultural space management emerged from a lengthy search for synergies and political solidarity that in turn envisaged concentrating most of the programmatic components "under one roof". However, this time around, the flexible-use model of a common multi-purpose assembly hall was set aside in favor of functionally differentiated and optimized infrastructures. This was a win-win strategy, as instead of fighting, the lobbying groups made it possible to not only reach their goals, but also to achieve the highest level of quality possible at that time.

Source: Copyright KKL Lucerne

When the collective definition of the goal becomes the means of achieving it

The examples illustrating our previous discussion mainly concerns two categories of architectural clients, which we can characterize as follows:

- Private builders (individuals, families, companies, clubs, etc.), acting for their own benefit, who usually have fairly precise ideas about programming. That this group of architectural patrons who "know what they want" may misjudge their true self-interest and may need professional advice, as we noted in the case of Adolf Loos' clientele, does not alter the fact that their needs strongly influence the building program from the very start. The availability of private financing introduces a further distinction. Dependency on mortgage loans, or sponsorship, in the case of architectural projects—as we have seen with Wagner's festival hall—can constrain the scope of the program as the program is being put together, and/or as it is transformed into architecture.

- Investors and property developers (banks, insurance companies, pension funds, and all kinds of capital investors), who undertake construction projects mainly for the sake of anticipated revenues, program their construction projects based on market analyses and economic forecasts, as we observed in passing in the case of the ARK 143 complex in Bern and Furglerstrasse in St. Gallen. This group does not follow any pre-set preferences, but rather supports those uses with the highest demand at a given time. Frequently, therefore, they prefer flexible architectural schemes that allow for subsequent shifts in programmatic components. In this case, the program is an adjustable container with variable contents.

A third category of builders should not go unmentioned, as it is of a specific nature. If private builders regard their programmatic desires as self-chosen goals, while investors consider their construction projects as a necessary means of capital utilization, the public sector is perhaps the only property developer that constitutes itself around and through its construction projects. This explains why the quality and transparency of the process are so important in the public sector:

- The public sector (municipalities, provinces, the federal government, public bodies such as universities, hospitals, and transit companies) must take account of the political consensus when compiling their building programs, and invest in extensive consultation in advance of construction projects in order to avoid obstructive complaints or negative votes. It is true that the authorities, or individual lobby groups, who are quite expert at gaining acceptance politically, have clear ideas about the needs they would like to meet with a construction project. But the duty to serve the public interest often requires strategic programmatic "packages" to be bundled to satisfy rival target groups at the same time. Such costly measures "buy" the political feasibility, as it were, of construction projects. Preparing the building program thus becomes an instrument of political action. The great challenge here is to link participation to ambition. Participatory processes should not be misused in order to do favors for everyone, regardless of the outcome, but rather to unite all forces, so that the very best can be achieved, something that could not come about without that alliance. The Culture and Congress Centre in Lucerne, which opened in 2000, is an example of such good fortune. The concept of a publicly managed cultural space was approved by three successive referendums, supporting the ambitious aspiration for a world-class concert hall.[25]

25 Sylvain Malfroy (1999), "Imagepflege nach aussen, Konfliktbewältigung nach innen. Architekturwettbewerbe und Stadtmarketing. Der Fall des Kultur- und Kongresszentrums (KKL) in Luzern", in *Schweizer Ingenieur und Architekt 23*, pp. 513–516.

Needs | "Each to their skills, each to their needs," was the great promise of the Socialist utopia and once a preconscious matter of course. It soon became material for theorization and negotiation. Decades later, based on user needs with universal demands and scientifically founded, it has solidified into an axiom of architectural design. In retrospect, we can see: What is considered to be an axiom, is itself socially and culturally defined, and therefore relatively and clearly subordinate to the passing of time – concretely effective, abstractly of limited value.

The New Human | Modern architecture is based on "the human", giving rise to the question of who this human is. It must be a different one than previously, as it presupposes a New Human. Beholden only to reason, emancipated from habits and conventions, all links to the past destroyed. Le Corbusier attests that this new contemporary has a new state of mind. But how new is new? How can we prevent the New Human from becoming a thing of the past as early as tomorrow? Human pathos becomes abstract, a dogma.

Function | From Latin *functio:* Performance, execution. Failure-free operation (functioning), correlation (mathematics, i.e. $y = x^2$), official position, area of responsibility, being. Diverse meanings, but always: An active connection creates a whole. For Goethe, function is an active state of being. For Louis Sullivan, whose "form follows function" is analogous with the development of a whole plant from a mere seed, it is organic. From a technical turn, it is wise to use one's scientific tendencies to counteract any capricious artistic tendencies. Abstract parameters dominated the functionalism of the 20th century, then sheer function, and then finally the bare economic profit of economic functionalism.

Purpose | The direct, one-way path from intention to result. Purpose guides action. Nothing happens without a reason, says Cicero; the brilliance of purpose lies in the future. This increases its normative power: The end justifies the means. Unconditional modernism chimes in: The end justifies the means. The unconditional modern-ism places means and expression beneath purpose. An unconditionalism that takes revenge when those set back rise up and demand a purpose. Without referencing a whole, the purpose forfeits its fundamental causality and must justify its framework of action.

SIA Standards | Taking sustainability into consideration, standards ensure building and facility safety and the functionality, durability, economic viability thereof in all phases of the life cycle. They delineate the rules of construction, document trusted knowledge, make knowledge gained from research accessible for practical use, and inspire ongoing research. These standards establish a legal basis and foundation of common understanding. Standards must be useful and applicable and actually implemented in practice (*utile, utilisable et utilisé*). They are framework conditions, yet still subject to change over time.

Tabula Rasa | From Latin *tabula:* Table and *radere:* To shave. A smooth wax tablet or empty page, in general: A clean slate. Philosopher John Locke compares the human mind at birth to a blank page, which is then inscribed by the experiences of life. Twentieth-century modernism proffered its designs with a similar lack of bias. Le Corbusier wished to tear apart conventional ideas of the heart and mind and begin anew with objectivity, only beholden to reason. Decoupled from its heritage, a new human appears.

Machine | From Greek *mĕchané:* Tool, artificial contraption, means. A mechanism that facilitates the achievement of a purpose through the flow of material, energy, or information. The purpose is a precondition. Technology and machines captivate the minds of the early 20th century. The smooth functioning of machines becomes an ideal, see the racecar of the Futurists, Le Corbusier's steam engine, Tatlin's machine art, or Jünger's total mobilization. A latecomer: High-tech and energy-conscious building.

Artificial Intelligence | Technology that attains self-organization through regulation and feedback. The only external input is in the first step. To what degree artificial intelligence is actually able to learn, i. e. to independently reflect on and modify the system, remains in dispute. Artificial intelligence must not be mistaken for artistic intelligence. The former is meant to replace the latter, for example, in parametric design. AI apologists are descended from the 20th-century enthrallment with machines and are carrying this tradition onwards—all the way to a self-generating modernism that will someday dispense with its own authors.

Organization | From Greek *órganon:* Instrument. Also organ, organism. Organization is the result-oriented collaboration of the individual parts of a whole. Although all work processes are organized, under scientific management (developed by Frederick Taylor), work processes are split into the smallest possible units of time to create repetitive processes. Mental work is divided from physical labor in order to rearrange these units into a new and improved organizational plan. This made a great impression during the 1920s: more than a few see in building not an aesthetic process, but mere organization.

Bauhaus | Most influential school of design of the 20th century. The fundamental doctrine (Klee, Kandinsky, Itten, Albers) was essential, and aimed for creative personalities through exercises in creativity and systematic carried out only for their own sake, instead of style, history, and academics. Bauhaus analyzed contemporary artistic tendencies and turned towards technical production methods. In a later phase, a scientific methodology is pursued. A paradoxical result of this is the formal canon of the International Style (Philip Johnson and Henry-Russell Hitchcock, 1932), which replaces what was once thought of as open end: creative activity became "Bauhaus Style".

PROGRAM

Modernism put function at the base of design. The zoning of city layouts into homogenous use areas that began with modernism was complemented by a guiding principle of creating fair traffic conditions in the city, and separating uses considered to compromise one another. The concept of use division, although still in effect in today's building ordinances, is now obsolete. This is also true of buildings. Societal processes of change are highly dynamic, and functional changes cannot be reconciled with permanent building. Since place is characterized by longevity, urban quality is solely dependent upon the physical impact of the buildings. Mixing different usages on the city level and having flexible structures on the building level are new guiding principles.

City Level

The specific value ratios of the area and volume of twelve buildings will be shown in floor plans and cross-sections, analyzed, and presented using a video beamer.

Specifications

Project work will be carried out in groups. The following building areas and volumes are to be analyzed:

- Floor area (FA)
- Net floor area (NFA)
- Structural area (SA)
- Usable floor area (UFA)
- Circulation area (CA)
- Service area (SA)
- Gross volume (GV)
- Average floor height (FH = GV/FA)
- Aboveground building envelope (BE)
- Window area
- Façade area

Economic Indicators (building efficiency):

- FA aboveground/UFA aboveground
- FA total/UFA total
- GV aboveground/UFA aboveground
- GV total/UFA total
- BE/UFA aboveground
- Window area/UFA aboveground
- Window area/façade area

The resulting values will be presented in a table and compared by type. The analyzed areas should be put in relation to one another, as various findings about the building can thus be attained and analyzed as economic indicators of building efficiency.

Requirements

- SIA (Swiss Society of Engineers and Architects) Norm 416

Goal
Calculation results will be compared and discussed. This will help students gain an awareness of how the proportions of the various areas of a building relate to one another and how important insights can be derived that are relevant to their own designs.

Rachel Whiteread: *Untitled (House)*, 1993, concrete, wood and steel (destroyed on January 11, 1994). Commissioned by Artangel, sponsored by Beck's

Photo credit: Sue Omerod

Gordon Bunshaft
SOM, Yale Rare Book Library,
New Haven Connecticut, 1963

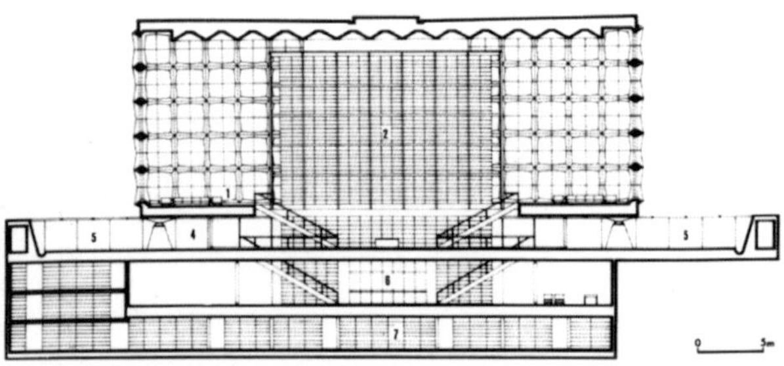

Gordon Bunshaft
SOM, Yale Rare Book Library,
New Haven Connecticut, 1963

Building Level

This exercise focuses on the analysis of architectural types and use distribution throughout a building. The selection of an architectural type must be seen in relation to the building site. The analysis and realization of a spatial program should result in a conclusive, well-structured model.

Specifications

- Surface line measurements of the building volume may not exceed 35 × 35 × 35 meters.
- The building should utilize the full 35-meter height capacity.
- At least 7,000 m^2 of aboveground FA must be planned, i.e. at least 5,040 m^2 aboveground UFA.
- The building must have at least two basement levels. Space (areas = UFA / floor height = ca. 3.5 m) will be allocated into public, semi-public, private, and secondary areas.
- Project work will be done in groups of two and presented on a DIN A0 plan.

The following must be submitted:
Building level plan
- Photo documentation of three important floors of the model
- One sectional view
- Two photographs of the volumetrics / photo model
- Area calculations

Models:
- Model 1:100

Requirements

- Spatial program
- Fire safety regulations 2015
- SIA Norm 416
- VSS Norms
- Table of design area calculations (Excel)

Goal

The selection of an architectural type requires a knowledge and analysis of typologies. The skills of organized abstraction and the subsequent spatial implementation are two crucial goals of this exercise.

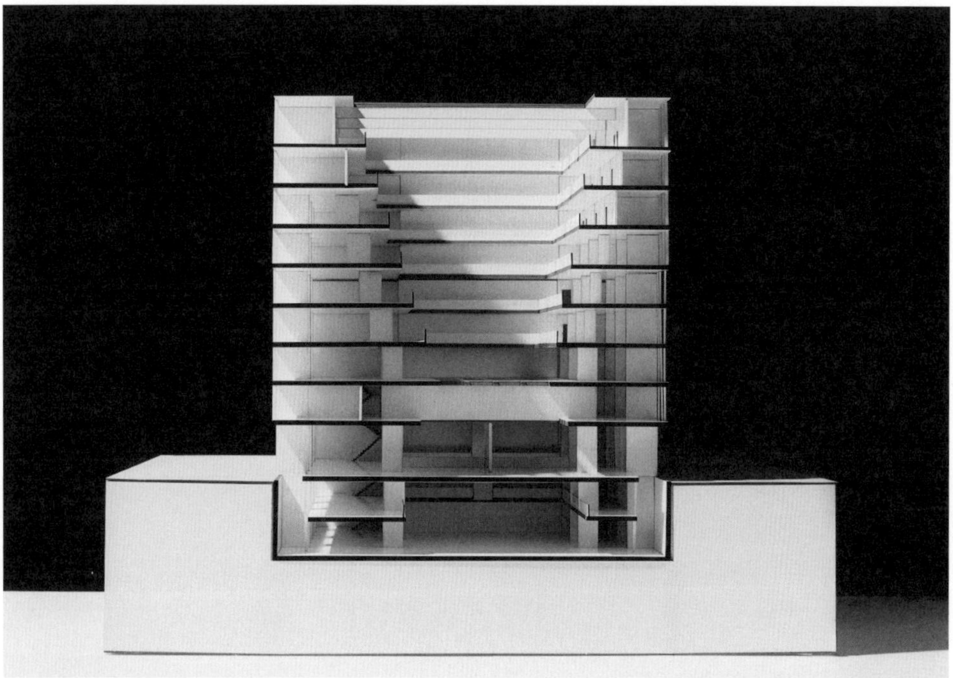

Section model
Joos Kündig
Iso Tambornino
15 SS

6

© Georg Aerni

SCHWEIZERISCHE HOCHSCHULE
FÜR DIE HOLZWIRTSCHAFT,
BIEL (1997–1999)
Architekten: Marcel Meili, Markus Peter Architekten AG, Zürich
Bauherrschaft: Kantonales Hochbauamt Bern

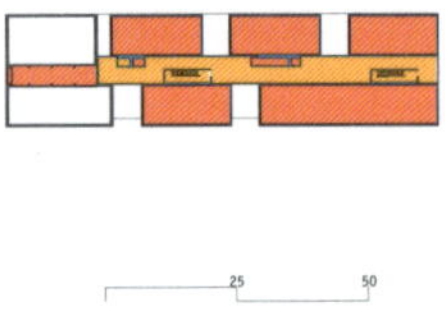

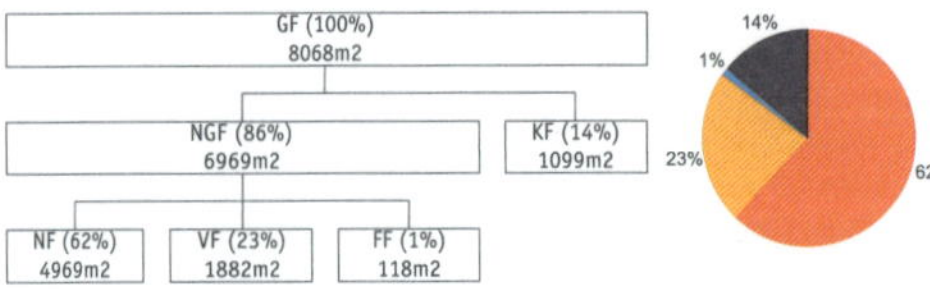

ÖKONOMISCHE INDIKATOREN

GF oberirdisch / NF oberirdisch
1.50
GF gesamt / NF gesamt 1.62
GV oberirdisch / NF oberirdisch

ÖKONOMISCHE INDIKATOREN

GF oberirdisch / NF oberirdisch 1.78
GF gesamt / NF gesamt 1.68
GV oberirdisch / NF oberirdisch 7.28
GV gesamt / NF gesamt 7.55

© Hannes Henz, Architekturfotograf, Zürich

VOLTA SCHULHAUS BASEL (1999–2000)
Architekten: Miller & Maranta dipl. Architekten ETH BSA SIA
Bauherrschaft: Kanton Basel-Stadt

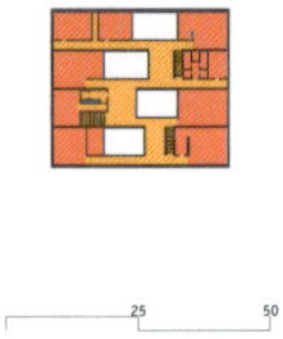

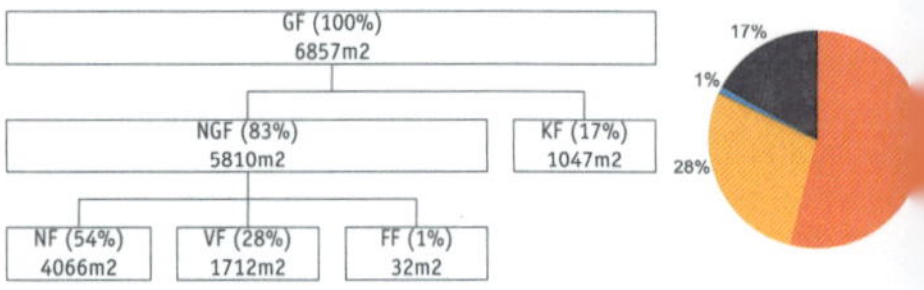

ÖKONOMISCHE INDIKATOREN

GF oberirdisch / NF oberirdisch 1.78
GF gesamt / NF gesamt 1.68
GV oberirdisch / NF oberirdisch 7.28
GV gesamt / NF gesamt 7.55

ÖKOLOGISCHE INDIKATOREN

HFL / NF oberirdisch 1.27
Fensterfläche / NF oberirdisch 0.29
Fensterfläche /Fassadenfläche
0.37

© Reinhard Zimmermann

BÜROGEBÄUDE ABB 706, BADEN (2001)
Architekten: Burkard Meyer Architekten BSA, Baden
Bauherrschaft: ABB Immobilien AG, Baden

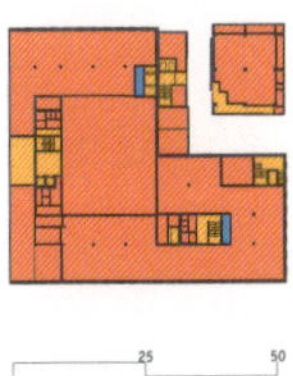

GF (100%) 17061m2

NGF (92%) 15700m2 — KF (8%) 1361m2

NF (81.1%) 13833m2 — VF (7.8%) 1325m2 — FF (3%) 542m2

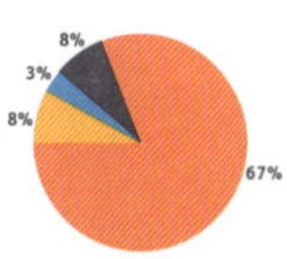

ÖKONOMISCHE INDIKATOREN

GF oberirdisch / NF oberirdisch	1.27
GF gesamt / NF gesamt	1.3
GV oberirdisch / NF oberirdisch	5.02
GV gesamt / NF gesamt	5.2

ÖKOLOGISCHE INDIKATOREN

HFL / NF oberirdisch	0.71
Fensterfläche / NF oberirdisch	0.18
Fensterfläche / Fassadenfläche	0.35

© Mario Carrieri

BÜROGEBÄUDE MIT RESTAURANT FABRIKSTRASSE 12, NOVARTIS CAMPUS, BASEL (2008)
Architekten: Vittorio Magnago Lampugnani & Jens Bohm
Bauherrschaft: Novartis

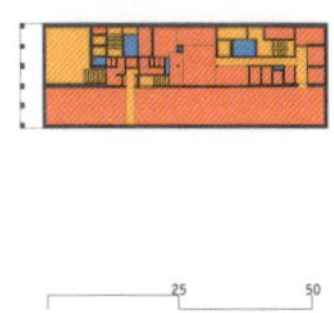

GF (100%) 7550m2

NGF (87%) 6555m2 — 13 (17%) 1047m2

NF (61.4%) 4637m2 — VF (19.9%) 1504m2 — FF (5%) 414m2

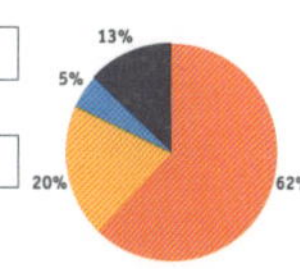

ÖKONOMISCHE INDIKATOREN

GF oberirdisch / NF oberirdisch	1.57
GF gesamt / NF gesamt	1.69
GV oberirdisch / NF oberirdisch	4.99
GV gesamt / NF gesamt	4.58

ÖKOLOGISCHE INDIKATOREN

HFL / NF oberirdisch	1.06
Fensterfläche / NF oberirdisch	0.44
Fensterfläche /Fassadenfläche	0.52

Benedikt Kowalewski
Jan Peters
12 SS

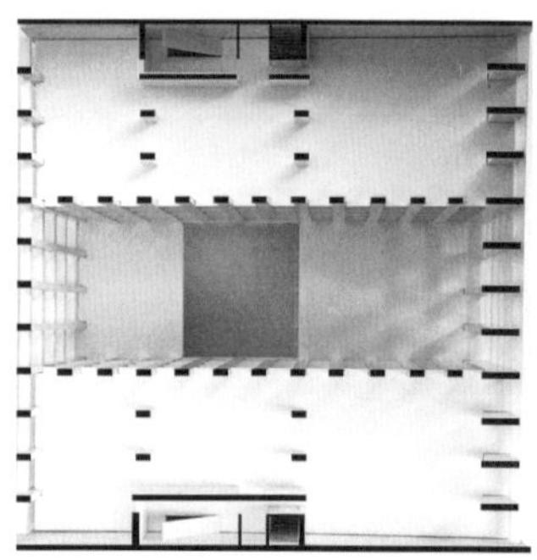

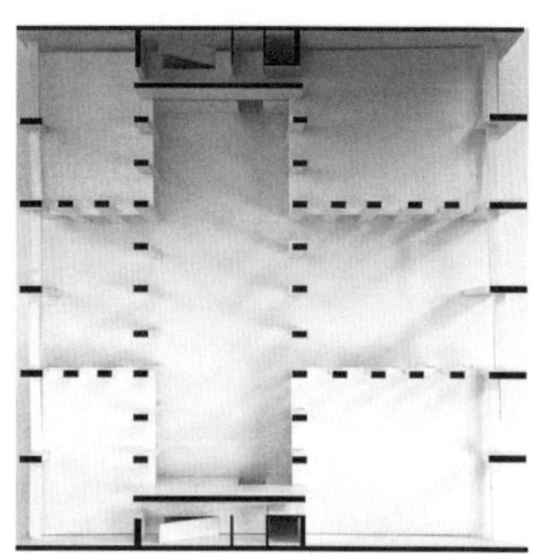

Samuel Klingele
Alexis Panoussopoulos
13 SS

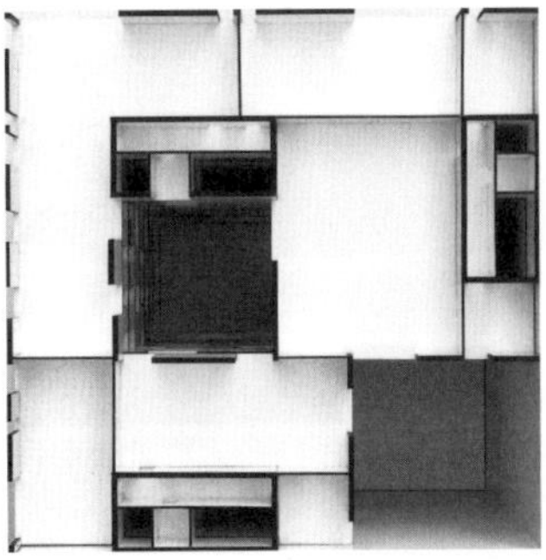

Achille Patà
Thomas Toffel
13 SS

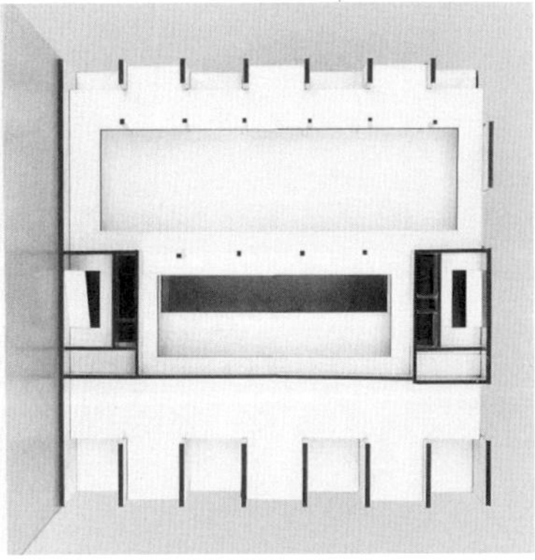

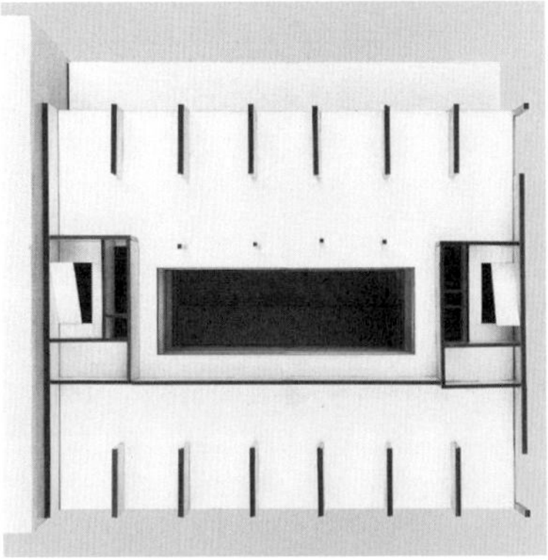

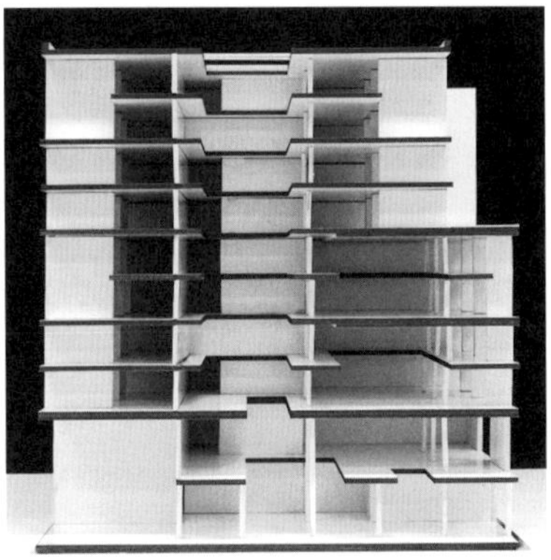

Valentina Sieber
Allegra Stucki
13 SS

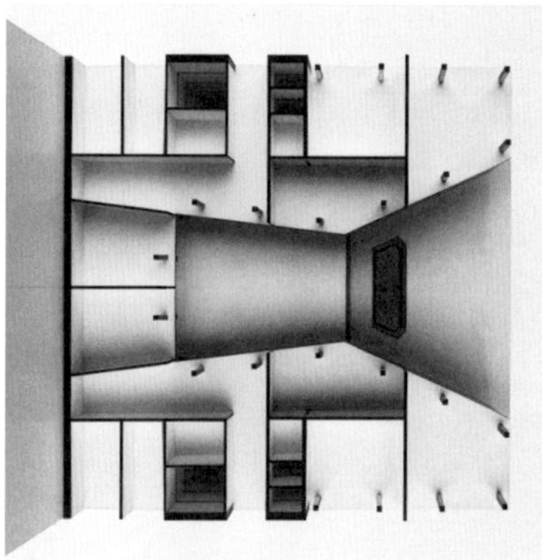

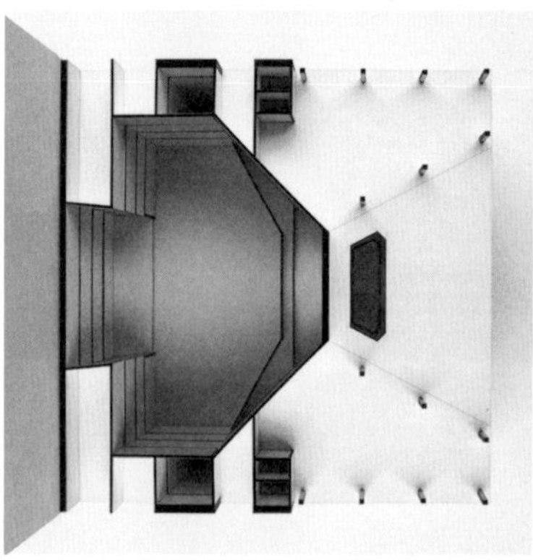

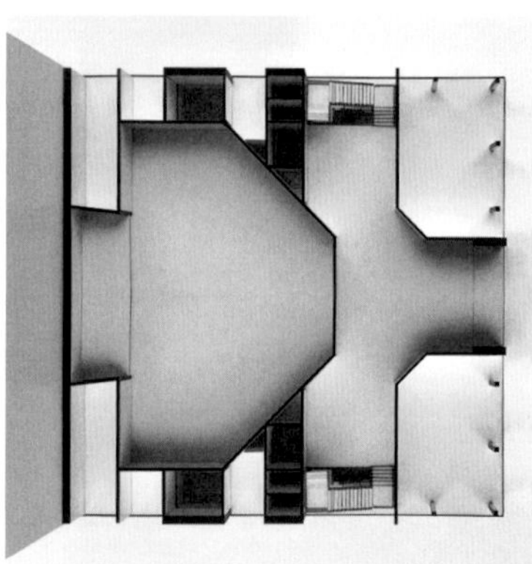

Eva Müller
Nina Stauffer
14 SS

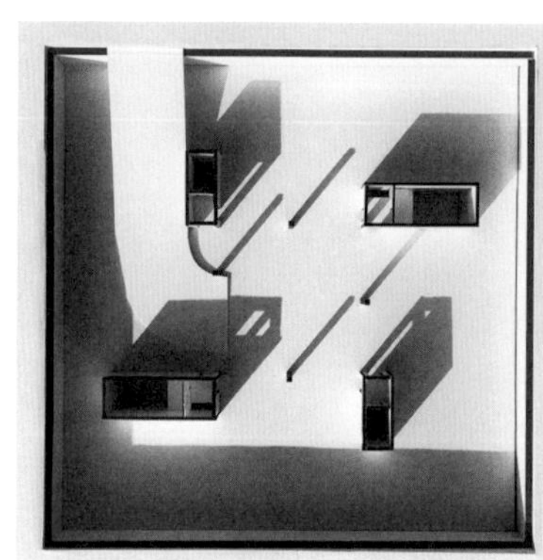

Yueqiu Wang
Yuda Zheng
13 SS

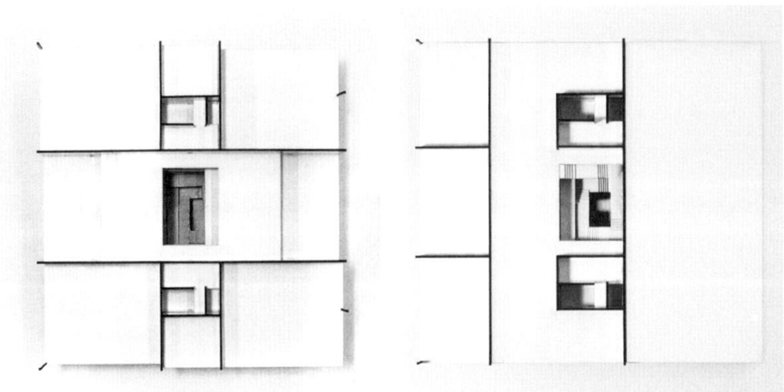

Timothy Allen
Okan Tan
16 ss

Mevion Famos
Manon Mottet
16 ss

6

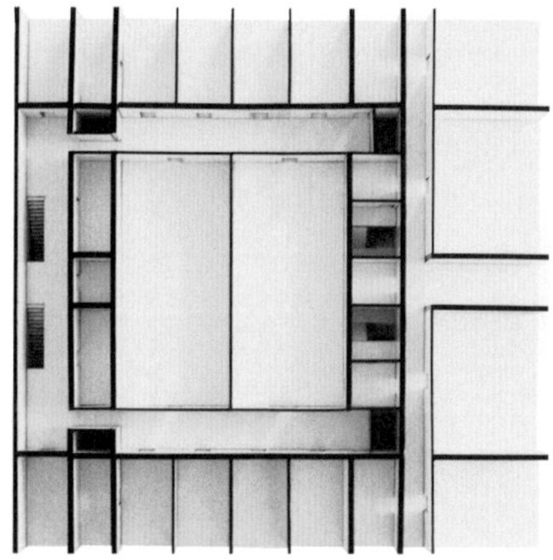

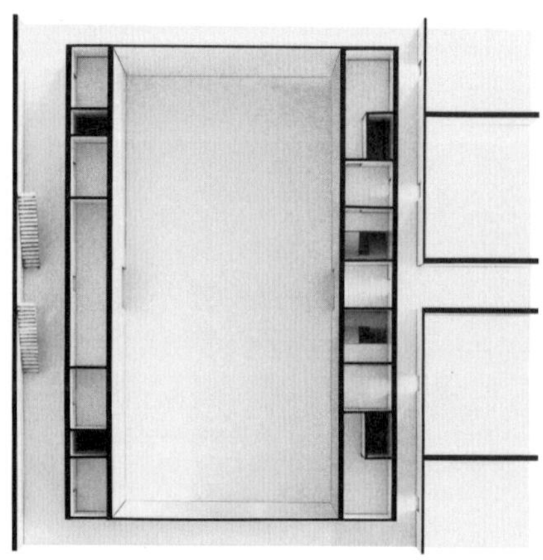

Katja Blumer
Giorgia Mini
16 ss

Maximilien Durel
Reto Habermacher
16 SS

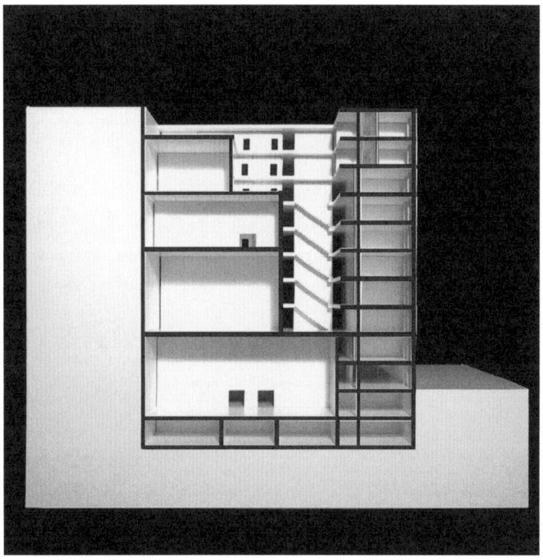

Pawel Bejm
Marco Fernandes Pires
17 SS

Timmy Huang
Joël Maître
17 SS

6

Julian Meier
Luca Sergi
16 ss

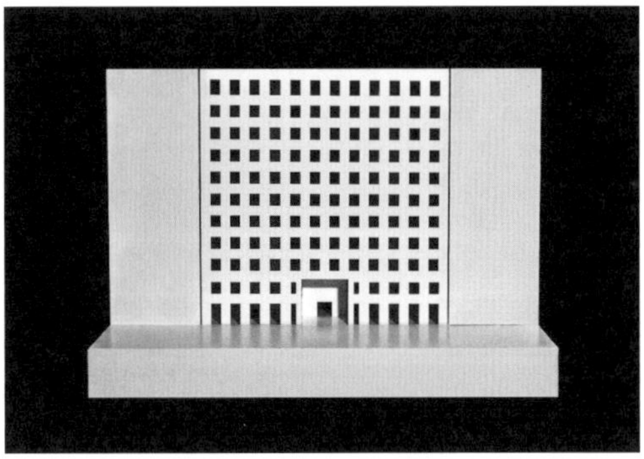

Benedikt Kowalewski
Jan Peters
12 SS

Joos Kündig
Iso Tambornino
15 SS

Nicolas Ganz
Sandro Lenherr
11 SS

Timothy Allen
Okan Tan
16 SS

6

Sebastian Heusser
Marcel Hodel
12 SS

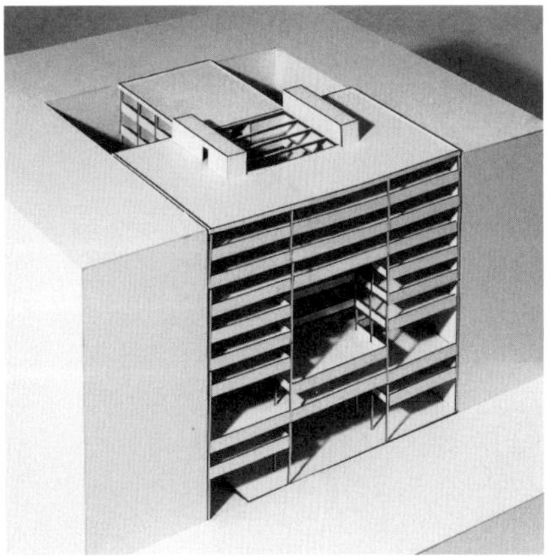

Stéphane Chau
Maurin Elmer
14 SS

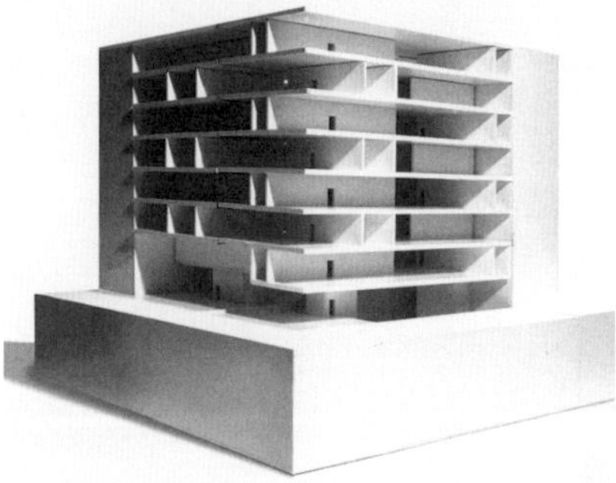

Jakob Junghanss
Fabian Kuonen
15 SS

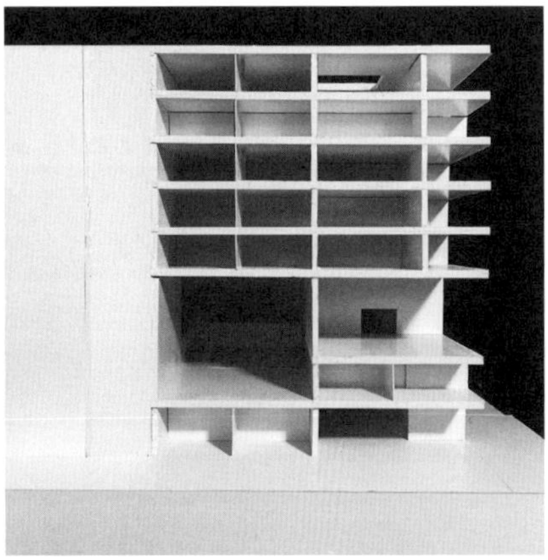

Maximilien Durel
Reto Habermacher
16 SS

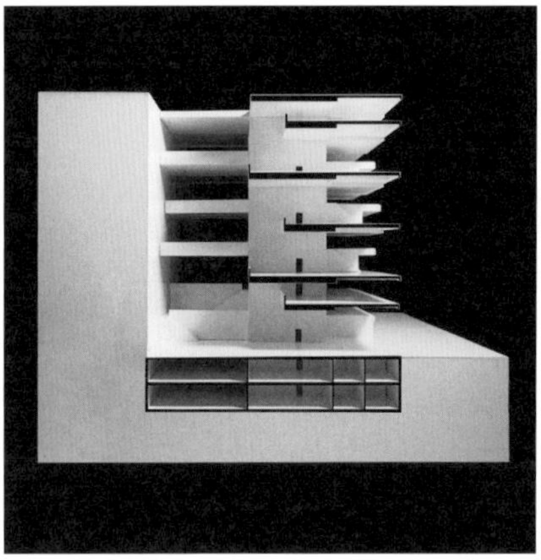

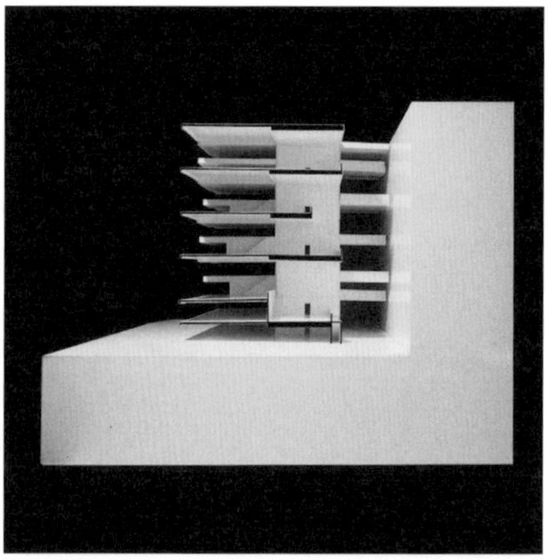

Patrick Perren
Rafael Schäfer
15 SS

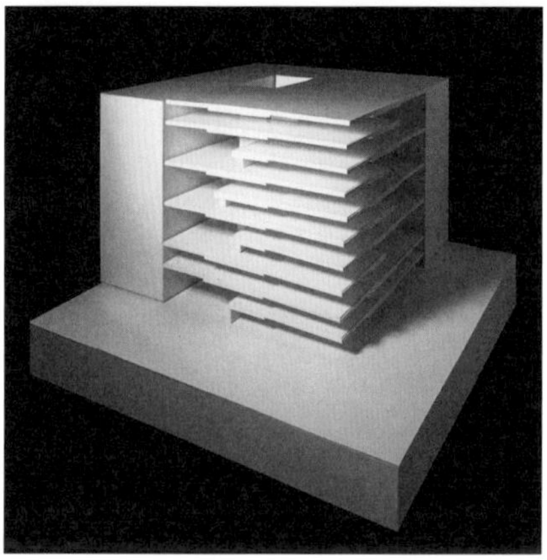

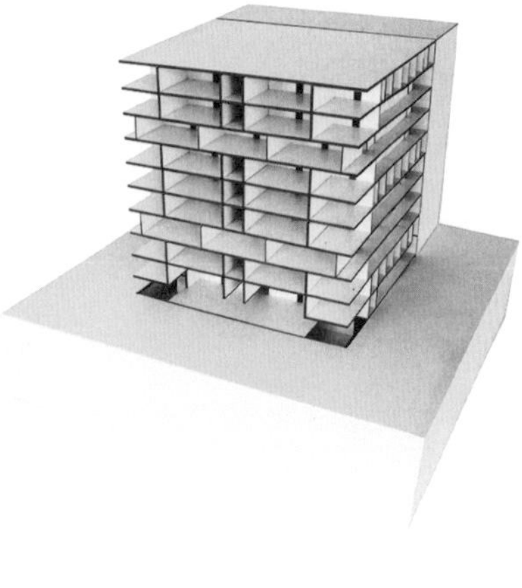

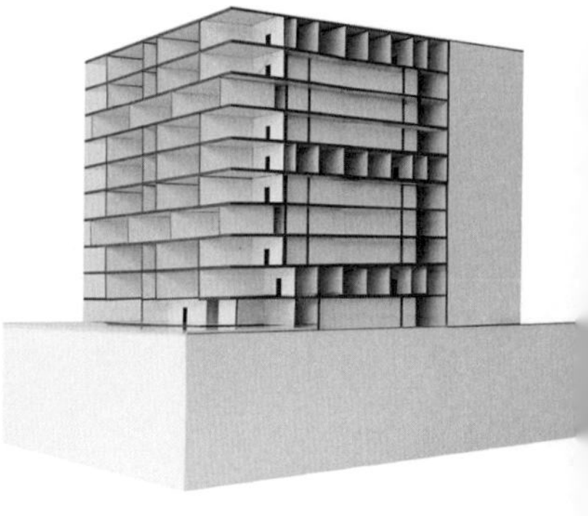

Katja Blumer
Giorgia Mini
16 SS

Lea Hottiger
Dimitri Kron
09 SS

6

Pawel Bejm
Marco Fernandes Pires
17 SS

Nina Feix
Petra Steinegger
15 SS

Samuel Klingele
Alexis Panoussopoulos
13 SS

6

Timmy Huang
Joël Maître
17 SS

Georg Aerni, 1826-4, Kwai Chung, 2000 © Georg Aerni

7

Place
Structure
Envelope
Program

While it is possible to ascribe physical presence to place—and in certain ways to structure and envelope as well—this is hard to do for program. The program is to the first three what the motor is to a boat and water. The program is the catalyst and drive; it provides reason and method. Something is launched, put into operation. Concept, decisions, and actions are main features; time is the dimension. When the program appears, it is free and unlimited, only to be limited and constrained by physical things. The self-setting program is undermined by being exposed to others, yet must be exposed, as it can only be staged in and through the other.

A driving force, the program is immediate and current, while place is static and enduring. The time frame of the program is the current one, while the physicality of place, structure, and envelope is timeless, or at least enduring. This indicates a definitive contrast. And modernism did indeed justify architecture through its program, proclaiming a break with all that is enduring. "A new architecture. An immense, devastating, brutal evolution has burned the bridges that link us with the past," (cited in Conrads, 1970, 92) stated Le Corbusier with the decisionistic pathos typical of the 1920s.

Shakespeare succinctly sums up the dilemma of the will expressed by the program: "The will is infinite and the execution confined," Is contrast everything? Is there not an equal amount of attraction in the game? The program does not originate in a vacuum; it draws the objects of its intentions from the reality of its time, it is bound to the things and the places. For Stephen Toulmin, this limitation is consequential: "All we can be called upon to do is to take a start from where we are, at the time we are there. [...] There is no way of cutting ourselves free of our conceptual inheritance: all we are required to do is use our experience critically and discriminatingly, refining and improving our inherited ideas, and determining more exactly the limits to their scope" (1990, 179).

Thusly, the program is structured by time, structure, and place. Does this mean the place is a timeless substance? It is quite apparent that place is subject to a steady state of change, created to a great degree by humans. In the words of Aldo Rossi: "Urban architecture—a human creation—is willed as such" (1982, 162). The place owes its concrete existence to human will, which one can, when it is structured, call program. Place gives program a—limited—opportunity to become reality.

Place and program reference each other. To give program priority is absurd, place must have precedence; it cannot be avoided—place is everywhere. The design will succeed when its connection with the place has been well prepared; this is when a programmatic breakthrough will occur, for place is not a timeless substance, rather, it is change and activity that has turned to stone.

It can happen that something doesn't become clear until it is already disappearing. On the relationship of the use and the operation of a building to its physical presence, Louis Kahn observed the following: "But when the building is a ruins and free of servants, its spirit emerges and tells of the miracle that a building was made" (cited from Latour, 1993, 109). (FA/MN)

Walls of Modernity and Beyond

Laurent Stalder

Linguistic usage has internalized closed space as a fundamental need. We talk about "our own four walls" and want a "roof over our heads". These expressions demonstrate a desire for intimacy or protection from bad or cold weather, which is intimately linked to an interior space that is closed on all sides. The classical theory of architecture, from antiquity via renaissance to modernity, has accommodated this fact. It has attributed a constitutive significance to the act of enclosure, symbolic with the plow, actual as a wall, placing material enclosure on all sides at the origin of architectural creation.[1]

A space without any opening, however, is a dungeon. It is therefore by no means a coincidence that perforating these space-enclosing walls with windows, doors, stairs, chimneys, and shafts has an equally firm place in architectural theory, which has always focused on the various apertures used to regulate light, air, people, and fluids.[2]

But this clear concept of an enclosed space with its separate, precisely placed apertures—windows and doors, stairwells and chimney pipes—has been undermined over the past 150 years by a number of different concepts that challenge the traditional understanding of architecture as a spatial art: the fluid space or the open plan of modernity, which not only interconnects individual rooms, but also dissolves the boundaries between the interior and the exterior; the transparent or "unprivate" house of the post-war period,[3] which transforms intimacy into extimacy (a place of constant accessibility);[4] the house as an interface;[5] or, most recently, the zero-emission building,[6] which aims to define the house as a junction between different infrastructures or energy flows. The closed and unified space, which could still be described as the consistent background of all possible relationships—be they constructive, social, legal, relating to energy politics or, most importantly,

7

[1] Cf. Fritz Neumeyer: "Mit dem Kopf durch die Wand. Annäherung an das Unwort Fassade", in: id. Hans Kollhoff [exhibition catalogue in the Galerie Max Hetzler, Berlin], Berlin, 1995, pp. 6–17.

[2] Cf. Werner Oechslin: "Leon Battista Albertis apertio—die Öffnung schlechthin = Leon Battista Alberti's Apertio—The Opening Absolute", in: *Daidalos* 13 (1984), pp. 29–39.

[3] Terence Riley: "The Un-Private House", in: *The Un-Private House*, New York, 1999, pp. 9–17.

[4] Georges Teyssot: "Fenster. Zwischen Intimität und Extimität", in: *Arch+* 191/192 (2009), pp. 52–59.

[5] Peter Sloterdijk: *Schäume, Band III: Sphären. Plurale Sphärologie*, Frankfurt am Main, 2004, pp. 501–516.

[6] Hansjürg Leibundgut: *LowEx Building Design. Für eine Zero-Emission Architecture*, Zurich, 2011, pp. 59–65.

aesthetics—in the early 20th century seems to have been dissolved in favor of an arrangement which now separately regulates, optimizes, and differentiates the different relationships at the threshold between the interior and the exterior, the private and the public, the safe and the unsafe, the pure and the impure, the developed and the undeveloped, the warm and the cold by means of a series of devices and components, individualizing them but also allowing them to be customized. Against this background, it has to come as a surprise that the history of modern architecture has mainly addressed the dissolution of the wall as a space-forming and tectonic component, ignoring a number of technologies like air curtains, coated glass, blinds and shutters, or air conditioning that constitute the contemporary terms of architectural design.

But what are the consequences of these new technologies for our understanding of architecture? What does it mean when the wall is no longer solely understood as a delimiting enclosure, but as a translucid, transparent, or opaque, breathing, permeable membrane, layer, or shell which no longer simply separates an interior and an exterior, but also connects them, and thus no longer divides as a boundary, but connects as a threshold, as a mi-lieu?

The beginnings of the extensive transfiguration of the environment by means of machines, devices, and tools, from agriculture through to architecture, can be dated to the mid-19th century.[7] That which comprehensively transforms architecture in this process is less its formal achievements, but a number of new specialized skills (e.g. in the field of hygiene), processes (for instance through electrification or hydro-development) and experts (like construction, mechanical, and sanitation engineers), managing the environment or the surroundings of buildings with a number of technologies.

This entails an exhaustive reorganization and redistribution in architecture and urban design.[8] The changes are visible on a number of different levels: on the political level, as this redistribution also constitutes a transfer of political responsi-

[7] The most exhaustive theoretical study of the environment and its consequences in architecture is still: Siegfried Giedion: *Mechanization Takes Command. A Contribution to Anonymous History*. New York 1948. Cf. Pedro Gomez (ed.): *Encyclopedia of Architectural Technology*, New York 1979; Cecil D. Elliot: *Technics and Architecture*, Cambridge, MA 1993.

[8] Illustrated in the example of Paris in: François Beguin: "Savoirs de la ville et de la maison au début tu 19ème siècle", in: Michel Foucault (ed.): *Politiques de l'habitat* (1800–1850), Paris, 1977, pp. 211–324, here pp. 247–251.

bility—think of the sanitation police that has the authority to enter private apartments in the name of the state—; on an urban design level, because from now on, the city is not only connected above ground, but also below ground, through an extensive network of infrastructures; or, precisely, on the architectural level—from construction to infrastructure to upgrading individual buildings with a number of devices that turn the buildings into proper "living machines",[9] "climate machines", or "comfort machines".[10]

At first glance, these interventions seem limited. Individual devices like the dumbwaiter, doorbell systems, water supply, lights, and so on lead their independent lives. The technological object within the house is abstract in its original form. It leads an autonomous existence, works according to its own laws and regardless of other objects. It is, above all, independent of the space-defining shell into which it implants itself, or the tectonic limits of which it pierces. In this primitive form, it constitutes a theoretical and material, since independent, unit. But little by little, the individual elements, components, and devices—for instance the sink, oven, and fridge in a modern kitchen, or air conditioning, artificial light, and curtain façade in the office building of the post-war period, or monolithic walls with storage capacity, upright windows with their automatic ventilation flaps, but also different sources of heat in the building (people and machines)—interlink to form a properly machine-like ensemble. Thus, the contemporary building has to be understood as a composite of different devices that need to be coordinated with each other, less in the form of compromise than because of their simultaneity.[11]

A perfect example in this respect is the history of air conditioning, which allows us to retrace the consequences of this development for architecture. The first experiments regarding the vital importance of air for the body stem from the mid-18th century, just like insights into the significance of proper ventilation for the comfort of interior spaces. But the first devices to

[9] Le Corbusier: *Vers une architecture*, ed. G. Crès, Paris, 1924 (1923), p. IX.

[10] Cf. Georges Vigarello: *Le sain et le malsain: santé et mieux-être depuis le Moyen Âge*, Paris, 1993, p. 212.

[11] Cf. Gilbert Simondon: *Du mode d'existence des objets techniques*, Paris, 1989 [1958], p. 21.

change the humidity and temperature of air only date from the first part of the 19th century, significantly appearing at the same time as modern meteorology based on the findings of physics and mathematical models. Initially, the first air conditioning systems, as described in the manuals of the early 19th century, were simple machines that compressed and expanded (and simultaneously cooled) air.[12] The breakthrough came at the turn of the century. While Mark Twain was still able to remark, in 1897, that everybody was talking about the weather but nobody was doing anything about it,[13] as early as 1906 a lithography studio patented an "Apparatus for Treating Air" for cooling, dehumidifying, and purifying air[14] that was able to mediate between two climatic parameters: the exterior climate with its seasonal variations, which could be recorded meticulously by means of meteorological maps, and an interior climate, which required uniform humidity and air temperature.[15] From the moment that air becomes a key category of comfort and can be studied and tested scientifically, it can also be specified according to characteristics like humidity, temperature, purity, warmth, and velocity. This analytical fragmentation of air, however, was also to lead to the converse possibility of planning different situations of comfort, regardless of time and place.

A pioneering insight for our modern understanding of our artificial environment is that from this point on, it was no longer humans who had to adapt to their environment, but it was the environment—regardless of climatic variation—that, thanks to the climate machine, could be adapted to the requirements of human comfort. This had been recognized as early as 1842 by the inventor of mechanical cooling, John Gorrie, who not only wanted to cool private homes and hospitals but also entire streets and squares with his ice machines.[16] While this proposition may have seemed naïve at the time, it nevertheless marks the start of the endeavor to totally control the human environment, the possibility of uniting "the antipodes by science", as the title page of a journal of climate technology

12 Cf. Bernard Hargengast: "John Gorrie: Pioneer of Cooling and Ice Making", in: *ASHRAE Journal* 33, 1991, p. 52.

13 Charles D. Warner, quoted in Gail Cooper, *Air-conditioning America: Engineers and the Controlled Environment, 1900–1960* [Johns Hopkins Studies in the History of Technology. New series, 23], Baltimore, MD 1998, p. 1.

14 "Apparatus for Treating Air": U.S. Patent 808 897, [2 January 1906].

15 Cf. Cooper: *Air-conditioning America*, pp. 23–28 (see Note 13). On the inventor of the "Apparatus for Treating Air", William H. Carrier, cf. Margaret Ingels: *William Haviland Carrier. Father of Air Conditioning*, Garden City, 1952.

16 Cf. Hargengast: *John Gorrie*, p. 60 (see Note 12).

aptly put it at the turn of the century.[17] From the 1950s, this concept is implemented on a large scale: through the combination of the sealed, sun-proof curtain façade and artificial lighting, the idea was to gain complete control over the interior climate at the touch of a button for the first time ever. Air conditioning system, artificial light, and curtain façade thus formed a mechanical ensemble that aimed to guarantee constant interior comfort. But the possibility to organize the interior space by means of a series of devices, and no longer exclusively through structural design techniques, had even more far-reaching consequences: air conditioning not only is the first machine that allows for the independence of the interior from its natural environment, but it is also one of the first user-friendly systems. Thus, mass production of climate devices in the post-war period completely changed our idea of comfort and simultaneously marked the beginnings of an interactive environment. In the course of less than 50 years, the transition from a centralized, hierarchically organized system to a decentralized system with standardized mass-produced devices with user-friendly customization was completed. This increasing individualization of comfort continues today in the supply and return air systems of today's ventilation technology, which are decentralized, digitally controlled, and synchronized with measurable harmful emissions.[18]

This development should also be reflected in the debates about architecture. While Le Corbusier still advocated a house for all countries and all climates, the house with an exact respiration, heated to 18 degrees and operated by a central "usine à air exact" in 1929,[19] Reyner Banham and François Dallegret, with their "environment bubble", proposed a portable "living package", a "survival backpack", adaptable to the individual needs of the modern nomad in 1965.[20] Here, the axiomatic principle of modern architecture as a spatial art with a geometrical order is replaced by an understanding of architecture as an individualized, topologically shaped space that forms an expression of

[17] *Ice and Refrigeration Illustrated* 34, 5 (1908), front cover.

[18] Cf. Hans Jürg Leibungut: *Lüftung*, online at: http://www.busy.arch.ethz.ch/education/arch_bach/tech_inst_I/03_Lueftung_111221.pdf (accessed on 23 August 2012); Ludger Hovestadt: "Elektrische Intelligenz", in: *Jenseits des Rasters. Architektur und Informationstechnologie. Anwendungen einer digitalen Architektonik*, Basel/Boston/Berlin 2010, pp. 244–249; Peter Widerlin: "Die Steuerung 2226", in: Dietmar Eberle and Florian Aicher: *Die Temperatur der Architektur: Portrait eines Energieoptimierten Hauses/Portrait of an Energy-optimized House: The Temperature of Architecture*, Birkhäuser, Basel, 2016, pp. 55–68.

[19] Le Corbusier: *Précisions sur un état présent de l'Architecture et de l'urbanisme*, Paris, 1930, p. 66.

[20] Reyer Banham/François Dallegret: "A Home is Not a House", *in: Arts in America* 2 (1965), pp. 70–79. Cf. Alessandra Ponte et. al.: *God & Co. François Dallegret Beyond the Bubble*, London, 2011.

performative requirements. This individualization, however, not only leads to the possibility of segmentation and the definition of specific atmospheres, but beyond that, it can be used for a possible physiological programming of the users, as for instance Philippe Rahm showed at the 2002 Biennale in Venice with his tellingly named installation *Hormonium*, in which he referenced the Swiss Alps to design an atmosphere with air quality, brightness, and temperature corresponding to that of the Swiss Alps at an altitude of 3,000 meters, and thus at least physiologically transferred the visitor into an artificial, temporally, and geographically removed atmosphere.[21] The resulting shifting of the boundaries between the interior and the exterior was tested with water vapor by Maria Eichhorn in her 2001 installation *Sea, Salt, Water, Climate...*, in which the visitors literally incorporated the atmosphere, breathing it in, and thus challenged the visual definition of the environment.[22] There, the latter is not defined by its geometrical boundaries, but in the truest sense by the quality of its atmosphere—the air surrounding the human being.

That which distinguishes the technological object is not only the tools but also the knowledge connected to the object of the technology.[23] Like no other device, air conditioning has achieved this for air, the characteristics of which—temperature, velocity, humidity, purity—it is able to control. But what does it mean to devise an architecture that is no longer understood and perceived only as an object in its durability, but judged according to its performance, an architecture that no longer consists of four walls and the roof over our heads, but of the environment which can be designed?

It is no coincidence that the engineer's definition of the house as a "machine à habiter" is contemporaneous with the upgrade of houses in the mid-19th century.[24] Regardless of the different functionalities and semantic nuances of the machine—aesthetics with Le Corbusier, climatic with Reyner Banham, electronic with interactive architecture—the distinguishing

[21] Cf. Federal Ministry of Culture (ed.): *Décosterd & Rahm: physiologische Architektur/ architettura fisiologica*, Basel, 2002.

[22] Hamburger Kunsthalle (ed.): *Meer, Salz, Wasser, Klima, Kammer, Nebel, Wolken, Luft, Staub, Atem, Küste, Brandung, Rauch:* [Ein-Räumen - Arbeiten im Museum, 20 October 2000 to 21 January 2001, Hamburger Kunsthalle], Hamburg, 2000.

[23] Martin Heidegger: "The Question Concerning Technology", in: *Basic Writings*, San Francisco, 1993, pp. 321–322.

[24] Georges Teyssot: *Die Krankheit des Domizils, Wohnen und Wohnbau 1800–1930*, Braunschweig/Wiesbaden, 1989, p. 50.

7

attribute of the machine is the fact that it allows to explicate and therefore to rethink, transform, improve, reject, and also shape the different purposes of architecture.[25] Using the example of Le Corbusier's architecture, Reyner Banham aptly showed that the technological achievements of his "machine à habiter" allowed for the dissolution of the traditional load-bearing, protective, insular wall into separate independent functional components: the glass wall against rain, the "brise-soleil" against sunlight, the "mur neutralisant" for climate control, or the soundproof wall against noise. In order to illustrate his thesis, Banham chose Le Corbusier's Armée du Salut building in Paris, which had been built in 1933 and was one of the first air-conditioned buildings in France; its façade had to be completely refurbished in 1952 to meet modern comfort requirements.[26] However, Le Corbusier's oeuvre in fact reflects the attempt of architectural modernity to objectivize its means and instruments. What Le Corbusier examined in *5 Points d'une Architecture Nouvelle* from a constructive perspective simultaneously takes place from a hygienic, visual, and acoustic point of view, for instance in experiments aiming to create climate-controlled interiors, like the sanatorium in Cleveland that treated diabetes patients with a higher concentration of oxygen,[27] on a purely visual level, like in the optically neutral space of the "white cube" of modern museums,[28] or on the acoustic level in the creation of acoustically neutral spaces beginning in the 1920s.[29] This individualization and compartmentalization of architecture into autonomized disciplines continued during the postwar period, and was also reflected in safety, energy, fire safety, and other laws and norms, and thus experienced a bureaucratization, but also an academization. The corresponding structure of the wall not only leads to specialization, but also to a segregation of its diverse elements and technological implements, such as ventilation, cooling, and light supply, as well as to the differentiation of partitioning options. There is no longer

25 Sloterdijk: *Schäume*, p. 501 (see Note 5).

26 Reyner Banham: *The Architecture of the Well-Tempered Environment*, London, 1969, pp. 154–159.

27 Shown in: Richard Döcker: *Terrassen Typ. Krankenhaus, Erholungsheim, Hotel, Bürohaus, Einfamilienhaus, Siedlungshaus, Miethaus und die Stadt*, Stuttgart 1929, p. 65. Cf. Cunningham Sanitarium—*The Encyclopedia of Cleveland History*, online: http://ech.case.edu/ech-cgi/article.pl?id=CS6 (accessed 23 August 2012).

28 Cf. Brian O'Doherty: *Inside the White Cube. The Ideology of the Gallery Space*, Santa Monica, 1986.

29 Cf. Sabine von Fischer: *Von der Konstruktion der Stille zur Konstruktion der Intimität*, in: Jens Schröter/Axel Volmar (eds): *Auditive Medienkulturen. Techniken des Hörens und Praktiken der Klanggestaltung*, Bielefeld, 2013.

a sharp distinction between the public and the private, the individual and the community, at the boundaries of the building, but this distinction now occurs over a series of different thresholds, as for instance in the Prada shop by Rem Koolhaas in Beverly Hills. Using visual and technological devices and RFID technology, the traditional wall with a door was amplified by a number of visual, climatic, and security thresholds, not only subdividing the boundary between interior and exterior but, by means of a number of screens that serve as mirrors and displays, the boundary between the digital and the analogue worlds, too.[30] And that these boundaries are no longer only differentiated in the spatial sense, but also in the temporal one, is shown in the Brasserie in the Seagram Building, where the images of the security camera above the revolving door are projected onto the screens at the bar, thus preceding guests as they enter the main hall and saunter down the catwalk.[31]

The previously unified but ambiguous and geometrically comprehensible space can now be subdivided into a series of multiform and mutually independent interstices that can no longer be organized only according to their tectonic boundaries, but, as the competition design for the expansion of the Kunstmuseum Basel by Made In shows, by a series of devices such as elevators, escalators, and lifting platforms.[32] In these designs, the distinction between the genres of device and architecture is obsolete, as they form part of the same ensemble that not only encompasses the building, but also the human being. The individual, formerly isolated devices and components have passed through a converging series that ranges from their abstract purpose as an independent technological object to their unique concreteness within an interconnected system that combines device, building, and user into a single entity.

Up until the final years of the 20th century, segmentation was seen as the only way of being modern.[33] Usually, the relationship between the technological object and technological

[30] Cf. Rem Koolhaas et al. (ed.): *Prada*, Milan, 2001.

[31] Cf. Aaron Betsky et al.: *Scanning: The Aberrant Architecture of Diller + Scofidio*, New York, 2003.

[32] Cf. Sabine von Fischer: "Tetris hoch vier: Wettbewerb Kunstmuseum Basel, Erweiterungsbau 'Burghof'", in: *Werk, Bauen + Wohnen 3* (2010), pp. 50–54.

[33] Cf. Caroline A. Jones: "The Mediated Sensorium", in: Caroline A. Jones (ed.): *Sensorium: Embodied Experience, Technology, and Contemporary Art, Cambridge,* MA 2006, pp. 5–49.

knowledge was all too quickly conceived as a causal one, which neglected the fact that, contrary to the technological object, which must respond to a specific problem, knowledge in fact opens a space of opportunity, thanks to which structural design issues no longer have to be understood only as a technocratic negotiation of different coefficients, but can contribute to the aesthetic design of different atmospheric spaces characterized by sound, visibility, or simply climate requirements. Examples are, for instance, the Learning Center in Lausanne by Sanaa, in which different space, noise, and climate boundaries dissolve into a variety of threshold spaces,[34] or the schoolhouse in Paspels by Valerio Olgiati, in which the classrooms are literally inserted between the walls. It is no coincidence that the interior and exterior walls in Paspels are visually developed as screens, too.[35] From this point of view, we also need to interpret more recent experiments with monolithic or seemingly monolithic walls less as a return to a traditional mode of construction, but rather understand them as an expression of explicit knowledge, for instance of the storage capacity of walls.[36]

However, this presentation, which addressed the technological upgrading of architecture with a series of prostheses, devices, and machines over the past 150 years, should not be construed as deterministic. It doesn't so much reflect the rationality of a more and more refined technological system, but rather the discursive field of modernity. The narratives of modernity, which form and organize space, have found their material crystallization in the many technological inventions supplementing the traditional art of building. While the once load-bearing, protective, insular wall guaranteed a clear distinction between an exterior and an interior space, its explication not only led to the possibility of its dissolution into individual, independent elements, but also to the possibility of staggering

[34] Cf. SANAA: Kazuo Sejima, Ryue Nishizawa, 2004–2008: *Topología Arquitectónica/ Architectural Topology*, Madrid, 2008.

[35] Cf. Paspels/Valerio Olgiati, Zurich, 1998.

[36] Cf. i. e. Alois Diethelm: "Magie der Mischung", *in: Werk, Bauen + Wohnen 92*, 1/2 (2005), pp. 10–15, here pp. 13–14.; Andrea Deplazes: *Nachhaltigkeit. Grundprinzipien der Architektur*, in: *Architektur konstruieren. Vom Rohmaterial zum Bauwerk. Ein Handbuch*, Basel: 2005/2008, pp. 315–319, and: "Low-Tech Ziegelbau" [Dietmar Eberle in Conversation with Florian Aicher], in: *Die Bauwelt 27–28 (2012)*, pp. 6–8; and: Dietmar Steiner: "Zurück zur Architektur", in: Dietmar Eberle and Florian Aicher: *Die Temperatur der Architektur: Portrait eines Energieoptimierten Hauses/Portrait of an Energy-optimized House: The Temperature of Architecture*, Birkhäuser, Basel, 2016, pp. 35–43.

the different boundaries into a sequence of multiform and mutually independent interstices, mi-lieux in the literal sense. But at this point, when boundaries can always be reset, it is no longer only the act of tectonic enclosure that constitutes the origin of the architectural activity, but, in a more comprehensive, existential sense, the shaping of one's individual environment•

This essay is a revised and updated version of my essay "Mauer, Maschine, Milieu", in: *GAM 9* (2013), pp. 154–165. I would like to thank Florian Aicher and Dietmar Eberle for their suggestions, in particular regarding the monolithic wall.

Solitaire | From French *solitaire:* Alone, lonely, a loner. A solitary tree stands outside the forest, a solitary building outside of a settlement. Originally reserved for special purposes (for example, a mill built at a flood-prone site), in particular for persons with political power. For this reason, often stately structures, such as fortresses, castles, or mansions. All façades of a solitaire are important, and in the case of Le Corbusier even all six: His elevated residences are "bathed" in green.

Closed Coverage | Built-up areas that present themselves as wall-like and contiguous when viewed from the public space of a street or square. In medieval cities, naturally grown developments with high-density construction of rear areas; in contemporary times, planned complexes with rear courtyards; in the Foundation Era, densification sometimes became unacceptable as the result of speculation ("stony Berlin"). The opposite of open building patterns in rows, solitary houses, and the like.

Block | A connected group of properties surrounded on all sides by streets and built along these streets in a closed construction pattern. The preferred building pattern of 19th-century urban planning, often with the building enclosure constructed in a similar building method, eaves height, and style. Surrounding interior courtyards and/or other developments. Often constructed by private corporations as investment properties. Contrasted by the special "worker's fortresses" of 1920s Vienna, subsidized housing developments built by the City of Vienna.

Row | Answering to the urban crisis at the end of the 19th century (industrialization and worker slums) garden cities surrounded by "green belts" emerged (Ebenezer Howard). Rows of houses and gardens promised sunlight, fresh air, and hygiene. During the 1920s, this concept was evolved into ribbon developments with multi-story apartment buildings, east-west lighting, and a shift away from blocks (above all in Germany, for example by Ernst May in Frankfurt, and Walter Gropius in Dessau and Karlsruhe). Starting in the 1960s, rows were also south-facing, aligning with the sun. Pure ribbon developments often lose urban advantages such as public squares and street spaces.

Courtyard | An open square belonging to the house and surrounded by buildings. Old German: Settlement site, enclosed space, encircled by a winding fence; from the wall to the barn to the house; only later did *court* take on the meaning of a site of noble assembly. Atrium houses, a Mediterranean residential type with a courtyard/fireplace, became popular both in cities (domus) and the countryside (villa). In the Iberian region: Patio. Initially, freestanding buildings around a work yard (*Paarhof,* a two-building farmstead) north of the Alps. Special noble forms: Court of honor, cloister/monastery, palazzo, castle building, barracks, prisons.

Hall | A large connected room largely unimpeded by installations; covered by a roof, in contrast to open atriums. Initially reserved for public and sacred uses due to the complexity of construction, for example agoras or basilicas, mostly church buildings and market halls since antiquity. Divided by naves or bays, or without pillars. The advent of industrialization and steel as a building material saw this type of room rapidly develop into factory halls, railway stations, warehouses, etc. The largest hall in the world—the Boeing Factory in Everett, Washington—covers almost 99 acres.

Central Corridor Building | In German, *Spänner* is used to describe the number of active to passive sections of a unit by number. A *vierspännige* carriage is drawn by four horses. In apartment buildings, *Spänner* is used for the number of dwelling units connected per floor to a corridor or stairwell. A double-unit is a corridor with two, a six-unit one with six apartments. Or: A one-hipped complex has two utility areas, a two-hipped three. Economic efficiency rises with the number, but there is an upper limit to the density.

Coherence | Correspondence of parts amongst one another and to the whole. Each type of settlement (i.e. city centers, suburbs, small towns, villages) has its own density, circulation, public space, uses (i.e. apartment buildings, villas, farmhouses, government or business buildings, factories), and building types (detached, closed, mixed). A good distribution, often following convention, creates coherence. Dissonance can arise through growth and shrinkage processes—for example, a farmyard in the city, or a factory in a services area.

Homogeneity | From Greek *homós:* Same and *genesis:* Formation. Of the same composition. Homogeneity describes the sameness of the elements of a system; something can be homogenous in contrast to heterogeneous. A homogenous volume is made up of a consistent structure and similar building elements. In architecture, these two terms are used to describe the appearance of materials, building structure, and urban fabric. Homogenous, in the sense of coherence, can be a positive value; the same is true of heterogeneous in the sense of diversity.

PLACE—STRUCTURE—ENVELOPE—PROGRAM

Variation (intermixing) and flexibility (diversity and change) relativize the primacy of function and effect a valorization of place and building structure. The requirements of the place influence new use concepts, new uses modify the place. Building structure and envelope type can function as catalyzers or as obstacles to flexible usage. The degree of interdependency increases.

Aerial view of the Imam Reza Shrine Complex (Mashhad, Iran) and the city surrounding it 1971.

IMG 42914 © Aga Khan Trust for Culture / Michel Écochard (photographer)

Concept model
Timothy Allen
16 ss

Building Level

This exercise will develop a preliminary draft for the final project. Aspects relevant to the urban context—volume, positioning, circulation, and façade—are confronted with the building program. Particular attention must be given to the ground floor area.

Specifications

This exercise will be carried out independently. The following must be submitted:

- A concept diagram or images of a concept model 1:500
- Figure-ground diagram 1:5,000
- Area plan, 1:1,000 with roof view and topography
- Section with adjacent buildings 1:500
- Ground floor plan 1:200/1:250
- Upstairs floor plans 1:500
- Façade concept and possibly images referencing built examples
- Written explanation
- Insertion model 1:500 in site model

Requirements

- Existing building plans
- SIA Norm 416

Goal

This exercise is a preparation for the final project. Students can individually choose the project "scenario". The project's place will remain the same from here on out, and work with it will be intensified.

Early ideas should be visualized abstractly using concept diagrams and models. The goal is to develop a concept, visualize it, and continue to think it through. The conventional methods of representation—site, floor plan, cross-sections, and façade—will continue to be required and these skills thus refined.

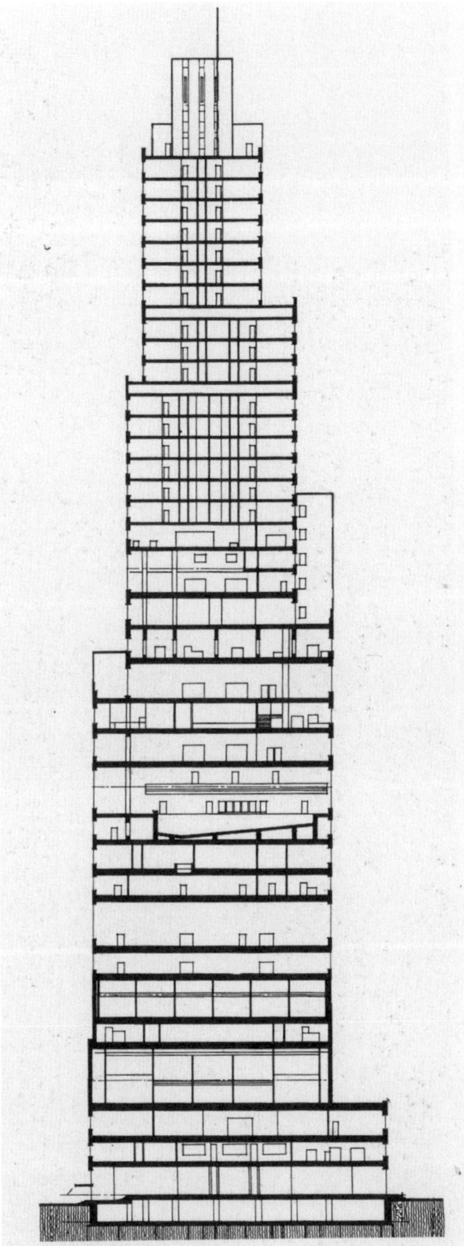

Starrett & Van Vleck,
Downtown Athletic Club,
New York, 1931

Source: Mario Campi, *Skyscrapers. An Architectural Type of Modern Urbanism*, Birkhäuser, 2000

Starrett & Van Vleck, Downtown Athletic Club, New York, 1931

MIDDLE AGES

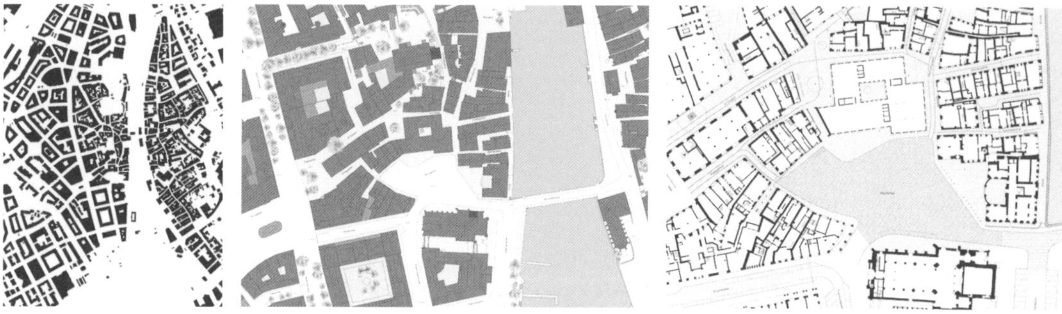

Nadia Raymann
15 SS

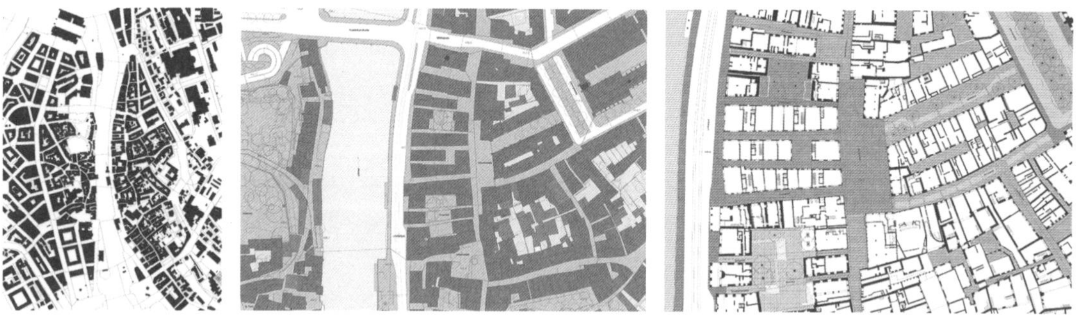

Rina Softa
11 SS

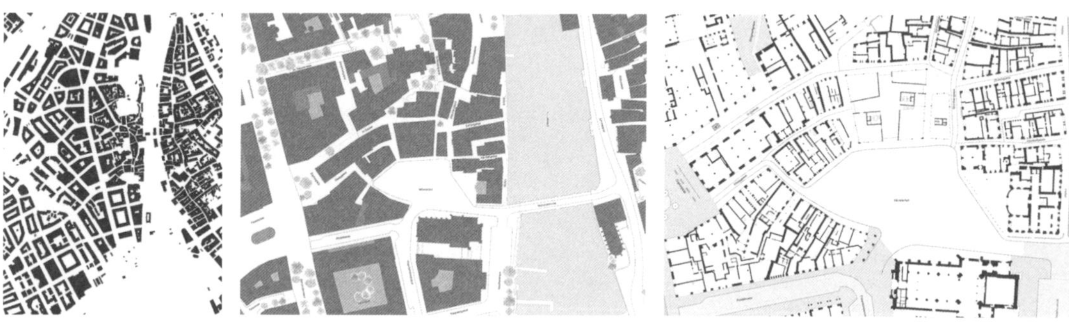

Deborah Truttmann
15 SS

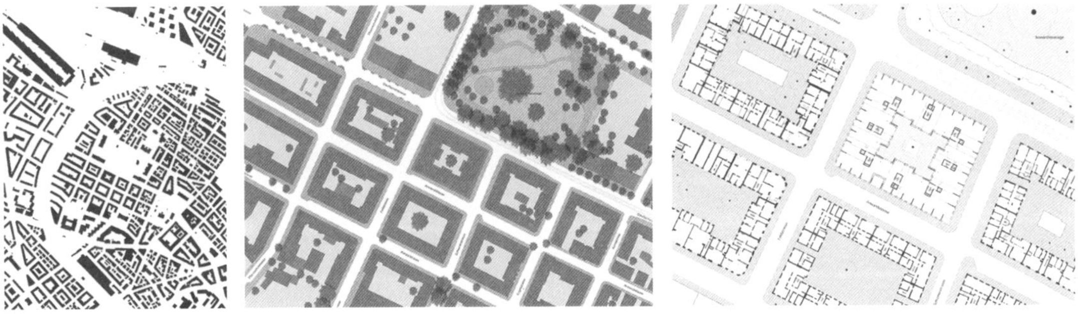

Leonie Lieberherr
11 SS

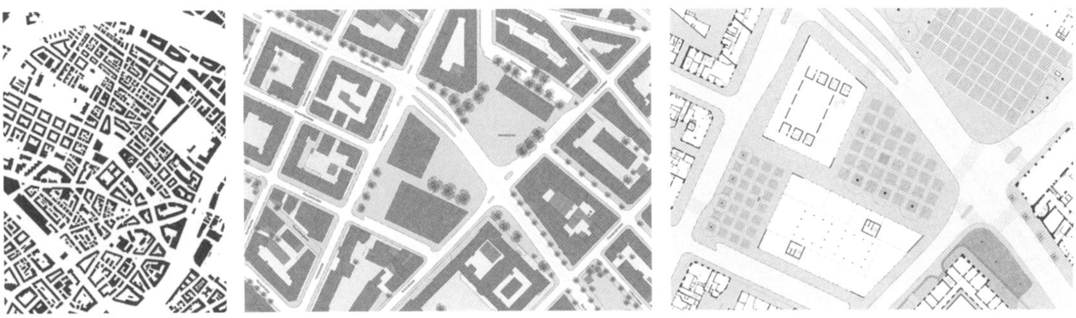

Patrick Perren
15 SS

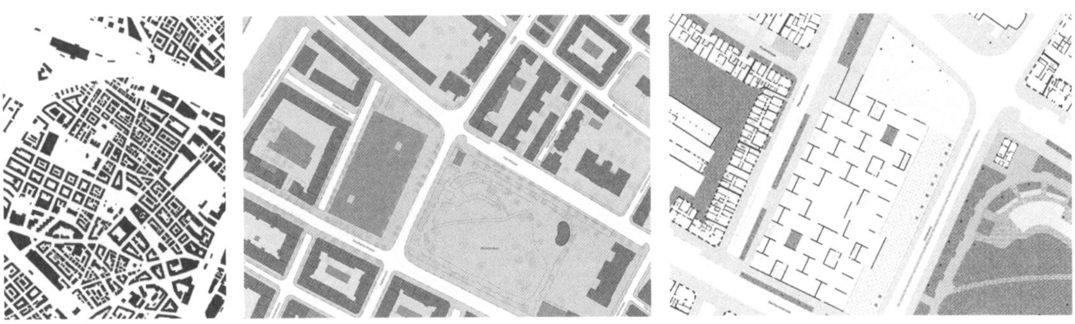

Thierry Vuattoux
16 SS

MODERNISM

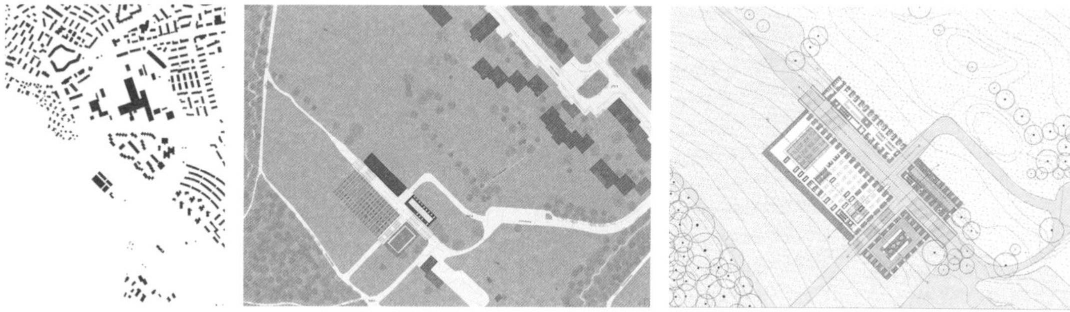

Cyrill Hirtz
16 SS

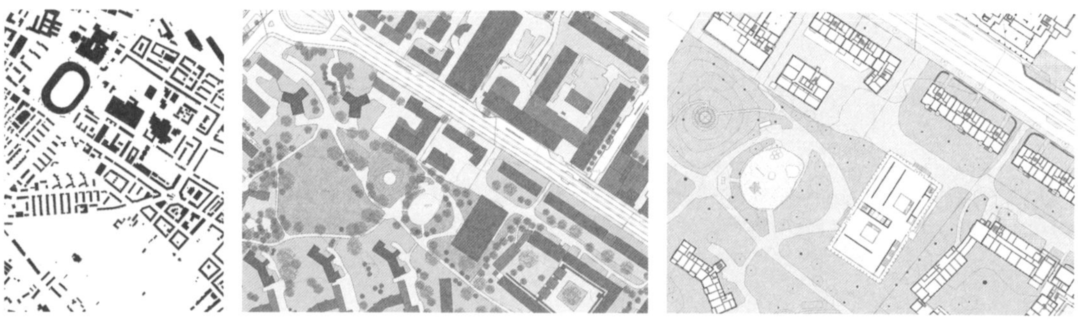

Viviane Zibung
15 SS

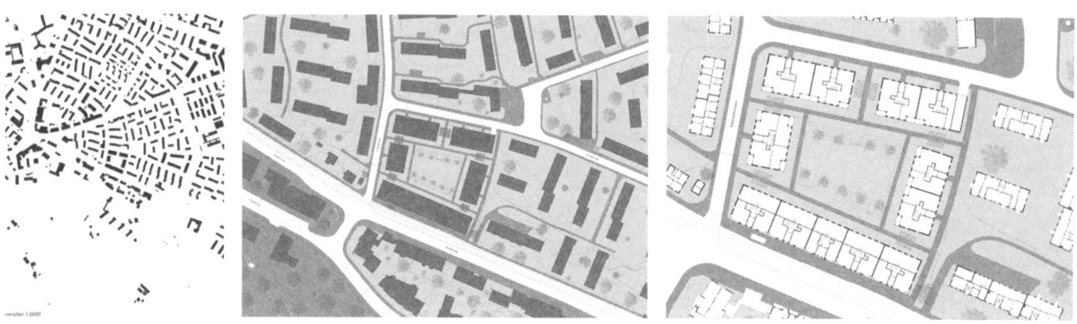

Sandro Lenherr
11 SS

MIDDLE AGES

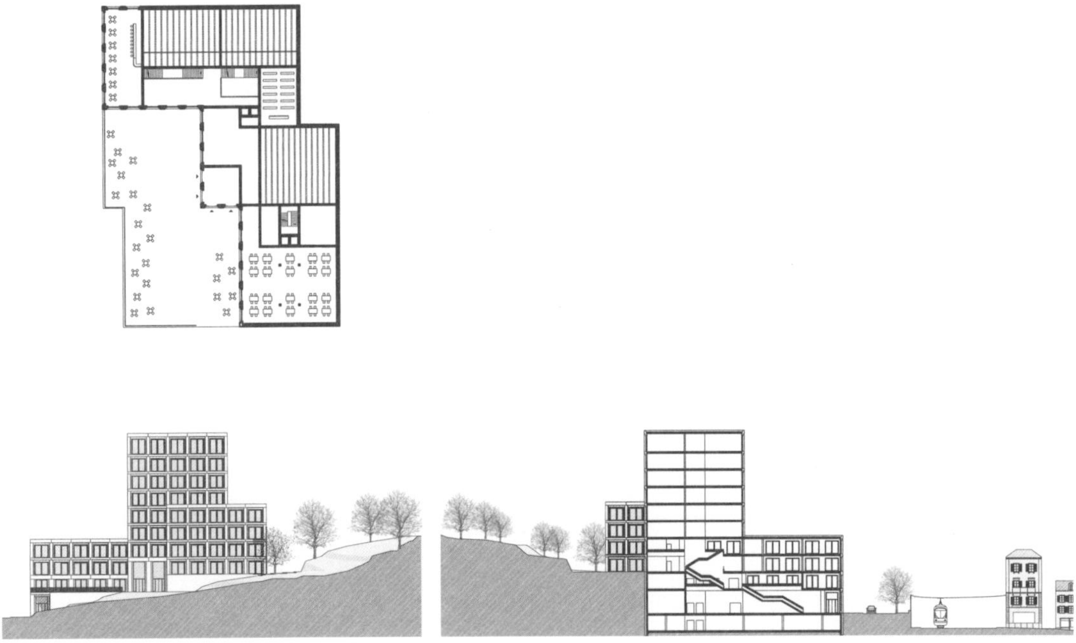

Marco Derendinger
14 SS

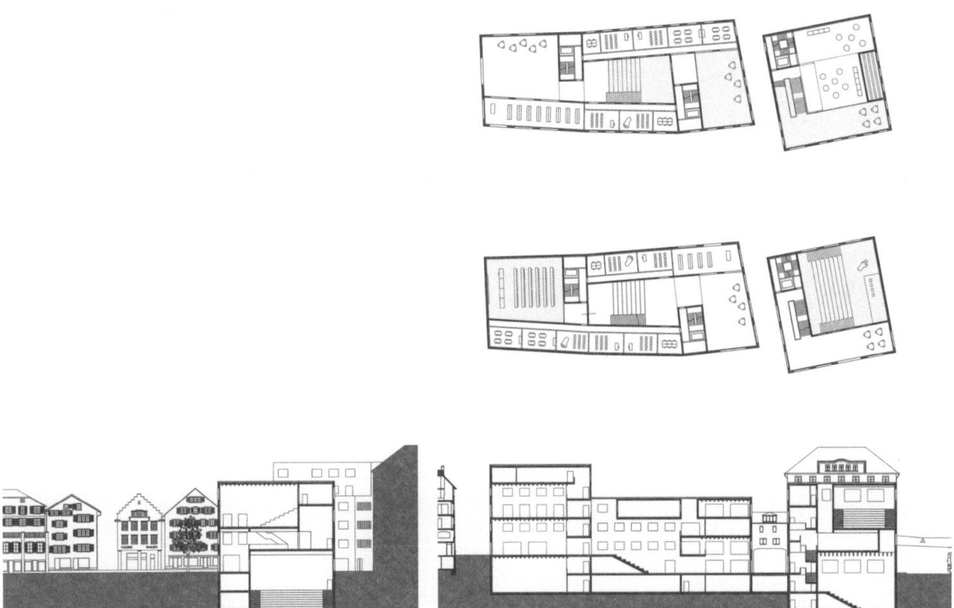

Noël Frozza
16 SS

MIDDLE AGES

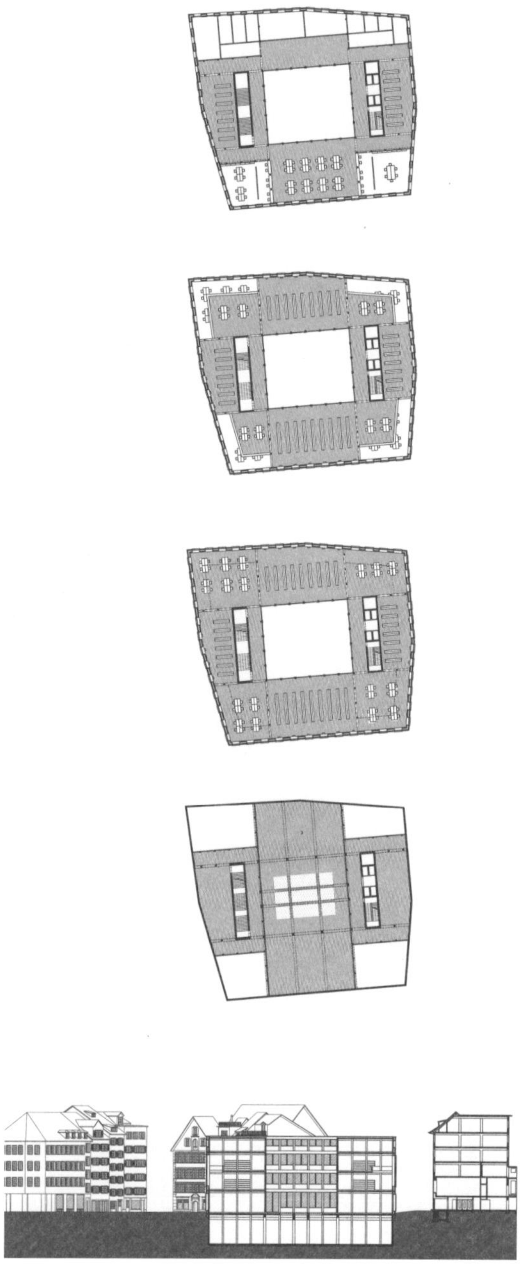

Katarina Savic
15 SS

Iso Tambornino
15 SS

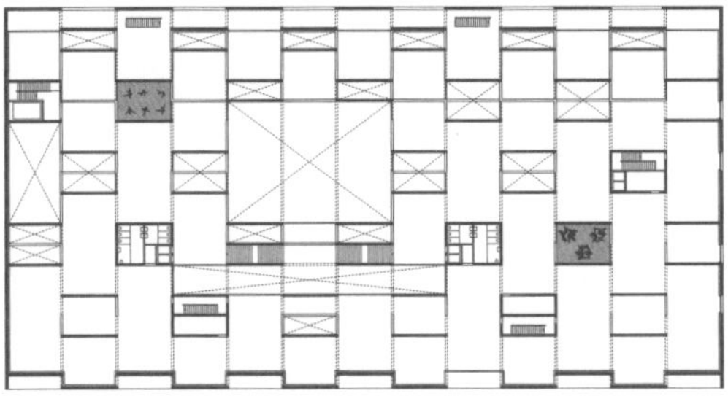

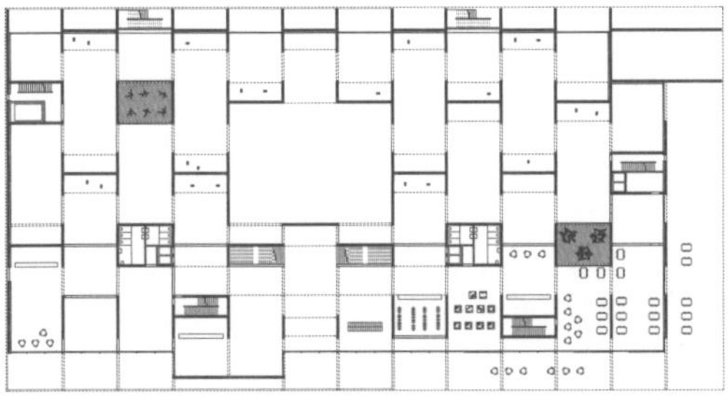

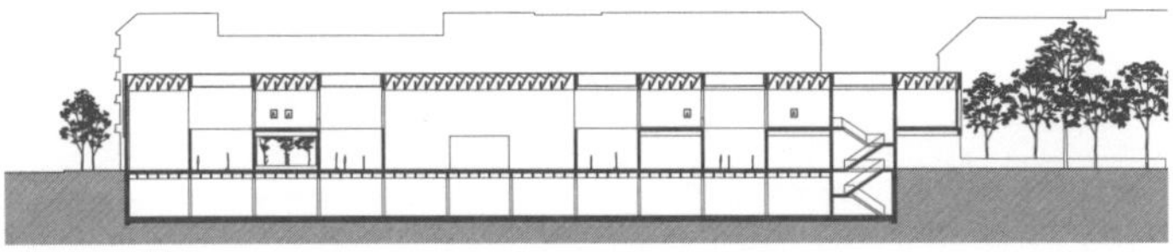

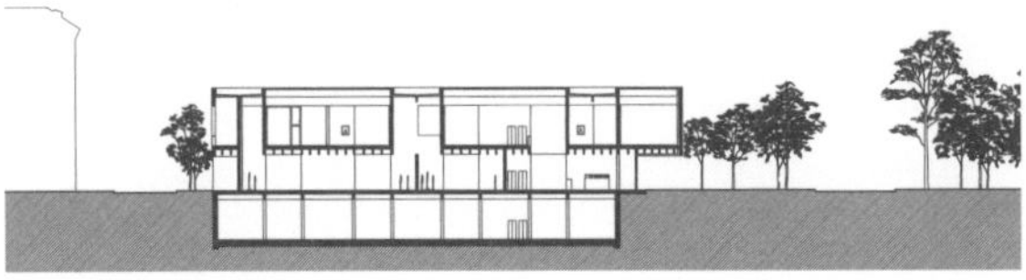

Thierry Vuattoux
16 ss

FOUNDATION ERA

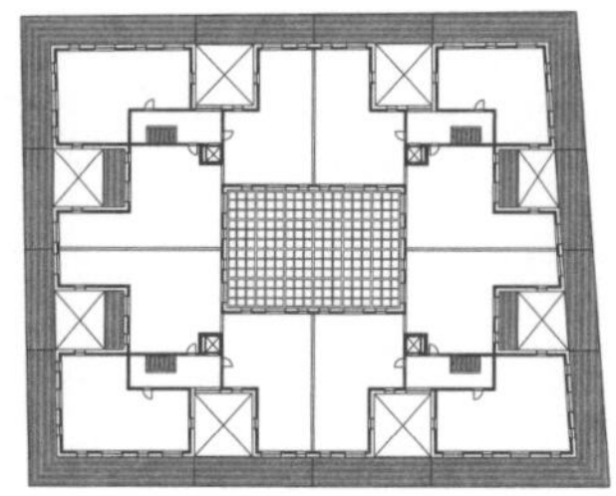

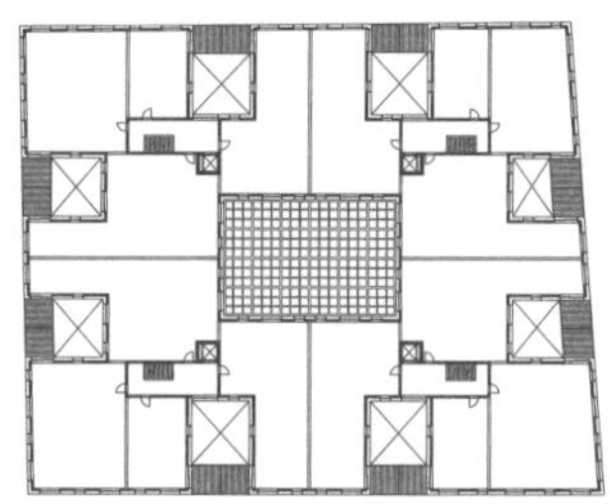

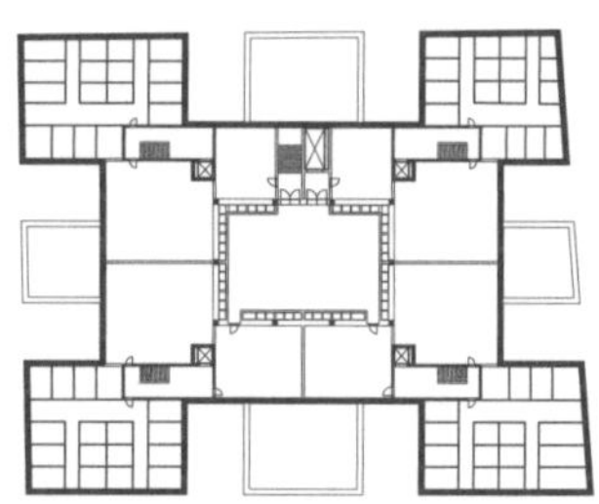

Elena Pilotto
12 SS

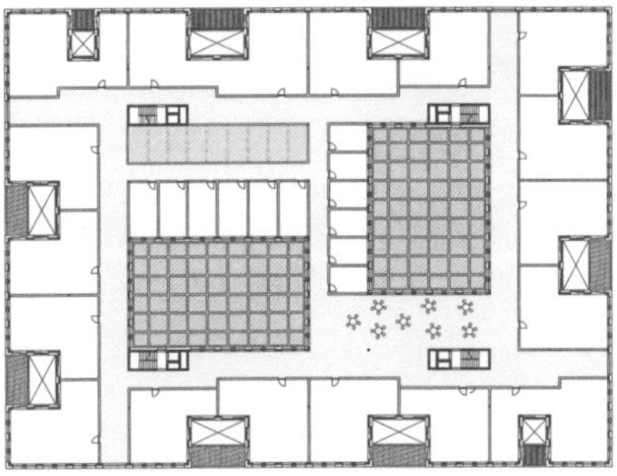
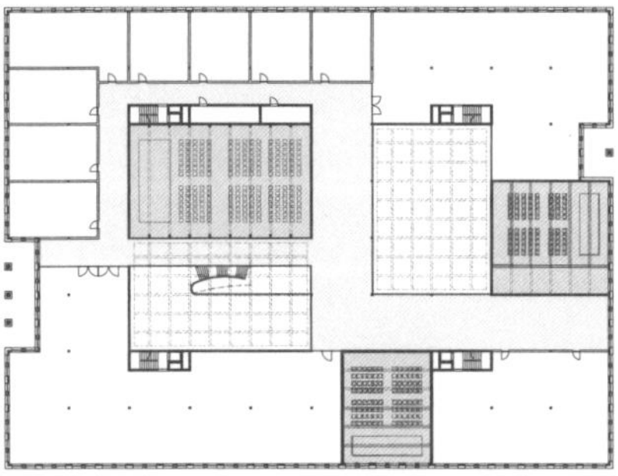
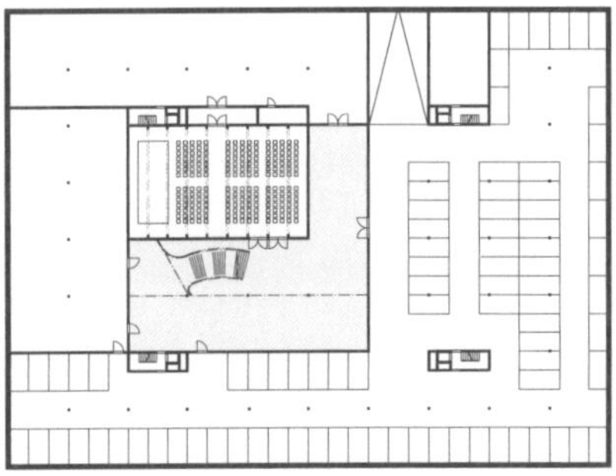
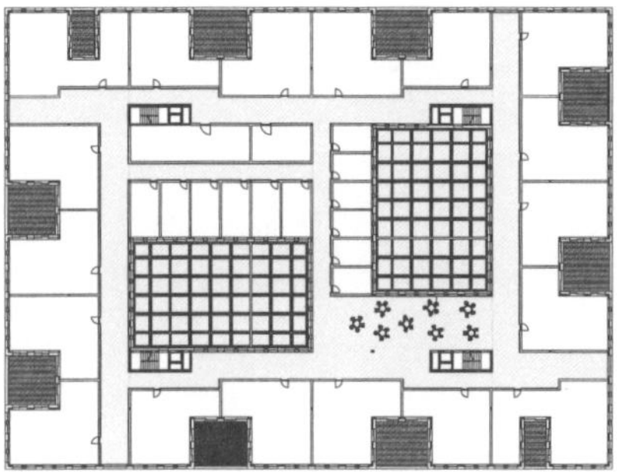
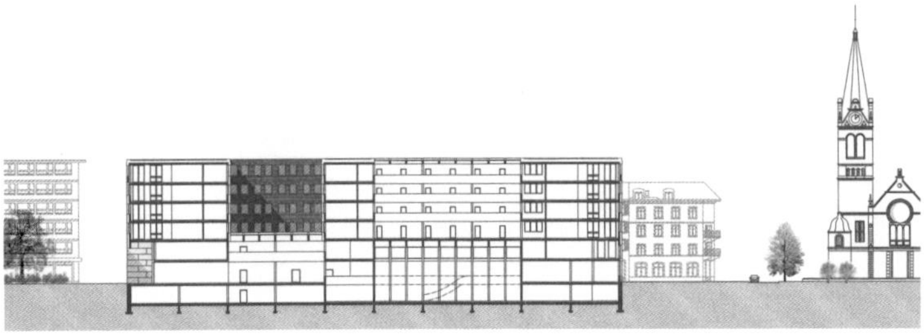
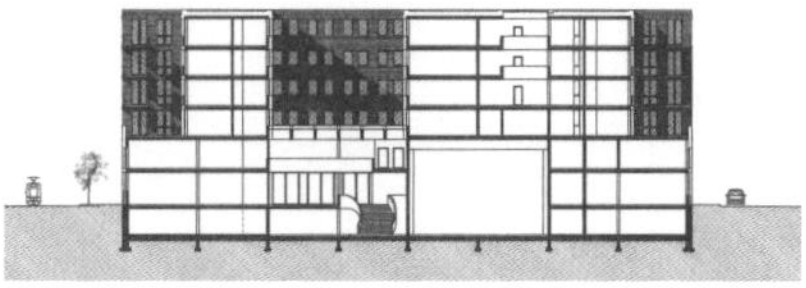

Maurin Elmer
14 SS

FOUNDATION ERA

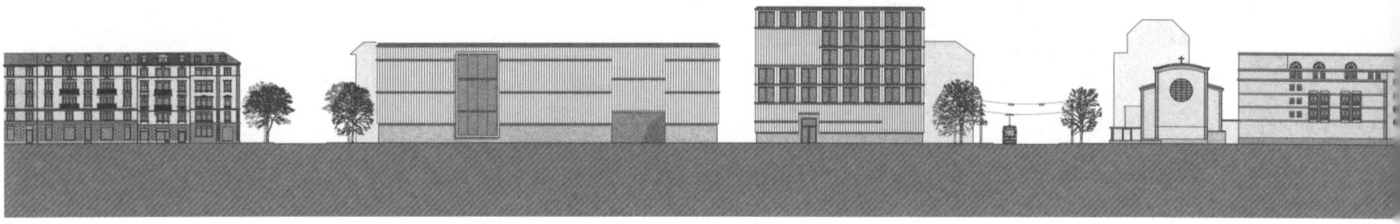

Julian Meier
16 SS

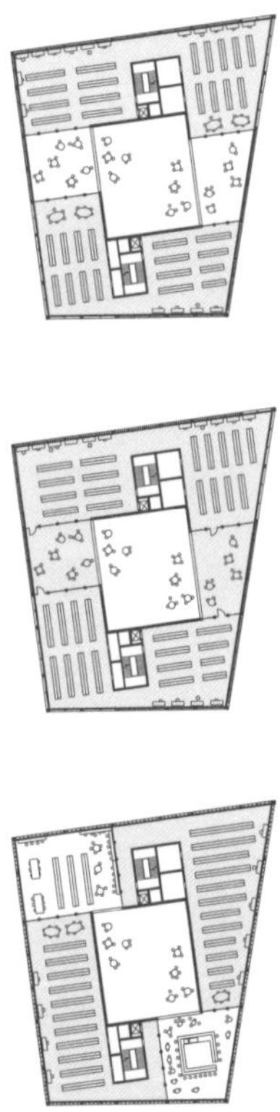

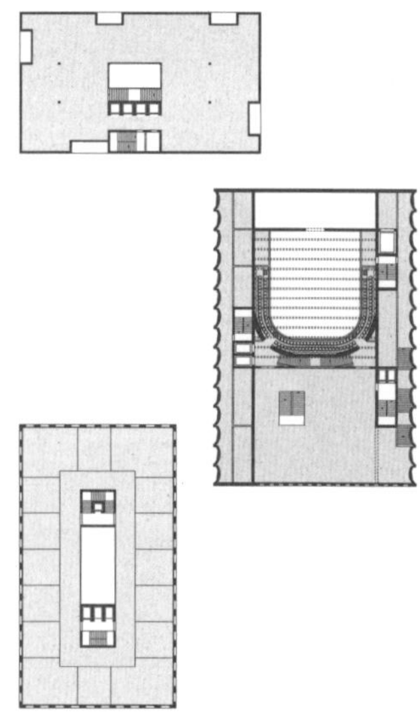

Timothy Allen
16 SS

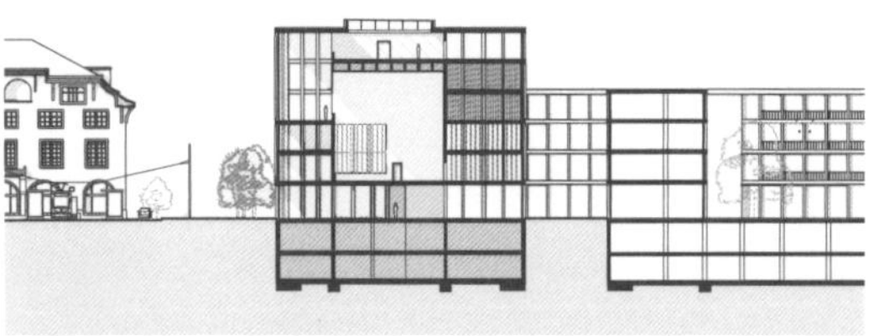

Daniela Gonzalez
15 SS

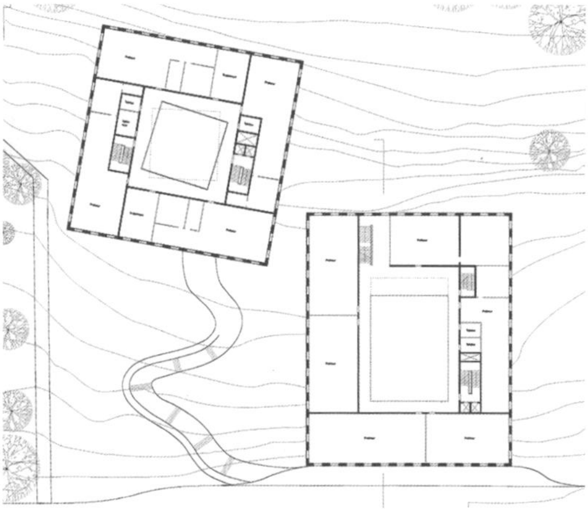

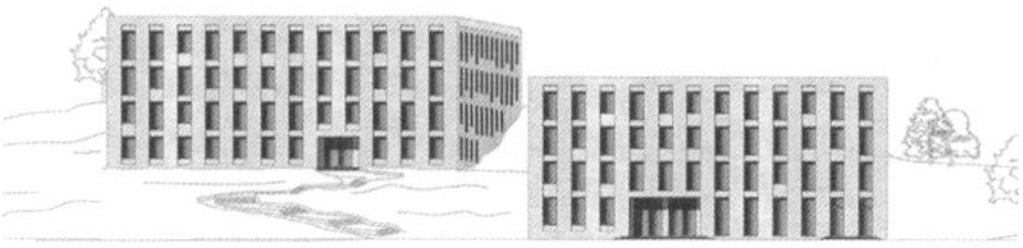

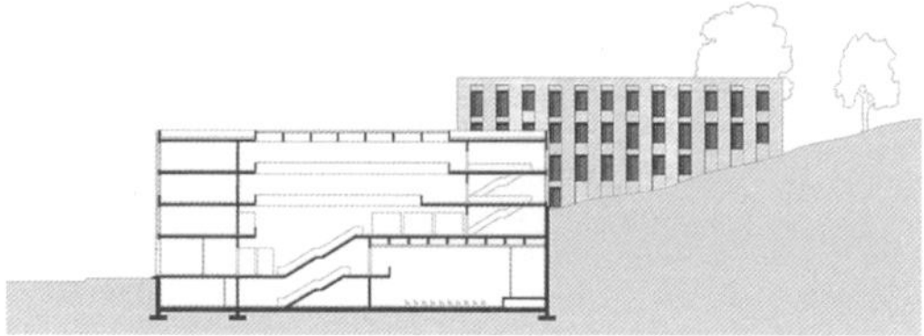

Cyril Angst
09 SS

MODERNISM

7

Lena Stäheli
11 SS

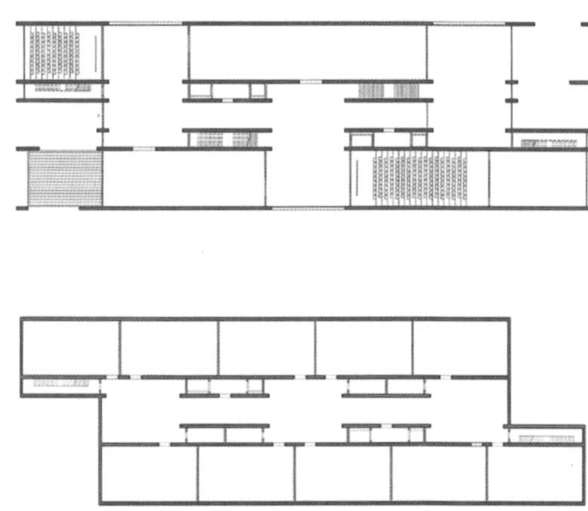

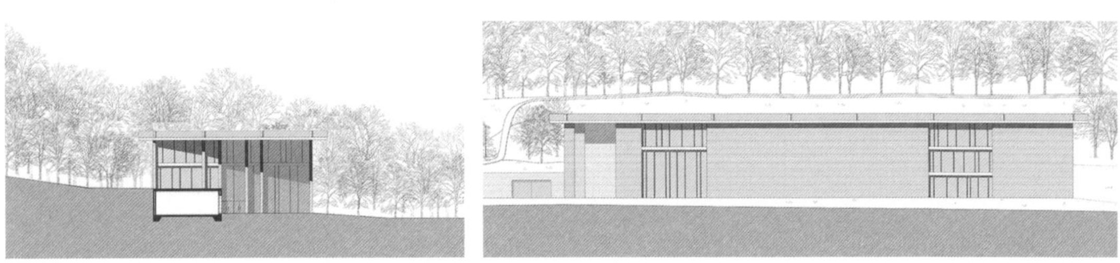

Lena Hächler
16 SS

MIDDLE AGES

Marco Derendinger
14 SS

Benjamin Graber
13 SS

MIDDLE AGES

Deborah Truttmann
15 SS

Noël Frozza
16 SS

Thierry Vuattoux
16 SS

Leonie Lieberherr
11 SS

Luca Rösch
14 SS

FOUNDATION ERA

Patrick Perren
15 SS

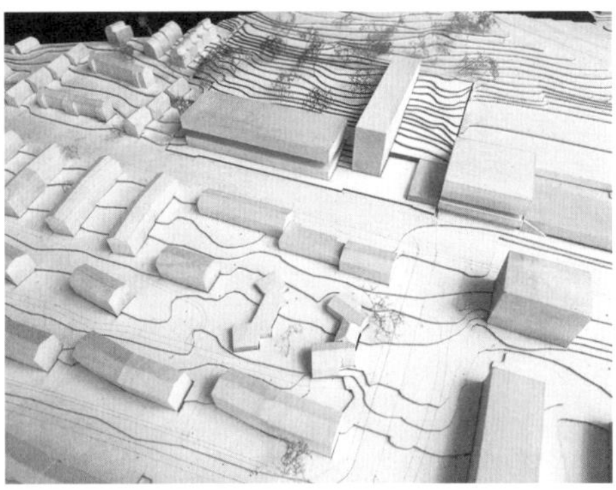

Eva Müller
14 SS

Tim Kappeler
16 SS

MODERNISM

Tiziana Schirmer
13 SS

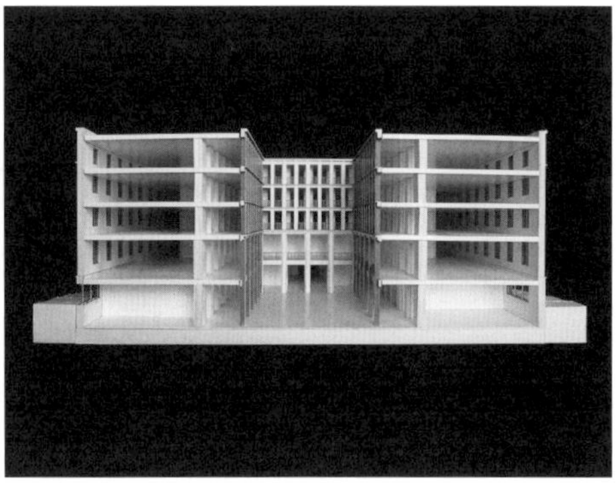

Benjamin Graber
13 SS

Adrian Gämperli
15 AS

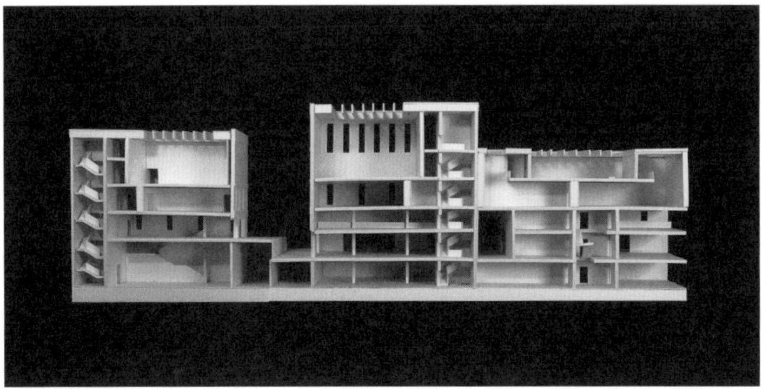

Carola Hartmann
16 SS

FOUNDATION ERA

Julian Ganz
09 SS

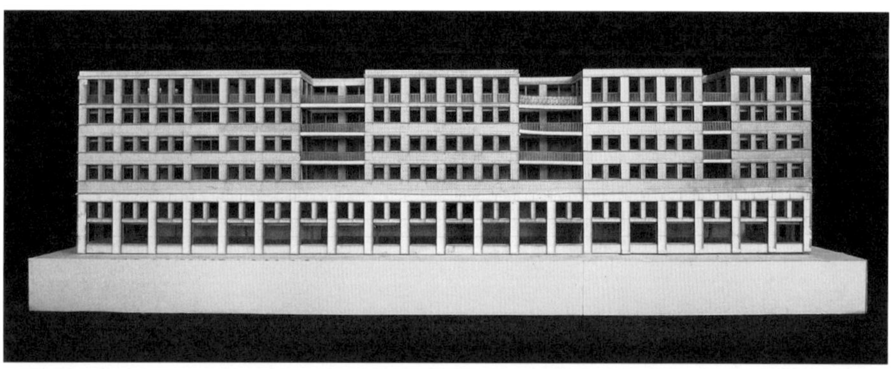

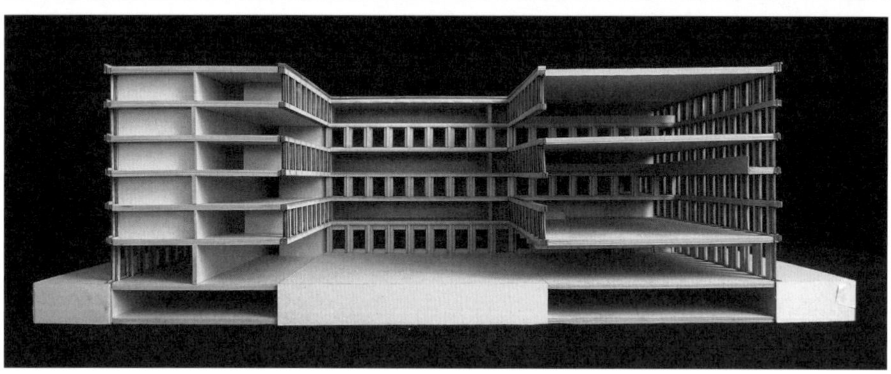

Michael Frefel
14 SS

Thierry Vuattoux
16 ss

7

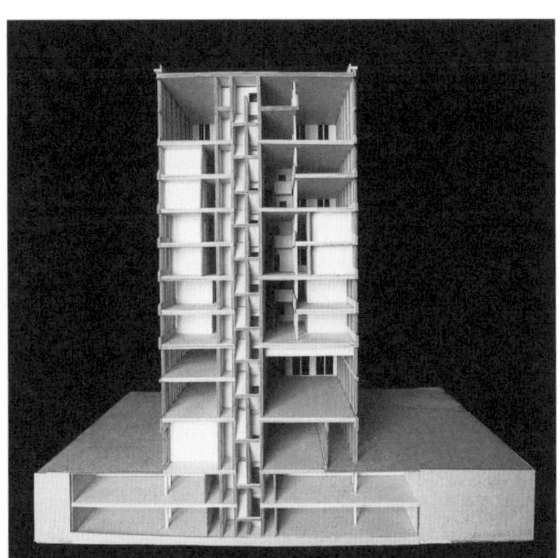

Jakob Junghanss
15 ss

FOUNDATION ERA

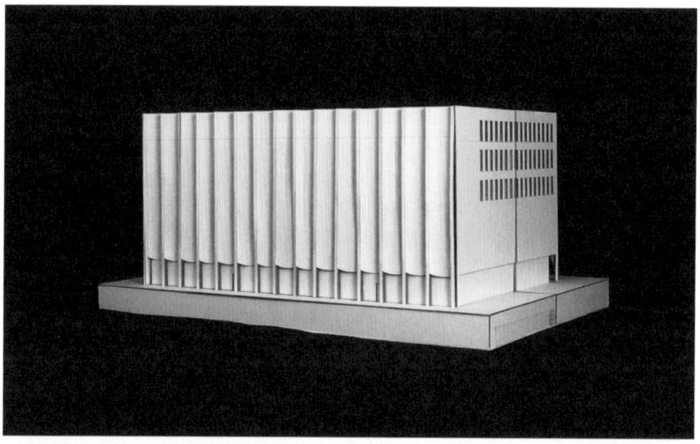

Timothy Allen
16 ss

Matthias Winter
09 SS

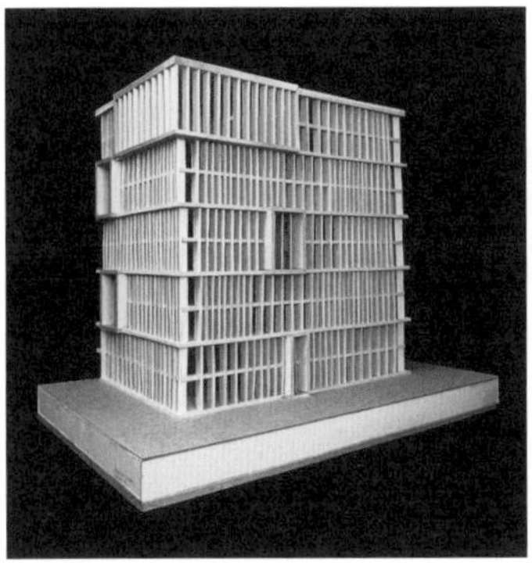
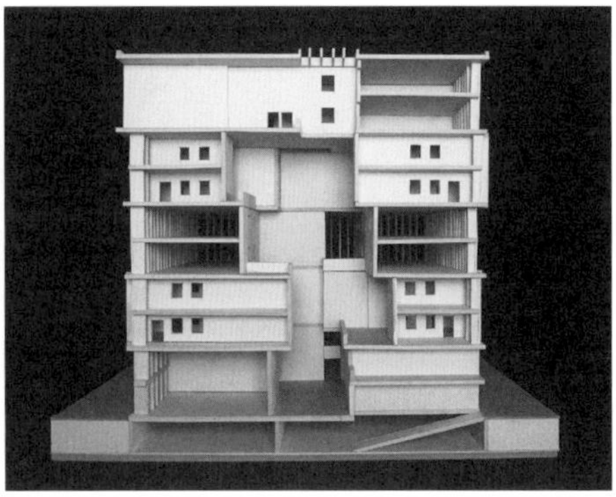

Geraldine Burger
13 SS

Marco Derendinger
14 SS

MODERNISM

Lea Grunder
14 SS

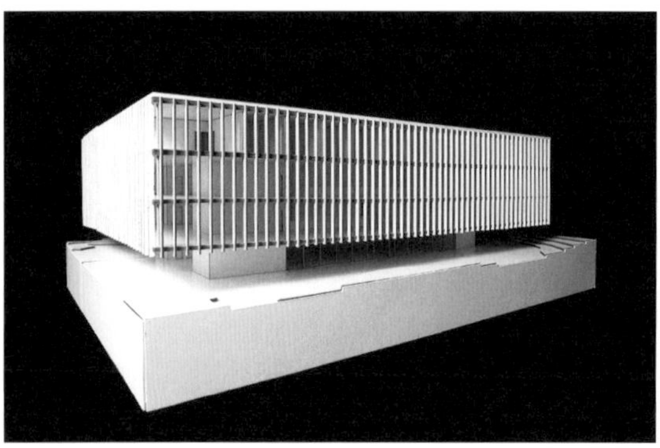
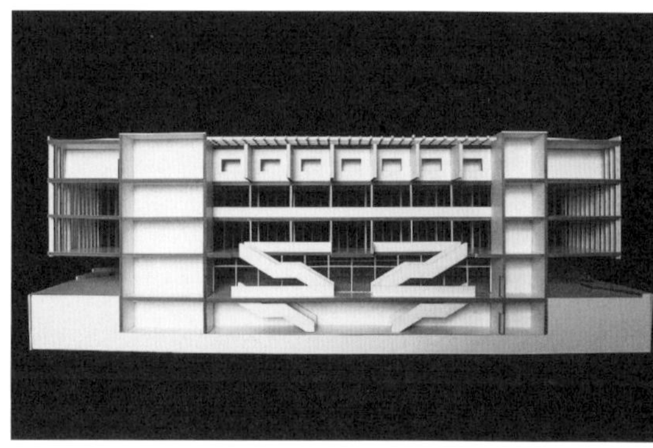

Alexandra Grieder
15 SS

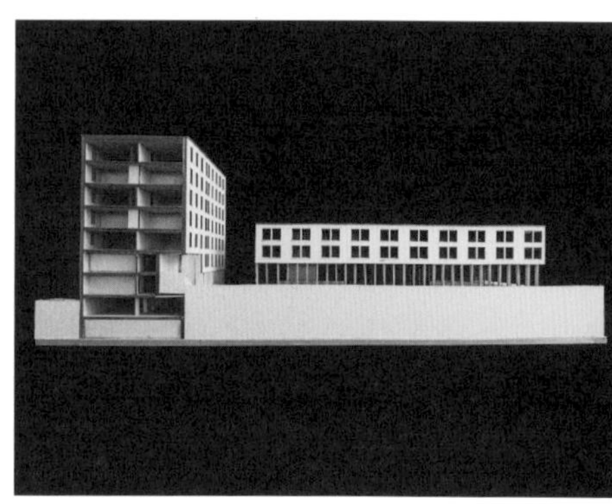

Eva Müller
14 SS

MIDDLE AGES

Thomas Meyer
09 SS

Françoise Vannotti
09 SS

MIDDLE AGES

Marco Derendinger
14 SS

Vincent Prenner
17 SS

Noël Frozza
16 SS

FOUNDATION ERA

Silvio Rutishauser
14 AS

Julian Meier
16 ss

Patrick Perren
15 ss

FOUNDATION ERA

Adrian Gämperli
16 ss

Timothy Allen
16 ss

Thierry Vuattoux
16 ss

MODERNISM

Tiziana Schirmer
13 SS

Sandro Lenherr
11 SS

Tobias Lutz
15 SS

MODERNISM

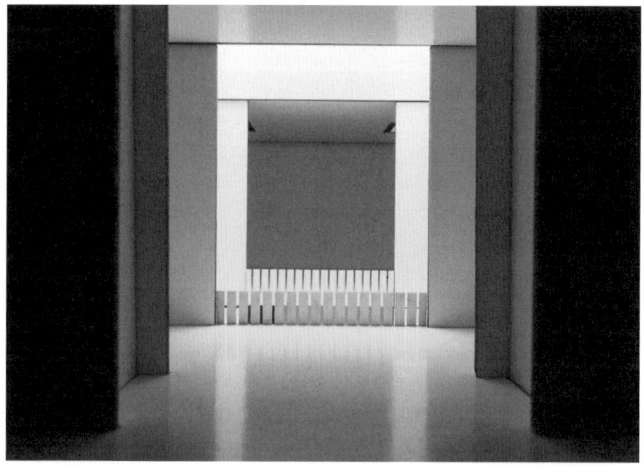

Daniel Zieliński
16 ss

Katrin Röthlin
16 ss

Christian Szalay
16 ss

Bas Princen, *Retreat (Palekh)*, 2003 © Bas Princen

8
Materiality

8 **Materiality**

One could speak of architecture as deliberate concreteness—material brought into form. The consistency of the volume, the materiality of the things is essential to architecture. The materiality of things and the consistency of the elements of architecture are first conveyed by the surface of the objects.

Is it that easy? The field of architectural objects alone is broad: They can be artifacts, artificial products, or natural materials; this includes physical phenomena such as sound and light, or fleeting substances like water and air; sensual impressions of materials—like hard/soft or porous/compact—must be named along with intellectual arrangements—such as the ordering of a grid, or artistic premises.

Is consistency part of the material uniqueness of a thing? Things are perceived, interpreted, desired, and detested—they are in a direct relationship with the actions of people and are occupied by intentions. In this way they gather meaning, become charged with emotion, acquire histories. According to this, things are an interplay of material, surface, and use. What happens with objective materiality when events impart things with situative meaning?

Material characteristics are communicated through surfaces. Surface is often looked at with mistrust—as fleeting, deceptive, only an appearance. Architecture theory plays a role in this, even Le Corbusier's definition of architecture as "the masterly, correct and magnificent play of masses brought together in light" (1986, 29) remains distanced. In this, all sensual materiality has disappeared—an earmark of the decidedly rationalistic schools of architecture. These, as a rule, target formal orders and constructive systems—thus the radical pre-eminence of columns and beams in Marc-Antoine Laugier's Primitive Hut.

Gottfried Semper, on the other hand, provides decided opposition. For him, architecture begins not with structure, but with texture, textiles, and material. And he asks: How is this done? These are people who choose two bands, tie them together, shaping them. Textiles can never be "objective" like stone. Shaping, giving the material a form, subjectively and thus seemingly—for Semper this is part of architecture. One can take from young Semper: In the discussion on polychromy, he took sides with color, with design, with the free will of the creative spirit: romantic revolts against the white rationality of the Classicists.

Seen this way, it is not surprising to read in his architectural teachings: "Every artistic creation, every artistic pleasure, presumes a certain carnival spirit, to put it in a modern way, the haze of carnival candles is the true atmosphere of art. The destruction of reality, of the material, is necessary" (2004, 438–9). His Natural History and Art History Museums in Vienna are proof of this—the opulence of the spatial envelope is overwhelming, space becomes a fantastic sheath. In art-obsessed Vienna, the interior spaces of Adolf Loos live on—in contrast to the asceticism of most of the façades of his buildings. This is where his battle against ornamentation unfolds; he becomes the taskmaster of modernism. His planar, solemnly gridded curtain façades are well removed from those of Semper.

This is not without challenge. Today, the key word is atmosphere. Ákos Moravánszky defines atmosphere as synesthesia—an all-experience of the space with all senses. The material, the sensual is back, and this in two ways. For one: a new culture of material, for building material and textiles. These are celebrated, while previously materials had melted into architecture. "I try to use materials like this in my work. I believe that they can assume a poetic quality in the context of an architectural object. [...] The tangibility, smell, and acoustic qualities are merely elements of the language that we are obliged to use," writes Peter Zumthor 2006, 10). This includes the use of new types of daily, dirtied, and used materials. On the other: The emotionalization of space. "Architecture must blaze," demanded Coop Himmelb(l)au almost 50 years ago.

If the extension of space through media proves to be an enrichment for the atmosphere will be shown by time. If synesthesia is part of its being, then activating all senses is a prerequisite.

8

The Porosity of Space

Eberhard Tröger

I have thoroughly inhabited [this house] as well. I believe it is the place in the world that I have lived in the most. And when I speak of other women, then I think that these other women also contain me; it is as if they and I, as if we, had the gift of porosity, of permeability. [...] All the women I see here are silent at first; I do not know what will become of them afterwards, but in the beginning they are silent for a long time. They are encrusted into the space, as if inserted into the walls, into the objects in the room. When I am here in this room, I have the feeling of not upsetting anything of a certain order, as if the space itself, the room, I mean, does not even detect my presence, the presence of a woman: it already had its place here. What I am most likely talking about is the silence of space.[1]

8

[1] Marguerite Duras, Michelle Porte: *Die Orte der Marguerite Duras*, Frankfurt am Main, 1982, p.14.

Silent Space

In 1976, the writer and filmmaker Marguerite Duras, then sixty-two, sat in her old country house in Neauphle-le-Château near Paris, and in a lengthy interview, spoke about the house's multivalent relationships with herself and her books and films. This was the only house that Duras, who grew up in Vietnam and later lived in Paris, had ever lived in intensely and for a long time. That is where she wrote her most important novels and many screenplays for her films. She identified herself and the protagonists of her works (who are almost always women) with this house. The "gift of porosity", which she ascribed to herself and those women, was transferred to the building and its spaces. For her, porosity has two fundamental qualities.

On the one hand, it effects a permeability, and on the other hand, it guarantees a great capacity for storage. As far as the women are concerned here, Duras means the ability to listen

Living room in the home of writer and filmmaker Marguerite Duras

Photos © Michelle Porte, *Les Lieux de Marguerite Duras*, Marguerite Duras et Michelle Porte, Minuit, 1977 without commenting, and to absorb the story of their counterpart in silence. Motherhood is perhaps the most fundamental example of this wordless exchange.[2] A child takes form in the mother's body and passes through it silently and naturally as part of its development, leaves it, and yet remains connected for life. The womb, perhaps the largest "pore" of the female body, is the first temporary "dwelling" of the still silent child. Communication occurs not verbally, but through physical exchange. Marguerite Duras also finds this non-verbal physical understanding in her own house. The women in her novels are "encrusted onto the space, as if inserted into the walls". Like Duras herself, they inhabited the rooms of their house(s) with her, remaining a silent presence. This house, too, has the "gift of porosity" that makes permeability and retention possible.

[2] In fact, as the basic element of everything physical, in this sense, the word *material* is related to the Latin word *mater*, meaning "mother".

8

In this sense, one could view the rooms and spaces of a house as its largest pores. Within these, histories are formed and, new people live and stay in them again and again, storing their lives in the rooms. They are caught up in the rooms and in their smaller configurations, like closets, niches, drawers, and shelves, and are ultimately retained in the pores of the plaster, the wood, the tiles, and in the seams of the drapery fabric.

Instead of pores, the French philosopher Gaston Bachelard speaks about "honeycombs" in which space, "through the long residencies" of its inhabitants, stores up "condensed time" like honey,[3] which then nourishes new life once again. This refers not only to the patina that accumulates in the pores of the material as a physical trace of life, but also the memories, feelings, and experiences of the inhabitants themselves, which the space absorbs and re-emits. When I have lived in a room long enough, it records me, my smell, my voice, my body, my habits, and my entire personality, so that I become a natural part of it. The room can then "remain silent", because its occupant always remains contained within it, regardless of actual physical presence. A calm matter-of-factness is engendered that reconnects space and occupant. The "gift of porosity" in man and material is crucial to this exchange. Both can be either open or closed, rough or

[3] Gaston Bachelard: *Poetik des Raumes*, Frankfurt am Main 2007, p. 35.

smooth, translucent or opaque. A person will perceive a space differently, depending on the degree of reciprocal permeability or capacity for retention.

Pores and Friction

In this sense, one might reach a different understanding of the materiality of architecture. Rather than talking about a particular type of stone, concrete, wood, ceramic, plastic, or metal, one might first understand the entire building as a material that possesses different degrees and qualities of porosity. If its architectural layout is composed on a small scale, as is often the case with residential buildings, it creates a large surface that comes very near to the body of the occupants, and generates great "friction". The tactile qualities of the walls, floors, ceilings, and objects in the space become even more important. And the material must be even more porous, so the inhabitants can breathe freely. If the architectural layout is more spacious, its materialization can modulate the character of the space more freely, because the dimensions of a room allow the occupant to breathe more deeply. A range of porosities can yield great permeability, but also a high density, whose various qualities complement each other.

Materials could be classified according to porosity and their relation to intimacy or anonymity. The greater the permeability and capacity for retention, the more a closer exchange between man and material becomes possible. Materials like wood, textiles, and even plaster all create such an intimate atmosphere. They provide a structure upon which the habits, the memories, and the life stories of the occupants can "encrust" themselves. They can absorb the traces of the occupants like a sponge and reproduce them in measures. These materials also affect the sound and smell of a room; they fully absorb the light, and they are warm and soft to the touch.

By contrast, there is an impersonal atmosphere in rooms furnished with materials like steel and glass, which gives the room a rather remote feeling. Due to the high density of the material, the traces of life bead up on them. They can thus become more heavily fortified with stories. Materials with glossy surfaces magnify this effect. They reflect the light almost unfiltered. A white color gives these materials a similar quality. For instance, the architects of classical modernism employed materials such as chrome, glass, and white paint to imbue their buildings with the bright look of cleanliness on the one hand, and on the other, the anonymous aura of transient internationality.[4]

[4] In modern architecture, these smooth and impermeable materials have often been combined with extremely soft and propous materials, such as deep pile rugs, raw silk curtains, natural stone, and highly grained wood. This close juxtaposition of anonymous detachment and intense intimacy served as a stimulus to material eroticism, as was achieved in the 1960s and 70s with combinations of materials such as high-gloss plastic and Flokati shag rugs.

8

In his well-known book, *In Praise of Shadows*, Tanizaki Jun'ichirō writes about the difference between soft, matte surfaces, which he attributes to Asian culture, and smooth, reflective, or white surfaces, which he believes are found predominantly in European culture: "When we see bright shiny things, we are generally seized with inner turmoil. [...] Of course, we do occasionally need silver kettles, sake bowls, and bottles as well, but they are never polished. On the contrary; one is happy when their shiny surface fades and they blacken with age." Matte, patinated surfaces may be regarded as signs of porosity, while a shine represents high density.

Anomalies and Misunderstandings

The mirror occupies a special place in this context. Mirrors also play an important role in Marguerite Duras' films. They signify a very special physical phenomenon. As a smooth, reflective surface, they have a very high density and thus a minimum level of porosity. Conversely, for Duras they are the maximization of the pore *par excellence*. They are like bottomless "holes" in which the (cinematic) image is caught and then released, as if from an infinite distance. The mirror thus does not store, but creates a hole for the fleeting, the detached, for "calling into question"; for coming and going without lingering.[5] It opens up space to infinity yet simultaneously seals it shut. Rather than displaying its own materiality, its reflects our personal image in virtual form and multiplies it. Mirrors are at once all materials and none at all.

[5] Duras, p. 74.

Glass is an even more architecturally significant material. Its density and transparency cause widespread misunderstanding that continues to impact our era to this day. In fact, it involves a contradiction that extends spatially beyond that of the mirror.

A very impermeable (i.e., small-pore) material, it feigns transparency by means of its transmissibility. We still frequently speak of the openness of glass façades. Yet it is one of the most impermeable materials we know. Its openness is based solely on an optical effect. This must not be underestimated, however, as it stands for the perception of an entire epoch and its fixation on visual stimuli, which is still growing.

The architects of classical modernism always strived for interior and exterior spaces that "flow" into one another. For them, a building should appear as porous as possible. Expanses of windows were designed for the temperate European climate along these lines, which, due to their sheer size, often had to be constructed as fixed glass. Those architects spoke about a framed view, which admittedly passes through the thin but extremely impermeable membrane of the windowpane. Inside and outside could only flow into one another visually, never physically. Today, this effect is being radically advanced by the virtual worlds from which we are also physically separated by the membrane of the computer screen. This visual notion of consumption is returning to architecture. Those who can afford to do so "open" their rooms through (non-operable) glass surfaces that make possible the protected consumption of the outside world. However, porosity, retention, and communication are no longer possible in this divided system. A building's occupants can interact with the environment visually at best. The window now becomes a screen.

Bubbles and Foam

In this way, the permeable pores close and become isolated bubbles that, together with adjacent bubbles, form a kind of foam. Each occupant now sits in their own impenetrable shell, closing themself off from their environment.[6] When many bubbles merge together in a foam structure, planar separating membranes form between them that strongly resemble fixed glazing in appearance and effect. Porosity and retention are then no longer possible. We can even find the image of the foam physically manifest at the material level. After window glass, building materials such as PU foam, cellular glass, foamed aluminum, and the like are currently among the most widely used façade materials. And in fact, these substances isolate building

[6] Peter Sloterdijk used this image to narrate the entire history of mankind from today's perspective in his spherical trilogy, *Bubbles, Globes, Foam.*

occupants energetically as well as socially. Materials like foam and glass do not allow the penetration of heat, air, odors, or most noises. Moreover, unlike porous materials, they can scarcely develop historicality. As they do not interact with their surroundings, they can neither change nor adapt themselves, nor record or retain any traces. They tend to stay the same and/or are destroyed by change. These aesthetics, which are ageless in a very special way, increasingly shape the face of our cities.

It is a paradox of Western society that we strive for the greatest possible amount of isolation in technology and energy as a positive goal, while on a psychosocial level we suffer from the increasing isolation of every individual, though we are increasingly tightly interconnected. The currently massive use of concrete clearly demonstrates this anxiety-ridden counterreaction. Because of its high density, concrete not only has very limited porosity; it also manifests a momentary state that is very difficult to change or reverse afterwards. The increasing freedom of action is counteracted structurally by increasing ossification and isolation.

Osmosis and Coma

In place of the smoothness of mirrors and glass, or the hardness of concrete, the history of architecture records centuries of efforts to increase the porosity of buildings by means of form, ornament, and decoration. The intricate shapes of stuccowork and stone masonry were vulnerable to deposits, and yet at the same time showed the ductility of their materials. There could be friction between the building and the city, and between space and its occupants. Today, however, these qualities are scarcely appreciated. What was once regarded as a precious patina is now seen as grime. Yet such deposits can still have a technical benefit. Untreated wood, for example, is initially very sensitive to moisture and dirt. It becomes mottled and swells up. After a certain period of use, or through weathering, the traces of time slowly accumulate in the pores and form a protective layer. Wood gradually reaches equilibrium with its surroundings and achieves a stable state that changes little afterwards. In contrast to painted material, its pores always remain open, permeable, and absorbent. The porous material becomes a semipermeable membrane that absorbs some substances, and lets others pass right through it.

This osmotic equilibrium between inside and outside is of fundamental significance. The material provides protection from unwelcome influences, but remains open to interaction and transformation.

The house in which Marguerite Duras lived, and about which she wrote, is an old French country house with a high tiled roof. The sandy plaster of the living room spreads across the high masonry; thick tufts of dried lavender from the previous summer lie above the door; spider webs hang from the dark beams of the attic; a soft blanket is draped over a low chaise lounge; and the slender doors with their gridded panes of glass open out onto the garden. The rooms have absorbed the personality and life story of their occupant and now exude her aura. Were we to see Marguerite Duras sitting at her table, that sense of unity would be established. In the present time, when we are more and more mobile and strive to dispense with baggage rather than accumulate it, we may find this image old-fashioned. Yet hardly anybody feels truly comfortable in perfectly smooth spaces. What sort of porosity, then, corresponds to contemporary society?

We are less encumbered, Western nations are cleaner and safer (at least superficially), and we are better interconnected than ever. For us to integrate and enjoy all these things, we need to have a well-calibrated, osmotic relationship with our environment.

The term *osmosis* physically describes the directed flow of tiny particles through a semi-permeable barrier layer. The material of this kind of membrane is such that it allows only certain selected particles to pass from one side to the other. It works on both sides, like a filter protecting against undesirable elements and only allowing the desired ones to pass, making them that much more enjoyable. In this way, a balance is established between interior and exterior, between private and public, and between protected and unprotected. A contemporary kind of porosity could thus offer spaces that are flexible and changeable, whose pores can easily adapt to their size and texture. They should be made of materials that facilitate a targeted interaction between inside and outside, as well as among occupants, building, and city, that can respond to different situations.

However, diffusive materials can no longer deploy their osmotic qualities if interaction is hindered by a cladding of less permeable materials, or if inherently very dense building materials are used. Complex building systems may then attempt to compensate mechanically for these shortcomings. However, such systems must be controlled automatically and cannot regulate themselves through direct interaction between inside and outside, or between building and user. While a porous building may communicate with its environment osmotically, an impermeable structure becomes a machine that obeys its own laws. The architectural body slips into a coma and must be artificially ventilated. Any irregularity or disturbance caused by its occupants can then lead to collapse. Thus, human appropriation is largely prohibited, and the city becomes an intensive care unit. Buildings like the Centre Pompidou in Paris or the Lloyds Building in London draw their aesthetic appeal from this image of sleek architecture on a technology drip. Although the cost of building systems has risen since then, the technology today has become invisible. It is no longer a living organism ventilated externally, but rather the building as a whole is a mechanized android. A psychotic relationship forms between an illusory entity and its users, whose inviolability causes a disconnect with reality and prevents communicative interaction. Interior and exterior, man and machine remain irreconcilably separated.

A Matter of Course

Utilized sensitively, impermeable materials such as glass, metal, and plastic may also become communicative elements of a building in a spatial sense. When employed in mechanically adjustable components, they allow a built structure's porosity to be variable. If the occupant can use their own strength to manipulate these components, as is true with operable windows and doors, for example, then the occupants themself becomes part of the osmotic system of the building. They can manually regulate the porosity of the building envelope in response to their own comfort or discomfort. By virtue of this contact, a wordless physical exchange takes place between humans and architecture.

A building in which the porosity of the materials and the variability of its spatial structure complement each other might thus—appropriately and distinctly—restore the intellectual and emotional unity between man and architecture.[7] Architecture could once again become tangible and emotive. It could record traces and develop historicality. Humankind could be "encrusted into the room" and become an integral part of the architecture, while at the same time remaining autonomous. Because its spatial fabric is readily comprehensible, such a porous building could develop an equable matter-of-factness that makes it approachable and communicative. Rather than tension, there could be a symbiotic balance between building, occupant, and environment. Architecture would become tranquil, "as if the space itself [...] doesn't even detect my presence: It already had its place here. What I am most likely talking about is the silence of space".[8]

7 Dietmar Eberle explored the qualities of a porous building without mechanical systems in his "2226" building in Lustenau. The theory of "open building" that he and John Habraken advocate is based on the idea of a spatially flexible and multilayered architecture which could be deemed structurally porous.

8 Duras, p. 14.

Material | In German, *Stoff,* from French *éstoffe:* Fabric, cloth, stuff. Related to Latin *stuppare:* to plug with cotton, mend. Today: Textiles, cloth, content. What is material is—in contrast to spiritual or intellectual—physical, concrete, sensual. Material comes in various aggregates, pure and mixed, and is in a state of flux. In German, the word *Stoffwechsel,* literally "material change", means metabolism, a process that is fundamental to human life. Semper interprets it as being cultural: Cultural techniques are created through the braiding, knotting, and tying of textiles that resurface in the ornamentation of stone buildings.

Surface | The enveloping skin of a volume; the dividing or boundary layer between interior and exterior. Mathematically only two-dimensional, objects actually have surfaces of various thicknesses, which gives them a sensual dimension that we mainly perceive through our sense of touch. The surface of glass has no volume, fluffy wool has more. This characteristic is not the same as that of the content; therefore, the surface is considered to be ostensible, deceptive. Husky, porous surfaces (rough wood) are considered more reliable, more authentic.

Nature | From Latin *nasci:* To originate, be born. Nature is a complex, dynamic structure; nature as the entire cosmos, or "the nature of a thing", its essence. What is for Plato the well-meshed universe, is for Aristotle an object of observation. This is where contemporary science joins in. Humanity together with its culture is the counterpart to nature. Ecology reflects on the relationship of the two, not in opposition, but in open and sensitive interplay. In constructivism, nature is merely a construct.

Patina | From Italian *patina:* A thin layer. A change in the appearance of a surface due to ageing. Proof of the age of things, sometimes unwanted (the yellowing of oil paintings through oxidization), sometimes desired (the patina of a bronze sculpture). In addition to the aesthetic and material reasons, patina also creates a protective layer and is therefore sometimes artificially encouraged (the green coloration of copper, rusting of iron, or anodizing of aluminum).

Light | It is not light that shines, but the illuminated, opined Goethe. Le Corbusier confirmed this by defining architecture as "the magnificent play of masses brought together in light". When light waves meet an object, it shines differently, depending on the surface. Its sculpturality emerges from the interplay with shadows. The more light the surface "swallows", making shaded areas visible, the more sculptural the volume becomes; the more light it reflects, the more bodiless it seems.

Porosity | From French *poreux:* Permeable, sponge-like, porous. Indicates the ratio of empty space to the total volume of a material. From a technical perspective, high porosity is desired above all for insulating materials. Porous materials seem warm to the touch, since air pockets conduct very little body heat when touched. Visually, the pores "swallow", the materials seem heavy. Since pores are often the result of erosion, porosity also has a temporal aspect. Such materials "swallow", store: Energy, time, and memory.

Atmosphere | The concordance of sensual (outer) and mental (inner) impressions at a specific place and specific time. In *The Poetics of Space*, Gaston Bachelard's observations revolve around a dialectics of inside and outside, an interplay which is neither clear nor limited. Poetic space expands objective space by imbuing it with inner life. When the two approach concordance, the result is an ambiance that is experienced as harmonious. The significance of this to architecture is increasing, in the case of atmosphere, for instance.

Senses | Senses are the media that convey the world to us. Aristotle counted five: Sight, hearing, smell, taste, and touch. Today, neuro-scientists have added several more: The senses of balance, pain, and internal stimuli. The hand shows: Senses always work together—the sense of touch and kinesthetic, passive and active. Senses create space (Edward T. Hall): Touch creates something different than hearing and seeing, focused sight something different than peripheral vision. The preference for sight in our culture causes other senses to be neglected; this reduction of sensual abundance means losing parts of the world.

Perception | Perception expands impression to create something that is true—in the interaction of intellect and senses. For Goethe, the mind and bodily and perceptive organs inform each other. Realization is for him a continual process in which seeing leads to observation, observation to reflection, reflection to combination—meaning that each attentive look can result in a theory. This in turn orders and evaluates the impressions of the senses—in other words: One only sees what one knows.

MATERIALITY

The materiality of things can result in the intensive experiencing of sensual qualities. This is true of the body and spaces of architecture. Physical proximity corresponds with bodily intimacy and is a precondition of atmosphere. From this, we can infer the privileged status of private spaces. The mood of buildings in an urban surrounding is more distanced in comparison. From this we derive the differentiation of the materiality of architecture and the materiality of the interior of the design. While the former is bound to the permanence of the place, the latter is aligned with the changing needs of the user.

City Level

A substantiated knowledge of the material and its characteristics, processing, and applications will be acquired.

Specifications

Project work will be done in groups of two. A detailed documentation and description of the chosen materials for floors, walls, ceilings, and detachable parts must be submitted:

- A textural photo documenting the materials
- A reference image documenting the materials implemented and processed in the context
- A technical description of the materials as follows:
- Description of materials/ substances
- Relevant material characteristics such as size (min./max. dimensions, strength, etc.), seams required, type of processing, use possibilities, surface quality, and maintenance
- Description of type of work required
- Relevant structural values for the floor, walls, and ceiling regarding thermal insulation (raw density, thermal conductivity, heat storage capacity) and fire safety (fire index)

Requirements

- Materials archive

Goal

To learn about the characteristics of materials and substances and about possibilities for processing and utilization.

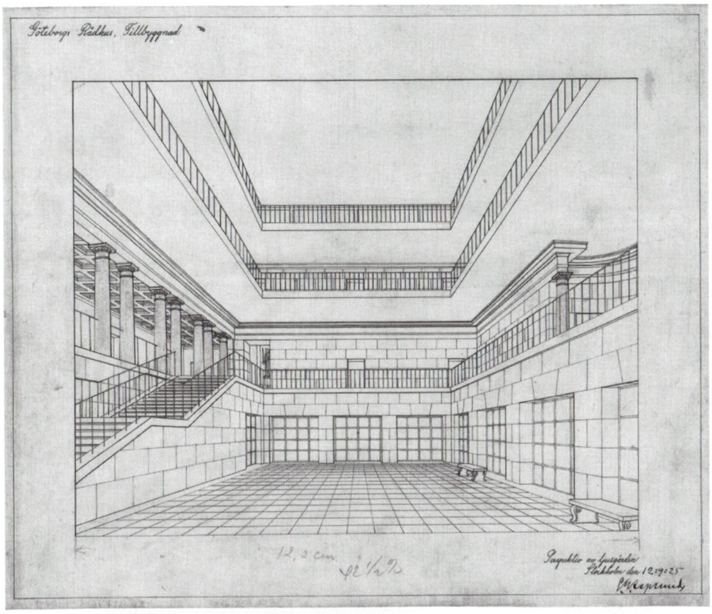

Gothenburg Law Courts Extension. Architect Gunnar Asplund. Perspective of the light well, 1925

The Centre for Architecture and Design, collection, ARK M, 1990

Gothenburg Law Courts Extension

Interior model
Jakob Junghanss
Fabian Kuonen
15 AS

Building Level

A flight of rooms from the previous assignment will be developed in detail. Room sequence, proportion, and character will be selected and adequate materials chosen. The model is an irreplaceable aspect of creating a realistic image of the design and verifying spatial phenomena. Lighting and spatial impressions in particular can be studied using a model.

Specifications

Project work will be done in groups of two. The following must be submitted:

- Floor plan and section schematic of the flight of rooms with a special focus on the relationship of interior and exterior 1:500
- Model, 1:20 or 1:33, with material representation
- Three interior photos with a focus on light, materials, and surface textures (model photos, not renderings).
- Written description of the concept with justification of materials choice

Requirements

- Crafting notebooks I–IV

Goal

To learn about the influence of material, surface, workmanship, and incoming light on the atmosphere of a room. The indoor climate must also be considered. Coherency and comfort are crucial criteria.

Adolf Loos, Villa Karma, Clarens VD, 1903–06, completed by Hugo Ehrlich 1912, bathroom

Christian Kerez I Haus Fosterstrasse I Zürich I 1998-2003

Sichtbeton

Wand: Ortbeton, Portlandzement (Normo 4)

Materialeigenschaften
Beton wird durch Mischung von Zuschlagstoffen, Zusatzmitteln, Zuschlag, Zement und Wasser hergestellt. Dabei macht der Anteil des Zuschlages rund 80% der Masse aus.
Der Beton nimmt die Druckkräfte auf, die Zugkräfte werden durch die Stahlbewehrung aufgenommen.

Verarbeitung
Die zu betonierenden Bauteile werden vor Ort mit Schalungstafeln geschalt, die Armierung eingelegt und in Etappen gegossen.
Nach dem Ausschalen wird der Beton geschliffen und poliert.

Arbeitsgattung
Maurerarbeiten

Bauphysikalische Kennwerte

Rohdichte	2400 kg/m3
Druckfestigkeit	42.5 - 62.5 N/mm2
Wärmeleitfähigkeit	1.8 W/mK
Wärmespeicherkapazität	1.1 kJ/kg K
Brandkennziffer	5.3

Gigon Guyer I Löwenbräukunst I Zürich I 2003-2013

Hartbetonbelag

Boden (öffentlicher Bereich): Hartbetonbelag

Materialeigenschaften
Bodenbelag aus Zement, Zuschlägen, Hartstoffen, Wasser, gegebenenfalls unter Beigabe von Zusätzen.
Hartbetonbeläge sind für leichte bis schwere Beanspruchungen geeignet. Sie sind wasserfest und weisen eine mittlere bis hohe Abrieb- und Schlagfestigkeit auf und sind nicht beständig gegen Säuren.

Verarbeitung
Bei der Verarbeitung von Hartbetonbelägen werden auf der Baustelle verschiedene Zuschlagstoffe beigegeben.
Während des Einbaus wird die Hartbetonmasse maschinell verdichtet und die Oberfläche geglättet.
Dadurch entsteht eine homogene, fugenlose, leicht glänzende Oberfläche.

Arbeitsgattung
Maurerarbeit

Bauphysikalische Kennwerte

Rohdichte	2400 kg/m3
Druckfestigkeit	50.00 bis 250.00 N/mm2
Wärmeleitfähigkeit	1.8 W/mK
Wärmespeicherkapazität	1.1 kJ/kg K
Brandkennziffer	6.3

Buchner Bründler I Wohnhaus Bläsiring I Basel I 2012

Klinker

Boden (privater Bereich): Klinker

Materialeigenschaften
Klinkerstein ist ein keramisches Bauprodukt, dass bis zur Sinterung gebrannt wurde. Er findet Einsatz als witterungsbeständige Vormauerziegel (Sichtmauerwerk) oder Pflasterklinker aufgrund seiner geringen Wasseraufnahmekapazität. Die Haupteigenschaften des gebrannten Klinkersteins sind dessen Frost- und Witterungsbeständigkeit. Er muss nachträglich nicht weiter behandelt werden.

Verarbeitung
Die Aufbereitung des Rohstoffs Ton erfolgt durch ein Zerkleinern der tonhaltigen Sedimente, einem Homogenisieren und anschliessendem Lagern in Sumpfhäusern, um die befeuchteten Tonminerale optimal aufzuschliessen. Die in Schneckenprozessen hergestellten Rohlinge werden an anschliessend bei 1100 °C bis 1300 °C gebrannt.

Arbeitsgattung
Maurerarbeiten

Bauphysikalische Kennwerte

Rohdichte	1.850.00 bis 2.100.00 kg/m3
Druckfestigkeit	60.00 N/mm2
Wärmeleitfähigkeit	0.810 bis 1.20 W/mK
Wärmespeicherkapazität	0.9 kJ/kg K
Brandkennziffer	6.2

Peter Zumthor I Haus und Atelier Zumthor I Haldenstein I 2005

Chromstahl I Unbehandelt

Detail (öffentlicher Breich): Türe, Handlauf, Fensterrahmen

Materialeigenschaften
Unbehandelter Chromstahl hat einen Chromanteil von ca 15 % und Nickelanteil von ca. 8 %.
Auch Nichtrostende austenitische Stähle gennant, sind die gebräuchlichsten rostfreien Stähle. Der Anwendung von nichtrostenden Stählen liegt der Wunsch zugrunde, neben der funktionalen Zuverlässigkeit Bauteile mit langer Lebensdauer, hoher Witterungsbeständigkeit und minimaler Unterhaltskosten zu erhalten.

Verarbeitung
Edelstahl wird aus Roheisen hergestellt. Roheisen selbst wird im Hochofen aus Eisenerz gewonnen.
Die metallischen Ausgangsstoffe werden in Öfen eingeschmolzen. Dazu dienen unterschiedliche Ofentypen; meist wird der Lichtbogenofen verwendet. Die beim unbehandelten (nicht vergüterten) Chromstahl prägende Oberflächenstruktur entsteht durch das Walzen der Bauteile.

Arbeitsgattung
Metallarbeiten

Bauphysikalische Kennwerte

Rohdichte	7.900.00 bis 8.100.00 kg/m3
Zugfestigkeit	500.00 bis 950.00 N/mm2
Wärmeleitfähigkeit	12.00 bis 15.00 W/mK
Wärmespeicherkapazität	450.00 bis 500.00 kJ/kg K
Brandkennziffer	6.1

David Chipperfield I Museum für moderne Literatur I Marbach am Neckar I 2002 - 2006

Birnbaumholz I Geölt

Detail (privater Breich): Treppe, Handlauf, Sitzbank, Türe, Briefkasten

Materialeigenschaften
Birnbaumholz ist ein schlichtes Holz. Es hat eine feine und gleichmässige Struktur und ist manchmal leicht geflammt. Durch ölen wird das Holz resistenter und bekommt einen dunklen Schimmer. Birnbaumholz ist hart, fest und zäh. Es hat eine ebenmässige Beschaffenheit und ist im trockenen Zustand sehr formbeständig. Aufgrund seiner geringen Witterungsbeständigkeit ist es vorallem in Innenbereich anzutreffen.

Verarbeitung
Birnbaumholz ist schwer spaltbar. Ansonsten lässt es sich mit allen Werkzeugen gut bearbeiten und ist für Oberflächenbearbeitungen unterschiedlicher Art sehr geeignet. Optische Unregelmässigkeiten wie Krümmung oder Jahrringstruktur halten sich bei dieser Holzgattung in Grenzen

Arbeitsgattung
Schreinerarbeiten

Bauphysikalische Kennwerte

Rohdichte	7.900.00 bis 8.100.00 kg/m3
Druckfestigkeit	41.00 bis 60.00 N/mm2
Schwindmass (tangential)	0.300 bis 0.360 % / 1% FÄ
Wärmespeicherkapazität	1,7 kJ/kg K
Brandkennziffer	5.3

Alvar Aalto I Gemeindezentrum I Säynätsalo I 1951

Leder I Rind

Detail Türgriff, Handlauf

Materialeigenschaften
Die Haut von Rindern eignet sich als Grundlage für praktisch alle Lederarten. Rindsleder ist das am weitesten verbreitete Leder der Welt. Das Narbenbild von Rindsleder zeigt eine gleichmässige Verteilung der Haarporen ohne typische Anordnungen. Die Fasern auf der Fleischseite sind sehr grob. Rindsleder ist stabil und besonders zugfest und können je nachdem wie viel Leder abgespalten wurde, dünn und leicht, aber auch sehr fest und schwer sein.

Verarbeitung
Rohleder wird vom Gerber erzeugt und anschliessen vom Sattelarbeitern weiter für die jeweiligen Produkte behandelt. Leder wird häufig zugeschnitten gehandelt, wobei das jeweilige, die Haut liefernde Tier die maximale Grösse vorgibt.

Arbeitsgattung
Gerber- und Sattlerarbeiten

Bauphysikalische Kennwerte

Rohdichte	400.00 bis 900.00 kg/m3
Zugfestigkeit	8.00 bis 25.00 N/mm2
max. verfügbare Grössen	3 bis 5 m2
durchschnittlicher Verschnitt	30% bis 45%

Lucio Crignola
Maximilian Fritz
14 SS

Alvaro Siza I Centro Deportivo de Alto I Panticosa I 2002

Kalkstein

Boden 1: Kalkstein

Materialeigenschaften
Als Kalkstein werden Sedimentgesteine bezeichnet, die überwiegend aus dem chemischen Stoff Calciumcarbonat in Form der Mineralien Calcit und Aragonit bestehen. In mehr oder minder schwankenden Anteilen kommen andere Minerale vor. In den meisten Fällen besitzen sie eine helle, graue bis graugelbe Farbe.

Verarbeitung/Oberflächenqualität
Vor allem dichte Kalksteine werden als leicht zu bearbeitende Naturwerksteine verwendet. Für die Baustoffindustrie ist Kalkstein einer der wichtigsten Rohstoffe. Dafür wird er in Kalkwerken aufbereitet und zu Branntkalk umgesetzt. Sehr reine Kalksteine sind Rohstoff für die chemische Industrie oder werden zu Terrazzo weiterverarbeitet

Arbeitsgattung
Bodenlegerarbeiten

Bauphysikalische Kennwerte

Rohdichte	2600kg bis 2900 kg/m3
Wärmeleitfähigkeit	1.0 bis 4.0 W/mK
Wärmespeicherkapazität	0.74 kJ/kg K
Druckfestigkeit	10.0 bis 80.0 N/mm2

Alvaro Siza I Igreja de Santa Maria I Canaveses I 1996

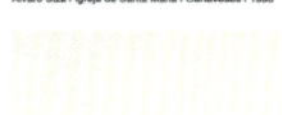

Weissputz

Wand 1 und Decke: Geglätteter Weissputz

Materialeigenschaften
Das Material hat eine eher matte, homogene Oberfläche, bestehend aus einem Bindemittel, feinen Zuschlägen und Wasser. Sie bringt Angenehme ästhetische Erscheinung und Regulierende Wirkung auf Feuchtigkeit und Raumklima hervor.

Verarbeitung/Oberflächenqualität
Feinkörniger Putz wird in angezogenem Zustand (schon etwas angebunden aber noch plastisch verformbar) geglättet. Durch den Oberflächendruck wird das gröbere Korn in die Tiefe gearbeitet und es kommt zu einer besseren Verzahnung der Gesteinskörner. Hierfür werden elastische Werkzeuge verwendet.

Arbeitsgattung
Gipser- und Malerarbeiten

Bauphysikalische Kennwerte

Rohdichte	1150 kg/m3
Wärmeleitfähigkeit	0.6 W/mK
Wärmespeicherkapazität	0.8 kJ/kg K
Druckfestigkeit	2 bis 4 N/mm2

Peter Zumthor I Kolumba Museum I Köln I 2007

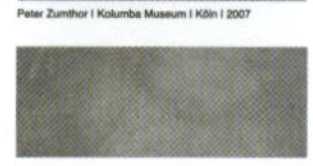

Beton

Boden 2: Geschliffenes Betonbodensystem (TERRAPLAN)

Materialeigenschaften
TERRAPLAN ist ein geschliffenes Betonbodensystem mit terrazzoähnlicher Optik. Die Betonrezeptur wird hinsichtlich der finalen Optik der Oberfläche speziell auf die gestalterischen Anforderungen abgestimmt. Die individuelle Komposition von Gesteinskörnung, Farb-Pigmente und Weisszement bestimmt maßgeblich das Erscheinungsbild des Bodens.

Verarbeitung/Oberflächenqualität
Durch moderne Trocken- und Nassschleifverfahren wird in einem mehrstufigen Prozess die finale Optik der Bodenoberfläche freigelegt. Durch die monolithische Bauweise entstehen hochwertige Oberflächen, die matt bis glänzend ausgeführt werden können.

Arbeitsgattung
Maurerarbeiten

Bauphysikalische Kennwerte

Rohdichte	2400 kg/m3
Wärmeleitfähigkeit	1.8 W/mK
Wärmespeicherkapazität	1.1 kJ/kg K
Druckfestigkeit	35 N/mm2

Darlington Meier I Mathilde Escher Heim I Zürich I 2010

Weisszement

Wand 2: Weisszement mit Farbzuschlag

Materialeigenschaften
Die Herstellung von Weißzement ist aufwändiger als diejenige von gewöhnlichem Portlandzement. Weißzemente werden aus sehr eisenarmen Rohstoffen hergestellt und müssen nach dem Brennen schnell gekühlt werden, um weiß zu bleiben. Weißzement wird hauptsächlich für Terrazzo, Sichtbeton und weißen Putz eingesetzt. Er eignet sich nicht nur für hellfarbige Zubereitungen, sondern lässt sich mit Farbpigmenten besser leichter einfärben.

Verarbeitung/Oberflächenqualität
Die Bauteile werden vor Ort mit Schalungstafeln geschalt, die Armierung eingelegt und in Etappen gegossen. Dadurch entstehen die Fugen an der Oberfläche. Nach dem Ausschalen können verschiedene Oberflächenbehandlungen angewender werden, wie zum Beispiel das Sandstrahlen.

Arbeitsgattung
Maurerarbeiten

Bauphysikalische Kennwerte

Rohdichte	2400 kg/m3
Wärmeleitfähigkeit	1.8 W/mK
Wärmespeicherkapazität	1.1 kJ/kg K
Druckfestigkeit	42 N/mm2

Le Corbusier I Notre Dame du Haut I Ronchamps I 1955

Weissputz

Wand 3: Grober Weissputz

Materialeigenschaften
Das Material hat eine eher raue, strukturierte Oberfläche, bestehend aus einem Bindemittel, feinen Zuschlägen und Wasser. Sie bringt Angenehme ästhetische Erscheinung und Regulierende Wirkung auf Feuchtigkeit und Raumklima hervor.

Verarbeitung/Oberflächenqualität
Feiner, dünnflüssiger Deckputz wird auf rauen, grobkörnigen Grundputz aufgezogen. Beim Überstreichen des noch feuchten Deckputzes entsteht sie grobe Struktur, welche auf die weisse Wand durch die Tiefe einen Schatten wirft.

Arbeitsgattung
Gipser- und Malerarbeiten

Bauphysikalische Kennwerte

Rohdichte	1050 kg/m3
Wärmeleitfähigkeit	0.6 W/mK
Wärmespeicherkapazität	0.8 kJ/kg K
Druckfestigkeit	2.5 bis 5 N/mm2

Peter Zumthor I Kunsthaus Bregenz I Bregenz I 1997

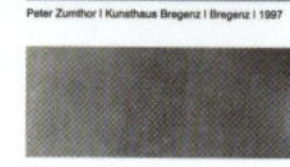

Stahl

Tür: Gebürsteter Stahl

Materialeigenschaften
Stahl ist eine metallische Legierung, deren Hauptsbestandteil aus Eisen besteht und mit den zusätzlichen Elementen Chrom, Aluminium und Silizium. Durch die gezielte Zugabe von Legierungselementen können die Eigenschaften auf einen grossen Anwendungsbereich ausgeweitet werden. Stahl wird oft im Bauwesen eingesetzt, da er sich durch eine grosse Form und Dimensionsstabilität auszeichnet und extrem hohe Belastungen aushält.

Verarbeitung/Oberflächenqualität
Das Eisen wird im Ofen mit den anderen metallischen Elementen zu Stahl geschmolzen. Er zeichnet sich durch eine glänzende Oberfläche aus. Der Stahl wird mit einer schwarzen Patina bestrichen. Es erhöht die Wetterbeständigkeit und erlaubt eine rostfreie Oberfläche zu haben.

Arbeitsgattung
Metallbauarbeiten

Bauphysikalische Kennwerte

Rohdichte	7900 kg/m3
Wärmeleitfähigkeit	40 bis 68 W/mK
Wärmespeicherkapazität	3800 kJ/kg K
Zugfestigkeit	340 bis 470 N/mm2

Noël Frozza
Thierry Vuattoux
16 SS

Louis Kahn I Exeter Library I New Hampshire I 1971

Backstein

Wand 1: Backstein Blockverband (6 Läufer, 1 Binderschicht)

Materialeigenschaften
Backstein ist ein keramisches Bauprodukt, dass bis zur Sinterung gebrannt wird. Hauptbestandteile ungebrannter Backstein-Rohmischungen sind natürliche Tonminerale. Die Haupteigenschaften des gebrannten Klinkersteins dessen Frost- und Witterungsbeständigkeit und geringe Wasseraufnahme. Je nach Beimischungen kann die Farbe zwischen Rot, Gelb, Weiss, Grau und Schwarz variieren. Der Backstein ist ein in Form gebrachtes und gebranntes Bauprodukt und muss nicht mehr bearbeitet werden.

Verarbeitung/Oberflächenqualität
Die Oberfläche des Backsteines wird nicht bearbeitet und bleibt unberührt. Die einzelnen Steine werden mit einer Mörtelfuge verbunden und zu einer Mauer aufgeschichtet. Der Verband der gewählt wird bestimmt die Stärke und Festigkeit der Mauer massgeblich und Fugenfarbe und Fugenausbildung beeinflussen den Charakter der Wandfläche massgeblich.

Arbeitsgattung
Maurerarbeiten

Bauphysikalische Kennwerte

Rohdichte	2100 kg/m3
Wärmeleitfähigkeit	1.2 W/mK
Wärmespeicherkapazität	0.9 kJ/kg K
Brandkennziffer	6

Ludwig Wittgenstein I Haus Wittgenstein I Wien I 1928

Kunststein gegossen

Boden 1: Terazzo Platten, gegossen

Materialeigenschaften
Kunststein ist ein Betonerzeugnis, das äusserlich nicht als Beton erscheint, sondern mit eigenen charakteristischen Gepräge in Struktur und Farbe Naturstein gleicht. Das Entfernen der Zementhaut und die Bearbeitung der Oberfläche lässt das typische Abbild der Schalung verschwinden. Die Zusammensetzung und Eigenschaften sind dem Beton sehr ähnlich, wichtigster Unterschied sind die Oberfläche sowie Zuschalgsstoffe und Bindemittel.

Verarbeitung/Oberflächenqualität
Kunststeinplatten werden im Industrieverfahren vorgefertigt und auf die Baustelle geliefert. Die Plattengrösse und Stärke kann nach Belieben ausgwählt werden. Somit kann eine sehr hohe Qualität erreicht werden. Die Oberfläche kann durch verschiedene Schalungsmöglichkeiten sehr fein und homogen gefertigt werden.

Arbeitsgattung
Maurerarbeiten

Bauphysikalische Kennwerte

Rohdichte	2600kg/m3
Wärmeleitfähigkeit	2 W/mK
Wärmespeicherkapazität	2.5kJ/kg K
Brandkennziffer	6

Louis Kahn I Nationalparlament I Dhaka I 1983

Sichtbeton

Decke 1: Ortbeton, Portlandzement

Materialeigenschaften
Beton ist ein zahflüssiges Gemenge, das durch die chemische Reaktion von Zement, Wasser, Zuschlagsstoffen und Zusatzstoffen innerhalb einer Schalung zu einem steinartigen Material erstarrt. Der Anteil der Zuschlagsstoffe beträgt 80% der Masse und gibt dem Beton seine Druckfestigkeit. Beton wird vorwiegend für Bauteile mit statischer Beanspruchung, meist mit Eisenstäben bewehrt, sogenannter Stahlbeton. Der Stahl gleicht dabei die schlechte Zugfestigkeit des unbewehrten Betons aus.

Verarbeitung/Oberflächenqualität
Die Decke ist eine Ortbetonkonstruktion mit einem Traggerüst, welches die Schalungstafeln abstützt. Die Decke wird armiert und in Etappen gegossen. Nach dem Erhärten des Betons wird die Schalung entfernt und die Oberflächenstruktur zeigt sich als Abbild der Schalung. Der Beton wird nicht weiter berarbeitet und kriegt seine endgültige Farbe und Festigkeit nach 28 Tagen.

Arbeitsgattung
Maurerarbeiten

Bauphysikalische Kennwerte

Rohdichte	2400kg/m3
Wärmeleitfähigkeit	1.8W/mK
Wärmespeicherkapazität	1.1kJ/kg K
Brandkennziffer	5.3
Druckfestigkeit	42.5 - 62.5 N/mm2

Caruso St John I Brick House I London I 2005

Stahl

Geländer: Stahl patiniert

Materialeigenschaften
Stahl ist eine metallische Legierung, deren Hauptbestandteil aus Eisen besteht und mit den zusätzlichen Elementen Chrom, Aluminium und Silizium. Durch die gezielte Zugabe von Legierungselementen können die Eigenschaften auf einen grossen Anwendungsbereich angepasst werden. Stahl wird oft im Bauwesen eingesetzt, da er sich durch eine grosse Form und Dimensionsstabilität auszeichnet und extrem hohe Belastungen aushält.

Verarbeitung/Oberflächenqualität
Das Eisen wird mit den anderen metallischen Elementen im Ofen geschmolzen zu Stahl. Er zeichnet sich durch glänzende Oberfläche aus. Der Stahl wird mit einer schwarzen Patina bestrichen. Es erhöht die Wetterbeständigkeit und erlaubt eine rostfreie, farbige Oberfläche zu haben.

Arbeitsgattung
Metallbauarbeiten

Bauphysikalische Kennwerte

Rohdichte	7800kg/m3
Wärmeleitfähigkeit	53W/mK
Wärmespeicherkapazität	0.9 kJ/kg K
Brandkennziffer	6

Jörg Boner I Haus Bärengraben I Baden I 2015

Sichtbeton I Bretterschalung

Wand 2: Ortbeton, Portlandzement (Normo 4)

Materialeigenschaften
Beton ist ein zahflüssiges Gemenge, das durch die chemische Reaktion von Zement, Wasser, Zuschlagsstoffen und Zusatzstoffen innerhalb einer Schalung zu einem steinartigen Material erstarrt. Der Anteil der Zuschlagsstoffe beträgt 80% der Masse und gibt dem Beton seine Druckfestigkeit. Beton wird vorwiegend für Bauteile mit statischer Beanspruchung, meist mit Eisenstäben bewehrt, sogenannter Stahlbeton. Der Stahl gleicht dabei die schlechte Zugfestigkeit des unbewehrten Betons aus.

Verarbeitung/Oberflächenqualität
Die Wände werden vor Ort mit hölzernen Schalungsbrettern geschalt, die Armierung eingelegt und in Etappen gegossen. Die Maserung des Holzes zeigt sich als Abbild der Schalung an der Oberfläche der Zementhaut. Die Leuchten werden als positive Form in die Schalung eingelegt, sodass die Öffnungen nach dem Ausschalen ein Teil der Architektur sind und keine zusätzlichen Elemente benötigt werden.

Arbeitsgattung
Maurerarbeiten

Bauphysikalische Kennwerte

Rohdichte	2400kg/m3
Wärmeleitfähigkeit	1.8W/mK
Wärmespeicherkapazität	1.1kJ/kg K
Brandkennziffer	5.3
Druckfestigkeit	42.5 - 62.5 N/mm2

Peter Zumthor I Kunsthaus Bregenz I Bregenz I 1997

Hartbeton

Boden 2: Hartbetonbelag

Materialeigenschaften
Beton ist ein zahflüssiges Gemenge, das durch die chemische Reaktion von Zement, Wasser, Zuschlagsstoffen und Zusatzstoffen innerhalb einer Schalung zu einem steinartigen Material erstarrt. Der Anteil der Zuschlagsstoffe beträgt 80% der Masse und gibt dem Beton seine Druckfestigkeit. Beton wird vorwiegend für Bauteile mit statischer Beanspruchung, meist mit Eisenstäben bewehrt, sogenannter Stahlbeton. Der Stahl gleicht dabei die schlechte Zugfestigkeit des unbewehrten Betons aus.

Verarbeitung/Oberflächenqualität
Bei der Verarbeitung von Hartbetonbelägen werden auf der Baustelle verschiedene Zuschlagsstoffe beigegeben. Während des Einbaus wird die Hartbetonmasse maschinell verdichtet und geglättet. Dadruch entsteht eine homogene fugenlose Oberfläche.

Arbeitsgattung
Maurerarbeiten

Bauphysikalische Kennwerte

Rohdichte	2400kg/m3
Wärmeleitfähigkeit	1.8W/mK
Wärmespeicherkapazität	1.1kJ/kg K
Brandkennziffer	5.3
Druckfestigkeit	42.5 - 62.5 N/mm2

Timothy Allen
Okan Tan
16 ss

Christian Kerez I Haus Forsterstrasse I Zürich I 1998-2003

Sichtbeton

Decke / Wand: Ortbeton, Portlandzement

Materialeigenschaften
Beton wird durch Mischung von Zuschlagstoffen, Zusatzmitteln, Zuschlag, Zement und Wasser hergestellt. Dabei beträgt der Anteil des Zuschlages rund 80% der Masse aus.
Der Beton nimmt die Druckkräfte auf, die Zugkräfte werden durch die Stahlbewehrung aufgenommen.

Verarbeitung/Oberflächenqualität
Die zu Betonierenden Bauteile werden vor Ort mit grossflächigen hölzernen Schalungstafeln geschalt, die Armierung eingelegt und in Etappen gegossen.
Nach dem Ausschalen wird die Oberfläche vom Schalungsabdruck befreit.

Arbeitsgattung
Baumeisterarbeiten

Bauphysikalische Kennwerte

Rohdichte	2400kg/m3
Wärmeleitfähigkeit	1.8W/mK
Wärmespeicherkapazität	1.1kJ/kg K
Brandkennziffer	6
Druckfestigkeit	40 - 60 N/mm2

Aldo Rossi I Gallaratese 2 I Milano I 1968-1973

Betonbodenbelag

Boden 1: Ortbeton, Rohbelag

Materialeigenschaften
Bodenbelag aus Zement, Zuschlägen, Hartstoffen, Wasser, gegebenenfalls unter Beigabe von Zusätzen.
Betonböden sind für leichte bis schwere Beanspruchungen geeignet. Sie sind wasserfest und weisen eine mittlere bis hohe Abrieb- und Schlagfestigkeit
auf und sind nicht beständig gegen Säuren.

Verarbeitung/Oberflächenqualität
Bei der Verarbeitung von Hartbetonbelägen werden auf der Baustelle verschiedene Zuschlagstoffe beigegeben. Während des Einbaus wird die Hartbetonmasse maschinell verdichtet und die Oberfläche geglättet.
Dadurch entsteht eine homogene, fugenlose, leicht glänzende Oberfläche.

Arbeitsgattung
Baumeisterarbeiten

Bauphysikalische Kennwerte

Rohdichte	2600kg/m3
Wärmeleitfähigkeit	1.6W/mK
Wärmespeicherkapazität	1.1kJ/kg K
Brandkennziffer	6
Druckfestigkeit	80 N/mm2

Arno Brandlhuber I Kirche St. Agnes I Berlin I 2011 - 2013

Klinkerfliesen

Boden 2: Steinzeugfliesen (Klinker)

Materialeigenschaften
Es handelt sich um ein vollkommen durchgesintertes und sehr kompaktes Produkt, dessen wesentliches Merkmal seine extrem niedrige Porosität mit einer Wasseraufnahme von < 0,5 % ist. Auf Grund der sehr geringen Wasseraufnahme ist Feinsteinzeug frostbeständig.

Verarbeitung/Oberflächenqualität
Unglasiertes Feinsteinzeug hat eine sehr gute Abriebbeständigkeit und eine hohe Bruchfestigkeit. Dadurch ist es hervorragend geeignet für Flächen mit intensiver Nutzung. Durch unterschiedlich gefärbte Keramikpulver oder durch lösliche Salze erhalten die Steine eine differenzierte Oberfläche.

Arbeitsgattung
Belagsarbeiten

Bauphysikalische Kennwerte

Rohdichte	2400kg/m3
Wärmeleitfähigkeit	4.8W/mK
Wärmespeicherkapazität	1.2kJ/kg K
Brandkennziffer	6
Druckfestigkeit	20 N/mm2

Arno Brandlhuber I Kirche St. Agnes I Berlin I 2011 - 2013

Beton sandgestrahlt

Treppe / Galerie: Ortbeton sandgestrahlt

Materialeigenschaften
Ein Gemisch aus Kies, Sand, Zement und Wasser. Um bestimmte Eigenschaften zu erreichen, werden je nach Anwendungsbereich Zusatzmittel (Verflüssiger, Luftporenbildner oder Verzögerer) sowie Farbstoffe hinzugefügt.

Verarbeitung/Oberflächenqualität
homegene, aufgeraute Oberfläche, Strapazierfähiger Beton.
Betonprodukte können oberflächlich Poren oder auch Haarrisse aufweisen. Die ausgehärteten Betonprodukte werden mit feinen Stahlkugeln (1 bis 2 mm), die mit enormer Geschwindigkeit gegen die Oberfläche geschleudert werden, aufgerauht. Die Zementhaut wird abgetragen, und die Zuschlagkörner treten hervor.

Arbeitsgattung
Oberflächenbehandlungsarbeiten

Bauphysikalische Kennwerte

Rohdichte	2400kg/m3
Wärmeleitfähigkeit	1.8W/mK
Wärmespeicherkapazität	1.1kJ/kg K
Brandkennziffer	6
Druckfestigkeit	40 - 60 N/mm2

Aldo Rossi I Gallaratese 2 I Milano I 1968-1973

Kalkputz

Stützen: Betonstützen mit Kalkverputz

Materialeigenschaften
Durch ihre hohe kapillare Leitfähigkeit und ihre unübertroffenen Diffusionseigenschaften können Kalkputze Luftfeuchtigkeit aufnehmen, zwischenspeichern und bei Bedarf wieder abgeben. Das verbessert spürbar das Raumklima.

Verarbeitung/Oberflächenqualität
Kalkputz wird zweilagig aufgebracht. Er ist kein Dünnputz und sollte mindestens 10mm dick sein. Der Deckputz als feinste Schicht versiegelt sozusagen den Grundputz und bestimmt durch seine Farbigkeit und Struktur das Aussehen der fertigen Wand.

Arbeitsgattung
Oberflächenbehandlungsarbeiten

Bauphysikalische Kennwerte

Rohdichte	1800kg/m3
Wärmeleitfähigkeit	0.8W/mK
Trockenrohdichte	1,3 kg/dm3
Diffusionswiderstandszahl	10

Kokai I House of the Tree Penthouse I Shenzhen I 2012

Sandstein

Treppenstufen: Sandsteinplatten überlappend

Materialeigenschaften
Sandstein ist ein klastisches Sedimentgestein mit einem Anteil von mindestens 50 % Sandkörnern. Die Sandkörner sind per Eigendefinition zwischen 0,063 und 2 mm groß und bestehen aus verschiedenen Mineralen, meistens jedoch aus Quarz. Sandstein ist relativ resistent gegen chemische Verwitterung.

Verarbeitung/Oberflächenqualität
homogene Oberfläche.
Sandsteine sind relativ weich und lassen sich leicht verarbeiten, besonders gleich nach der Gewinnung im noch bergfeuchten Zustand. Trocknen die Sandsteine, so steigt ihre Festigkeit an. Aufgrund ihrer Vielseitigkeit hinsichtlich Farbe und Härte werden Sandsteine seit Jahrhunderten als Bau-, Schleif- oder Schmuckmaterial verwendet.

Arbeitsgattung
Ausbauarbeiten

Bauphysikalische Kennwerte

Rohdichte	2500kg/m3
Wärmeleitfähigkeit	4.7W/mK
Wärmespeicherkapazität	1.2kJ/kg K
Brandkennziffer	6
Druckfestigkeit	38 - 109 N/mm2
Biegezugfestigkeit	6 N/mm2

Marc Hunziker
Katarina Savic
15 ss

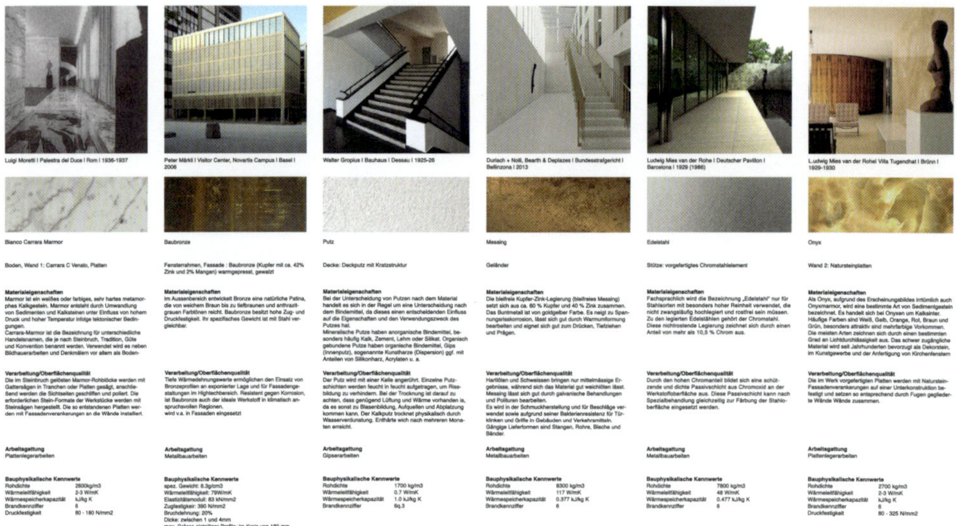

8

Robin Schlumpf
Daniel Zieliński
16 ss

Alana Elayashy
Christian Szalay
16 ss

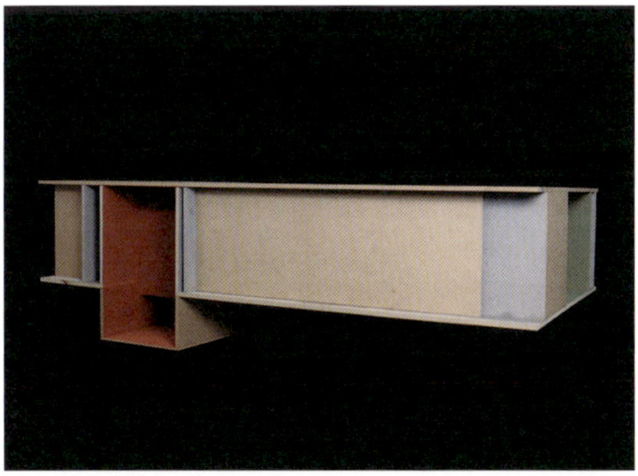

Sohpie Ballweg
Philipp Bleuel
17 SS

Mara Huber
Beatrice Kiser
17 SS

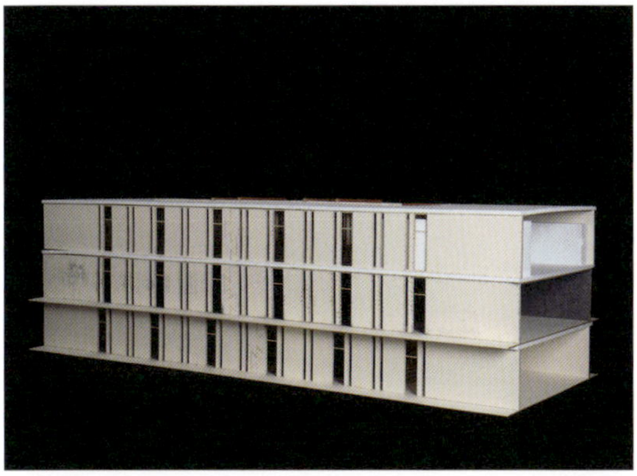

Rémy Carron
Samuel Dayer
17 SS

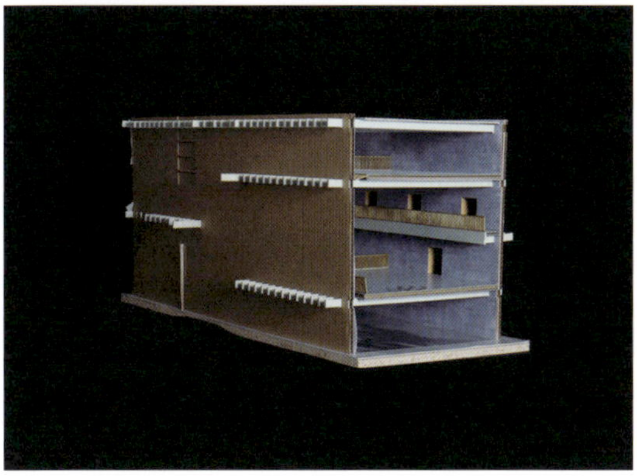

Maximilian Dietschi
Marius Mildner
17 SS

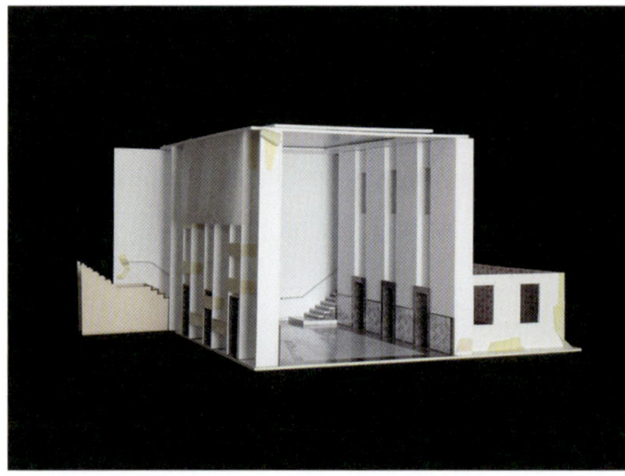

Nicola Merz
Vincent Prenner
17 SS

Louis Strologo
Darius Tabatabay
17 SS

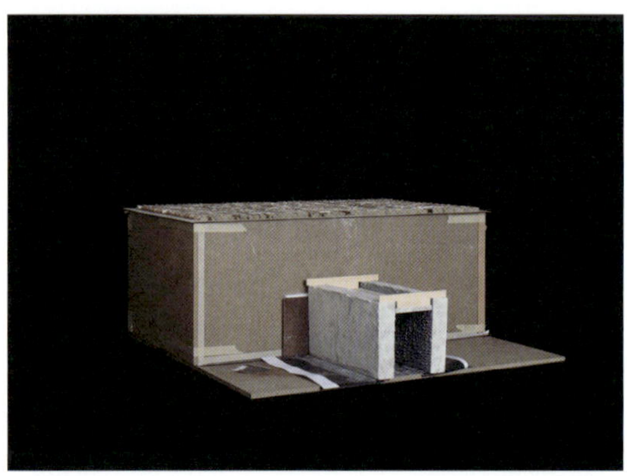

Larissa Strub
Lucie Vauthey
17 SS

Marko Mrcarica
Li Andrew Xingjian
17 SS

Mario Sommer
Andrea Zarn
10 SS

Claudio Arpagaus
Valentin Buchwalder
12 SS

Mira Elsohn
Maximilian Fink
12 SS

Timon Ritscher
Louis Thomet
12 SS

8

8

Elena Pilotto
Lino Saam
12 SS

Raphael Disler
Benjamin Graber
13 SS

8

8

Eva Müller
Nina Stauffer
14 SS

Marc Hunziker
Katarina Savic
15 SS

8

Alcide Bähler
Timon Dönz
15 SS

Joos Kündig
Iso Tambornino
15 SS

Jakob Junghanss
Fabian Kuonen
15 SS

Mevion Famos
Manon Mottet
16 ss

Julien Graf
Reto Habermacher
16 ss

8

Robin Schlumpf
Daniel Zieliński
16 ss

Maximilien Durel
Cyrill Hirtz
16 ss

Kerstin Spiekermann
Nicolas Wild
16 ss

Pawel Bejm
Fortunat Cavigelli
17 ss

Rémy Carron
Samuel Dayer
17 SS

Mara Huber
Beatrice Kiser
17 SS

Nicola Merz
Vincent Prenner
17 SS

Andreas Gursky, Copan 2002, C-Print, 206 × 262 × 6.2 cm
Courtesy of Sprüth Magers Berleri London

9

Place Structure Envelope Program Materiality

With this ninth and final step, the project has reached its maximum completion. From urban conditions to the structural formation of the building, from user options to user surfaces, all imaginable aspects have been integrated into a whole—not merely organized, but also not really composed. The first doesn't really live up to the extent of the complexity, the second emphasizes artistic ambitions over paying dues.

The whole has—as defined by Aristotle—a beginning, middle, and an end. Even when a building stands in a spatial and temporal context that has a formative effect and can be very broadly interpreted, the building is located at a place and is completed. This differentiates it from a wholly open structure thought of as a framework for everything and everywhere. It is especially determined by the cultural presence of the place. Within this framework, user options are, of course, to be kept flexible.

The whole integrates the parts and the steps in a way so as to create a meaningful figure. Alberti defines it classically: "that reasoned harmony of all the parts within a body, so that nothing may be added, taken away, or altered, but for the worse" (1755). Even when the project is developed from one step to the next, the individual steps are related to one another. And it is by no means as if the developments disappear in some way—to the contrary: With each step, one turns back to the steps that came before, for they appear in a different light, the concepts gaining in depth and enrichment.

This unfolding ensures that the design and the built object have the fullness that distinguishes good architecture. This is true indiscriminate of the differentiation between place, structure, and envelope, which emphasize the permanent side of architecture and its public role, and program and materiality, which highlight the changing, private aspects. In any case, it is this process of bringing-into-harmony that imbues the design with quality and the building with identity.

The classical definition of such a whole speaks of connections—between the parts themselves and to the whole. Appropriateness and balance are in demand, and result in a harmony seen in rhythm and proportion. Even if the classical canon is today questioned, the idea of unity remains alive. The significance of connections was reemphasized during the late 20th century from a wholly new perspective: that of ecology.

Here, also, relationships are highlighted. There is nothing that has no effect; the slightest flap of a butterfly's wings can trigger a catastrophic flood; forces evoke counterforces; the system adapts to change; things are moving. Ecological systems are characterized by reflexivity, unpredictability, and dynamic balance.

Social systems can also be described this way. On the one hand, the connections of convention and sociocultural acceptance, on the other, the actions of humans, which are only predictable to a certain degree and in a dynamic balance. Building cannot be thought in any other way, for it is an action dynamic and, as such, is always tied to conditions. When the actions unfold within this context, is aware of its ties, it is—according to the proverb—"not to preserve the ashes but to pass on the flame," and the dynamic takes the form of continued building, and built identity is the result. (FA/MN)

Workday, Sunday

Dietmar Eberle

Architecture is one of the forces that brings order to our artificial life—to a degree that is apparently increasing. And this in times when other effective orders are buckling under the rapidly mounting speed of change—such as the way we deal with time. We have long since carried the day into night. The strength with which the regulation of time persists is astonishing, for example in the division of workdays and Sundays. It seems natural then to consider the field of architecture in this regard.

The German *Duden* dictionary states plainly that the workday is a day on which work is permissible, in contrast to the *working day*, a day on which work is actually carried out, and in contrast to Sundays and public holidays, when work is forbidden. This elevates those days above the majority of ordinary days, while the workday is "a day like every other". An early dictionary defines this everyday as "everyday life, a common day, a weekday: in contrast to Sundays and holidays."[1]

9

Does this mean the workday is the everyday? This is the case in many respects, as the everyday lacks the decisive contrast that turns the workday into Sunday. The everyday says it is "one like every other", it is uniform, indifferent. On the other hand, the workday, with *work*, with *doing*, stands in opposition to Sundays and holidays and their celebration. The workday is about working, about getting off work, resting—ordinary things that are part of everyday life. Sunday is about church, museum visits, the soccer field—sermons, aesthetics, and spectacles.

On Doing

The workday is when you get your hands dirty, rarely safeguarded by reasons of beauty. But workdays have their own rule of law. Those who live according to it are aware of this. Rainer Werner Fassbinder was such a workday person who reportedly said that whoever is busy is right.

[1] Johann Heinrich Campe: *Wörterbuch der deutschen Sprache*, 1807. Cited in: Klaus Laermann, *Alltags-Zeit*, Course Book 41, Berlin, 1975, p. 88.

The workday has a character of being-in-the-world, and is determined by the flow of time. The workday is doing, creating, making, and functioning; it is growth and development, reality, and possibility; the workday has the nature of an event. The things of the workday are the kind with which one interacts, about which one worries.

The things of the workday have different temporal dimensions. There are those that are subject to direct consumption, direct access; alternately, there are things that last longer, are intended to be long-lasting. Working daily using one's own abilities relies on the economy of means. This is why persistence and endurance are so highly rated. This can also be observed in actual doing: In the workday, continuity and practice are the setting for seizing opportunities.

The workday takes place through dealing with things in space. This is a living space, not an abstract space. It is not a room that is simply there, and then the workday takes place in it. Neither does the workday create a space—the workday is already spatial from the start. As Maurice Merleau-Ponty emphasized, human existence is spatial, just as space is existential. Lived space is not geometric space. This has consequences for building and for buildings. August Schmarsow called attention to the fact that buildings are dependent upon our behavior: "This interaction with the building originates with our own bodies, and its effect always returns to them."[2]

These are not two geometrical objects that oppose one another—we are here, and the building is there. We have always taken part in space, actively and passively, in our time, "lock, stock, and barrel". The term "subjective body" (German: *Leib*) addresses this difference to the neutral object/objective body. The body is the subjective body: with all the senses, in motion, relating to its environment, mindful of its possibilities and its past. "My body is a thing-origin, a zero point of orientation. [...] It is the measure of all spatial conditions. [...] My body exists where it has something to do," says Merleau-Ponty.[3]

[2] August Schmarsow: *Unser Verhältnis zu den Bildenden Künsten. Sechs Vorträge Über Kunst und Erziehung.* Teubner, Leipzig, 1903, p. 105.

[3] Maurice Merleau-Ponty, *Vorlesungen.* Cited in: Stephan Günzel, *Maurice Merlau-Ponty, Werk und Wirkung,* Vienna 2007, p. 69.

This contamination though circumstance, the environment, and corporeality characterizes the workday in exceptional ways. Sunday, on the other hand, stands for peace, tidiness, and spirituality. Further juxtapositions can be associated along these lines:

THE WORKDAY UNIVERSE	THE SUNDAY UNIVERSE
things	concept
context	object
practice	theory
concrete	abstract
in flux	final
convention	inspiration
boundary	openness
variation	creation
craftsmanship	design

The workday is despised as heavy, laborious, ordinary, and monotonous. Sunday, on the other hand, still leads the stroller "from gray city walls [...] towards the sun, towards freedom". The light aftertaste of Sunday sermons ranks well above "everyday twaddle" (Gotthold Lessing). Henri Lefebvre has argued against this: this world evidences "a power hidden in the seeming banality of everyday life, something that is exceptional in its ordinariness".[4]

[4] Henri Lefebvre: *Everyday Life in the Modern World.* Cited in: Ben Highmore: *Das Alltägliche bewohnen*, in: *Daidalos 75*, Berlin 1999, p. 40.

The world of workdays takes up the bulk of our time. In terms of construction, 95% of all buildings are used on workdays, the remainder on Sundays. The miscalculation of these conditions inevitably leads to the mistaken notions of people who prefer to be active on Sunday.

Characteristics

The workday deals with the things that are necessary for living. It is conducive to work, reproduction, exchange, consumption, recreation. This takes place concretely, in places that can be named, by specific people with goals. For Henri Lefebvre, the workday possesses: "Ego, bed, bedroom, dwelling, house. [...] It embraces the loci of passion, of action and of lived situations, and thus immediately implies time. Consequently it may be qualified in various ways: it may be directional, situational or relational, because it is essentially qualitative, fluid and dynamic."[5] In contrast to Sunday with its prominent objects and monuments, the workday is exposed to influences. What is decisive are not settled terms, but concrete things. Friedrich Nietzsche wrote, "above all things there standeth the heaven of chance, the heaven of innocence, the heaven of hazard, the heaven of wantonness." [6] The workday is concrete, casual, rakish.

Sunday is set aside for the sermon, for truth, and for beauty. Consistent with its emphasis on the conceptual, it is abstract, authoritative, clean, and perfect. While here the order of rational inferences of cause and effect dominates rational thought, the workday is marked by the constant alternation of unarticulated and pre-conscious conventions and reflexive acts of will. The French sociologist Michel de Certeau attributes an anarchic potential to this world. He recognizes "microbial, unique, and divergent practices of [...] proliferating lawlessness, linked by illegible yet robust tactics, so interconnected that they have become routine events and inconspicuous creativity [...] smaller instrumentalities, little artifices of discipline, small but infallible engines." [7] We will return to this later.

The psychiatrist Wolfgang Blankenburg considers these "small, infallible machines" essential for a successful life; one cannot thoroughly think through every action, but rather must be able to rely on convention: "Natural self-understanding and self-sufficiency/self-reliance are related to one another dialectically. The self-determination of the self-reliant man stands out from the anonymous sea of all that happens 'by itself' and understands itself 'of itself', and yet remains related to it at the same time. There is a reciprocal relationship between self-awareness and self-reliance. Self-reliance is based on the self-evident and at the same time negates it."[8]

Workday time is similarly grounded: concrete, experienced time, a certain kind of time (like daily chores), moment, duration. It is tied to specific fields of activity, provides orientation, is designed for the long term, constancy; it is self-contained and

[5] Henri Lefebvre: *The Production of Space*, Oxford / Cambridge, 1991, p. 42.

[6] Friedrich Nietzsche: *Also sprach Zarathustra*, Munich, 1967, p. 166.

[7] Michel de Certeau: *Praktiken im Raum*, Paris, 1980. Cited in: Jörg Dünne und Stephan Günzel: *Raumtheorie*, Berlin, 2006.

[8] Wolfgang Blankenburg: *Der Verlust der natürlichen Selbstverständlichkeit*, Berlin, 2012, p. 124.

has a beginning and an end. Moments of subsistence and craftsmanship remain effectual. This is opposed to time that is bound in every respect: fragmented into the smallest identical units, featureless, numerable, linear, monotonous, clocked—the prerequisite for becoming synchronized to new mechanisms, predictable, off limits.

Place

This is the calculating time of modernism, as boundless as its space. By contrast, the time and space of the workday are close at hand. Martin Heidegger calls this material world that is shaped by man and his actions, and that is here, "existence", which is characterized by dealing with things: "To be 'at hand' has a different affinity that is not determined by measuring distances. This affinity is governed by careful, 'calculating', handling and use. [...] The availability of the environment is not at hand for an eternal observer removed from existence, but is encountered in the carefully attentive everyday life of existence."[9]

9

9 Martin Heidegger: *Sein und Zeit,* Tübingen, 1963, p. 102, 106.

At hand are the things that are dealt with, which are carefully attentive. Such things form places, as Martin Heidegger explained in his lecture to architects titled *Building, Dwelling,*

Ghosts and the City
Giotto (Giotto di Bondone 1266–1337), The Legend of St. Francis

Source: Scala Archives, Florence

Thinking (1954), using the example of a bridge: "The bridge is a thing and only that. Only? As this thing it gathers the fourfold. [...] It swings over the river, connects the existing shores, brings electricity and shore and land to the vicissitudes of each other. [...] The bridge is always and ever differently guiding."[10] Places are made, and spaces form, out of things like the bridge.

This interplay of thing and place is fundamental, so it is natural to look for the precise beginning of design there. Design must secure the setting in order for this to succeed. Scandinavian architecture has a feel for this context, as the Danish architect Kay Fisker says: "The human, the use, and the wear that give charm to the ordinary house should guide us. We must give the common ordinary house the respect it deserves. It gets us nowhere to set lonely monoliths of outstanding architecture in the landscape if their surroundings are unsightly and horrible. First the architectural setting must be in order."[11]

[10] Martin Heidegger: *Poetry, Language, Thought*, translated by Albert Hofstadter, Harper Colophon Books, New York, 1971, p. 6.

[11] Kay Fisker: *Persondyrkelse eller anonymitet*. In *Arkitekten 26* (1964). Cited in: Erik Nygaard: "Kay Fisker und die funktionale Tradition". In: *Die Architektur, die Tradition und der Ort*, Vittorio M. Lampugnani (ed.), Stuttgart/Munich, 2000, p. 193.

Structure

Structure forms the setting for any architecture, just as what is naturally self-evident forms the setting for its own spontaneity, and as place and context form the setting for the individual building. In the architecture of the workday, it describes the possible limits to practical value. Structure is the built fabric of construction and enclosure—for humans and their media. An extension of the concept of structure is to understand it in the sense of basic spatial frameworks that connect to make complex figures.

Poised at the start of the term's career is the crisis of classical modernism, the breakup of CIAM 1953 in Aix-en-Provence, and the formation of Team X. A few years earlier, Georges Candilis had attracted attention with his residential buildings in Casablanca and other projects linked to traditional settlements in the Maghreb—a three-dimensional scaffold filled with life by the users that is completed only by appropriation. This interplay of structure and infill would soon become the main paradigm. Yona Friedman, one of Candilis' protagonists, put it this way: “The buildings that constitute the cities must be treated as skeleton frames, to be filled in as desired. The way the frames are fitted out is up to each resident.”[12]

In the 1960s, it became clear that structure was not solely meant to be structural and spatial. In one case, it was interpreted as a social structure; in another, a temporal one. Aldo van Eyck, founding member of Team X and the leading proponent of Dutch structuralism, put it this way: “Man is always and everywhere the same. His spirit remains unchanged. However, he developed it differently, according to the environment. Modern architecture [...] is so far gone, that it lost sight of what is not different and new, but old and eternal.”[13]

In his 1964 exhibition “Architecture Without Architects” at MoMa in New York and in his book of the same name, Bernhard Rudofsky wrote: “Collective architecture is a communal art that

[12] Yona Friedman: “Die 10 Prinzipien des Raumstadtbaus”, lecture Essen 1962. Cited in: Ulrich Conrads: *Programme und Manifeste zur Architektur des 20. Jahrhunderts*, Braunschweig, 1975, p. 176.

[13] Aldo van Eyck: speech at the 1959 CIAM Congress in Otterlo. Cited in: Kenneth Frampton, *Die Architektur der Moderne*, Frankfurt/Vienna, 1995, p. 234.

9

The Inside of the Outside and the Outside of the Inside, façade of the Florence Cathedral, design by Bernardo Bagatelli, a. k. a. Poccetti (1548–1612)

Source: Museo die Opera di Santa Maria del Fiore/ Rafaello Benici/Archivi Alinari, Florence is not the product of a few intellectuals or specialists, but consists of the spontaneous and continuous activity of a whole people, supported by a common heritage, influenced by common experience. [...] The beauty of this architecture (we recognize today) is the result of a rare understanding of how to deal with practical problems. The forms of the buildings, sometimes handed down through a hundred generations, like those of the tools, are of lasting value."[14] Out of this grew the notion of typology, mostly anonymized. The task of further developing and deepening that anonymous knowledge is comprised precisely in the architecture of the workday.

[14] Bernard Rudofsky: *Architektur ohne Architekten*, Salzburg, Vienna, 1989, p. 8.

Envelope, Public Sphere, and User

The boundary between interior and exterior, cold and warm, private and public, which protects and conceals private and intimate spaces, and at once displays and represents social and public spaces, has its own physical quality. European urban architecture is actually characterized by the fact that the side on display to the public has an opulent physicality. Its appearance is determined in terms of public space, not the building's interior. This is diametrically opposed to a fundamental dogma of modernity.

In contrast to this, Gottfried Semper, architecture theoretician and one of the most important architects of the 19th century, not only validated the autonomy of the envelope and the wall, but also deemed it the primary element of architecture. He thought about the wall as a garment, covering, or clothing; it was certain to him "that the use of coarse tissue as a means of separating the 'home', the inner life, from the external life, preceded the simply constructed wall, stone, or any other material."[15] He stated further: "The cladding of the walls was the original, the essence of its spatial, architectural meaning; the wall itself was secondary."[16] It follows that: "The technique of the wall

[15] Gottfried Semper: *Der Stil in den technischen und tektonischen Künsten oder praktische Ästhetik*, Vol. 1, Frankfurt, 1860, p. 228.

[16] Gottfried Semper: *Vergleichende Baulehre*, 1849. Cited in: Heidrun Laudel: *Gottfried Semper, Architektur und Stil,* Dresden, 1991, p. 105.

builder [...] must have and retain the most important and enduring influence on the stylistic development of architecture itself, and that it must be regarded as a primordial technique."[17]

[17] Semper, *Der Stil*, p. 233.

Hence, the wall is autonomous, it is primary, and it is so as something cladded. It is that way because Semper adds decoration to the fabric, and the fabric and the decoration are equally necessary—in textile art (*Textrin*) the two are synchronized. And decoration is not an accessory, because it gives expression to "the true and legitimate representation of the spatial concept".[18] Semper sees representation, which occurs in public space, in the original forms of festivity and celebration, and he uses the word "commemorate"—meaning collective remembrance. Here he makes clear that architecture is a matter of public life and history.

[18] Ibid., p. 229.

The connection to place, the dialogue with place, is therefore compelling. Representation is not about turning an interior to the exterior, but speaking the language of the place, the use of conventions, the unfolding of its potential. Conventions characterize the always changing character of cities, for example. That is what creates their atmosphere and thus their playability.

User and Program

Playability—game, festivity, celebration: that is Semper. Festivity and workday? The paintings of Pieter Bruegel the Elder—for example, *Children's Games* from 1560—show how festival, play, and the workday are not opposed. Deepening this opposition is reserved for the modern age. In de Certeau's anarchic "inconspicuous creativity and the little artifices", the interplay lives on. The opposition is brittle and becomes noticeable. New actors make themselves noticeable on the stage of the built work: the passersby. Public space as defined by building envelopes is their habitat. Its durability, its conventions ensure its playability. These passersby are the users of the 21st century.

Contrasting to this are the users of classical modernism: These users are meant to define the structure of the building and its outer form through function—an abstraction that is interpreted in their best interest by the architect (the "New Human"). By the time structuralism emerged, this user had become an actor who appropriates the space, who defines its function, who, by making use of it in an own way, produces the very real nature of the space—the user consumes the space productively, and becomes a producer. "Without production, there is no consumption; but also, without consumption, there is no production, as production would be so pointless. [...] Production creates the

The Poetry of Construction, Marco Zanuso, sketch

Source: Archivio del Moderno, Accademia di Architettura Universita della Svizzera italiana, Mendrisio material as an external object for consumption."[19] The person who uses the spaces determines their own program, produces, and ultimately designs the space; their grasping reach is now the predominant spatial relationship. The use of a space is detached from the built structure; this is already reality outside of Central Europe.

[19] Karl Marx: *Grundrisse der Kritik der politischen Ökonomie*, reprint Moscow 1939–41, Frankfurt 1972, p. 12.

Surface, Materials, Sensuality

Consumptive production is a term of political economy that has its counterpart in productive consumption. Both interact to form the metabolism of the workday, the working person, and the consumer, mediated by things that occur as products or consumer goods. "In production, the person is objectified; in consumption, the thing is subjectified; [...] without consumption, there is no production."[20]

[20] Ibid., p. 11.

This metabolism of the workday takes place within a context, against the background of the place. It happens against the backdrop of a structure that makes it possible, and within the framework of public space, which is formed by plastic envelopes, by façades. The metabolism is a living event, an activity. As production, it is building, consuming, expending, enjoying, squandering. Consumption and consuming—that is the surface, sheer superficiality. This, too, is part of architecture.

Materiality and sensuality establish the intrinsic value of the surface. It has its own value and its own quality in comparison to envelope and space—sensuality is its medium, comfort its purpose. At the same time, comfort is understood as an atmosphere that provides well-being, and which can be modified by the user through their own actions—on a workday. This is opposed to the luxury of possessing objects—on a Sunday, such as the possession of spiritual worth.

Sensuality—the answer to the surface—is itself an active relationship. Modern neurology has long since abandoned the idea that passive perception is opposed to the active will. Rather, reception is action, action is reception. The gaze is directed, the grasping hand feels the object.

The consequences for the relationship between construction and the user: if the body and its behavior was a chief concern for August Schmarsow, half a century later, the French philosopher Gaston Bachelard, in his *Poetics of Space*, focused on our

Modern man in the distorted mirror of his own projections, Roy Lichtenstein, *Stepping Out*, 1978

behavior, things, and space. "The experienced building is not a lifeless box. Inhabited space transcends geometric space."[21] "Pleasing things rise to a higher level of reality than indifferent things, the things defined by mere geometrical reality. They not only take their place in a certain order, but in a communication of order. Domestic labor spins connecting threats from one thing to another..."[22] The fact that these "connecting threads" are not mysticism becomes clear when he describes how they are spun through careful daily routines: "Henri Bosco says, 'The soft wax penetrated this smooth material under the pressure of the hands and the useful warmth of the canvas. Slowly, the tabletop took on a dark luster. That ray seemed to emanate from the hundred-year-old whitewood, from the actual heart of the dead tree, drawn out by magnetic rubbing, which eventually spread over the surface like a new light. The old fingers, loaded with magical powers, the magnanimous palm, drew latent vital powers from the massive block of lifeless fibers. What took place before my astonished eyes was the creation of a thing."[23]

But not only are reception and action intertwined. Memory and vistas, past and future, are involved in every process of perception. And the reception is never confined to one sense—neurologically an interconnection always takes place. "Each of the one billion nerve cells (in the human brain) sends its information to about 10,000 others. Distribution takes place; that is, the divergence of information. There is one point and ten thousand others: each of these nerve cells receives information from ten thousand others: the principle of convergence. Divergence and convergence. The architecture of this system of the brain is generally very different from that of modern thinking machines."[24] The sense awareness does not only have the five classic senses of seeing, hearing, smelling, tasting, and touch; today there is also temperature sense, feeling of pain, sense of balance, bodily awareness; finally, there is memory and vision. Like any awareness, this can also be formed, unfolded. Artistic practices do this, as Gaston Bachelard explains: "Every poet of furniture instinctively knows that the interior of a closet is deep. The interior of

[21] Gaston Bachelard: *Poetik des Raumes*, Munich 1960, p. 78.

[22] Ibid., p. 98.

9

[23] Ibid., p. 97.

[24] Ernst Pöppel: "Im Kopf", in: *Über Denken*, Rotis, 1999, p. 24.

the closet is an intimate space, a space that does not open for just any whim. […] With lavender, the story of the seasons permeates the closet. The lavender alone brings a sense of duration to the hierarchy of linens. One need not wait until they are put to use […] 'The closet is full of laundry. There are even moonbeams that I can unfold.' With the verses of André Breton, the image is now heightened to a level of excess a rational mind no longer wants to acknowledge. But excess is always on the apex of a living image."[25]

[25] Bachelard: *Poetik*, p. 110.

The excess of the senses, material presence, variety, and abundance—this makes for an animated surface. When Gottfried Semper maintained: "Every artistic creation, on the one hand, every enjoyment of art requires a certain carnival spirit—carnival candlelight is the true atmosphere of art,"[26] he was addressing festivity and smoke, and that was meant for architecture. His Vienna museums provide an impressive testimony. This was also true of the great purist Adolf Loos two generations later—with his interiors! Another generation later, the game of materials found a master in Carlo Scarpa, complemented by virtuosity in the detail. It is this interplay of materiality, details, approachability, and social interaction that makes up the atmosphere—for Gernot Boehme it is "the common reality of the perceiver and the perceived".[27]

[26] Semper, *Der Stil*, p. 231.

[27] Gernot Böhme: *Atmosphäre. Essays zur neuen Ästhetik*, Frankfurt, 1995, p. 34.

Fundamentals, Rules

The "pampered things", the things that gain their own brilliancy by being handled, are common in the workday at home, but that can hardly be said for the opulence of the surface. A modestly-sized space like the Kärntner Bar in Vienna by Loos lives from the mastery of the use of materials, but added to that are scale, proportion, and geometry. Those are the foundations of architectural design that are rightly called timeless. These basics apply equally to both the workday and Sunday. Not only are they effective in the workday; they originate there. For a long time, division and composition, the foundations of proportion and geometry, were carried out with cord and ruler, and followed the economy of simple workaday operations. But the evolution of these operations into doctrines—such as the triangulation of a gothic cathedral, the quadrature of a façade by Alberti, and Le Corbusier's Modulor—unfolds their blooms in Sunday architecture. It remains true that these basic principles are valid in all spheres of architectural creation.

The rules and regulations that apply there are the rules of technology, such as building construction, statics, and building physics; the rules of the discipline of architecture, formulated in the theory and history of the discipline; the rules of society, such as sociology, economics, and psychology; the rules of form-giving, whether it is the precision of gestalt theory or the signif-

Diversity and richness of surfaces, Josef Frank, material design "Fruit Tree", ca. 1943–45.

icance of semiotics. Added to this are new rules of digital media and the new geometries they create. In any case, these rules must be coordinated with what practice brings to regulation: the particularity of place, the features of conventions, the practice of use, dealing with things. Architectural order never exists unto itself, as Vittorio Lampugnani explains: "Architecture must be modest and follow its own internal immanent utopia: that of order. An architectural structure always contains a dialectic of order and disorder; it is the result of the collaboration between the project and reality."[28] Paul Valéry also takes this up, adding a dimension fundamental to architecture, namely durability: "The body thus compels us to desire what is useful or simply comfortable; the soul demands of us beauty; but, in its laws and in its accidents, the rest of the world obliges us to regard every work as a continuation of its work."[29]

Thus, workday and Sunday are germane—secular, useful, concrete and spiritual, purposeless, abstract, long valid. It is wrong if only the one counts, if pointless appearances surrender to the splendor of use. This is due to human use—concrete, bodily; no abstraction of the "new human".

If we try to transfer Sunday to the workday, to push the workday through Sunday, then we fail in the acceptance of architecture, and architecture becomes a phenomenon of preliminary design or the outer layer.

Building for the workday means taking account of their concerns, timeless rules and regulations. No new recipe for architecture, no new dogma, and it is called "workday architecture". Architecture is not art; it is not conceptual. It stays with the orders of discipline, set in scene in a place, as a background for the people who make use of it. Actually old, and yet new, in a world where overpowering "signature buildings" are what count. Contrary to this trend, we should demand along with Frank-Berthold Raith that: "architects acknowledge their extensive

[28] Vittorio M. Lampugnani: *Architektur als Kultur*, Cologne, 1986, p. 338.

[29] Paul Valerie: *Eupalinos*. Frankfurt, 1973, p. 99.

impotence not only with regard to the production of buildings, but also with regard to their reception, i.e., the consumption of architecture. [...] Architecture is not a cosmology, but it can contribute to the continuous differentiation of the web of cultural meaning."[30]

[30] Frank-Bernhard Raith: "Das Alltagsleben der Architektur", in: *Daidalos75*, Berlin, 1999, p. 14.

To begin architecture with the place, the context—a web of events—does not mean taking a view of the whole form, but rather to comprehend it in execution, as an event. Architecture, to modify a passage by Bernard Tschumi, is not conditioned by the design, but is the design of conditions. The design emanates from the place, does not replicate it, but wins new options for it in the struggle. Something like this is suggested in the "most minimal intervention possible" of Lucius Burckhardt.

The same humility applies to the most important audience of architecture: the user. Gone is the notion of a single, ideal user; a new figure takes on importance: the passer-by. Walter Benjamin pointed out that architecture is perceived "in dispersion and through the collective"—tactile and visual, less "by means of attention than by habit; less through actively noticing than by casual observation."[31] This corresponds to the valorization of peripheral versus focused vision, as undertaken by E. T. Hall, supplemented by a revaluation of the senses of proximity (touch, smell, hearing), which are important to the workday.[32]

9

[31] Walter Benjamin: *Das Kunstwerk im Zeitalter seiner technischen Reproduzierbarkeit.* Frankfurt, 1976, p. 47.

[32] Edward T. Hall: *Die Sprache des Raumes*, Düsseldorf, 1976.

A Signpost

A reversal of design practice? Revaluation of its elements and moments? Actually old, and yet new? There are probably only a few architects who knew how to span the arc between architectural practice on the cutting edge and its contemplation as much as Josef Frank. Born near Vienna in 1885, he studied with Alberti, launched his architectural practice in 1910, and became one of the most important architects in the design of Viennese housing estates; along with private commissions built in the spirit of Viennese modernism that attracted attention. He is a co-founder of the Austrian Werkbund and became the director of the Werkbundsiedlung Wien in 1931. During this time, the notion of "architecture as symbol" emerged, the first billing of dogmatic modernism. After emigrating in 1933, he lived in Sweden, built very little, and resorted to creating a literary and graphic work, ranging from visionary architecture to textile designs. His many textile designs are still an unexplored treasure.

Frank found himself committed to a European architecture that evolved timeless ideas of proportion and harmony tailored to the human form and its behavior. This culture, according to his perhaps most famous statement, spans "the entirety of history as we know it. This thought alone could be the foundation of modern architecture."[33] The consequence of this, which is contained in every abstract idealization, is radical: "Today, those who want to create something vital must not neglect things and push them aside for the sake of any sort of principle. [...] Those who want to create something vital today must take on all that is alive today. The whole spirit of the age, with all its sentimentality and exaggerations, together with its tastelessness, which are nevertheless at least alive. [...] It is time to finally realize that there are no definitive goals."[34]

This openness to the ordinary things of life is met with an impressive self-observation: "I know very well that no system suffices for that, because it requires intuition."[35] And, "The purpose of a building cannot be expressed in words. It is not actually for cooking, eating, working, or sleeping, but for living.[36] Every building is dependent on a great many things that do not allow for a merely calculated form, because the sense of well-being one experiences in it depends on the sensibility of the designer, which the engineer does not possess."[37]

[33] Josef Frank: *Architektur als Symbol*, Vienna, 1931 (reprint 1981), p. 166.

[34] Ibid., pp. 171–172.

[35] Ibid., p. 172.

[36] Ibid., p. 150.

[37] Ibid., p. 57.

9

Beauty | Not a concept, but, as Nietzsche says, only a word? In contrast, Augustine: The truth – that, which exceeds our scattered knowledge – shines forth in beauty. For the Pythagoreans it is number, scale, proportion, music, and harmony. Alberti joins in to define it as something to which nothing may be added, taken away, or altered, but for the worse. Friedrich Schiller's personal perspective is that beauty is for the feeling heart. And for Christian Morgenstern it is everything that one sees with love. So it is an activity? Nietzsche knew that beauty is no accident, that starting at the right point is crucial—with the body, with strength, logic, and intoxication. And yet, what remains is merely a veil.

Art | Art, according to Immanuel Kant, aims for disinterested satisfaction. Self-development is its measure, freedom its requirement. Adolf Loos confirms that, in contrast to architecture, a work of art is brought into the world without there being a need for it. A building must meet a need. A work of art has no responsibility to anyone, a building to everyone. The aim of a work of art is to make us feel uncomfortable, a building is there for our comfort. Architecture must stay away from art. But does this unconditional contrast do justice to architecture? What, then, is the art of building?

Originality | From Latin *origo*: Original; true, unadulterated, unique. The origin is creation; drawing on this, the artistic genius of romanticism pushed up against rational enlightenment and brought with it, according to Johann Gottfried Herder, the beating heart into position to counter the head. Not everlasting reason but the vital powers of each person and their place are the truth, and from this point of view, the best most genius minds are not found in the study—they act from within themselves, with true originality. Respect for property must also be paid to the environment, which sets it apart from arbitrary originality.

Appropriateness | Appropriateness is a criterion of proportionality, that deliberates measures in light of the intention, means in light of the aspired result. Appropriateness is obligatory, without being objective: in a specific case, measures, means, and intention are to be reconciled with each other. The whole created in this way – a building, for example – is made of up individual pieces. Individual identity, general connectedness: putting both into the right scale creates appropriateness. Appropriateness, in Latin *decorum*, is for Vitruvius a fundamental aspect of architectural beauty.

Standpoint | Human agency—including recognition—is neither an instinctive nor a passive act. It is intentional; there is always an actor, and this includes a standpoint. In the 20th century, Kant's realization was radicalized: With Heidegger, we as agents with our standpoint are always the world that we open, which, for its part, comes to meet us. Both face the world; architecture and standpoint are inseparably related to one another. As impossible as it is to think of architecture as being objective, it is equally impossible to have a free-floating standpoint.

Sustainability | Can be traced back to the Central European forestry management of the 18th century. In order to prevent further depletion, no more wood was to be cut than grew back or was planted. A guiding principle of resource management with the goal of maintaining a stable system—the careful handling of resources. Today's understanding of sustainability rests upon three pillars: Society, economy, and ecology. Became a political approach with the Brundtland Report in 1987.

Contemporaneity | According to Mies van der Rohe, the keyword for modernity in architecture is "the will of the epoch translated into space" – to create form from the nature of the task and the methods of our time. Architecture goes with the times; however, time is not purpose but instead produces the available means. Modernity contrasts this: Since the *Querelle des Anciens et des Modernes*, it has been accepted that the past as such should be shaken off. For the radicals of the 1920s, there was only our time: the age of machines. However, colleagues soon began to object to the living and seating machines.

Synthesis | From Greek *synthesis:* Aggregation, combination. Ever since the first great treatise on architecture, Vitruvius' *Ten Books on Architecture* (written in the year 1 b.c.), the delivery of synthesis has been demanded of the art. *Utilitas, firmitas,* and *venustas* are the three principles upon which the entirety of architecture rests. This says two things: 1. A preference for the one or the other misses the very core of architecture – the synthesis. And 2. Each of these three elements is fundamental; none can be drawn from the other; connection counts, and none can be the foundation of architecture alone.

Rationality | From Latin *ratio:* Reason. Reason-based thinking and acting of various types, for example the priority of reason (logic) over empiricism, and confirmability of each step of thinking or acting. Grounds other than reason (religion, tradition) are discarded. Since the rejection of a normative antiquity (*Querelle des Anciens et des Modernes*, late 17th century): equated with modernism (also architecture), for example, the radical functionalism of Carlo Lodoli (1690–1761). A unique variety: In 20th-century Italy, architecture with basic geometrical shapes.

PLACE—STRUCTURE—ENVELOPE—
PROGRAM—MATERIALITY

In this final exercise, the knowledge acquired will be used to bring all topics together and merge them into an independent project. The progression of instructional topics helps to accurately prioritize the various demands on architecture and to develop a personal approach to assignment and place. The specific conditions of the place on the one hand, and the generally formulated typological examples on the other, create two poles between which the project creator can freely move and develop something new. In this way, something specific, contemporary, and better can emerge from a generality.

Façade model
Pablo Vuillemin
14 SS

Building Level

The final project builds on the preparatory work completed in Exercise 7. A building or building ensemble will be planned in an urban situation. The existing buildings will be completely or partially demolished, fictitiously at least. An urban development concept will be developed. The concept must outline the treatment of the existing plot structure and the urban master plan. In the following steps, the structure, circulation, and layout of the usable floor areas according to the spatial allocation program will be clarified, and a façade developed that shows the intervention in its urban context. The materiality of a flight of rooms must be established with a focus on the resulting atmosphere.

Specialization

The final project will be completed independently. The following must be submitted:

Plan 1 City Level
- Written description and project stamp
- Photos of insertion model 1:500
- Figure-ground diagram 1:5,000
- Area plan 1:1,000 including roof perspectives and topography
- Ground floor plan 1:500 with open spaces and footprints of the surrounding buildings
- A representative façade view 1:200/1:250

Plan 2 Building Level
- Area calculations and representation according to SIA 416
- Table of parameters
- Model photos of the materiality of a flight of rooms
- Standard floor plan 1:200/1:250
- Floor plans 1:500
- A representative cross-section 1:200/1:250 including context
- Diagram, pictogram, schematic, etc. explaining the concept

Models
- Insertion model 1:500
- Sectional model 1:75/1:50

Requirements

- Figure-ground diagram 1:5,000
- Area plan 1:1,000
- Ground floor plan 1:500
- Site model 1:500
- Plans of existing structures
- Spatial allocation program
- Table of areas and list of parameters
- Crafting notebooks I–IV
- General norms

Goal

The final exercise of this one-year course brings the previous exercises on Place, Structure, Envelope, Program, and Materiality and their interactions together to create a final project. The skills acquired during these two semesters enable students to solve these complex tasks. The incremental accomplishment of these complex tasks teaches a methodical approach. Networked thinking, simultaneity, and maintaining sustainability are indispensable aspects of this method.

The sections and steps of this program are integrated in such a way so as to create a meaningful whole. Even when the project is developed from one step to the next, the individual steps are related to one another. And it is by no means as if the developments disappear in some way—to the contrary: With each step, one turns back to the steps that came before, for they appear in a different light, the concepts gaining in depth and enrichment.

This unfolding ensures that the design and the built object have the fullness that distinguishes good architecture. This is true indiscriminate of the differentiation between place, structure, and envelope, which emphasize the permanent side of architecture and its public role, and program and materiality, which highlight the changing, private aspects. In any case, it is this process of bringing-into-harmony that imbues the design with quality and the building with identity.

Carlo Scarpa, Casa e studio Gallo, Vicenza, 1962–65, interior

Vaclav Sedy © CISA-A. Palladio

Giovanni Muzio, Ca'Brutta, Milan, 1919–22

© Gabriele Basilico/Archivio Gabriele Basilico, Milan

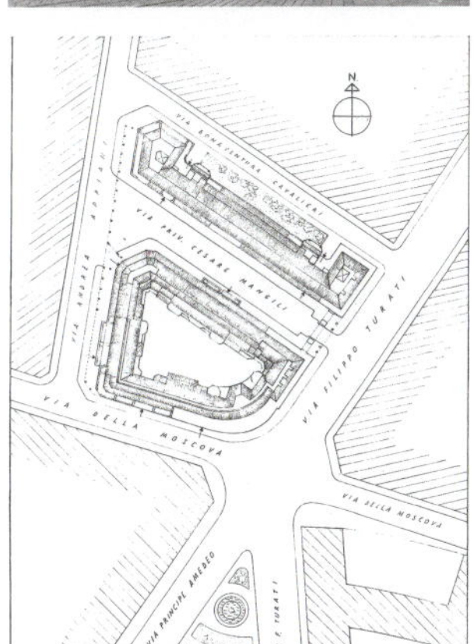

Giovanni Muzio, Ca'Brutta, Milan, 1919–22
Quartiere Moscova – Milan 1922
Planimetria 1:500

© Archivio Muzio

MIDDLE AGES

Marco Derendinger
14 SS

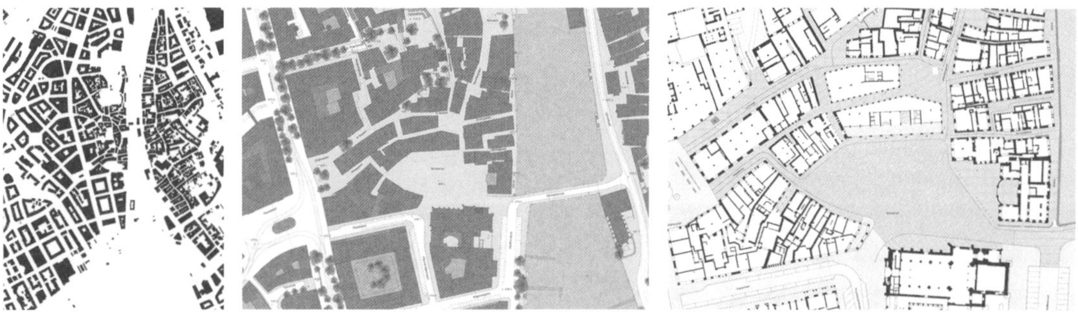

Silvio Rutishauser
15 SS

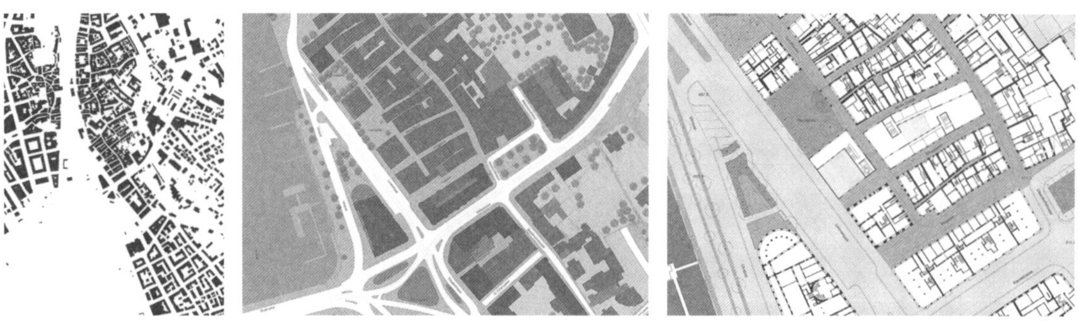

Noël Frozza
15 SS

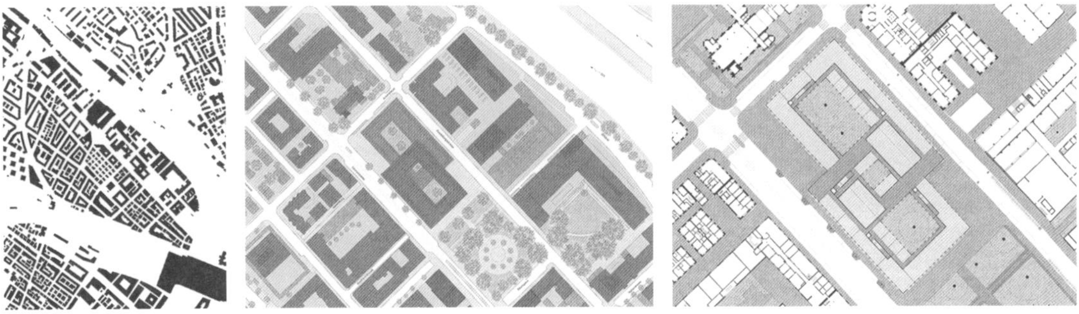

Luca Rösch
14 ss

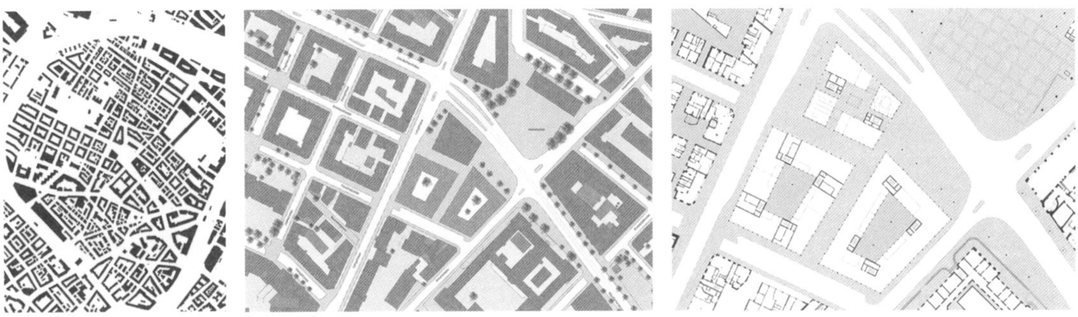

Daniela Gonzalez
15 ss

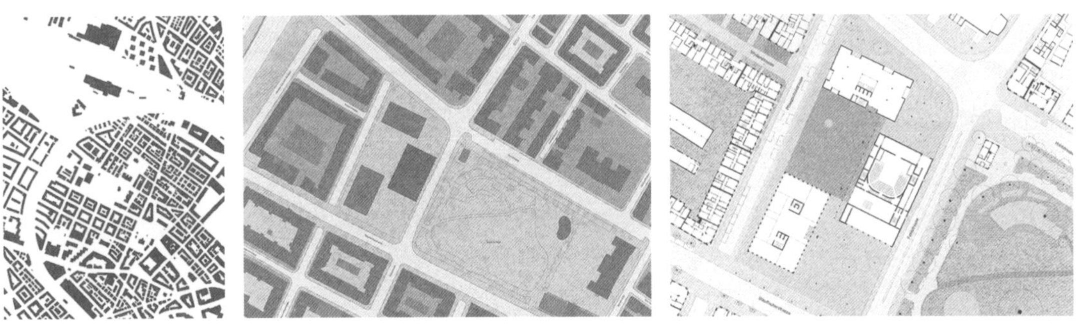

Timothy Allen
16 ss

MODERNISM

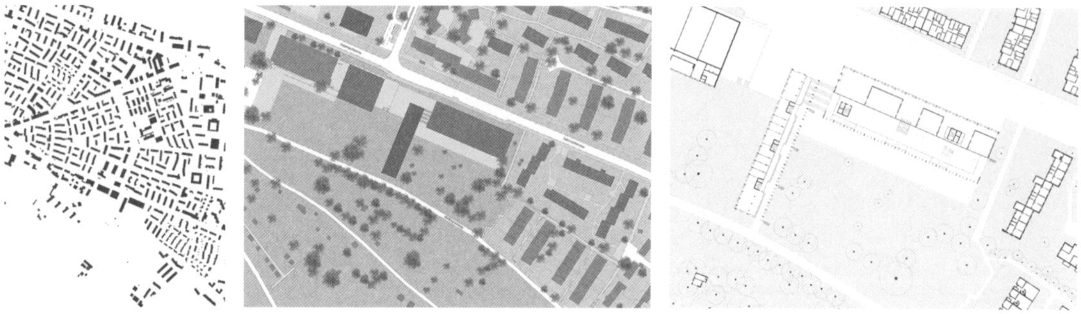

Eva Müller
14 SS

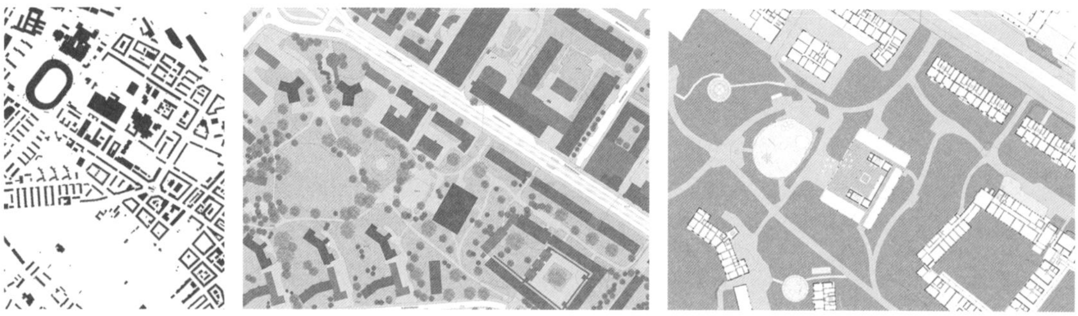

Jan Helmchen
15 SS

Christian Szalay
16 SS

MIDDLE AGES

Françoise Vannotti
09 SS

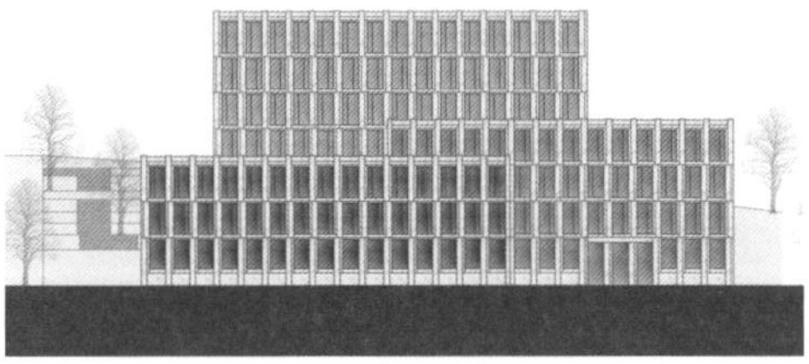

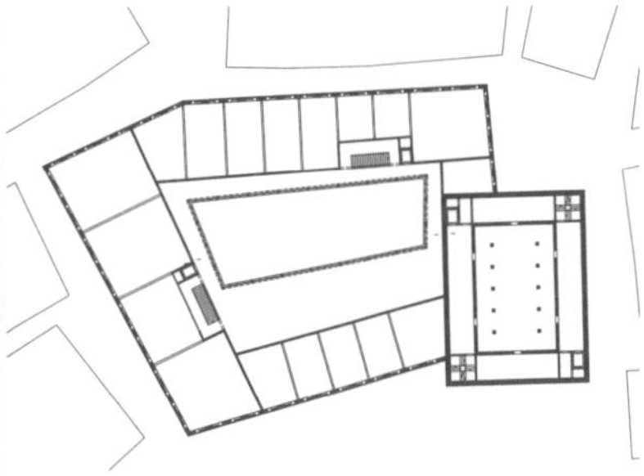

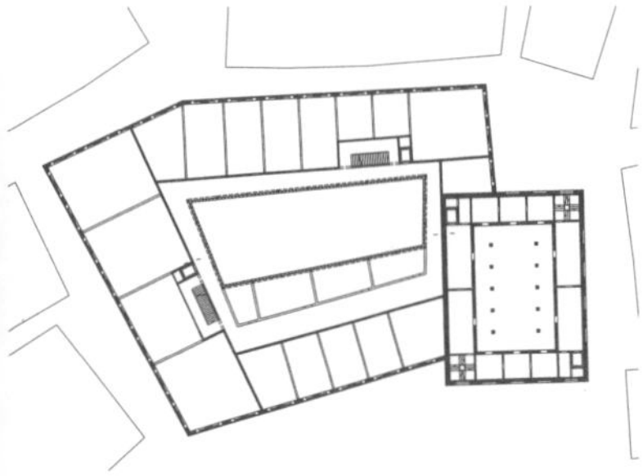

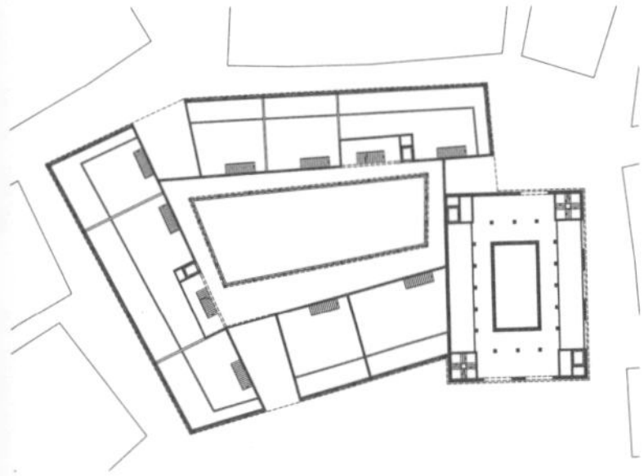

Vanessa Feri
17 SS

MIDDLE AGES

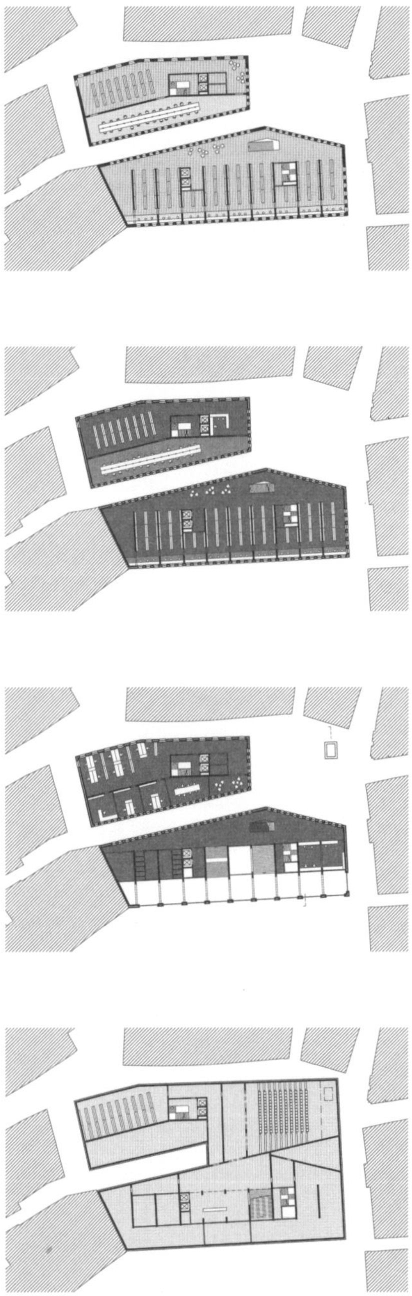

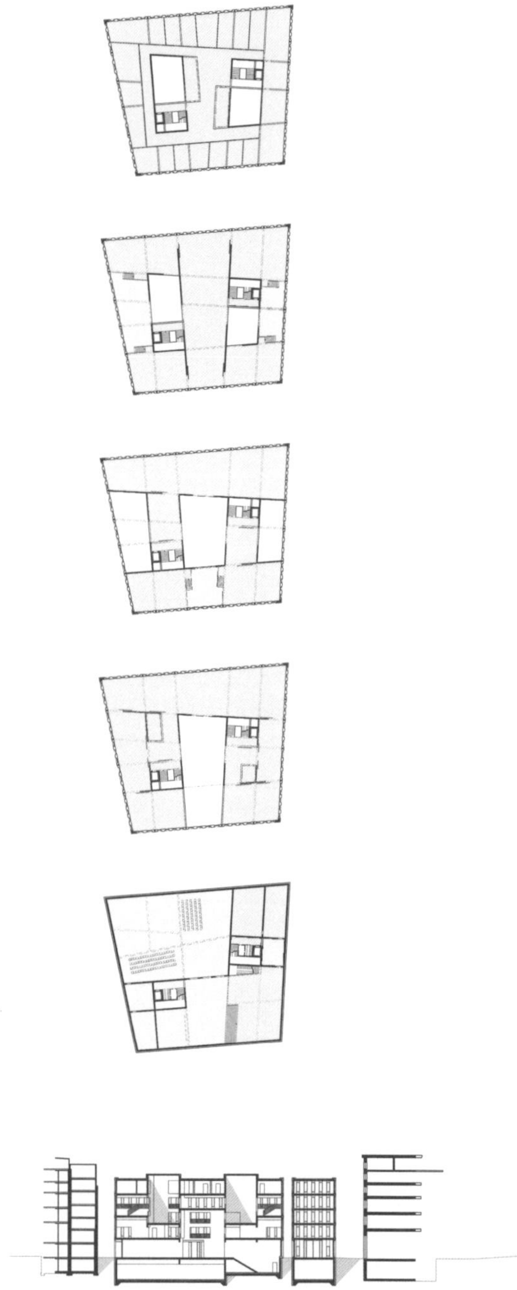

Silvio Rutishauser
15 SS

Deborah Truttmann
15 SS

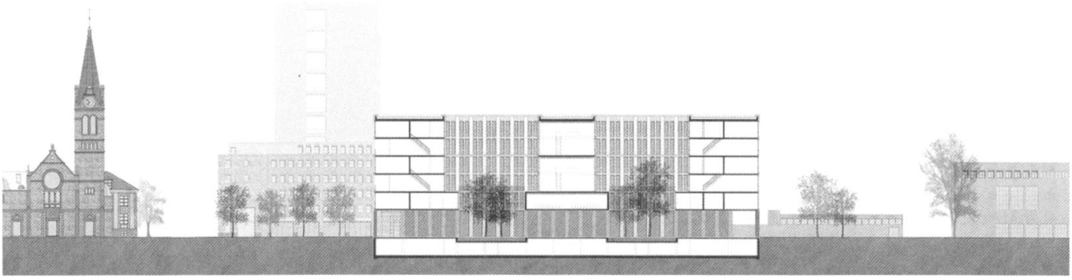

Nadine Weger
14 ss

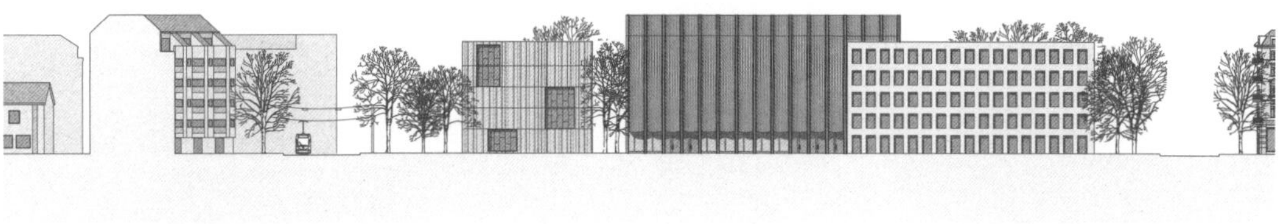

Timothy Allen
16 ss

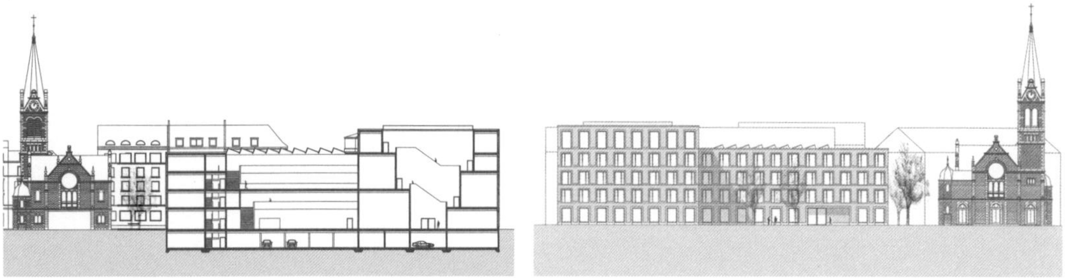

Matthias Winter
09 ss

FOUNDATION ERA

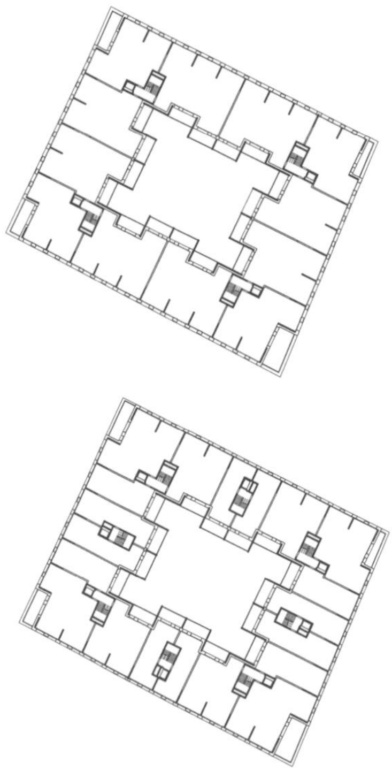

Leonie Lieberherr
11 SS

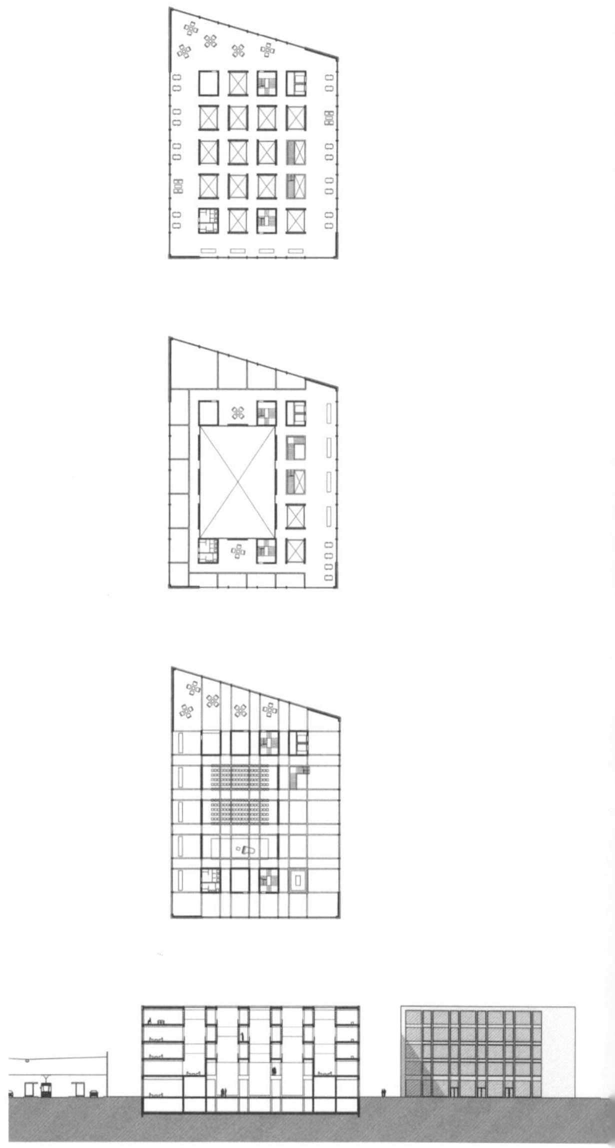

Patrick Perren
15 SS

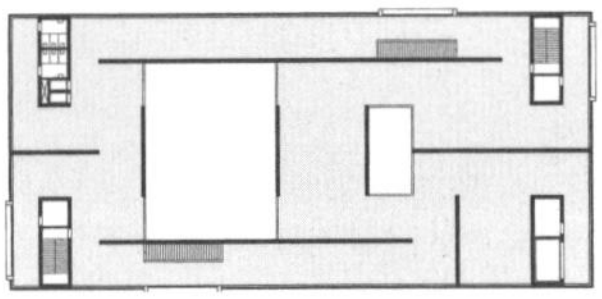

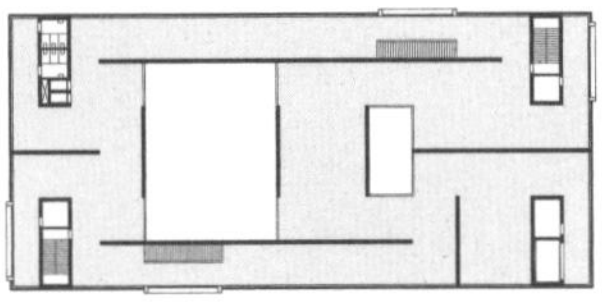

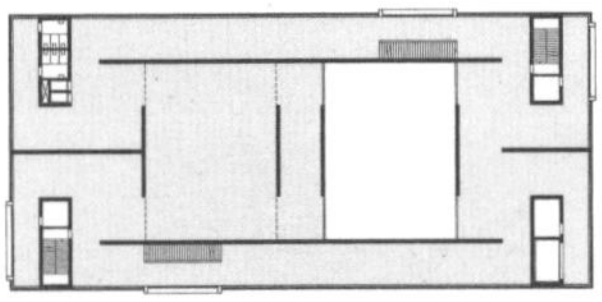

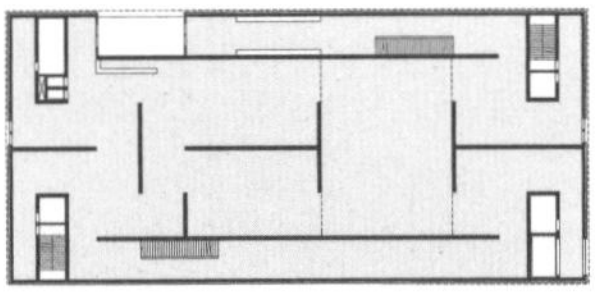

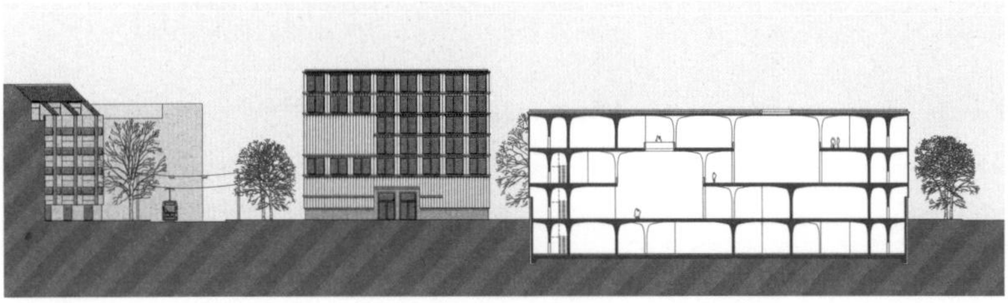

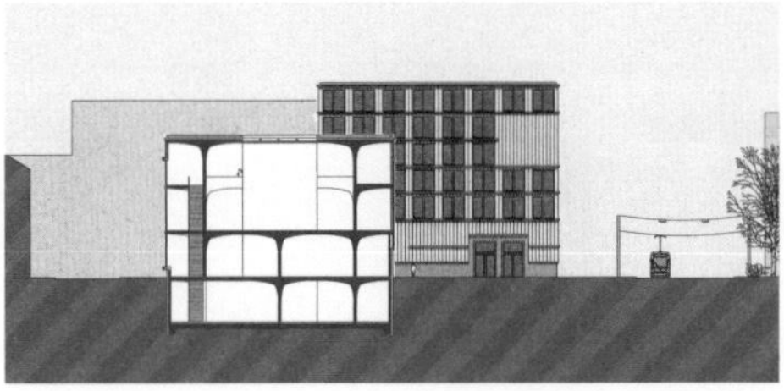

Julian Meier
16 ss

MODERNISM

Alcide Bähler
15 SS

Lea Gfeller
12 AS

Tobias Lutz
15 SS

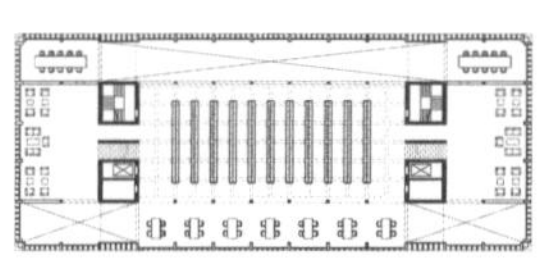

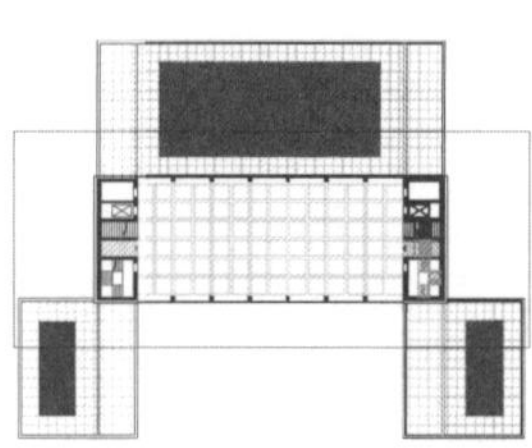

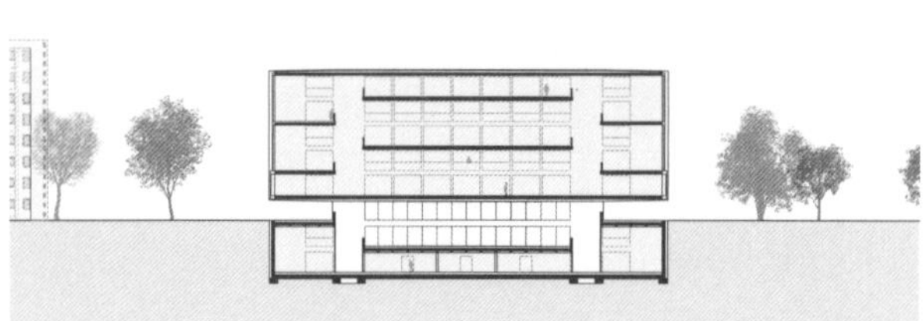

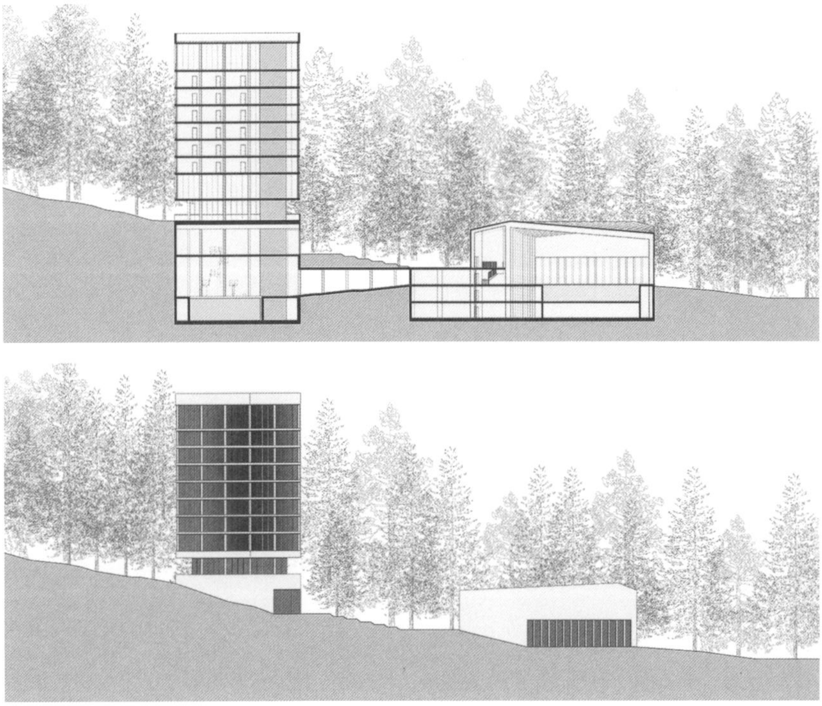

Katrin Röthlin
16 ss

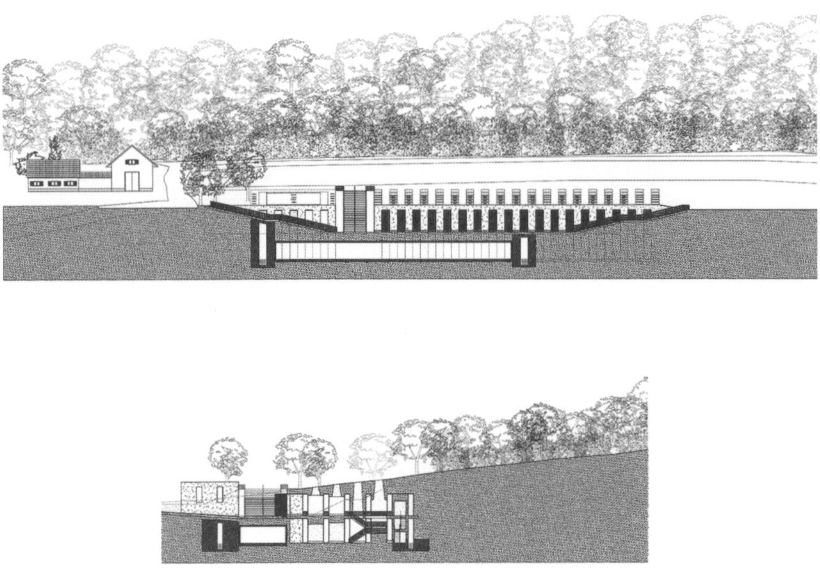

Cyrill Hirtz
16 ss

MODERNISM

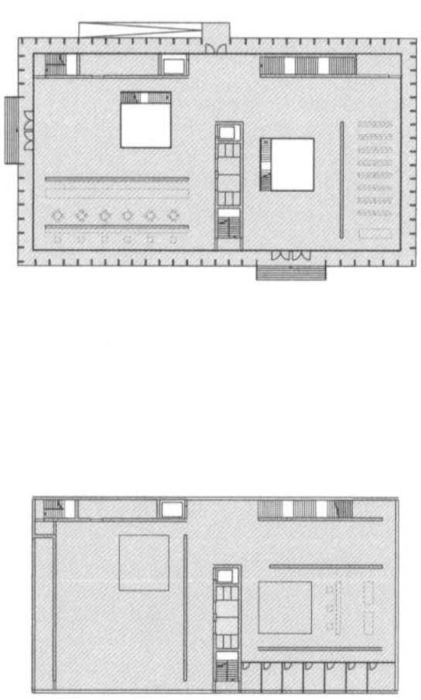

Viviane Zibung
15 ss

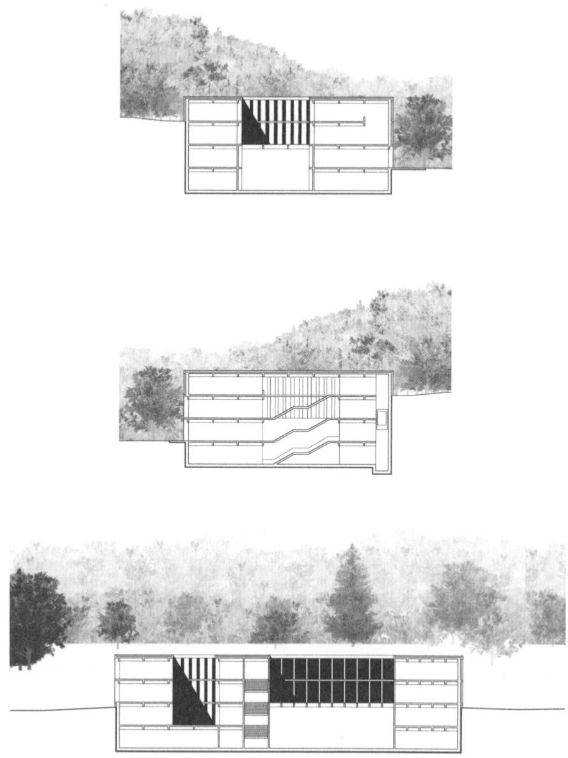

Christian Szalay
16 ss

MIDDLE AGES

Silvio Rutishauser
15 SS

MIDDLE AGES

Sara Finzi-Longo
16 SS

Erich Schäli
17 SS

Christoph Zingg
12 SS

Viviane Zibung
15 SS

FOUNDATION ERA

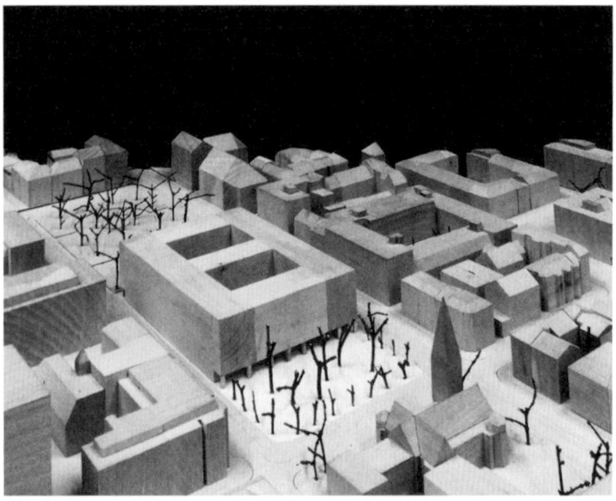

Nadine Weger
14 SS

Julian Meier
16 SS

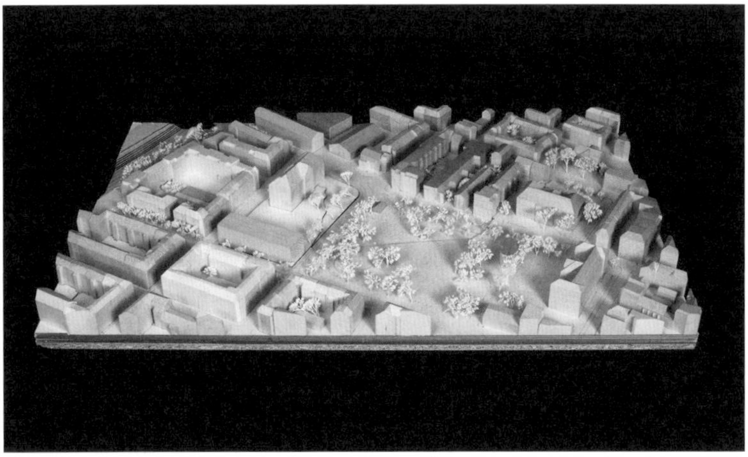

Nirvan Karim
15 AS

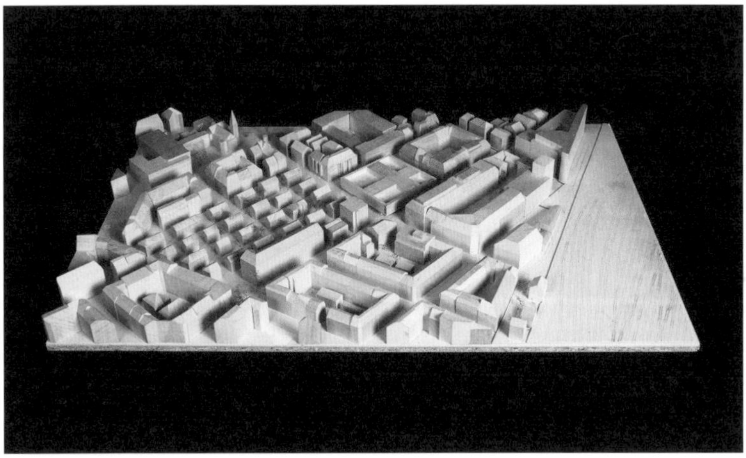

Lucia Bernini
17 SS

MODERNISM

Lisa Neuenschwander
17 SS

Timmy Huang
17 SS

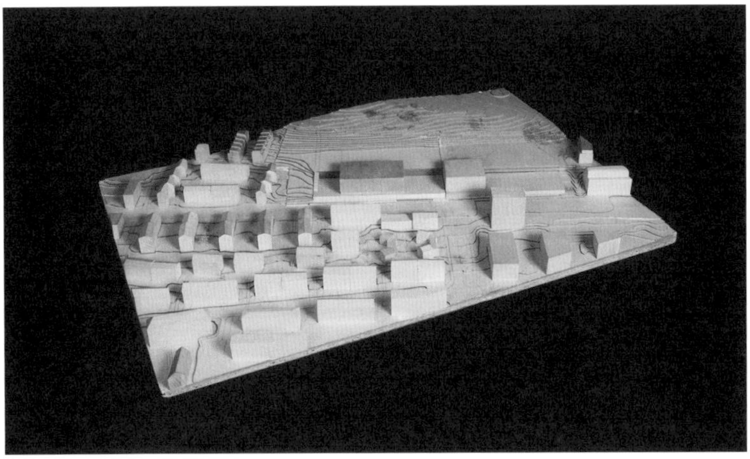

Fortunat Cavigelli
17 ss

Daniel Zieliński
16 ss

MODERNISM

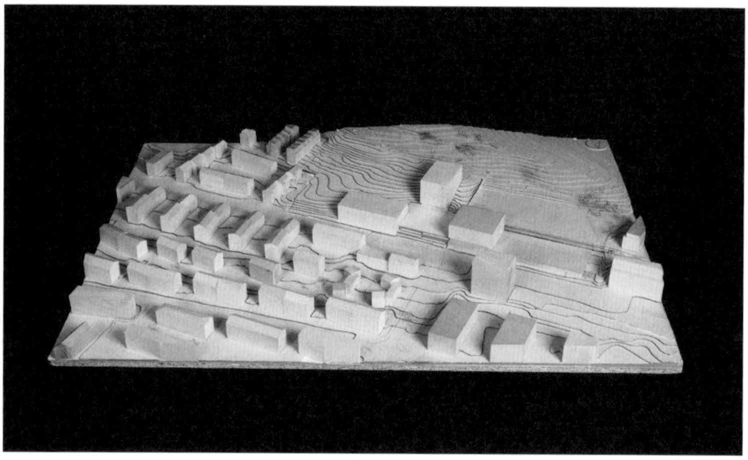

Nina Rohrer
17 SS

Christian Szalay
16 SS

MIDDLE AGES

Nadia Raymann
15 ss

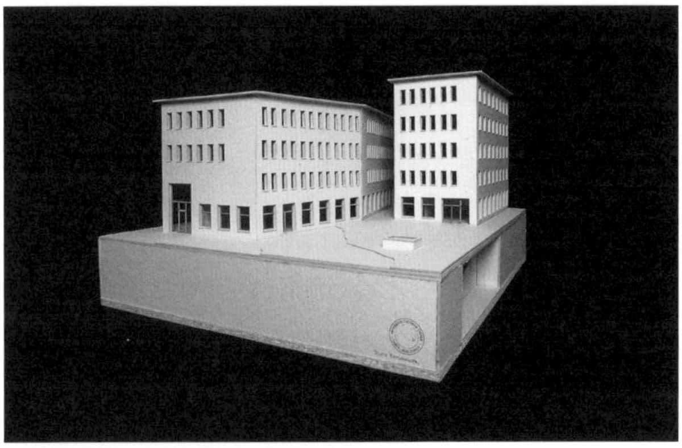

Silvio Rutishauser
15 ss

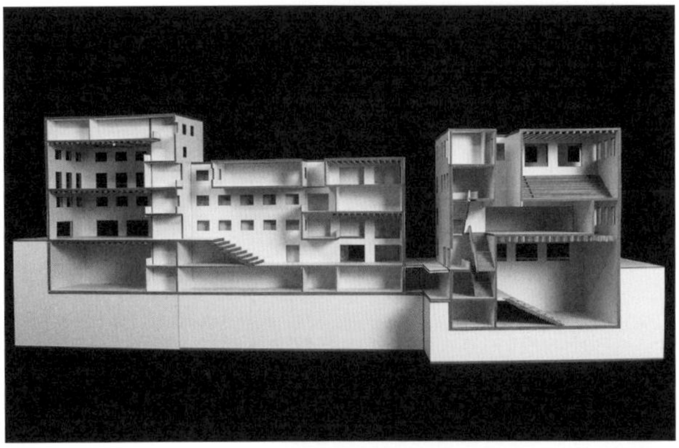

Noël Frozza
16 ss

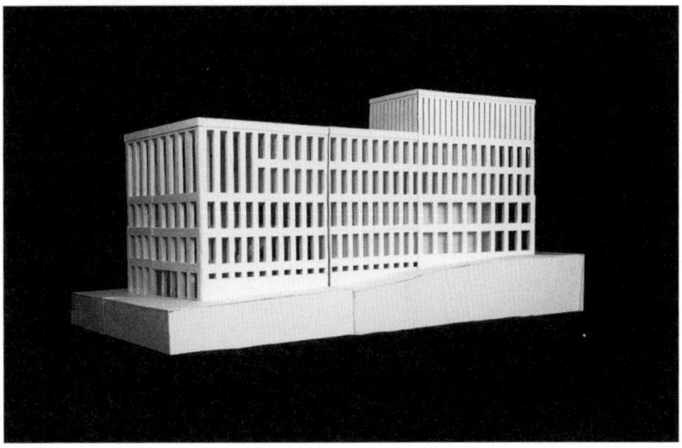

Sara Finzi-Longo
16 ss

FOUNDATION ERA

Nadine Weger
14 SS

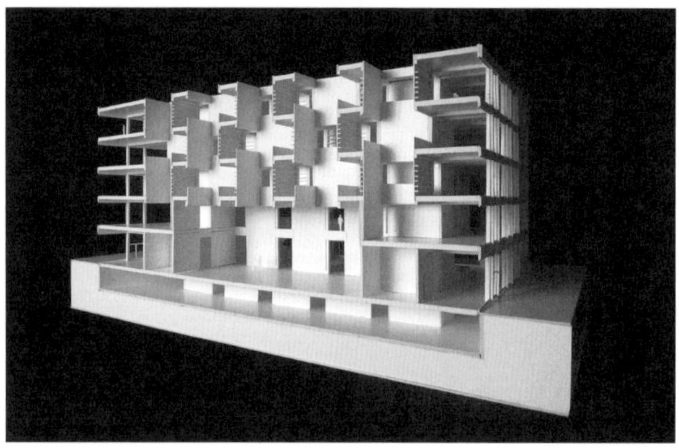

Patrick Perren
15 SS

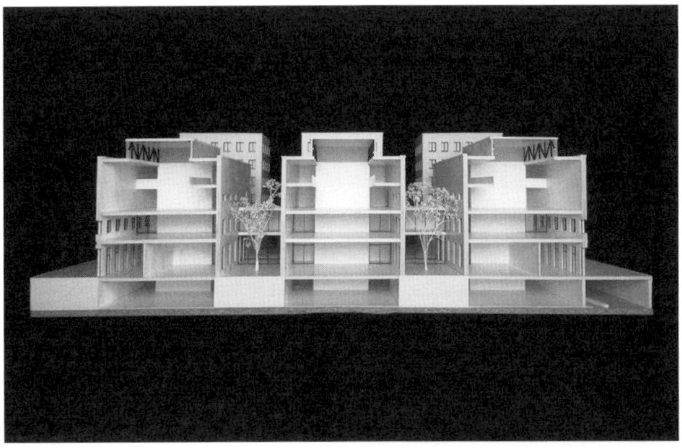

Yueqiu Wang
13 SS

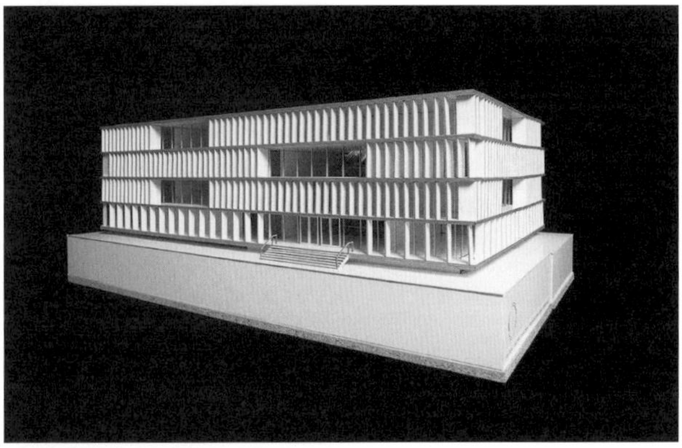

Viviane Zibung
15 SS

Maximilien Durel
15 AS

Grégoire Bridel
16 AS

MIDDLE AGES

Sophie Ballweg
Philipp Bleuel
17 SS

Isabel von Bechtolsheim
Rafael Zulauf
13 SS

Lucio Crignola
Maximillian Fritz
14 SS

Jan Honegger
Ekaterine Scholz
17 SS

Marius Mildner
Maximilian Rietschel
17 SS

FOUNDATION ERA

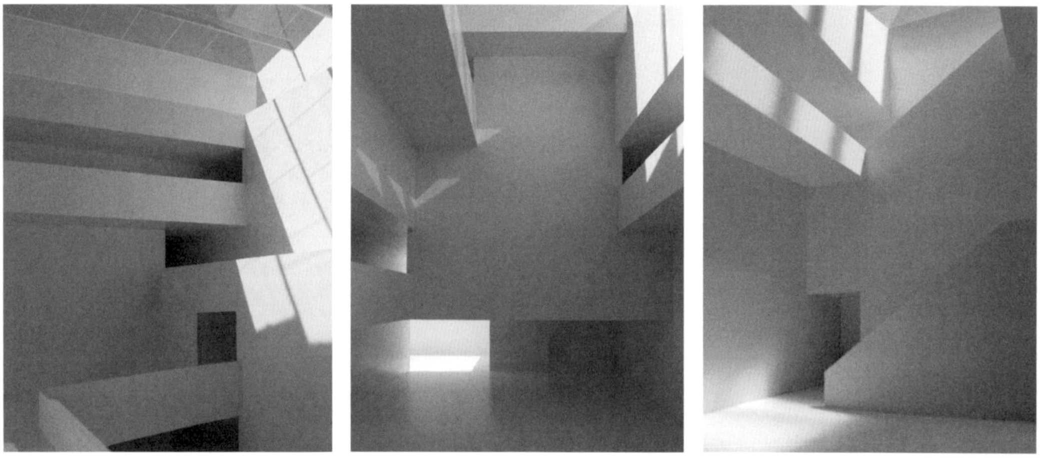

Matthias Winter
09 SS

Fatma Graca
Valentina Grazioli
14 SS

Lisa Lo
Raphael Stähelin
11 SS

Thomas Meyer
09 SS

FOUNDATION ERA

Fabian Reiner
15 SS

Artai Sanchez Keller
16 ss

MODERNISM

Micha Weber
08 ss

Timothy Allen
Okan Tan
16 ss

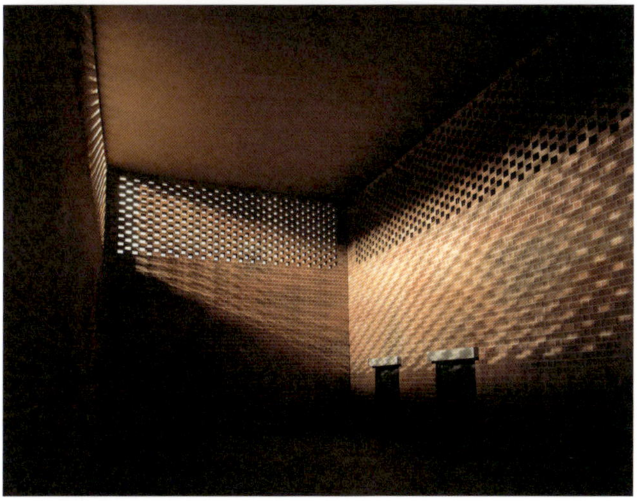

Jana Bohnenblust
Ming Fung Ki
17 SS

MODERNISM

Cyrill Hirtz
16 ss

Students at work

Final evaluation
Autumn Semeste

Learning Behavior in an Architectural Teaching Studio: What to teach and how to Learn?

Jia Beisi

An architectural teaching studio is a basic learning environment in architectural schools. The studio aims to effectively transform knowledge through interaction between teachers and students. The effectiveness of studio teaching is based on program design, which not only pertains to the content, but also to the management of interaction. This study addresses a general problem in architectural education and introduces David A. Kolb's experiential learning theory. This theory consists of two dimensions of process, namely, prehension and transformation. According to N. John Habraken, ordinary architectural prototypes in prehension are more important than exceptional architectural examples. Transformation is a frequent and consistent process of reflection in action and/or Donald Schön's theory of learning-by-doing. According to Kolb's theory, students can be divided into four different learning style categories. Architecture tends to favor the type of learning dubbed "the accommodator", because the discipline actively employs concepts of learning-by-doing. The team chaired by Prof. Eberle will explore the teaching program and its organization.

1 *Studio Environment and Debate*

An architectural teaching studio (or simply "studio")[1] is the most important component of the architectural school learning environment. The studio is the center of teaching and learning and distinguishes an architectural school from other professional schools. The studio is a complex social environment where ideas, skills, and architectural thinking are presented, evaluated, and transmitted through interaction between

[1] In architectural schools, the studio is a place where students work on design projects and are evaluated by teachers and tutors. The studio was called a drawing room at the École des Beaux-Arts of 19th-century France. In Bauhaus, in the early 20th century, it was called a workshop, while post-World War II American architectural schools named it a laboratory. The definition of a studio in this study was adopted from the writings of Donald Schön (1985).

students and studio teachers. Simulations of real cities and buildings are designed, improved, and transformed in the studio. The role of the design studio in student learning can be summarized in three aspects:

(a) to learn and practice architectural visualization and representation skills
(b) to learn and practice architectural languages
(c) to learn architectural thinking.

Regardless of the definitions of "language" and "architectural thinking", the studio is a unique learning environment with an inherent tradition and is considered an important form of education. According to Schön,[2] the studio is a setting in which students can acquire competence. The studio is where the learning-by-doing traditions of project-based education were developed.

The studio, which is intended to be a simulation of the reality of the built environment as well as a socially interactive and creative environment, has two interrelated and fundamental problems. First, it may not necessarily be a successful and accurate simulation of reality. Some architectural schools are unaware of the common and shared values of the ordinary environment, the issues of time and transformation, and distributions of responsibility. The second challenge is the effectiveness of knowledge transfer from teachers to students. In the studios of some architectural schools, design ideas remain abstract and teachers fail to represent these ideas in spatial and technical design and to train skills. There are two interrelated problems:

(1) There is a gap between reality and the imitations of reality in the studio.
(2) There is a gap between what is taught by tutors and what is learned by students.

[2] Donald A. Schön: *The Design Studio*, RIBA Publications Limited, England, 1985, pp. 5–6.

The content and organization of the studio has been questioned before. This study focuses on the gaps in organization. The issues of studio effectiveness are global and in the context of general education. World market changes since the 1960s have challenged professional education. The focus on education has shifted from "teachers teaching in lectures and in the studio", to "students (...) self-learning from multifold resources, and think[ing] critically about important bodies of knowledge".[3] A common understanding among educationalists is that teaching methods and assessments should be geared towards producing learners who possess high-level thinking skills. Problem-based learning (PBL) has gradually been adopted in both professional and non-professional education as an effective tool for enhancing educational improvement. This approach emphasizes the development of learning skills, or "how to learn" instead of knowledge content or "what to learn".[4] PBL has effected four significant changes in education. First, PBL shifts the educational focus from teaching to learning, which increases student motivation. Second, educational objectives shift from professional training to life-long learning and holistic education. Third, PBL shifts teaching from generic standardized approaches "for the masses" to an approach that deliberately encourages the development of students' individuality, thereby encouraging genuine and original creation rather than imitation. Fourth, PBL shifts learning methods from subject-based teaching to the integrated application of knowledge.[5]

The PBL education model does not directly address the issues of architectural school studios but instead calls for a deeper understanding of the specific character of the architectural studio and identifies avenues for improvement.

2 *Kolb's Experiential Learning Model*

American educator and philosopher John Dewey directly influenced a number of key theoretical figures in education in the 20th century. Dewey described learning as a dialectic process that integrates experiences, concepts, observations, and

[3] Jia Beisi: "Problem-based Learning in Crossing University Joint Studio of Architecture", *Time+Architecture* (in Chinese) 13, 2001, pp. 55–56.

[4] Jia Beisi: "Evaluation of an Architectural Studio with Problem-based Learning (PBL) Concept", Proceedings of the Chinese Conference on Architectural Education, 23–25 October 2002, Wuhan, organized by the National Supervision Commission for Education in Architecture and the Central China University of Science and Technology, 2002, pp. 96–102.

[5] Ibid, p. 166.

action. “The crucial educational problem is that of procuring the postponement of immediate action upon desire until observation and judgment have intervened”.[6]

Kolb combined the works of Dewey, Kurt Lewin, and Jean Piaget to identify the common themes that characterize experiential learning processes. He also adapted Carl Jung’s theory that people can be characterized by psychological types, but rejected the static interpretations of their descriptions of individuals. He assumed a contextualist view towards individual differences, suggesting: “Stable and enduring patterns of human individuality arise from consistent patterns of transaction between the individual and his or her environment. The way we process the possibilities of each new emerging event determines the range of choices and decisions we see. The choices and decisions we make, to some extent, determine the events we live through, and these events influence our future choices. Thus, people create themselves through their choice of the actual occasions they live through. In Tyler’s words, to some degree we write our own ‘programs.’ Human individuality results from the pattern or ‘program’ created by our choices and their consequences”.[7] He and his colleagues developed the experiential learning model (Figure 1), which illustrates the following aspects of the learning process:

(1) the two basic structural dimensions of the learning process,
(2) the four different learning styles, and
(3) the spiral progression towards high-level knowledge.

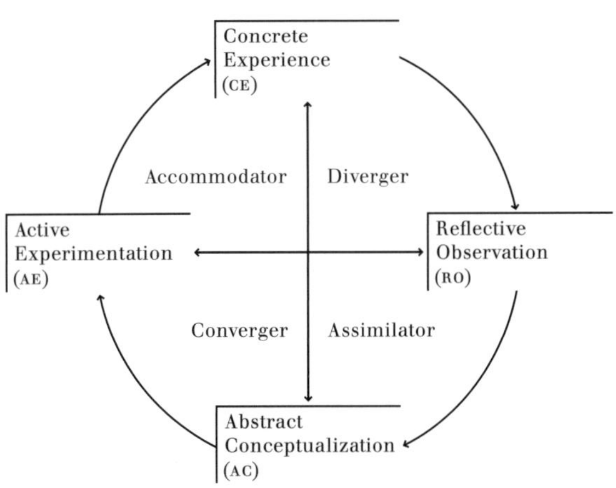

Figure 1. Kolb’s experiential learning model

[6] Dewey, cited in: David A. Kolb: *Experience as the Source of Learning and Development*, Prentice-Hall, Inc., New Jersey, 1984, p. 22.

[7] David A. Kolb: *Experience as the Source of Learning and Development*, Prentice-Hall, Inc., New Jersey, 1984, p. 64.

(1) *The dimensions of the learning process*

Learning is the process wherein knowledge is created through the transformation of experience in "a four-stage cycle involving four adaptive learning modes, namely, concrete experience, reflective observation, abstract conceptualization and active experimentation".[8] In this model, concrete experience/abstract conceptualization and active experimentation/reflective observation are two distinct dimensions. The first is the *prehension dimension* (vertical axis in the model) and includes two dialectically opposed modes of grasping experience, namely, through direct apprehension of immediate concrete experience and through indirect comprehension of abstract representations of experience. Both dimensions are sources of knowledge. One dimension deals with the actual world, which is tangible and can be felt through immediate experience in a process called apprehension. The other dimension refers to abstract statements, theories, concepts, and symbolic representations of the real world, which can be understood through comprehension. The second dimension in Kolb's model is the *transformation dimension* (horizontal axis in the model), which includes two dialectically opposed modes of transforming experience, namely, via intentional reflection and extensional action. Learning is the process wherein proposed knowledge is created through the transformation of experience, either through direct apprehension of immediate experience or abstract representation of experience.

[8] Ibid., p. 40.

(2) *The four learning styles*

Kolb further classified four basic types of learning activity based on the different knowledge sources and transformations. Learning and transforming concrete experience through reflection is called *divergence*. Learning by conceptualization through reflection and observation is called *assimilation*. *Convergence* pertains to learning through experimentation on concepts. *Accommodation* occurs when concrete experience is obtained from experimentation results. Some students show strong skills in one or two of the four learning activities, whereas they demonstrate relatively weak abilities in other activities. A student's learning style is described using his or her strongest activity. The following is a description of the characteristics of the four basic learning styles based on research and clinical observations of LSI score patterns.[9]

[9] Ibid., pp. 77–78, 93.

- *Divergent learning* pertains to one's imaginative ability and awareness of meaning and values. Some students may have a strong ability to view concrete situations from different perspectives and organize relationships into a meaningful *gestalt*. This orientation emphasizes adaptation through observation rather than action. Students perform well in situations that call for the generation of alternative ideas and implications, as in "brainstorming" sessions. Students who are oriented towards divergence are interested in people. They tend to be imaginative and emotion-oriented, sensitive to people's feelings and values, listen with an open mind, gather information, and envision the implications of ambiguous situations.

- The greatest strength of *assimilation learning* is centered on inductive reasoning and ability to create theoretical models and assimilate disparate observations into an integrated explanation. This orientation is less focused on people than on ideas and abstract concepts. Ideas are not strongly judged by their practical value. Theories under this orientation should be logically sound and precise. Assimilation is related to thinking competencies, namely, organizing information, building conceptual models, testing theories and ideas, designing experiments, and analyzing quantitative data.

- Students with a *convergent learning* style have strong problem-solving, decision-making, and practical application skills. They excel in situations that involve conventional intelligence tests, where a question or problem has a single correct answer or solution. Knowledge is organized using hypothetical–deductive reasoning and focuses on a specific problem. Students with convergent learning are skilled in controlling their emotional expression. They prefer dealing with technical tasks and problems rather than with social and interpersonal issues. A convergent learning style is associated with decision skills, such as creating new ways of thinking and doing, experimenting with new ideas, choosing the best solution to a problem, setting goals, and making decisions.

- *Accommodative learning* focuses on ways of doing things, carrying out plans and tasks, and getting involved in new experiences. Students with this approach are interested in seeking opportunities, taking risks, and action. Students can adapt to immediate changes in circumstance and are most likely to discard plans and theories. People with an accommodative orientation tend to solve problems intuitively through trial and error and by relying heavily on other people for information rather than on their own analytic ability. They commit themselves to objectives, influence and lead others, engage in personal involvement, and deal with people.

(3) *The spiral progression towards knowledge*

Learning is an ongoing process towards attaining a high level of knowledge. The best learner achieves balanced strengths in all four learning styles.

Prehension and transformation should be implemented to enable students to learn design in the studio. This approach should be adopted because design involves similar sequences of learning activities. Stephen Kirk analyzed Alva Aalto's design process and suggested the following decision-making process when creating a model:

First, a design problem is composed of many—as well as conflicting—points of view, objectives, functional requirements, and individuals. Second, a period of absorbing this diffuse and immense amount of data takes place and the designer must reach a point of appreciation—not necessarily understanding—of the entire problem. Next, the designer reaches deep within a creative reservoir to generate a large number of ideas and potential solutions. Finally, some form of synthesis or process of discrimination occurs that allows these ideas to be brought into balance to address the original problem statement.[10]

[10] Stephen J Kirk und Kent F. Spreckelmeyer: *Creative Design Decisions: A Systematic Approach to Problem Solving in Architecture,* Van Nostrand Reinhold Company, New York, 1988, p. 9.

This process can result in design alternatives and requires an evaluation procedure. Evaluation results are then integrated into another round of decision-making. The decision-making model suggested by Kirk consists of five steps:

(1) information and analysis
(2) speculation (alternative)
(3) evaluation
(4) synthesis
(5) recommendation.

Recommendation must be checked against the initial contextual constraints. A critical feature of this process is its cyclical and expanding character. As Kirk writes: "Not only is the methodology used at each point in the facility cycle, but it is also a repetitive sequence of decision-making events".[11] This pattern of spiral movement is similar to Kolb's learning process.

[11] Ibid., p. 41.

In the studio, students are continuously polishing their skills in design methodology. The repetitive process involves an expanding cycle of analysis, speculation, evaluation, synthesis, and recommendation. In addition to its simulative nature, this process also involves teacher participation.

Kolb's theory is significant, given that it clearly describes how professional education can become a constraint to personal creativity. This theory also suggests ways to resolve the problem. Professional training is one of the strongest forces that shapes a student's learning style: "Each task we face requires a corresponding set of skills for effective performance. The effective matching of task demands and personal skills results in an adaptive competence".[12] According to Kolb, professional education encounters serious problems in a rapidly changing society: "The fixed person for the fixed duties, who in older societies was such a godsend, in the future will be a public danger".[13] To resolve this problem, Kolb suggests that three classes of learning objectives be considered in curriculum design. These classes include content objectives, learning style objectives, and growth and creativity objectives. Only content objectives—or "what to teach"—are considered explicitly. To improve the effectiveness of professional teaching, a learning style should be appropriate to the given profession. In addition to specialized developmental training, teachers should formulate objectives for the growth and creativity of their students. Students should experience different learning styles, as well as the tension and conflict involved in these styles, because it is only "from the resolution of these tensions that creativity springs".[14]

[12] Ibid., p. 93.

[13] Whitehead 1926, cited in: ibid., p. 183.

[14] Ibid., p. 202.

3 *Prehension Dimension Issues in the Architectural Studio*

According to Kolb, a learning process should include the vertical dimension of prehension (concrete experience vs. abstract conception) and the horizontal dimension of transformation (reflection vs. experimentation). Concrete experience is most effectively learned through personal experience, whereas abstraction of knowledge can be taught in lectures. Reality is not explored in the studio. Similarly, only the principles of reality are taught in lecture rooms.

John Habraken suggests the need to build up knowledge of the everyday environment in three aspects:

(1) how values are shared in environmental design
(2) how change and permanence sustain the environment
(3) how the distribution of design responsibilities can make it bloom.[15]

[15] John Habraken: "Questions That Will Not Go Away: Some Remarks on Long-term Trends in Architecture and Their Impact on Architectural Education", *Shaping the European Higher Architectural Education Area – Transactions in Architectural Education No. 18*, Art if Text S.A., Greece, 2003, p. 39.

Knowledge pertains to the present and the past and should be organized in such a way that its implications are possible in the future. Habraken also suggests learning skills and methods of cooperation. Skills include creating variations on an accepted typology, using agreed-upon patterns, and setting up a system of parts and relations to create different forms in the same style. The knowledge and skills proposed by Habraken are subjects of learning and not located in the horizontal dimension or the dimension of knowledge transformation. This type of knowledge belongs to the vertical dimension and abstraction concept because knowledge and skills are structured.

According to Habraken, studios are no longer capable of imitating reality and the shared built environment when teaching, the studios separate designers from reality. Common reality is represented by three essential aspects:

(1) Sharing of values: A good environment has qualities shared by all buildings in the same locality. In contrast, only special buildings are studied in a studio.
(2) Change and transformation: Good architecture should be able to adapt to changes over time. A permanent building must be finely grained and adaptable.
(3) Distribution of design responsibility: To sustain everyday environments, design must allow different parties to take care of things on different levels in the environmental hierarchy, as complex project design tasks must be distributed among members of design teams. The architect is not only the designer

of creative entities, but also a coordinator for an information dependent process of decision-making in collaboration with other team members. "The very idea of 'architecture' as a self-contained and single-centered act does not apply to work in everyday environment".[16]

[16] Ibid., p. 37.

Habraken addresses the subject of teaching in the studio. Jeremy Till identified a few famous architectural schools, such as Walter Gropius in 1920s Bauhaus, Louis Kahn in the 1950s, Penn Boyarksy in the 1970s, and the Architectural Association, Peter Cook, and the Bartlett School of Architecture in the 1990s. He also indicated differences in their appearances and essential similarities in their operation. Students in these schools dutifully and often painfully copied the actions and forms of the studio master. Thus, architectural education in these schools effectively removed students from reality, thereby "instigating a denial of the ordinary in the pursuit of the extraordinary",[17] a finding similar to that of Habraken.

[17] Jeremy Till: *Lost Judgment,* EAA Prize 2003–2005, *http://www.openhouse-int.com/competition.html*, 2005.

4 *Transformation Dimension Issues in the Architectural Studio*

According to a comprehensive survey conducted by Kolb and his colleagues, the preferred learning style in architecture is accommodative learning. A good architectural student or architect is an accommodator (Fig. 2).

To explore studio teaching and learning, we investigated the transformation of knowledge, or the horizontal dimension. The studio is a place for transforming knowledge. Concrete experience and abstractions can be learned in the studio through the actions of reflection, observation, and experimentation. According to Schön, a studio is filled with learning-by-doing or reflection-in-action: "Sometimes our spontaneous knowing-in-action yields unexpected outcomes and we react to the surprise by a kind of thinking what we are doing while we are doing it, a process I call reflection-in-action".[18]

Donald Schön was a professor and researcher at MIT and a consultant for several governmental agencies and private industries. Given his research findings on architectural studios, he was regarded as a key figure who made significant contributions to architectural education. He believed that a studio is a supplementary method for teaching students to deal with situations of uncertainty, complexity, and uniqueness in actual practice.[19]

He believed that studio teaching is essential to architecture as well as other fields of professional education.

- "The gap between a description of designing and the knowing-in-action that corresponds to it must be filled by reflection-in-action."
- "Designing depends on recognition of design qualities, which must be learned by doing."
- "Because designing is a creative process in which a designer comes to see and do things in new ways, no prior description of it can take the place of learning by doing".[20]

[18] Donald A. Schön: *The Design Studio*, RIBA Publications Limited, England, 1985, p. 23.

[19] Ibid., p. 20.

[20] Ibid., p. 190.

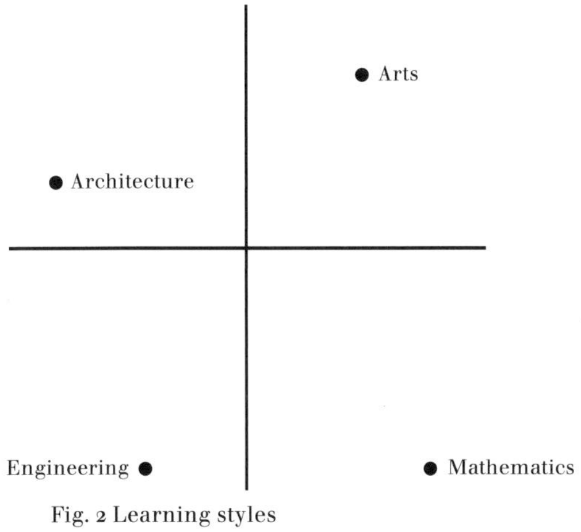

Fig. 2 Learning styles related to typical disciplines; abstraction of Kolb's survey findings.

Studio teaching involves sequences and repetitive actions, namely, experiments and reflections on the result of experiments. Experiments in the studio mean "liking and unliking the experience of laboratory science." Studio projects occur in particular situations and under certain demands, which is similar to in the real world. However, a studio project is confined and continuously evaluated and developed at a pace much faster than in the actual world. Studio experiments differ from laboratory experiments because many potential answers to a design question can be explored almost at the same time using sketches. According to Schön, a studio consists of actions that function in three ways:

(1) to test new understandings ("What is going on here?")
(2) to explore new phenomena ("What looks odd here?")
(3) to affirm or negate moves in an attempt to improve things ("How can we get this under control?") [21]

[21] Ibid., pp. 25–26.

Students in the studio learn to "combine reflection and action, on-the-spot, often under stress – to examine understandings and appreciations. (…) Telling, demonstrating, questioning, translating into performance, reflective imitation, criticism, all may be 'chained' in various combinations, in such a way that the later events of doing, telling, translating and reflecting build on earlier ones."[22] Schön confirmed that a studio consists of one of the two dimensions of the learning model, namely, transformation of knowledge through reflection and experiment.

[22] Ibid., p. 76.

As Schön observed, an experiment is processed by the sketches, drawings, and models made by students and tutors, whereas reflection is mainly represented in verbal conversation. Transformation of knowledge can occur in the studio only when both demonstration and conversation are conducted smoothly and effectively. "For the student, every attempt at translating instruction into action is an experiment that tests his construction of the instructor's meaning. (…) For the studio teacher, every utterance is the output of an attempt to read the test of the student's performance for its content of understanding and problems. What he chooses to say to the student tests his reading."[23] Therefore, reflection-in-action is interactive. [23]Ibid., p. 69.

According to Schön, a studio is confined to the horizontal dimension. Students need to imitate the tutor's demonstration. Schön illustrated the following typical reflective imitation process:

(1) a student perceives the actions of the tutor
(2) a student imitates the tutor
(3) a student reflects on his or her performance
(4) a student internalizes his or her performance and makes it his or her own.[24] [24]Ibid., p. 74.

Schön believed that, in the beginning, students should give up their own conceptions and methods about design in order to learn design: "A good student is capable of willing suspension of disbelief."[25] A tutor should bring his or her own experience and conceptualization of design to fill the gap. This process means that the vertical dimension is mostly represented by the conceptions and experience of the tutor. [25]Ibid., p. 58.

Schön recognized the ignorance of students about their experiences and beliefs in learning-by-reflective imitation, something he believed to be inevitable:

> *Although, in any particular interaction between student and studio master, the various types of ambiguity, vagueness or obscurity may not arise, the potential for them is inherent in the studio situation. The premise of the studio is that the student must begin to design before he knows what he is doing so that, in the light of this experience, the studio master's demonstrations and descriptions may begin to have meaning for him, and thereby help him to teach himself to design. (...) They must do this in spite of the potential for ambiguity, vagueness, or inexpressibility inherent in much of what they wish to communicate about.*[26] [26]Ibid., p. 62.

According to Schön, reflective imitation is the only way of learning in the studio that should be adopted by students: "Moreover, they may need to unlearn other ways of learning which interfere with this one."[27]

[27] Ibid., p. 75.

Till did not clearly demonstrate how studios should change, but he suggested that teachers should act as examiners and the students given the responsibility of finding answers. He addressed the necessity for students to develop their own structure of thinking, build a self-critical response, and form their own judgments and intentions.[28] He suggested the possibility of students developing different ways of learning in the studio, thus transforming the studio instead of simply passing the burden of prehension dimension on to the teachers. (Fig. 3)

[28] Jeremy Till: *Lost Judgment*, EAA Prize 2003–2005, *http://www.openhouse-int.com/competition.html*, 2005.

5 *Conclusion*

The problems faced by architectural education in studio teaching are also problems in general professional education. An investigation into educational theories and changes in current educational thinking provides insights into studios in architectural schools. Kolb suggested a learning process consisting of two structural dimensions, namely, *prehension* and *transformation.*

Prehension comprehends two dialectically opposed modes of grasping experience, namely, concrete experience and abstract conceptualization. According to Habraken, prehension dimension training should focus on the ordinary built environment rather than on signature or exceptional buildings. Handicapped studio teaching generates conflicts between reality and imitations of reality in the studio subjects, as well as conflicts between the teaching of tutors and the learning of students. A studio can be improved by addressing the values of prehension dimension in two ways. First, studio subjects and programs should be restructured to ensure their resemblance to reality and the built environment. Habraken defined reality as the process of sharing values in the common environment, changes

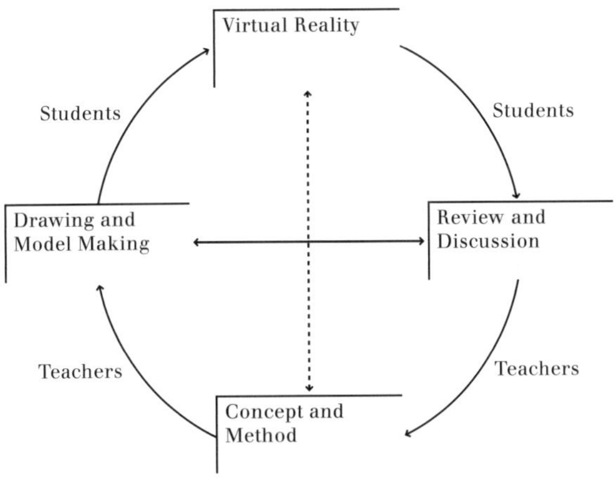

Fig. 3 Knowledge transformation in the studio

and permanence of the structure, and distribution of design responsibility. Second, the focus of the studio should shift from the teacher to the students. Direct contact with the everyday environment of students can be recognized and integrated into education. Students should develop a sensitivity to the environment on their own.

In Kolb's model, the *transformation dimension* comprehends two dialectically opposed modes of transforming experience, namely, reflective observation and active experimentation. A typical studio researched by Schön operates in the transformation dimension. The quality of the studio depends on the quality of active experimentation by the student, including the consistent provision and revision of sketches, models, and drawings that represent reality and concepts. The quality of the studio also depends on the quality of reflections and observations of the teacher on student experimentation as shown in the sketches, models, and drawings. Student experimentation is crucial to knowledge transformation because without a sketch or model, the teacher has nothing to reflect or observe and thus cannot provide feedback. The learning process of students cannot start without creating these outputs. According to Schön, a typical transformation of knowledge or learning in a studio is called reflection-in-action.

The analysis of the relationship between Kolb's learning model and Schön's theory of the learning studio explains why a good architect tends to become an accommodator, or why architecture tends to shape students into accommodators. This finding is attributed to the fact that accommodators are likely to perform experiments that facilitate reflection-in-action. A well-structured and intensive program characterized by frequent, well-prepared presentations by students and effective feedback by teachers is essential to cultivating an accommodating culture in the studio. This book demonstrates an example of these teaching programs•

Architecture and Computer Science, Computer Science and Architecture

Michele Lanza
Marcello Nasso

M.N. | This book is an attempt to systematize the teaching of architecture. Are there parallels to the methods and topics seen in the computer sciences?

M.L. | In software engineering, as in architecture, we deal with the question of how to build, maintain, and evolve large systems.

Unlike in architecture, software has no place—no up and down, no left and right. Everything is everywhere and nowhere at once. There are no distances and the place where something is done or written is not relevant. At run time, when the system is executed, all distances collapse into practically nothing.

Yet there is indeed a structure. The entire thing must be organized and given a structure. This is why we speak of *software architecture.*

M.N. | In computer science, the structure is defined by the software architecture. What does software architecture involve?

M.L. | It involves the structuring of systems: How systems are divided into subsystems and again into sub-subsystems and how these systems and subsystems communicate with each other. That is software architecture. It creates an order.

M.N. | This is what architecture does as well. A city or a building is conceived in the same way—a city by using master plans and building types, buildings by using construction systems and building components.

What differentiates software engineering from architecture besides its lack of place?

M.L. | The other difference I see is that in architecture there is always a thought process that leads to a concrete result in the end. For the engineer and the master builder who build the system, these are the plans. This means that in the end there is a model and an implementation of the model. In software engineering, this difference doesn't exist.

Nobody designs a system that is implemented by someone else. Although this is attempted, what is actually happening is the implementation of a model. The source code is what is physically and effectively written in the end. In this sense, it is a model of the system.

M.N. | What form does this model of a system have?

M.L. | Currently, it is in writing.

M.N. | Does this mean language?

M.L. | Exactly. What is presented at the end, what the programmer sees, is many lines of text, written in a specific programming language, which the machine can understand. And therein lies the intellectual complexity of programming. What programmers actually do is write structured systems in a complex manner.

What they actually see are many lines of source code, packed in files.

The problem is that millions of lines in thousands of files are needed in order to master the necessary complexity. Abstraction and the mastery thereof are the skills that, in the end, make a truly great programmer. Programming is abstraction at a very high level.

In his book *The Mythical Man-Month,* Fred Brooks says that programmers, like poets, are not far from pure thought. They build castles in the sky that are made of air, simply by allowing their imagination to prevail. He wrote this in 1975.

M.N. | That is a very personal vision of the big picture. In order to build a large system, a collective is necessary: many different actors with shared visions and the goal of together creating a large whole. Seen from this point of view, the metaphor of the romantic poet no longer seems to work.

M.L. | Two thirds—and thus the great majority—of complex software projects involving multiple actors go awry. They don't mess up for technical reasons—they mess up because of human error.

M.N. | Because the actors can't make themselves understood?

M.L. | Yes, due to communication difficulties—from person to person, not from person to machine. The topics that must be communicated are simply too abstract.

And then, human nature must be factored in as well. Something we call Conway's Law says that systems designed by organizations are constrained to produce designs that are similar to the communication structures of the organizations that write them. If you are in, you understand; if you are out, you don't.

There is a system that organizes things—which parts go where. That is software architecture.

Another problem is the unbelievably high turnover that takes place in the software industry. Programmers change their jobs with great frequency and leave artifacts behind that other people, people who did not write these things themselves, then have to understand. It's as if the architect of a building would change five times while it's being built.

M.N. | The question is, can "good" systems overcome this, and is there is a super-system in normal institutions?

M.L. | Usually not.

M.N. | But there should be one—an overarching structure that acts as a net to catch knowledge.

M.L. | That only exists in organizations that can afford it. The key term here is *mission critical software*. NASA, for example, functions this way. Launching a rocket costs billions. If you are doing it, you have enough money to nail down a near perfect system. But it requires more time and large sums of money.

In the modern software industry, where everything is defined with marketability in mind, it's not affordable. It's not an advantage to write good or nice software, or to write beautiful software. The mere fact that the software is being written is already highly meaningful.

The first software engineering conference was held in 1968 in Garmisch, sponsored by NATO. There, the term *software crisis* was brought to the forefront. This was in recognition of the fact that the software industry was in a crisis, in a crisis of complexity. This crisis has not ended. It is still there and has grown even stronger. It's a vicious circle: The better the means of writing software become, the longer the systems live.

M.N. | Not how something is done is interesting, but that something is done. It is not about the inherent beauty of a system, but that the system has even been built. Unfortunately, this is familiar in architecture as well.

And yet: What is beauty anyway?

M.L. | For me, designing software means keeping all that is essential and throwing out all else.

Simplicity is beautiful. Simple code is beautiful. In Richard Gabriel's book, *Patterns of Software*, he talks about habitability in a similar context—the habitability of software. In this book, he says that there are systems in which it is wonderful to program, that are beautiful to look at, and which are comfortable to be in.

It's about how easy it is to make changes. Changes constantly have to be made. Ugly systems are systems in which changes, no matter how small, waste a huge amount of energy. In a beautiful system, it is clear what one must do, when one must do it, and how to do it. There is beauty on a linguistic level. There are beautiful lines of code where someone use the right variables and named the things as they should be named. It is also possible to write ugly things, by using variables that are really something else, or simply by giving things the wrong names. This makes systems much more difficult to understand.

In extreme programming, there is also the concept of egoless programming. This means that one doesn't write for oneself, but for someone else. One therefore tries to write in a way that is as easy as possible for someone else to understand.

M.N.| But as an ordinary user, I never see what the programmer has written. The result is communicated to me through an interface and thus in an entirely different way.

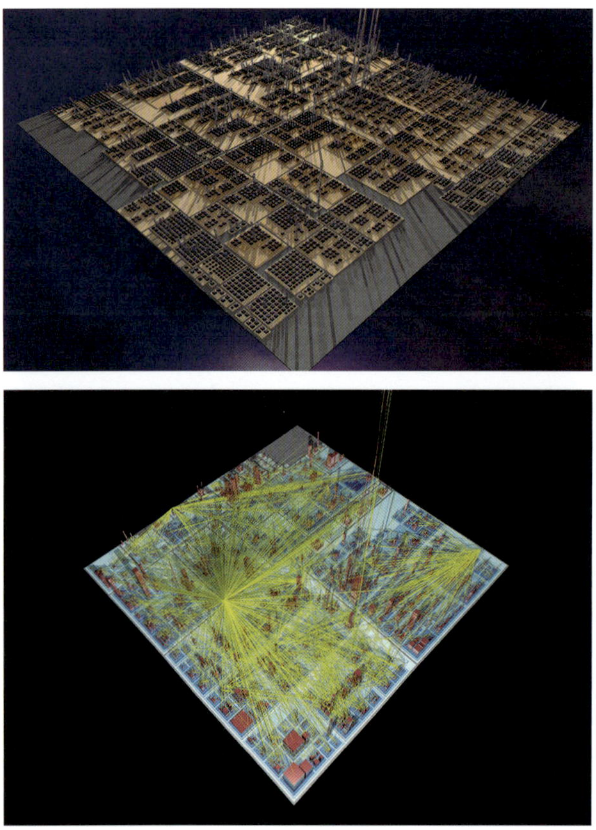

Michele Lanza, visualizations of the codes and metrics of different dimensions using various languages (Java, C++, Smalltalk, CSharp). The visualization takes the form of a city, improving general comprehension and potentially enabling any problems that arise to be more quickly understood. Each subsystem is a city district, within which buildings represent each individual file in the system.

M.L. | Exactly, now we are talking about the skin. This can be reduced to what we call the user interface. This is the part of the system seen in the end by the user. What I mean is that even if, for example Windows Vista is 80 million lines of source code, what the user sees at the end is windows, buttons, and graphic design—it's just the skin of the system.

M.N. | Isn't using a user interface to operate a system relatively new?

M.L. | Yes. The very first computers were not user interface-based. The first user interfaces showed up in the 1960s and even more in the 1970s. This is due to the fact that, before then, there were no users. The few people who used computers back then had the word computer in their job title. They knew how to use them and thus didn't need a user interface. It was not until computer science became mainstream in the 1980s and 1990s that user interfaces really became necessary—for people who wanted nothing to do with programming: the users.

M.N. | The interface is comparable to what we call the skin or the envelope in architecture. Another analogy is theater—in theater, it would be the stage, where everything happens.

M.L. | I understand what you are getting at. Your allegory describes the perfect interface. It would be what you don't see. It would be ideal to use an everyday language, without resorting to the crutch of an interface. But the machine just isn't smart enough for that. In order to obtain a such understanding, the machine would have to be intelligent—but it isn't.

M.N. | What is intelligence?

M.L. | Self-awareness. It has no self-awareness. The machine is not aware of itself.

M.N. | HAL 9000, the fictitious computer on the Spaceship Discovery in Stanley Kubrick's film *2001: An Odyssey in Space* from 1968, has a consciousness. The film is built up so that in the beginning, the machine is only an abstract technical construction, but then through the course of the film it develops an increasingly clear sense of self-awareness.

M.L. | At this point in time, that is simply impossible. There are people who believe in what we call singularity, which refers to machines developing a sense of self-awareness. There are people who say that this could happen within the next 15 to 20 years. But there were also people who said the same thing in 1965, and more than 15 years have passed since then. In my opinion, it currently still doesn't look possible.

M.N. | And so much for insight on the state of computer science. The parallels to architectural development are obvious, however, differences between the two disciplines are also becoming clear. Let's focus on these.

M.L. | Another difference to architecture is that there are no borders, no physical borders. There are thus no recognized rules that determine how software systems must be structured. There is no rulebook that one can or should follow. There's no difference between good and evil, so to speak. In the end, what the user sees, is in any case something totally different. One can design a system incredibly badly; but if the user interface is convincing, then the system is convincing.

M.N. | I understand: There are no rules and regulations. Are there schools of thought, methods, or theories?

M.L. | There are process theories. These relate to how one can methodically approach the design of a system. In these fields, there are also models. There is, for example, the waterfall model. This is when one thing is done after the other.

Waterfall is in reference to the methodology. Waterfall. Software engineering is often compared to conventional engineering or to civil engineering. In this, the metaphor of building a bridge is used. It is necessary to coordinate numerous persons. In the end, a result is produced that is useful to humans in some way.

But the difference that causes the metaphor to fall apart is this: When you start to build a system, the context then changes within a very short period of time. This happens continually. This means that when we describe designing a software system with the metaphor of building a bridge, we have to add the following: While the bridge is being constructed, the landmasses the bridge is meant to join are continually shifting. If you rigidly stick to a plan, you risk the end result being a bridge that joins nothing.

The metaphor only works if it is clear from the very beginning that the context will not change and when all requirements are clear from the very beginning. However, in the last fifty years of the field, it has become evident that it is impossible to fully anticipate the context. One has noticed: The context is continuously changing.

However, a different approach is also possible, one that emerged in the 1990s. It is called agile software development and encompasses various methodologies, for example, extreme programming. This recognizes that change is the most important factor and that one should not try to build systems that are resistant to change. Change is accepted as matter of fact.

Since this, various means of building systems have existed. Most of them follow an onion model – one creates skin after skin and in this way creates interactive steps or types that are strongly based on prototypes.

How is this different from architecture? In computer science, prototyping is cheap, because it's not physical. One can take a prototype and continue to develop it. In architecture, this would mean that one would start constructing a building in order to understand how it should not be done, and then tear it down again in order to build it the right way.

M.N.| In architecture, models and systems are not the same thing. It is possible to develop prototypes into context-specific building typologies using models. The two and three-dimensional graphical representations and the building of physical models at various scales are the means of simulation we use to avoid as many mistakes and misunderstandings as possible.

In addition to this, a great number of things are made differently, depending on the site or craftsmanship, or choice of industrial production method.

A house in a village should be similar to the neighboring house. Each house has its own identity, yet it is related to the house next to it and is part of a greater whole. The same is true for the parts that make up the different buildings.

M.L.| That is different from in the computer sciences. To quote Fred Brooks again: "There are no two identical parts in a software system."

In architecture some parts are indeed identical. As you just described, buildings are based upon conceptually identical components. In computer science and software engineering, each line is written by hand.

M.N.| Are there any machines or programs that can support programmers by writing entire passages?

M.L.| Yes, there are. This is called model-driven engineering. One tries to create models and then a machine generates the source code at the push of a button. But the whole thing is just a vision that doesn't really work for two reasons: The first reason is that what it is possible to generate using such machines is by definition incomplete. It always has to be retroactively improved by hand. One can create skeleton programs, but the missing parts have to be inserted by hand. The other reason is the modeling languages. These are very complex—so complex that the models are more complex than that which the models are trying to model.

M.N. | What is the difference between a model and a program in computer science?

M.L. | A program is made up of source code. Source code is a high-level representation, a representation of what the computer is churning through on a deeper level in order to be able to execute something. A model is a mental representation of a program. It is not the program itself. Yet some say that the program is the model. And others say that the model can be used to generate a program.

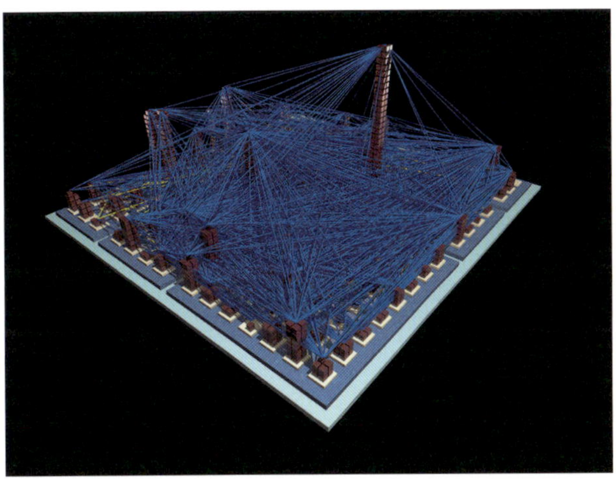

Michele Lanza, a program visualized using CodeCity, a visualization system developed by a research team led by Lanza. Problems that could lead to a program crash are seen as very high buildings, hugely out of proportion in comparison to the other buildings. These "health maps" indicate the areas in which program architecture must be improved.

M.N. | For architecture, two analogous approaches can be discerned. There is functionalism on the one hand, which has been tied to modernism since the late 19th century. The arguments of this school are: The current use of the building, which in architecture we also call the program, generates the form. Rationalism argues against this, saying that the program is the result of the form and thus the structure.

Buildings with a set destination are often occupied differently all of a sudden. I'm thinking of basilicas—a building type developed by Romans. It was originally used for large public meetings, legal trials in particular. Then it became a house of God for Christians, since this type of structure permitted a great number of people to collect under one roof. The structural capacity defined the building typology, not its function.

M.L. | This is not a problem in computer science, since it isn't physical—the costs of building something are not comparable in software. And there is theoretically nothing lost.

From the 1920s to 1960s, computer hardware was much more important that the software. Nixon purportedly once asked how much the software that flew Apollo 11 to the moon weighed. Since this time, hardware has made increasingly significant leaps, and has become less and less important physically. In comparison, software is much more important, in fact endlessly more important. One has practically limitless space, an endless space within which to develop systems.

M.N. | We have talked about the absence of a place, the meaning of structures and systems, the necessity of the skin as an interface, and the ambivalence of models of programs. What about materiality?

M.L. | In this area, the crucial difference is plain and simply that, as mentioned before, there is no attrition. Materials are used: If people walk across a floor for hundreds of years, the floor is changed; a line of code, however, doesn't age in the same way, it never gets old. Architecture is subject to gravity, software isn't.

The system disintegrates nevertheless. This isn't because of the system, but because the reality outside of the system is changing. A system that is by definition immortal and interminable suffers from the fact that reality is not in a standstill. A system that is as it is and stays that way will very quickly become obsolete. It will no longer meet the needs of reality.

It must be adapted. There is indeed erosion, but it comes from without, not within. The elements are intrinsically non-deformable. With time, the system itself makes itself obsolete.

M.N. | What is the oldest system that exists?

M.L. | What is a system? When I think about modern software, there are no systems older than 50 years old that have survived.

Large banking systems are sometimes 30 to 40 years old. In computers, that is an eternity, dozens of programmer generations.

Language is added into all this. Software systems are written in a programming language. These are languages that were developed in order to be able to more easily communicate with the machine. These languages are continually being invented, and many simply die off and are gone. It is currently estimated that about 9,000 programming languages are in existence. Of these, 20 or 30 are actually used—the others are meaningless. New programming languages will rise up and replace the ones that are common today. But the systems will still be there. This is also a human resources problem: These systems, some of which are 30 or 40 years old, can only be understood by a very few people.

Another difference to architecture, to its materiality, is connected to the aspect of accountability. In modern software engineering, there is no accountability for a false application. In architecture, someone is held responsible for damages. If a software system has an error and, for example, an airplane crashes because of it, a programmer is still not held responsible for it. This has never been regulated.

M.N.| Is that a good thing?

M.L.| That's a good question. I think it's generally a bad thing. The field of computer science has failed as a whole when it comes to creating a professional image. Today, anybody can claim to be a computer person. I don't think anybody can just claim to be an architect and legally start building.

M.N.| Wouldn't it be enough to differentiate people with a high level of know-how from those without?

M.L.| When a field has no boundaries that define what falls within it and what is out of bounds, then it is difficult to continue developing it. If today, for example, there is a call for environmentally sustainable development, then it is clear to whom one can go in the field of construction.

When attempts are made to make the field of computer science more professional, nobody knows who to turn to. Only a very few are actually professionally educated. I think that the majority of source code on this planet was written by amateurs.

M.N.| It's no different in architecture. Only a very few architectures and cities were built by architects.

M.L.| There are a great many parallels between architecture and software engineering. They are both about complex structures. Complex structures that change over time, that must change, must be converted. These are structures that, at the end of the day, were built for people. I believe that architecture has adopted very little of use from software engineering while, in contrast, software engineering has taken on many useful aspects of architecture. I think the entire field still lies fallow.

On the State of Architecture

Arno Lederer

During the last hundred years, architects haven't liked talking about beauty. They had a hard time applying that particular quality to architecture. Once everything became calculable, architecture had to keep up. Function, purpose, and economy have properties that can be calculated. Beauty, on the other hand, comes about as the result of a coherent scientific and technical method of calculation practically on its own. Moreover, calculation itself became a paragon of beauty, and it was left up to machines, especially in the first half of the 20th century. Buildings assumed the shapes of aircraft and vehicles, though in their essence they are the opposite of mobility. Architects really liked being photographed with their cars in front of the buildings they designed.

The preference for methods of quantification over beauty is consistent with the enormous value placed on the technical designer, the engineer. This became the ideal figure during that era, the new primitive savage who creates from the here and now, with no cultural baggage.

A great number of architects still pay homage to this scientific and technical notion, cladding it in another garment, not wanting to see its inherent contradiction. People are still fascinated by forms and façades that look so breathtaking, as if gravity is no problem. In the meantime, a simple dwelling is expected to be a power station; once again a building becomes the ideal image of the free-floating colonization of space.

It is apparent to everyone that this architecture dissociates itself from what existed up until the end of the 19th century: the Vitruvian tradition that had given continuity to architecture for many centuries. To be sure, the relatively well-read citizen could tell the difference between styles from antiquity to the Renaissance, Baroque, or even the eclecticism of the late 19th century, but everything was based on the canon of *Baukunst in fünf Jahrtausenden*[1] (Architecture in Five Millennia), as Hans Koepf named his widely read history of architecture.

[1] Hans Köpf: *Baukunst in fünf Jahrtausenden*, Kohlhammer Verlag, Stuttgart, 1997.

The great debate in architecture theory and criticism concerns the question of whether it was right to break with that canon, or whether we should return to architecture as it was understood before the rupture of modernism. This is directly related to the perception of the architect as it has been treated since antiquity, and is opposed to that of the engineer, which didn't emerge until the 18th century and was mainly developed during the 19th century.

The first architect to systematically consider this profession, the Roman architectural writer Vitruvius, was reportedly a fairly mediocre architect. Was this related to the fact that he described the architect as a man who knew something about everything, but never everything about that something? He seemed to be marked by something unfinished. "As for men upon whom nature has bestowed so much ingenuity, acuteness, and memory that they are able to have a thorough knowledge of geometry, astronomy, music, and the other arts, they go beyond the functions of architects and become pure mathematicians."[2] If Vitruvius were a child of the last two centuries, we could safely assume he would have replaced the mathematician with the engineer.

[2] Vitruvius: *Ten Books on Architecture*, Book 1, London, 1914.

He himself opposed another ideal to quantifiable perfection: the type of the universally engaged person in which thought and action, philosophy, art, and practical technical knowledge are united. For him, the thinking that views architecture as an explanatory model of the world is part and parcel of the architectural work. This self-reflection of the guild was not conducive to architecture during moments of upheaval in the 20th century and even after the devastating destruction of this period. The last comprehensive project of this type at the beginning of the last ten decades, namely that of Friedrich Ostendorf, came to a standstill halfway through when Ostendorf died in World War I. Architects only began to put their thoughts down on paper in the early phase of postmodernism.

The profession of the engineer as we understand it today is a child of industrialization. There are no Vitruvius, Albertis, or Schinkels in the history of engineering. Perhaps the pursuit of and training in systematic and theoretical treatments of technical questions and propositions also gives less rise to aesthetic and philosophical discourse.[3] Or perhaps being goal-directed, working with numbers and facts, leaves no room for interpretations or questions of conviction. Engineers are people of modernity; architects are a kind of pre-modern people.

Architecture had little to offer in response to the unstoppable triumphal march of science and technology. The temptation to let engineers lead the way was great, and their actions guaranteed that things would move forward on the path to progress. Certainly a dazzling concept: definitely justified when it came to medical advances; more than questionable in the development of military technology; ambivalent in everyday life—if we look at traveling across the country in modern intercity express trains, for example. And yet, the engineer who figures things out is trusted. At best, the architect can be believed. But that is the thing about faith.

In the pre-modern era, people believed more than they knew, and today, we know more than we believe.

How little this trade-off does for architecture is shown by an example from the world of today's social engineering. How are major architectural projects decided today, in competition juries, for instance? A committee is formed, and as a prerequisite for a decision, it commissions a group of experts from various specialized disciplines who compile long lists of quanti-

3 One engineer has done literary work on his profession: Heinrich Seidel, 1843–1906, designed the Anhalter Bahnhof and the Yorckbrücken in Berlin. As an author, he wrote the book *Leberecht Hühnchen*, a tale of an engineer who lives modestly and who "knows the art of being happy". Seidel also wrote the engineer's song, whose first line is, "Nothing is too hard for the engineer...", which became the motto of Gyro Gearloose.

fiable details. The study of floor plans and sections is replaced by numbers that produce a statement about energy values, emergency exit widths, and costs. The specialists are concerned not with the whole, but with details divorced from context. And these details say nothing at all about the actual quality of the design proposal.

Because this group does not want to, nor is it able to read the plans, it calls for a second decisionmaking aid: a visualization. Yet this is still not about the whole, but rather a more or less clever advertisement, with an illustration that is no more than a work of temptation. It shows the building as it can never really exist, with blue skies, snappy cars, and happy young bystanders.

If the image suits the viewer's taste and matches favorable values in the preliminary review, it will become the favorite, no matter how miserable the architecture is.

Taste is a question of judgment, to quote Schiller. However, the ability to judge requires knowledge. Acquired knowledge, the knowledge of feeling, which comes from the experience of years of working with the subject, and with the thing that connects them both: education. Responsibility is also part of judgment—delegating it to specialists, on the other hand, is an excuse. In this respect, one can simply say that our society's taste is miserable where architecture is concerned.

One needs only look at the curricula of architecture faculties: the course of study often includes subjects belonging to technical sciences, economics, law, or the social sciences. Packed to the gills with detailed knowledge, the students are also supposed to learn how to design. Artistic design, or any artistic subjects at all, literature, music, theater—i.e. everything we group under the rubric of culture—have a different value. Apparently, these are subjects one is meant to acquire as a sideline, during one's spare time.

For more than 25 years now, we have had excellent machines intended to lighten and improve the work of architects. Let's be honest: has anyone actually been able to determine whether these blessings have improved the architecture of our buildings and cities?

The machine, a creation of technology and science, is pitted against subjective arbitrariness. Adolf Loos wrote about the state of our profession in 1921, following the aesthetic frenzy of the *fin de siècle:* "Architecture does not belong among the arts. Only a very small portion of architecture belongs to art: the tomb and the monument. Everything that serves a purpose should be excluded from the realm of art!"[4] A few years later, Hannes Meyer put it this way: "The new building is [...] a product of industry, and as such, it is a work of specialists. The architect was an artist and is now becoming a specialist in organization."[5]

Since then, architects, bolstered by this supposed theory, have argued outside of artistic content. Their creations of form are presumably buttressed by quantifiable values, function, economics, and technology. Helpless against the solid proof of engineers, who have established themselves as specialists in all these fields as a trusted partner in constructing the city and the building, architecture is going into retirement.

In return, there is the promise of efficiency. How does that look? The fact is—to cite just one example—that since the 1980s, the auxiliary costs for construction have increased by more than 30 percent. Incidentally, the cost of construction alone has risen by more than 40 percent over the past twenty years, as a large daily newspaper recently reported. It attributed this to increasing technical demands, such as fire protection, cost optimization, and energy conservation—to say nothing of the rise of the "intelligent house".

4 Adolf Loos: *Trotzdem*, 1900–1930, ed. Adolf Opel, reprint Prachner, Vienna, 1982, p. 78.

5 Hannes Meyer: *bauhaus, Zeitschrift für Gestaltung*, Dessau, 2, 1928, pp. 12–13.

Do the facts bear this out? Here's one example from our own practice: we founded our office back in 1979. Soon afterwards, we won a competition for a building complex with housing, a branch bank, a library, and shops, located in a downtown area. A conservative estimate of the cost today would be between 25 and 30 million euros. At that time, I was 32 years old, had to sell my car because I needed the money, and thought it was fantastic that I had a photocopier that could make copies in muted colors of text typed on a typewriter. The drafting equipment was a true luxury: we had bought it at Charette in New York. Three consulting engineers stood at our side: the surveyor, the structural engineer, and a mechanical engineer. The clients sighed over the high auxiliary costs, which amounted to 18 percent of the cost of construction—modest, by today's standards. But compared to what we build today, the buildings are no better or worse. It was only cheaper, the decisions were easier, and we were the ones in charge.

When we invite the engineers and architectural consultants involved in a design project to a meeting, there are often 20 or more people sitting together, trying to get to a common denominator in the babel of jargon. The same happens with provincial and city officials and private construction companies. The true art of architecture consists in the ability to get past the many individual specializations that each contribute to the failure of architecture according to their powers of assertion, with their musts, shoulds, and wants, in order to do justice to the notion of building culture. But building culture means thinking in a holistic context. It can be improved only by people who, in the Vitruvian sense, know a little about everything, but never a lot about one thing. Specialists are the enemy of building culture. It belongs in the hands of generalists.

Today, architects are reduced to relying on specialists for the look of a design. Is it any surprise that the critique of our cities as inhospitable isn't even close to nearing an end, but rather on the rise? There are certainly enough buildings in the nation that work wonderfully, have the best data readings, and yet people wonder why no one really wants to live in them. Why is this? Because a building is not a machine. After all, one doesn't look for a life partner by looking at blood counts. And instructors and professors who use charts sorted by different criteria to give out twenty grades from 1 to 6 in order to calculate the final grade with the average do not belong in schools and universities.

That is the subject of Max Frisch's great novel *Homo faber*,[6] which describes the fate of Walter Faber, an engineer who, believing only in numbers and technical progress, fails miserably as a human being. The idea of saving the world with technology is absurd. It will fail just as much using art alone. Frisch opposes *homo faber*, "man the maker", to *homo luden*, "man at play", as described by Schiller in his letters on aesthetic education.

Homo faber is equally and equitably dependent on homo ludens, because the overall view, the unfolding of all components into an organic whole—that is what beauty is—overtaxes technology, and it calls for architects, with imagination and responsibility. It would be disastrous, as Martin Heidegger noted, if one day, "only calculating thought were valued and practiced."[7]

Alberti, whose *Ten Books on Architecture* has been one of the most important books of architectural theory for half a millennium, writes in the ninth volume about the seriousness and difficulty of the profession of architecture:

"Doubtless Architecture is a very noble Science, not fit for every Head. He ought to be a Man of a fine Genius, of a great Application, of the best Education, of thorough Experience, and especially of strong Sense and sound Judgement, that presumes to

[6] Max Frisch: *Homo faber*, Frankfurt (Suhrkamp), 1977 *(Note: Max Frisch is not the first person to deal with the failure of the engineer.* The Tunnel *is the title of a novel by Bernhard Kellermann, 1879–1951, which is about an engineer in the early 20th century who wants to build a tunnel from Europe to America and gets it done, resulting not only in a tremendous number of deaths, but also leading to his ruin. The book was published by S. Fischer in 1913.)*

[7] Martin Heidegger: *Gelassenheit*, Messkircher speech 1955

declare himself an Architect. (…) For though Building is a Matter of Necessity, yet convenient Building is both of Necessity and Utility too: But to build in such a Manner, that the Generous shall commend you, and the Frugal not blame you, is the Work only of a prudent, wise and learned Architect."[8]

And today? Have a look at the German fee schedule for architects and engineers, passed into law by parliament. This text, plus the commentary, is several hundred pages long. The word "beauty" is nowhere to be found. Nor the idea that experience and education distinguish architects, or that they are wise and judicious artists. Architects are paid according to technical and economic data. Whether the building is beautiful, whether it adds cultural value to the city, whether it isn't silent, as Paul Valéry says, still talks, or rather sings, does not seem to be of interest to politics and business.[9]

If one were to compare language to architecture, one might say that the producing of ordinary market-oriented design that shapes everyday life is like writing instruction manuals. Sometimes it is prose; very rarely is it poetry. Poems belong to the fine yet barely cherished genres of art. Prose can be art, but most of the time it is not. Instruction manuals would fail at their purpose if they were art.

Those three levels were always contained in architecture. But it has been robbed of poetry. A building that is no more than a technical implementation of a number-based spatial program is like an ordinary instruction manual, which lacks any interpretation. By contrast, a poem is free and open to the play of interpretation and structure—and isn't that what pleases us about it?

We can speak of architecture if it offers more than a single possibility of interpretation. Poetry is needed to make that possible; it must not be reduced to a taboo. Let us at least commit ourselves to the notion of architecture! Think about the second word! Isn't that what is really demanded of our profession—contrary to all appearances? It would be this: the state of architecture.

[8] Leon Battista Alberti: *The Architecture of Leon Batista Alberti in Ten Books*, printed by Edward Owen, 1755; Book IX, Chapter X, p. 687.

[9] Paul Valéry: *Eupalinos: or, The architect.* Oxford University Press, 1932.

When we presented the founder of a large trading company with our design for a new company headquarters some time ago, the critical comments and concerns—or rather, the know-it-all attitudes—of the numerous consultants involved in the project were unmistakable. Our client listened attentively. Then he ended the conversation by saying that he did not care about any of it. The only thing that mattered to him was whether the design was sound and beautiful. Since then, some of those consultants are no longer involved in the project. This gives us hope

• • •

Aicher, Florian
Born 1954 in Ulm, Germany. Studied architecture at the National School of Architecture in Stuttgart, freelance architect since 1983, mainly for remodeling. Architectural publishing and teaching, most recently for Spittal/Drau Technical College.

Beisi, Jia
Born 1963. Professor of Architecture at the University of Hong Kong. Studied Architecture at the Nanjing Institute of Technology and ETH Zurich. Research on the history and theory of architecture and living in Switzerland and in China; numerous publications. Teaching at the University of Hong Kong since 1996. Director of Baumschlager Eberle Hong Kong Ltd., most recent project a 370,000-square-meter business and residential center in Wuhan.

Caruso, Adam
Born in Montreal, Canada. Studied Architecture at McGill University. Founded an architecture firm together with Peter St John in 1990. First international acclaim: New Art Gallery in Walsall in 1995; followed by the Millbank Project at Tate Britain, Nottingham Contemporary, Gasgosian Galleries in London, Paris, and Hong Kong, and most recently Bremer Landesbank, among others. Teaching in England since 1990 and guest lecturer at the Accademia di architettura in Mendrisio, the Graduate School of Design at Harvard University, and the London School of Economics. Appointed Professor of Architecture and Construction at the ETH Zurich in 2011.

Eberle, Dietmar
Born 1952 in Hittisau, Austria. Studied Architecture at the TU Wien. Freelance architect since 1979, co-founder of the Vorarlberger Baukünstler group, of the Baumschlager Eberle firm in 1984, which today has subsidiaries in 9 nations. Teaching since 1983, most recently as professor at the ETH Zurich. AIA member.

Hauser, Franziska
Born 1977 in Karlsruhe, Germany. Studied Architecture in Karlsruhe and Mendrisio. Architect at Baumschlager Eberle and kcap since 2005. Assistant for the Professorship of Dietmar Eberle at the ETH Zurich since 2009.

Lanza, Michele
Born 1973 in Avellino, Italy. 1993–1999: Studied Informatics in Bern, Switzerland. 1999–2003: Doctoral studies in Computer Science, awarded the Ernst Denert Foundation Software Engineering Prize. 2004: Post-doctorate at the University of Zurich. 2004–present Founding member and professor of the Department of Informatics at the Università della Svizzera italiana (USI) in Lugano, Switzerland. Faculty Dean since 2013.

Lederer, Arno
Born 1947 in Stuttgart. Studied Architecture in Stuttgart and Vienna. Freelance architect since 1979 (today Lederer Ragnarsdóttir Oei), mainly working on public cultural buildings, urban development, and on juries. Taught from 1985–2014, most recently at the University of Stuttgart.

Magnago Lampugnani, Vittorio
Born in 1951. Studied Architecture at the University La Sapienza in Rome and the University of Stuttgart, graduating in 1977. After an assistant position at the Institute for the Fundamentals of Modern Architecture and Design in Stuttgart, he became a scientific consultant for the International Building Exhibition Berlin (IBA) from 1980–1984. In 1990, he began editing the magazine *Domus* and directing the German Architecture Museum in Frankfurt am Main, which he ran until 1995. He has been a professor at the Graduate School of Design at Harvard University and was Professor of the History of Urban Development at ETH Zurich from 1994–2016. He manages architectural firms in Milan and Zurich. He is currently a Fellow at the Berlin Institute for Advanced Study and has published numerous works on the history and theory of architecture and the city.

Malfroy, Sylvain
Born 1955 in Lausanne, Switzerland. Architectural historian, studied Philosophy at the University of Lausanne. Teaching and research positions at Swiss universities and colleges with an emphasis on the fields of urban morphology, landscape aesthetics, and architectural design theory. Currently a lecturer at the Department of Architecture of ZHAW Winterthur and the Geneva University of Music Neuenburg.

Meyer, Adrian
Born in 1942. Studied Architecture, partner of Burkard Meyer in Baden. Professor of Architecture and Design at the ETH Zurich from 1994–2008. Head of darch from 2001–2003. Author of numerous publications, including *Stadt und Architektur, Konkret/Concrete, Architecture: A Synoptic Vision.* He has been teaching as a guest at the TU Wien since 2008.

Nasso, Marcello
Born 1974 in German-speaking Switzerland. 1999–2005: Studied at the Accademia di Architettura in Mendrisio, Università della Svizzera Italiana. 2007: Founded Marcello Nasso Architekten in Zurich. 2009–2015: Academic Associate and Superior Academic Associate at the Professorship of Dietmar Eberle, Department of Architecture, ETH Zurich. 2012: Lecturer at the Uni Cagliari Summer School. 2013–2015: Employed at *Domus* Milan. 2015–present: Various residential projects.

Neumeyer, Fritz
Born in 1946. Studied Architecture at the TU Berlin, graduated 1977, habilitation 1986. 1987–1989: Research Fellow at the Getty Center for the History of Arts and the Humanities, Santa Monica, California. 1989–1992: Professor of Building History at the TU Dortmund; Jean Labatut Professor of Architecture and Urbanism at Princeton University. 1993–2012: Professor of Architectural Theory at TU Berlin. Publications include *The Artless Word: Mies van der Rohe on the Building Art; Der Klang der Steine, Nietzsches Architekturen, Bauen beim Wort genommen – Quellenschriften zur Architekturtheorie.*

Pálffy, András
Born 1954 in Budapest. Studied Architecture at the TU Wien. 1974–1985: Professor of Architecture since 2002, Head of the Institute for Architecture and Design TU Wien. Lived in Rome from 1978–1985. Building of exhibition spaces for contemporary art, Generali Foundation, 1994, first builder of the architectural ideas of Jabornegg & Pálffy, developed over years. Designing and teaching in Vienna since 1985. President and Director of the Secession Artists Union in Vienna from 2007–2014. Currently planning the renovation and refurbishment of the Austrian Parliament building.

Šik, Miroslav
Born 1953 in Prague. Doctorate in Architecture, professor at ETH Zurich. Emigrated to Switzerland in 1968. 1973–1979: Studied Architecture at ETH Zurich under A. Rossi and M. Campi. 1986–1991: Initiator of *Analoge Architektur*. Architectural firm in Zurich since 1988. Professor at ETH Zurich since 1999. Awarded the Heinrich Tessenow Prize in 2005. Swiss representative at the Venice Architecture Biennale 2012. Publications include *Analoge Architektur* (1988), *Old – New, de Audibus 2*, essays and interviews from 1987–2001 (2002); *Analoge Altneue Architektur 1983–2016* (2018). Buildings include St. Antonius Catholic Center Egg 1990–2003, Morges Conference and Hotel Center 1995, Zurich Musician's Residence 1997, Church of Baden 2007, Haldenstein Center 2008, Zug Senior Citizen's Residence 2013, Hunzikerareal Residences Zurich 2015.

Stalder, Laurent
Born in 1970. Professor of Architectural Theory, Institute of Architectural History and Theory, ETH Zurich. Research field: Architectural history and theory of the 19th–21st centuries at the crossroads of technological history. Key publications include *Hermann Muthesius: Das Landhaus als kulturgeschichtlicher Entwurf* (2009), *Schwellenatlas* (2009), *Fritz Haller. Architekt und Forscher* (2015).

Tröger, Eberhard
Born 1969 in Hof an der Saale, Switzerland. Architect, lecturer, author, and artist. 1990–1996: Studied Architecture at the TU Berlin, 1991–2001: ETH Zurich (gta), 2010: General Commissioner of the German Pavilion at the Venice Biennale. Lecturer on design at ZHAW in Winterthur since 2013. Head of the Spatial Design program at the ZHdK in Zurich since 2014. Books: *Sehnsucht* (2010); *What Architects Desire* (2010); *Touch Me!* (2011); *Density & Atmosphere*, (2014). Also publishes in specialized journals and works as a freelance artist.

A

Marc Augé: *Orte und Nichtorte,* Frankfurt, 1994

B

Gaston Bachelard: *Poetik des Raumes,* Munich, 1960

Adolf Behne: *Der moderne Zweckbau,* Berlin, 1964 (1926)

Adolf Behne: *Neues Wohnen, neues Bauen,* Leipzig, 1927

Adolf Behne: *Die Stile Europas,* Leipzig, 1930

Reiner Benham: *Die Revolution der Architektur,* Hamburg, 1964

Werner Blaser: *Mies van der Rohe,* Zurich, 1965

Gerhard R. Blomeyer, Barbara Tietze: *In Opposition zur Moderne,* Braunschweig/Wiesbaden, 1980

Gernot Böhme: *Architektur und Atmosphäre,* Munich, 2006

Uwe Bresan: *Stifters Rosenhaus,* Leinfelden-Echterdingen, 2016

Gerda Breuer (ed.): *Ästhetik der schönen Genügsamkeit oder Arts and Crafts als Lebensform,* Braunschweig/Wiesbaden, 1998

Lucius Burckhardt: *Wer plant die Planung?,* Kassel, 1980

Lucius Burckhardt: *Der kleinstmögliche Eingriff,* Kassel, 2013

C

Ulrich Conrads: *Programme und Manifeste zur Architektur des 20. Jahrhunderts,* Berlin/Munich, 1964

D

Andreas Denk, Uwe Schröder, Rainer Schützeichel (eds.): *Architektur Raum Theorie,* Tübingen/Berlin, 2016

Werner Durth: *Deutsche Architekten, Biographische Verflechtungen 1900–1970,* Braunschweig/Wiesbaden, 1986

E

Dietmar Eberle: *Von der Stadt zum Haus. Eine Entwurfslehre,* Zurich, 2007

Dietmar Eberle, Eberhard Tröger: *Dichte Atmosphäre,* Basel, 2015

Bernd Evers (ed.), Christof Thoenes et al.: *Architekturtheorie,* Cologne, 2003

F

Theodor Fischer: *Zwei Vorträge über Proportion,* Munich, 1956

Theodor Fischer: *Sechs Vorträge über Stadtbaukunst,* Munich, 2012

Kenneth Frampton: *Die Architektur der Moderne,* Stuttgart, 1983

Kenneth Frampton: *Grundlagen der Architektur,* Munich/Stuttgart, 1993

Kenneth Frampton: *Die Entwicklung der Architektur im 20. Jahrhundert,* Vienna/New York, 2007

Josef Frank: *Architektur als Symbol,* Vienna, 1931

Eduard Führ et al.: *Architektur im Zwischenreich von Kunst und Alltag,* Münster/New York/Munich/Berlin, 1997

Eduard Führ: *Bauen und Wohnen, Martin Heideggers Grundlegung einer Phänomenologie der Architektur,* Münster/New York/Munich/Berlin, 2000

G

Hans-Georg Gadamer: *Die Wahrheit des Kunstwerks (1960), Gesammelte Werke,* Tübingen, 1987

Georg Germann: *Einführung in die Geschichte der Architekturtheorie,* Darmstadt, 1987

Johann Wolfgang von Goethe: *Von deutscher Baukunst,* Camburg, 1945

Johann Wolfgang von Goethe: *Anschauendes Denken, Goethes Schriften zur Naturwissenschaft,* Frankfurt, 1981

Walter Gropius: *Architektur. Wege zu einer optischen Kunst,* Frankfurt/Hamburg, 1956

Ute Guzzoni: *Der andere Heidegger,* Freiburg/Munich, 2009

H

Edward T. Hall: *Die Sprache des Raumes,* Düsseldorf, 1976

Martin Heidegger: *Holzwege,* Frankfurt, 1950

Martin Heidegger: *Der Feldweg,* Frankfurt, 1953

Martin Heidegger: "Bauen Wohnen Denken", in: *Vorträge und Aufsätze,* Pfullingen, 1954

Martin Heidegger: *Gelassenheit,* Freiburg/Munich, 2014

Agnes Heller: *Das Alltagsleben,* Frankfurt, 1981

I

Lukas Imhof: *Midcomfort,* Vienna, 2013

J

Jane Jacobs: *Tod und Leben großer amerikanischer Städte,* Gütersloh, 1963

Ernst Jünger: *Der Arbeiter,* Hamburg, 1932

K

Hans-Joachim Kadatz: *Seemanns Lexikon der Architektur,* Leipzig, 1994

Emil Kaufmann: *Von Ledoux bis Le Corbusier,* Stuttgart, 1985

Hans Kollhoff: *Über Tektonik in der Baukunst,* Braunschweig/Wiesbaden, 1993

Hans Kollhoff: *Architektur: Schein und Wirklichkeit,* Springe, 2014

Hans Kollhoff, Helga Timmermann, Fritz Neumeyer, Ivan Němec: *Architektur,* Munich, 2002

Hanno-Walter Kruft: *Geschichte der Architekturtheorie,* Munich, 1986

L

Vittorio M. Lampugnani: *Architektur und Städtebau des 20. Jahrhunderts,* Stuttgart, 1980

Vittorio M. Lampugnani: *Architektur als Kultur,* Cologne, 1986

Vittorio M. Lampugnani, Claus Baldus: *Das Abenteuer der Ideen. Architektur und Philosophie,* Berlin, 1987

Vittorio M. Lampugnani: *Die Modernität des Dauerhaften,* Berlin, 1995

Alessandra Latour: *Louis I. Kahn – Die Architektur und die Stille.* Basel, 1993

Le Corbusier: *Ausblick auf eine Architektur,* Gütersloh/Berlin, 1969

Henry Lefèbvre: *Die Revolution der Städte,* Munich, 1972

Rudolf zur Lippe: *Neue Betrachtung der Wirklichkeit,* Hamburg, 1974

Adolf Loos: *Trotzdem,* Vienna, 1931

M

Máté Major: *Geschichte der Architektur,* Budapest, 1974

Wolfgang Meisenheimer: *Das Denken des Leibes und der architektonische Raum,* Cologne, 2004

Hannes Meyer: *Bauen und Gesellschaft,* Dresden, 1980

Barbara Miller-Lane: *Architektur und Politik in Deutschland 1918–1945,* Braunschweig, 1986

Ákos Moravánszky: *Architekturtheorie im 20. Jahrhundert,* Basel, 2015

Ákos Moravánszky: *Lehrgerüste,* Zurich, 2015

Ákos Moravánszky (ed.): *Precisions,* Berlin, 2008

William Morris: *Wie wir leben und wie wir leben könnten,* Cologne, 1983

N

Fritz Neumeyer: *Mies van der Rohe. Das kunstlose Wort,* Berlin, 1986

Fritz Neumeyer: *Quellentexte zur Architekturtheorie,* Munich/Berlin/London/New York, 2002

Christian Norberg-Schulz: *Genius Loci. Landschaft, Lebensraum, Baukunst,* Stuttgart, 1991

O

Philipp Oswald et al.: *Bauhausstreit 1990–2009,* Ostfildern, 2009

P

Juhani Pallasmaa: *Die Augen der Haut,* Los Angeles, 2013

Georges Perec: *Träume von Räumen,* Bremen, 1990

Ute Poerschke: *Funktionen und Formen – Architekturtheorie der Moderne,* Bielefeld, 2014

Julius Posener: *Aufsätze und Vorträge,* Braunschweig/Wiesbaden, 1981

R

Aldo Rossi: *Wissenschaftliche Selbstbiographie,* Bern, 1988

Aldo Rossi: *Die Architektur der Stadt,* Düsseldorf, 1973

Colin Rowe, Fred Koetter: *Collage City,* Basel/Boston/Berlin, 1997

Bernard Rudofsky: *Architektur ohne Architekten. Eine Einführung in die anonyme Architektur,* Salzburg, 1993

S

Friedrich Schiller: *Über die ästhetische Erziehung des Menschen in einer Reihe von Briefen,* Munich, 1967

August Schmarsow: *Unser Verhältnis zu den bildenden Künsten,* Leipzig, 1903

Alfred Schmidt: *Der Begriff der Natur in der Lehre von Marx,* Frankfurt, 1962

Paul Schmitthenner, *Baugestaltung,* Stuttgart, 1932

Fritz Schumacher: *Strömungen in deutscher Baukunst seit 1800,* Cologne, 1935

Fritz Schumacher: *Der Geist der Baukunst,* Stuttgart, 1938

Fritz Schumacher: *Grundlagen für das Studium der Baukunst,* Munich, 1947

Fritz Schumacher: *Lesebuch für Baumeister,* Berlin, 1947

Gottfried Semper: *Der Stil in den technischen und tektonischen Künsten,* Vol. I & II, Munich, 1863

Miroslav Šik: *Altneue Gedanken, Texte und Gespräche 1987–2001,* Lucerne, 2002

Camillo Sitte: *Der Städtebau nach seinen künstlerischen Grundsätzen,* Basel/Boston/Berlin, 2001

T

Heinrich Tessenow: *Hausbau und dergleichen,* Berlin, 1920

Stephen Toulmin: *Cosmopolis,* Frankfurt, 1991

Alexander Tzonis: *Das verbaute Leben,* Düsseldorf, 1973

Alexander Tzonis, Liane Lefaivre: *Architektur in Europa seit 1968,* Frankfurt, 1992

U

Oswald Mathias Ungers: *Architekturlehre,* Aachen, 2006

V

Paul Valéry: *Eupalinos oder Der Architekt,* Frankfurt, 1973

Marcus Vitruvius Pollio: *Baukunst,* Zurich/Munich, 1987

Adolf M. Vogt et al.: *Architektur 1940–1980,* Frankfurt/Vienna/Berlin, 1980

W

Anni Wagner: *Von Ädikula bis Zwerggalerie. 100 Begriffe der Architektur in Bildern,* Munich, 1975

Gert Walden: *Baumschlager Eberle Annäherungen,* Vienna, 2010

Maria Welzig: *Josef Frank,* Vienna, 1998

Z

Beatrix Zug: *Die Anthropologie des Raumes in der Architekturtheorie des frühen 20. Jahrhunderts,* Tübingen/Berlin, 2006

Peter Zumthor: *Architektur Denken,* Basel, 2006

I, Florian Aicher, the editor, am thankful for the support I received for the production of this volume through the professorship of Dietmar Eberle from Franziska Hauser, Pascal Hofmann, Stefan Roggo, and Mathias Stritt. Special thanks go to Ute Guzzoni, Markus Koch, Matthias Mulitzer, Rainer Schützeichel, and Thomas Valena for the countless conversations and essential information.

The final version is the result of several years of preparation by Marcello Nasso; a very special thank you for his cooperation, availability, and intense dedication to this preparatory work. Many of the topic texts are the result of this collaboration, marked with FA/MN. I, Florian Aicher, am responsible for the development of the remaining texts and terminology.

Jia Beisi | Hubert Bischoff | Elisabeth Blum | Elisabeth Boesch | Roger Boltshauser | Othmar Bucher | Marianne Burkhalter | Adam Caruso | Dalila Chebbi | Beat Consoni | Sabrina Contratto | Jürg Conzett | Zita Cotti | Einar Dahle | Max Dudler | Piet Eckert | Philipp Esch | Carl Fingerhuth | Dietrich Fink | Annette Gigon | Lorenzo Giuliani | Silvia Gmür | Patrick Gmür | Niklaus Graber | Hans-Ullrich Grassmann | Andreas Hagmann | Thomas Hasler | Deborah Hauptmann | Christine Hawley | Hans Hesse | Andreas Hild | Sabina Hubacher | Eduard Hueber | Marius Hug | Lukas Huggenberger | Louisa Hutton | Dieter Jüngling | Johannes Käferstein | Gabriele G. Kiefer | Thomas Kohlhammer | Hilde Leon | Claudine Lorenz | Chris Luebkeman | Paola Maranta | Daniele Marques | Josep Lluís Mateo | Christoph Mathys | Marcel Meili | Adrian Meyer | Quintus Miller | Meinrad Morger | Victorine Müller | Barbara Neff | Bettina Neumann | András Pálffy | Lilian Pfaff | Ivan Reimann | Franz Romero | Alain Roserens | Flora Ruchat-Roncati | Yvonne Rudolf | Arthur Rüegg | Matthias Sauerbruch | Rita Schiess | Christian Schmid | Margherita Spiluttini | Annette Spiro | Volker Staab | Laurent Stalder | Jakob Steib | Erich G. Steinmayr | Petra Stojanik | Marc Syfrig | Hadi Teherani | Peter Thule Kristensen | Philip Ursprung | Paola Viganò | Günther Vogt | Ingemar Vollenweider | Thomas von Ballmoos | Wang Wei Jen | Gesine Weinmiller | Yasky Yuval | Gundula Zach | Marco Zünd

Library of Congress
Control Number: 2018937456

Bibliographic information published by the German National Library

The German National Library lists this publication in the Deutsche Nationalbibliografie; detailed bibliographic data are available on the Internet at http://dnb.dnb.de.

ISBN 978-3-0356- 0632-4
(Hardcover)

ISBN 978-3-0356- 0633-1
(Softcover)

This publication is also available as an eBook
(ISBN PDF 978-3-0356-1099-4)

and in a German language edition
(ISBN Hardcover 978-3-0356-0621-8,
ISBN Softcover 978-3-0356-0622-5,
eBook 978-3-0356-0662-1).

P. O. Box 44,
4009 Basel, Switzerland
Part of Walter de Gruyter GmbH,
Berlin/Boston

9 8 7 6 5 4 3 2 1
www.birkhauser.com

EDITORS

Dietmar Eberle
Florian Aicher

EDITORIAL TEAM

Franziska Hauser
Pascal Hofmann
Marcello Nasso
Stefan Roggo
Mathias Stritt
ETH Zurich
CH-Zurich

ACQUISITIONS EDITOR

David Marold
Birkhäuser Verlag
A-Vienna

PROJECT AND PRODUCTION EDITOR

Angelika Heller
Birkhäuser Verlag
A-Vienna

TRANSLATION FROM GERMAN INTO ENGLISH

Word Up!

PHOTO EDITOR

Dominique Jahn
CH-Zurich

DESIGN

Gottschalk+Ash Int'l
CH-Zurich

PRINTING

Holzhausen Druck GmbH
A-Wolkersdorf